W9-DFH-871

North Star Country

UPSTATE NEW YORK AND THE CRUSADE

FOR AFRICAN AMERICAN FREEDOM

Milton C. Sernett

 Syracuse University Press

Copyright © 2002 by Syracuse University Press

Syracuse, New York 13244-5160

All Rights Reserved

First Edition 2002

02   03   04   05   06   07   6   5   4   3   2

The paper used in this publication meets the minimum
requirements of American National Standard for Information
Sciences—Permanence of Paper for Printed Library Materials,
ANSI Z39.48-1984. ∞   ™

LIBRARY OF CONGRESS CATALOGING-IN-PUBLICATION DATA

Sernett, Milton C., 1942–
    North star country : upstate New York and the crusade for African
American freedom / Milton C. Sernett.—1st ed.
        p.   cm.
    Includes bibliographical references and index.
    ISBN 0-8156-2914-1 (alk. paper)—ISBN 0-8156-2915-x (pbk. : alk. paper)
    1. Antislavery movements—New York (State)—History—19th century.
2. Slavery and the church—New York (State)—History—19th century.
3. Abolitionists—New York (State)—History—19th century.   4. African
American abolitionists—New York (State)—History—19th century.
5. African Americans—Civil rights—New York (State)—History—
19th century.   6. New York (State)—Politics and government—1775–1865.
7. New York (State)—Race relations.   I. Title.
E445.N56 S47 2001
326´.8´0974709034—dc21

                                                            00-068773

Manufactured in the United States of America

I kept my eye on the bright North Star and thought of liberty.

—Refrain from a fugitive's song

MILTON C. SERNETT is professor of African
American Studies and History at Syracuse
University. He is the author of *Abolition's
Axe: Beriah Green, Oneida Institute, and the
Black Freedom Struggle; Black Religion and
American Evangelicalism: White Protestants,
Plantation Missions, and the Flowering of
Negro Christianity, 1787–1865;* and *Bound for
the Promised Land: African American Religion
and the Great Migration.* He is the editor of
*African American Religious History: A Docu-
mentary History.*

Contents

Illustrations

Acknowledgments

In the course of the struggle to make freedom's star shine more brightly on their communities, their region, and the nation as a whole, abolitionists formed bonds of friendship with others who had similar reform interests. These intimate circles provided support and encouragement, though they were not free of debate and differences. While preparing this book, I encountered others who believe the story of Upstate New York to be important to the larger story of the American experience. Their friendship and encouragement during what was, at times, an overwhelming challenge has made North Star Country *a better book.*

Scholarship is a collective endeavor in which we scholars build upon the work of our predecessors. Much of the research I have incorporated into the following story draws on primary sources that others have diligently preserved and made available to researchers and on articles and books that are either not easily accessible or are out of print. I am particularly grateful for the pioneering work Monroe Fordham has done over more than two decades with the journal *Afro-Americans in New York Life and History.*

A word of appreciation is also due to the many custodians of local (public and private) historical societies, libraries, and archives whose concern for preserving evidence pertaining to the African American experience in New York State has resulted in easier access to the existing materials than was possible a generation ago.

Carol Kammen read an early draft of this book and nudged the project along at Syracuse University Press. Along with many others, she convinced me that there existed a need to bring the scattered fragments of the freedom story together for a new generation of readers, in the classroom and beyond.

David Ramsey, journalist and history enthusiast, saw the manuscript as useful to a readership wider than the circles of professional historians within which I have moved for a quarter century.

Robert Shear sparked renewed public interest in the regional freedom story by creating his Internet site on the central New York State Freedom Trail.

An ever-helpful supportive circle of specialists answered my frequent queries. Bonnie Ryan, for example, helped me sort out the evidence related to the Harriet Tubman property. Chris Densmore assisted me with matters pertaining to western New York State. Melody Mitchell shared information about the African American presence in Peterboro and vicinity and was also ready with a word of encouragement. Judith Wellman's star shines especially brightly in the constellation of friends and associates who aided the cause. She read the manuscript carefully, provided constant support, and shared information about her exciting research concerning the Underground Railroad in Oswego County. Sarah Elbert also provided helpful and perceptive comments on a draft of the manuscript. Winston Grady-Willis, a fellow historian and colleague in the Department of African American Studies at Syracuse University, gave generously of his time and affirmed my belief that narrative history has a place among academic historians. Judge Hugh Humphreys, a marvelous storyteller and historical investigator whose passion for good history and good writing is unflagging, helped more than I, as his friend, had a right to ask or expect. His detailed and pointed remarks, editorial suggestions, and gentle prodding kept me true to the course.

Finally, I wish to remember all the friends of liberty in Upstate New York who undertook, with whatever resources they possessed, the task of making the region a place where the North Star of freedom could shine. It is most appropriate to make that remembrance on this day, the 150th anniversary celebration of the bold rescue, performed by the friends of freedom in Syracuse, of the fugitive some called William Henry and others knew as Jerry.

Milton C. Sernett
Cazenovia, New York
October 1, 2001

Introduction

*Borrowing from the masthead of Frederick Douglass's famous newspaper,
I have christened Upstate New York "North Star Country" in this book.
In its most literal sense, the North Star was the astronomical reference
point used by freedom-seekers on the Underground Railroad. But the
North Star was also emblematic of the freedom struggle itself, a moral
enterprise which began in the wake of the Upstate New York's evangelical
awakening during the 1820s and which did not cease until the passing
away of the abolitionist generation during the 1870s. James W. C. Pennington, known as the fugitive blacksmith, welcomed Douglass's* North
Star *and, upon receiving the first issue, wrote, "My taste is well suited to
the style of the 'Star.' The name, I think, is a happy one, indeed. There
cannot, to my mind, be a more appropriate name. Let it be then, what the
Polar Star is in the heavens—brilliant, dignified, standing in bold relief,
and, above all, so constant to its position, that the bewildered mariner is
sure of his reckoning if he can but fix his eye upon it. So it is also to the flying bondsman; and so may the 'North Star' ever be."*[1]

In May 1847, Frederick Douglass, in the company of William
Lloyd Garrison, attended the thirteenth annual meeting of the
American Anti-Slavery Society (AASS) in New York City. Since
its formation in 1833, the AASS had espoused the Garrisonian philosophy of immediate, unconditional, and uncompensated emancipation. Now the abolitionists gathered to hear—once again—the
call to battle. Despite the split in abolitionist ranks seven years earlier which resulted in the formation of the rival American and Foreign Anti-Slavery Society, Garrison took the podium, confident that
New England, more specifically Boston, was still the epicenter of the
abolitionist movement.

As Garrison spoke, the crowd began to chant, "Douglass, Douglass," an indication that Garrison's protégé, as biographer William McFeely phrased it, "was getting to be more than Boston could contain or be comfortable with."[2] When it was Douglass's turn to speak, he described slavery as "a system so demoralizing and inhuman, so impious and atheistical, so hostile to the cause of liberty and Christianity throughout the world" that it was everyone's duty to destroy it. Garrison reported, "Douglass was eminently successful in his speech, and was warmly applauded from beginning to end."[3]

Douglass still counted himself a loyal Garrisonian, but he was looking beyond New England and the circle of Boston immediatists for a base of operations. He intended to start another abolitionist newspaper, one that would give him an editorial voice of his own. Douglass was explicit about his motives: "It is neither a reflection on the fidelity, nor a disparagement of the ability of our friends and fellow-laborers, to assert what 'common sense affirms and only folly denies,' that the man who has *suffered the wrong* is the man to *demand redress,*—that the man STRUCK is the man to CRY OUT— and that he who has *endured the cruel pangs of Slavery* is the man to advocate Liberty."[4]

In early fall, Douglass set plans in motion to launch his paper in Upstate New York—a decision that was to have important consequences for him and for the region I am calling North Star Country in honor of his paper and all it symbolized. On October 28, 1847, Douglas wrote to Amy Post, a Quaker woman from Rochester whom he had met on his first trip to Upstate New York in 1843, "I have finally decided on publishing the *North Star* in Rochester and to make that city my future home."[5] Dedicated to the victims of oppression, the first issue of the *North Star* appeared on December 3, 1847. Rochester remained Douglass's home for the next quarter century. His decision to relocate to Upstate New York proved to be a wise one for, by the 1840s, the region rivaled New England in importance to the continuing battle against slavery. Douglass lived until 1895, but he did not move out of Rochester until 1872 when he took up residence in Washington, D.C.

This book tells the story of how the Empire State's central and western area, once termed the Burned-over District in reference to the successive religious revivals sweeping it in the 1820s, participated in the crusade for black freedom, a crusade born of religious revivals and continuing through

Frederick Douglass (1818–1895). From a rarely published daguerreotype, this image of Douglass probably dates from the late 1840s. Douglass resided in North Star Country for a quarter century and was an eloquent and courageous witness for freedom. He was also one of the principal actors in the intimate circle of reformers who worked out of the old Burned-over District. *Courtesy of the Onondaga Historical Association.*

Office of the *North Star,* Rochester. Frederick Douglass opened an office in the Talman block of downtown Rochester at 25 Buffalo Street (now E. Main Street). This view dates from after the Civil War. *Reproduced from the Rochester Historical Society's Publication Series Volume XIV [1936].*

the Civil War into the 1870s, when many of the veteran abolitionists passed from the scene.

This theme first tugged at me in early spring 1995 when I was far from the hills and valleys of Upstate New York and suffering from a serious case of *heimweh,* a word that Swiss soldiers stationed at the Vatican in the sixteenth century used to mean homesickness. While I was a senior Fulbright scholar at the Free University in Berlin, Germany, I gave illustrated talks about the abolitionist movement of the Burned-over District. This term has been associated with the part of New York State west of the Adirondacks and the Catskills since the publication of Whitney Cross's classic book, *The Burned-over District: The Social and Intellectual History of Enthu-siastic Religion in Western New York, 1800–1850,* almost a half century ago.[6] I did have the good sense to hide most of my regional chauvinism in the celebration of Upstate New York history by reminding my European listeners that many contemporary Americans were also unfamiliar with the region's role as a threshold of freedom before the Civil War.

Before I moved to Syracuse from the Midwest in 1975, my emotive connections with New York's Burned-over District were with scraps of its history as diverse as Cooperstown's National Baseball Hall of Fame, Mark Twain's house in Elmira, and, of course, the celebrated Erie Canal. I knew more about the strange odyssey of the Cardiff Giant—now in repose at the Farmers' Museum in Cooperstown but originally hewn from a stone quarry in my natal state of Iowa—than I did about Gerrit Smith of Peterboro, who was surely one of the most important and least chronicled American abolitionists.[7] Since 1991, when I moved to Cazenovia in Madison County, I have visited Peterboro, which is located about ten miles to the east, many times. Through the research I have done for this book, I now understand what the African American abolitionist Henry H. Garnet meant when he remarked, in 1848, "there are yet two places where slaveholders cannot come—Heaven and Peterboro."[8]

In the early 1980s, I came upon the shadowy figure of Beriah Green while rereading *The Souls of Black Folk,* by W. E. B. DuBois, the preeminent African American scholar of the twentieth century and heir to abolitionist activism. In the chapter titled, "The Faith of the Fathers," DuBois sings a song of praise for his mentor Alexander Crummell, one of the most important black activist intellectuals of the nineteenth century. According to DuBois, Crummell told him how strenuously Beriah Green labored to remove the veil of racial prejudice from Oneida Institute, located in Whitesboro, Oneida County, when Crummell was a student there in the mid-1830s.[9] I began a quest to understand, and then remedy, why it was that Beriah Green, who presided over the inaugural assembly of the AASS in December 1833, merited only a passing reference in the existing canon of abolition studies. This quest resulted in the publication of *Abolition's Axe: Beriah Green, Oneida Institute, and the Black Freedom Struggle* in 1986.[10]

North Star Country uses a wider lens than that employed in *Abolition's Axe,* one that brings a larger cast of characters into view. Though the story that follows encompasses the western two-thirds of New York State, commonly called Upstate New York or central and western New York, my narrative highlights a core area along the Erie Canal from Utica to Rochester: the heart and soul of New York State's old Burned-over District. In addition, the fascinating, often heroic, and sometimes cantankerous cast of characters moved from Upstate New York onto other stages. Beriah Green lectured in Tappan Hall in New York City, freedom-seekers found refuge in Canada West (now Ontario), Gerrit Smith sought to influence affairs in the nation's capital, Susan B. Anthony and Elizabeth Cady Stanton went to London for the 1840 world antislavery gathering, coconspirators of John Brown headed down to Virginia, brash young men marched off to Civil War battlefields, and idealistic young teachers went into the war-ravaged South to instruct those who had come out of the House of Bondage.

Frederick Douglass was correct. The black freedom crusade did not end when President Abraham Lincoln signed the Emancipation Proclamation or when victorious Yankee soldiers stacked arms and returned home. Many of the pioneering abolitionists who took up the torch of *immediatism* in the 1830s either retired from the crusade after the Civil War or passed away. However, as the concluding part of my narrative makes clear, a new and younger phalanx followed in their footsteps, convinced that securing the liberty of the newly freed slaves was critical to the abolitionist mission.

This book incorporates a thematic timeline of more than a half century. On July 5, 1827, Nathaniel Paul's oration celebrated the end of slavery in New York State (see the discussion in chapter 2). His speech symbolizes the optimism found in the opening scenes of the main part of our story. In 1869, Edmonia Highgate's return to Syracuse and her tragic death illustrate the demise of the post–Civil War effort of the abolitionists to extend the freedom crusade beyond emancipation.

To comprehend the significance of these events, I have extended the timeline both backward and forward. Thus, by way of prologue, chapter 1 examines the pre-1827 presence of African Americans in the crucible of Upstate New York's emerging regional and religious identity. The epilogue sketches out post–Civil War developments, gives attention to how African Americans fared in North Star Country after the passage of the Thirteenth Amendment, which abolished slavery, and examines efforts to perpetuate the abolitionist legacy.

Abolitionism takes on multiple meanings in my account of how the black freedom question played out in Upstate New York. I am interested in going beyond chronicling a self-contained reform movement with a consistent ideology and set cast of characters.

In the early chapters of this book, I focus on the emergence of immediatism within a cultural region defined by revivalism and reform in the 1820s and 1830s. The antislavery voices we hear in these chapters belong to what has been traditionally thought of as *movement abolitionism;* that is, to reformers who were in harmony with the Garrisonian moral suasionists. But there were other, equally important expressions of antislavery sentiment in Upstate New York.

Chapter 4 explores the rifts caused by the debate about slavery and race when ecclesiastical abolitionists took the fight into America's churches. Chapter 5 concentrates on political abolitionism and the birth of the Liberty Party in North Star Country. Chapter 6 is transitional: in the turbulent 1850s, the national turmoil over how to check the expansion of slavery widened the arena in which freedom's advocates fought. It also brought traditional movement abolitionism into tension with anti-Southern sectionalism and set the allies for freedom on a collision course with agents of the federal government. My narrative of the Underground Railroad (chapter 7) highlights the contributions of self-defined abolitionists as well as those who did not identify with any faction of movement abolitionism. In chapter 8, where the focus is John Brown's relationship with North Star Country personalities, *radical abolitionism* comes to the forefront. Chapter 9, "Battlefields and Home Fronts," shows the abolitionist impulse to be diffused, unarticulated, and unintentional, as in the case of Yankee soldiers who fought only to put down the South. What began as a clash between the white South and the white North was transformed into a freedom war by the participation, on and off the battlefield, of African Americans and their radical allies. *North Star Country's* epilogue tracks the pursuit of freedom for African Americans into the early Reconstruction period, when there was still hope that the end of this country's bloodiest conflict would give rise to a more egalitarian America.

I need to make three additional clarifications about this attempt to recapitulate the black freedom crusade from the vantage point of Upstate New York. First, the presence of African Americans in this region defined the emancipation struggle in ways that were richer and more powerful than allowed for by traditional treatments of movement abolitionism, which portrayed it as the work of a minority of white males. Samuel R. Ward, the black abolitionist and clergyman, claimed that racial prejudice was "less active and less bitter" in western New York "than in any other portion of the United States." Nevertheless, Ward regarded the region as "the very battle ground of impartial Freedom" because African Americans would be expected to achieve more there than in places where they were "overlooked, neglected and despised."[11] Ward, like Frederick Douglass, lived in North Star Country for most of the years that he was an abolitionist activist. In the narrative to follow, African Americans have a central role, not just as slaves and fugitives, but as principals in the freedom campaign; sometimes as partners with white reformers and, at other times, as independent actors.

Second, the women of Upstate New York made many contributions to the antislavery effort. In the process, they challenged the gender-based restrictions assigned to them during the antebellum decades. Charles G. Finney's revivalist preaching stressed that individuals must take moral responsibility for their actions, good as well as bad. By breaking with Calvinistic determinism, Finney reasserted the importance of free will for women as well as men.

Third, this book is about the moral choices made by Upstate New Yorkers of all religious persuasions—and none at all—when they were confronted by claims for African American liberty. Should one become an abolitionist or not? What must Christians do about slavery? How should the ballot box be used? Is it morally imperative to assist a fugitive? Should one think of John Brown as a misguided fanatic or a martyr for freedom's cause? In the struggle with the South, what is there to fight (and die) for? How can good people extend the freedom crusade beyond the Civil War?

These questions, and many others, troubled the consciences of residents in the Burned-over District. Then, as now, the slavery question generated intense self-examination regarding the most mundane aspects of daily life. In 1836, fourteen-year-old Elizabeth Smith affirmed: "I do not eat the products of slave labor but Aunt Rebecca has been very kind to me and has got me some other sugar. Once I was helping Aunt to make [?] out of slave sugar, or I knew nothing to the contrary, and I got a little on my finger when without thinking I put it in my mouth, but spit it out."[12] (Elizabeth Smith,

Gerrit Smith's feminist daughter, is credited with inventing the bloomer dress.) By reexamining the importance of individuals as moral actors, we discover how many inhabitants of the western two-thirds of New York State were twice born: first as converts to evangelicalism and second to immediatism.

I hope that readers of this book will arrive at the conclusion that New York State's Burned-over District deserves to be equally well-remembered as North Star Country—an accolade confirmed by Frederick Douglass's decision to settle in Rochester and, in the aggregate, by the moral choices of those who joined him in advancing the cause of freedom. When I apply "North Star Country" to Upstate New York, I do so with the understanding that there were other regions in the republic where freedom's allies could be found. *North Star Country,* however, is the story of the black freedom crusade, in its multiple dimensions, in a place I have called home for a quarter century. I hope that re-presenting the dramatic struggle to destroy slavery from the vantage point of Upstate New York will stimulate renewed interest in the history of reform and an appreciation for the importance of the African American presence in the region. The poet T. S. Eliot wrote, "And the end of all our exploring / Will be to arrive where we started / And know the place for the first time."[13]

North Star Country

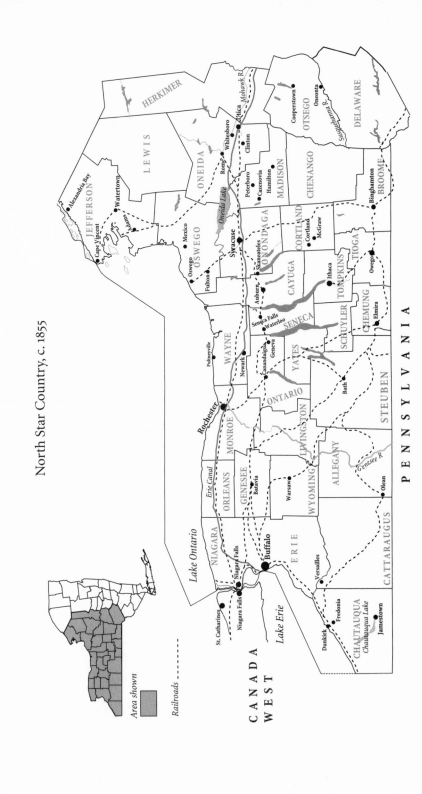

North Star Country, c. 1855

1. Slavery and the Burned-over District

"Everywhere that slavery exists," Austin Steward said of his years in Steuben County, "it is nothing but slavery. I found it just as hard to be beaten over the head with a piece of iron in New York as it was in Virginia."[1] Steward, who eventually made his home in Rochester, was one of approximately forty slaves that Captain William Helm brought to central New York State in 1804, first to Sodus Bay and then to Bath. Helm, a Virginian, was one of a small number of slaveholders who attempted to import the plantation system into Upstate New York after the Revolutionary War.[2]

Other African Americans were held in the region when it was sparsely populated by whites. Some of the first African Americans may have arrived in service to pioneer explorers and settlers. A few escapees found refuge among the resident Native Americans.[3] For the earliest African presence in what was to become New York State, we need to look back to the seventeenth century.

The slave population of colonial New York originated with the import of Africans by the Dutch. The population escalated after 1664 when the English took control of what had been known as New Netherland.[4] Those who worked the land of the old Dutch patroon estates along the Hudson River experienced something akin to the bondage underpinning the plantation economy of the southeastern seaboard. The typical slaveholder in the mid–Hudson River valley, whether Dutch or German, kept his slaves in his own household, with basements made up to accommodate them.[5]

Isabella Baumfree, who later took the name Sojourner Truth, is perhaps the best known of the African descendants who experienced slavery in the lower Hudson River valley. In 1797 she was born into slavery near the Hudson River in Ulster County. She was bought and sold at the whim of whites just as African Americans were in Richmond's Old Slave Mart. She performed domestic duties, such as cleaning and cooking, as did most female slaves in post-colonial New York. She also plowed, hoed, and reaped the fields.[6] Male slaves worked as farm hands, porters, bakers, carriage drivers, and were skilled at a variety of crafts.

The Dutch did not trouble with elaborate race-based legal codes and took a casual attitude toward the system of slavery, providing minimal legal distinctions between the categories of slave and free. A category of *half-free* allowed some individuals to be rewarded for long and faithful service with the equivalent of personal liberty, in exchange for the payment of, for example, "thirty schepels of maize or wheat and one fat hog, valued at twenty gilders."[7] Race-based codes did not prevent free blacks in New Netherland from making a living, and some "owned" white indentured servants.

Under English rule, however, black slaves found their lives more restricted. Slave couples were often forced to live apart. In 1702, "An Act for the Regulating of Slaves" prohibited those Africans held as slaves from carrying weapons, buying or selling anything, and, unless authorized by their masters, participating in social activities. During the colonial period several outbreaks of anti-black hysteria took place because of fears of slave insurrection. This hysteria was most notable in connection with two uprisings, one during 1712 and one during 1741, in Manhattan.[8] As a consequence, British colonial authorities redoubled their control efforts. In summing up the colonial period, David Kobrin writes, "New York's slave population was probably more widely diffused among the white population than in any other English colony. Although some masters owned bands of over 30 slaves, in the closing years of the colonial period few individuals owned more than 10 slaves, and the average master had between one and three slaves in his household."[9]

The Treaty of Paris in 1783 did not bring universal emancipation, although the political ideals of the American Revolution led some slaveholders to voluntarily manumit a small number of blacks. More significantly, some liberal-minded American patriots yoked Enlightenment notions of individual rights together with Christian teachings about the equality of souls and formed the New York Manumission Society in 1785.

Several prominent New Yorkers, including John Jay (later the first president of the society), Alexander Hamilton, Philip Schuyler, and Governor Lewis Morris, supported the New York Manumission Society's efforts to obtain emancipation by legislative action. The society attempted to thwart the illegal import and export of slaves for sale, assisted free blacks held in bondage illegally, promoted boycotts of merchants who profited from the slave trade, and established schools for black children and black adults. Although the society stimulated the growth of antislavery sentiment in New York, it lacked the sharp critique of Southern slavery that abolitionists would voice after 1831.[10] Only the Quakers, or Society of Friends, who issued the first protest against slavery in colonial New York at a meeting in Purchase during 1767, made a good faith effort to rid their communities of the sin of slavery. Several Quaker congregations went so far as to compensate individuals who had been held as slaves by the congregation's members.[11]

In 1790, the first federal census enumerated 21,329 individuals in the category of *slave* in New York State. Albany, New York, Queens, and Ulster Counties accounted for more than half of this number.

Ontario County was the only one of the thirty-two counties I have included in my demarcation of North Star Country that existed by 1790. It was formed in 1789 out of Montgomery County, covering the territory west of Seneca Lake and bordered by Lake Ontario to the north and Pennsylvania to the south. Known as Genesee Country, the area attracted additional white settlers, including some Southern planters, after the Seneca Nation signed over land rights in a deal arranged by land speculator Robert Morris in 1797. The 1790 census enumerated ten slaves and six free persons in Ontario County, out of only 1,075 inhabitants. Ontario County later shrank in size as other counties were carved out of it.[12]

By 1800, what was to become the Burned-over District, and later North Star Country, contained 351 slaves and 373 free persons of color. In 1810, the counts were 975 and 1,423, respectively. For reasons not entirely clear from the records, by 1820 the number of slaves in central and western New York State had declined to 662 while the number of free persons increased to 3,289.[13]

The opponents of slavery from New York State achieved partial success after the American Revolution via the passage of gradual emancipation measures. The Gradual Emancipation Act of 1799 stipulated that African

Americans born of slave mothers in New York State after July 4, 1799, were to be considered indentured servants. They had to serve their masters until the age of twenty-eight, if they were male, or the age of twenty-five, if they were female. They were then considered "free colored persons." In 1817, New York State enacted another gradual abolition law. It provided that slaves born before July 4, 1799, were to be freed on July 4, 1827. This prepared the way for universal emancipation in 1827.[14]

Austin Steward was one of a small number of African Americans in Upstate New York who went from the status of slave to free person before 1827. Determined to become his "own possessor," Steward considered running away or obtaining his freedom by joining the army. When he learned that Captain Helm had violated an 1801 state statute that prevented masters from hiring out their slaves to escape the provisions of the Gradual Emancipation Act, he sued for his freedom, with the aid of New York Manumission Society members. One of them took Steward into his own family in 1815, when Austin was about twenty-two. "I cannot describe to a free man, what a proud manly feeling came over me," Steward wrote in his autobiography, "when I hired to Mr. C. [Otis Comstock] and made my first bargain, nor when I assumed the dignity of collecting my own earnings."[15] In 1817, Steward settled in Rochester, where he operated a grocery and dry goods business. He is believed to have been Rochester's earliest black business owner and property owner.[16]

Some slaves in Upstate New York obtained their freedom by running away, long before there was anything like an organized network of friends for a fugitive and long before statewide emancipation. Peter Wheeler, a slave from Ludlowville, Cayuga County, fled his master's grasp in 1806. He said of his emotions at that time, "I now began to feel somethin' like a man, and the dignity of a human being began to creep over me, and I enjoyed my liberty when I got it, I can tell you."[17]

A few individuals managed to accumulate sufficient funds to purchase their own freedom. By working as a lumberman and hostler in the town of Caroline, Tompkins County, Peter Webb amassed $350. In 1818, he obtained the following affidavit signed by his owner: "This is to certify that I have this day agreed to discharge my man, Peter, known by the name of Peter Webb, from all further servitude as a slave; that he is free to act for himself as a free man from this time forward."[18] Webb later married, farmed for

Engraved by J. C. Buttre from an Ambrotype

Austin Steward (1793–1869). Remembered as the founder of Rochester's earliest black-owned business, Steward sold meats and other groceries from his store on E. Main Street. On July 5, 1827, Steward delivered the speech at Rochester's celebration of Emancipation Day (the end of slavery in New York State). *Courtesy of the Rochester Public Library.*

himself, raised a large family, and helped organize the African Methodist Episcopal Zion Congregation in Ithaca during 1833.[19]

Most slaves of the early national period were not as fortunate as Peter Webb. Thomas James's owner, Asa Kimball of Canajoharie, Montgomery County, once traded him for a yoke of oxen. James fled to Youngstown, Niagara County, and worked on Canada's Welland Canal. He then returned to the United States, thinking that his stay in the Province of Upper Canada, where slavery had been abolished by the Imperial Act of 1793, made him free under American law.[20] This was not the case; when James, at age nineteen, settled in Rochester in 1823, he was technically, at least, a runaway and subject to reenslavement. His legal status, and that of the 10,088 individuals the 1820 federal census counted as slaves in New York State,[21] was comparable to the condition of hundreds of thousands who languished under the whip of the Southern slave driver. Because of a brief autobiography James wrote and published in pamphlet form, we know something of the day-to-day struggles he experienced when the number of African Americans in Upstate New York was small.[22]

Free blacks in Upstate New York, as elsewhere in the North, had few economic and educational opportunities as the early national period (1789–1825) drew to a close. Public schools for free blacks did not exist, and most private schools barred their doors to the children of free blacks. A few charity schools, sponsored by manumission societies or religious groups opposed to slavery, sought to link emancipation with education. Utica and Geneva held Sunday schools for blacks in 1815 and 1816, respectively.

Austin Steward attended a manumission-sponsored academy in Ontario County. Of that experience he wrote, "With my books under my arm, and money of my own earning in my pocket, I stepped loftily along toward Farmington, where I determined to attend the Academy." Though Austin spent three winters "with pleasure and profit" at the school, he confessed, with chagrin, that at the age of twenty-three he was "yet to learn what most boys of eight years knew."[23]

Thomas James tells us that he knew nothing of "letters or religion" until, at age nineteen, he settled in Rochester and attended a Sunday school for "colored youths" opened by Mr. Freeman on Buffalo Street (now West Main Street). In 1828, James started his own school for "colored children" on Favor Street and began holding religious meetings. A year later he commenced preaching, and in 1830 he purchased property at Favor and Spring Streets on which to build a church. In May 1833, Bishop Christopher Rush of the African Methodist Episcopal Zion Church (a denomination organized during 1822 in New York City) ordained him. "I had been called Tom as a Slave," James commented, "and they called me Jim at the warehouse [of the Hudson and Erie line along the Erie Canal]. I put both together when I reached manhood, and was ordained as Rev. Thomas James."[24]

As was true in the downstate area, free blacks occupied the narrowest of niches in the emerging post-colonial economic order. Thus, few blacks were able to qualify for the elective franchise by amassing property worth $100. Given the extent of racial discrimination north of the Mason-Dixon Line, the fact that African Americans had the right to vote prior to the legal end of slavery in New York State may seem surprising. Before 1821, "every male inhabitant of full age" who satisfied residence and property requirements was allowed to vote. After 1821, the property restriction was removed from white males but kept for black males, who were required to own a freehold worth at least $250 in excess of all debts. Republicans apparently feared that the eligible African American electorate would, despite its small size, throw votes to the Republicans' Federalist opponents and provide the critical margin in close elections. The tightening of restrictions resulted in the virtual disfranchisement of free blacks in New York State. In 1826, a property tax list showed that only 298 of 39,999 blacks in the state (.007 percent) qualified under the property requirements.[25]

Though the end of slavery in 1827 did not remove all forms of legalized discrimination against them in New York State, African Americans viewed July 4th of that year as a significant step forward. To avoid any conflict with the festivities marking Independence Day, state-wide black emancipation was observed on July 5th.

The principal festivities were held in Albany, the state capital. According to the *Albany Argus and City Gazette,* a procession led by "African bands and Marshals" and followed by "state officers, the Judiciary, Senate, members of Congress, members of Cincinnati, revolutionary worthies and citizens" made its way to the Second Baptist Church. One suspects that not a few of the black marchers keenly felt the irony of the moment—it had taken a half century for the egalitarian rhetoric of the American Revolution to be applied to them.

On July 5, 1827, Reverend Nathaniel Paul stood in the pulpit of the Second Baptist Church to reflect on the meaning of emancipation in New York State. Brightly colored banners bearing the names of some of the stalwart advocates of state emancipation hung in the church. Celebrants, black and white, crowded in to hear what this black preacher had to say. Paul had been pastor of Second Baptist, Albany's only African American church, for seven years, but he had never felt so overwhelmed with the high responsibility of the preacher's task as he did at that moment. It was his duty to probe the deepest meaning of emancipation in New York State so that the "good story" could be preserved in the communal memory "to our children and to our children's children, down to the latest posterity."

After reviewing the long history of black suffering, beginning with the tears of the oppressed on the slave ships, the black preacher asked the hardest question of all: "Tell me, ye mighty waters, why did ye sustain the ponderous load of misery? or speak, ye winds, and say why it was that ye executed your office to waft them onward to the still more dismal state; and ye proud waves, why did you refuse to lend your aid and to have overwhelmed them with your billows?" Echoing the theological insight given to Job in the Bible, Paul sought an answer to the dilemma of the suffering of the innocent in God's "sovereign prerogative to bring good out of evil." Thus, it was all the more important to recognize the historic significance of what had transpired in the lives of black New Yorkers. "Under the Almighty," Paul declaimed, "we are enabled to recognize the fourth day of the present month, as the day in which the cause of justice and humanity have triumphed over tyranny and oppression, and slavery is forever banished from the state of New York."[26]

Orators outside the state capital did not draw as large a crowd as Paul had, but the spirit of celebration, mixed with concern about what the future might hold, was the same. The *Ithaca Chronicle* reported, with a note of sarcasm, that because blacks had taken a holiday to observe emancipation day, "Every man must be his own servant for the day; and many fair hands are constrained to engage in culinary and household matters."[27] In Rochester, Austin Steward participated in a celebration replete with band music and booming cannon. In his address, Steward asserted, "Let us as one man, on this day resolve that hence-forth, by continual endeavors to do good to all mankind, we will claim for ourselves the attention and respect which as men we should possess."[28]

Steward's well-being, and that of other blacks in Upstate New York, would depend in large measure on the character the region would develop as it became more populated. Prior to the American Revolution, the westward advance of white settlement had come into conflict with the Iroquois Confederacy. But after the peace of 1783, New York frontiersmen moved into the Mohawk River valley, the central Finger Lakes, the Genesee Valley, and the Ontario lake plain. Before long, farms, villages, and towns dotted the map. Within forty years the age of the frontier had come to an end. In 1820, more than 700,000 inhabitants, most of which were of European descent, lived west of the 1783 frontier line. Except for parts of central and western New York State that had questionable agricultural potential, such as the Tug Hill Upland and the western Adirondacks, the region had achieved a measure of economic and cultural maturity.[29]

The emergence of what we are calling North Star Country as a distinct region was accelerated by the opening of DeWitt Clinton's celebrated ditch: the Erie Canal. Construction of the canal that was meant to link Albany and Buffalo began on July 4, 1818. When it was completed in October 1825, the 363-mile artery fostered economic development and the cultural integration of central New York State with western New York State. The cost of a ton of produce that was carried between Albany and Buffalo was reduced from $100 to $12, including tolls. Wheat from the bread-basket farms of the Genesee Valley could be brought to flour mills in Rochester, processed, and then sent by canal boat to Albany and by ship to the markets of New York City.[30] Immigrants, in turn, flowed into North Star Country along the canal. Many of them came from parts of New England plagued by agricultural recession. These canal travelers were following the call to the new lands of the West—a call many others had heeded since the 1790s when hundreds of thousands of acres that had been distributed to Revolutionary War veterans were sold to speculators and land companies.[31]

The historians who described the social composition of the population beyond the 1783 frontier line write of Yankees and Yorkers.[32] Yorkers came north from Pennsylvania or New Jersey, or west from eastern (downstate) New York. They settled primarily in the Southern Tier. Yankees, the larger of the two migrant streams, were natives of New England. Many of them hailed from Vermont, and they tended to cluster together in Upstate New York towns. Settlers from Massachusetts and Connecticut, particularly from the western portions of those states, likewise flocked into the nineteen

New York counties that comprised the post-1783 region of settlement expansion. Some of these Yankees settled in Upstate New York only to remove to Ohio's Western Reserve, which the State of Connecticut claimed, or to lower Michigan. Both regions became hotbeds of antislavery activity after 1830.

The process by which the New York frontier was peopled by Yankees and Yorkers was not an orderly one. In the first decades of settlement, the communities lacked a homogeneous identity. Nevertheless, a regional culture gradually emerged, one which was dominated by the values and traditions imported from New England. As the distinguished historical geographer Donald Meinig argues, "when western New York was opened for settlement in the first decade of the republic, New Englanders migrated and settled in such numbers upon so wide an extent of country during this community-forming period as to stamp an indelible Yankee imprint upon the subsequent history and character of all Upstate beyond the Hudson and Middle Mohawk valleys."[33] Even the architectural look of many of the towns and villages reminded passing travelers of New England. It is not surprising that some thought of Upstate New York as New England Extended.

In addition to serving as a channel for the diffusion of Yankee culture and values, the Erie Canal, together with its feeder canals, stimulated the commercial development of Upstate New York. By the time Andrew Jackson was elected in 1828 and the Democrats had achieved ascendancy on the national scene, Upstate New York was no longer a region of isolated farms. Flour milling in Rochester, the salt business in Syracuse, textile manufacturing in Utica—all signified a more complex economic order, which was further accelerated by the construction of the first railroads.[34]

Historians who have examined this process of regional integration in greater detail, and with much more precision, than can be done here underscore the cultural consequences. Mary P. Ryan examined changes in family patterns in Oneida County. She concluded that, by the 1820s, there was a significant trend away from the agrarian patriarchal model and toward a more town-centered middle-class-family model in which women exercised more independence by involving themselves in a variety of reform and benevolent causes.[35] Paul E. Johnson studied Rochester and found that the emerging manufacturing economy fostered starker class divisions as well as debates over community values among Upstate New

Yorkers. He argued that the Rochester revival of 1830–1831 (of which more will be said shortly) was fundamentally a "middle-class solution to problems of class, legitimacy, and order."[36]

As fundamental as canals and railroads were to giving Upstate New York a regional identity, another kind of event took place near the village of Adams, in Jefferson County, on a Sabbath evening in the autumn of 1821. This event would affix the label Burned-over District to the cultural core of North Star Country.

On October 10 of that year, a young lawyer by the name of Charles Grandison Finney (1792–1875) walked into the woods north of town with a heavy heart. Finney's family homestead was in nearby Henderson, a part of northern New York State that was sparsely settled and that had retained much of the character of the raw frontier. Although Finney's grandson characterized the famous revivalist's youthful years as those of a splendid pagan,[37] and although Finney himself described his preconversion life as given over to one sin or another, this young man was no Saul on the road to Damascus. However, he was anxious about the state of his soul. This anxiety was born of a recent flare-up of religious awakenings in which individuals in the area had been encouraged to ask themselves if they were truly converted.

On that fateful October morning, Finney left the law office of Wright and Wardwell in an agitated state. As he later related, upon finding a remote spot in a large wooded tract, he resolved to "give my heart to God, or I never will come down from there." Finney knelt. The hours passed. "I prayed," he wrote, "till my mind became so full that, before I was aware of it, I was on my feet and tripping up the ascent toward the road." Full of joy and peace, this young lawyer found a new calling: he would become a preacher. Finney returned to his law office, took out his bass viol, and played and sang hymns, still in a state of great emotional upheaval. Another wave of intense religious feeling passed over him and he experienced "a mighty baptism of the Holy Ghost." When a client came in to remind Finney that his services were needed the next morning in court, Finney replied, "Deacon Barney, I have a retainer from the Lord Jesus Christ to plead his cause, and I cannot plead yours."[38]

Following his conversion, Finney became a Presbyterian minister. Church leaders commissioned him "to labor in the Northern parts of the

Country of Jefferson and such other destitute places in that vicinity as his discretion shall dictate."[39] This lawyer-turned-revivalist was not the only itinerant evangelist in Upstate New York, but he had gifts others did not: a vigorous physique, a personable manner, a powerful voice, and, above all, remarkable eyes. Many of the converted who came under his sway remembered Finney's deep blue magnetic eyes. He seemed to be able to look directly into the souls of those to be converted, breaking down resistance to the gospel message. His grandson described his eyes as "large and blue, at times mild as an April sky, and at others, cold and penetrating as polished steel."[40]

Finney sermonized that everyone, church member or not, needed to make a personal decision for the Lord. Finney broke with the traditional Calvinist doctrine of original sin, which was pessimistic about human nature, by emphasizing free will; that is, the individual's ability to respond willingly to the offer of divine grace. This belief liberated the evangelist from the gloomy Calvinist doctrine which asserts that because God knows who will be saved and who will be damned, one's spiritual fate is predetermined. Building upon the earlier insights of Puritan theologian Jonathan Edwards and his followers, the New Divinity preachers of New England, Finney stressed that humans have free will and therefore can choose for God. In other words, they can *choose* good over evil.

The significance of this revelation may be difficult to appreciate at our current distance from the cultural crucible of the Burned-over District. We are not familiar with the religious language of the 1820s, and the contemporary age is not one in which the question of free will is commonly discussed. By underscoring the power of moral agency, Finney accented the importance of choosing, "Gospel salvation seemed to me to be an offer of something to be accepted; and that it was full and complete; and that all that was necessary on my part, was to get my own consent to give up my sins, and accept Christ."[41] And if thousands accepted this understanding of Christian conversion, what were the social consequences? Michael Barkun, a political scientist and close student of millenarian movements, provides this useful interpretation of the link between "getting" saved and saving the world:

> Individuals might save themselves, or rather open themselves up to God's saving grace. While in theory this might happen at any time, it was more likely to happen under the prodding of a skilled revivalist, who knows how to arouse a

Charles G. Finney (1792–1875). Finney was an evangelical preacher and revivalist who sparked a religious awakening in Upstate New York during the late 1820s and early 1830s. The awakening prepared the way for the abolitionist campaign. Although he was averse to a direct attack upon slavery by political means, Finney believed that human bondage was sinful. *Courtesy of the Oneida County Historical Society at Utica, N.Y.*

sense of despair while at the same time holding out the possibility of transformation. As predestination reinforced the social hierarchy of the colonial village, so revivalists' conversions harmonized with the new Jacksonian social mobility. Increasingly, all things were deemed possible, including freeing the world from sin by the exercise of possible initiative.[42]

One wonders if Finney realized how powerful his sermons were and how potentially disruptive they were to existing social arrangements, especially when they were heard by people trying to make sense of the economic, political, and cultural changes transforming the Burned-over District, the area across which the revivalist moved with such intensity for about a decade.

The evangelist with the "large and prominent blue eyes" began preaching in the remote parts of northern New York State but reaped a more bountiful harvest in the upper Mohawk River valley. Thousands experienced conversion. Finney felt himself "pulled 40 ways at once." The Utica revivals, which took place from 1825 to 1827, were especially spectacular.[43] Rochester fell under the spell of Finney's preaching in the winter of 1830–1831. Finney capped off his work in Rochester with a five-day "protracted meeting" during which hundreds of new converts were made through revivals that lasted from sunrise to sunset.[44] Before Finney left Upstate New York to seek an even larger harvest in Philadelphia, Boston, and New York City, hardly any community, of whatever size, was left untouched, directly or indirectly, by the sparks of revivalism. John L. Hammond estimates that between 1825 and 1835 at least 1,343 revivals took place in New York State. These were concentrated in central and western New York State during 1829–1832.[45]

Although some critics tarred Finney with the brush of the crude frontier revivalist, he was not an unlettered camp meeting preacher. Unlike the purveyors of religious excitement who were associated with the Second Great Awakening in places like Cane Ridge, Kentucky, and points further west in Ohio and Indiana, Finney did not encourage or practice spiritual pyrotechnics. As historian Whitney R. Cross wrote in his classic account of the Burned-over District, "No agonizing souls fell in the aisle, no raptured ones shouted hallelujahs. Rather, despite his doses of hell-fire, the great evangelist, 'in an unclerical suit of grey,' acted like a lawyer arguing . . . before a court and jury, talking wit, verve, and informality."[46]

As a young man, Henry Stanton heard Finney when the revivalist campaigned in Rochester. Many years later, after his long career as an abolitionist, Stanton recalled, "I listened. It did not sound like preaching, but like a lawyer arguing a case . . . The discourse was a chain of logic . . . I have heard many celebrated pulpit orators in various parts of the world. Taken all in all, I never knew the superior of Charles G. Finney."[47]

Elizabeth Cady, the future Elizabeth Cady Stanton and women's rights crusader, also attended some of Finney's protracted meetings. She wrote in her memoirs,

> I can see him now, his great eyes rolling around the congregation and his arms flying about in the air like those of a windmill. One evening he described hell and the devil and the long procession of sinners being swept down the rapids, about to make the awful plunge into the burning depths of liquid fire below, and the rejoicing hosts in the inferno coming up to meet them with the shouts of the devils echoing through the vaulted arches.

Finney suddenly stopped, pointed at the procession he was rhetorically creating, and said, "There, do you not see them!" Mesmerized by the revivalist's dramatization, young Elizabeth jumped up and looked in the direction Finney pointed. That night she slept fitfully. Visions of the damned haunted her. She suffered from depression for some time thereafter. "To change the current of my thoughts," the future feminist pioneer recalled, "a trip was planned to Niagra, and it was decided that the subject of religion was to be tabooed altogether."[48]

Pulpiteers of the old school, including the Reverend George Gale, under whose gaze Finney sat while unconverted in Adams, customarily read their sermons. Finney improvised and often addressed individuals by name, calling upon them to come to Jesus. He persuaded women to give testimony in public, something highly unusual in an age when women were supposed to keep silent in so-called promiscuous assemblies. Under Finney's influence, hundreds of small prayer groups were organized, new churches were started, and scores of men and women committed themselves to evangelical work and benevolent campaigns such as the temperance movement. Evangelicals sought to reinforce the sanctity of the Sabbath by restricting secular activity; to promote Christian education and foreign and domestic missions; and, most importantly, as we shall soon see, to abolish slavery. Finney's methods, which were emulated by others, came to be called new measures. The firestorm of revivals that engulfed Upstate New York during the twelve-year period of 1825 to 1837 belongs to the general outbreak of religious enthusiasm and moral passion known as the Second Great Awakening.[49]

Finney's influence on the region I have defined as North Star Country was both profound and enduring.[50] Although the revivalist moved to the post of theological professor at Ohio's Oberlin College in 1835, he would not be forgotten in the churches of the Burned-over District. Of him, Whitney Cross said,

> Charles Finney has seemed to some historians, as to many of his contemporaries, to be one of those rare individuals who of their own unaided force may on occasion significantly transform the destinies of masses of people. His influence was indeed extraordinary. His example probably contributed more to the complexion of ensuing events than did any of the other coincident phenomena which introduced the distinctive phase of Burned-over District history.[51]

As to the boundaries of the region that felt the impact of revivalism, Cross wrote, "No exact geographical sense can be assigned to the phrase. It simply meant the place where enthusiasts flourished. But convenience dictates an arbitrary boundary located to include the major expressions of spirit identified by the term. For my purposes I have defined the Burned-over District as that portion of New York State lying west of the Catskill and Adirondack Mountains."[52] As we explore the transformation of New York's Burned-over District into North Star Country, our regional boundaries are approximately the same. Lakes Ontario and Erie serve as the northern and western borders; the Pennsylvania line is the southern border; and the Catskill and Adirondack Mountains mark the eastern boundary of this roughly thirty-two-county area.[53]

There were other burned-over districts in the nation, regions where revivals and reform campaigns of one kind or another flourished. Parts of western New England and the West (formerly the Northwest Territory) also witnessed eruptions of religious enthusiasm. Vermont, for example, had its own burned-over district.[54] But there was something about Finney territory that was singular. Historian Judith Wellman writes, "It also spawned Mormonism, Millerism, and the organized women's rights movements. It welcomed the Shakers, the Oneida perfectionists, and Fourierist groups, and it nurtured abolitionists, temperance people, dress reformers, water cure enthusiasts, peace advocates, educational reformers, asylum-builders, and anti–tight-lacing societies. Although it was not the only reform area in America, it remained a vibrant, churning center of the storm for three decades and more."[55] To this list we should append the 1848 spirit rappings that were conducted by the Fox sisters in Hydeville and later in Rochester.

Spiritualists formed religious communes along the Finger Lakes, and spiritualist groups still dot the Upstate New York landscape. For example, the Temple of Truth Church, Inc., meets for worship at Freeville in Tompkins County. The Shakers established a colony in 1826 at Sodus on Lake Ontario and later moved to Groveland, about fifty miles to the southwest in Livingston County. Residents of the Burned-over District also dabbled in the pseudoscience of phrenology. Prison reform, which culminated in the progressive prison system at the state facility in Auburn, the anti-Masonic movement, and educational experiments that emphasized manual labor and curricular reform likewise benefited from burnt-over zeal.

The feeling that the whole self could be purged of the weaknesses of the flesh and thereby strengthened for the war on worldly evil was so intense that some Upstate New Yorkers, including, as we shall see, a number of prominent abolitionists, adopted various health regimens. These regimens included taking the water cure and following the diet popularized by Sylvester Graham, the namesake of the graham cracker.[56]

Whether searching for a higher moral plane as members of utopian groups such as the one led by John Humphrey Noyes near Sherrill in Oneida County, or participating in new religious movements like Mormonism and Millerism, those affected by the *isms* had much in common. They sought a better world through the perfection of the self. Noyes went so far down the perfectionist path that he ended up denying the reality of sin or, more precisely, trying to operate the Oneida community as if human beings did not need the checks and balances of basic institutions such as family, church, and government.[57] Although most leaders of the new religious movements were not radical ultraists like Noyes and his followers, they did intend to reshape the inner self, turning loose the human will and thereby human potential. In the wake of Finney's crusade, people were changed and then set about attempting to change the world around them. In his "Instructions to Converts," Finney set a lofty goal. The newly converted should "aim at being holy, and not rest satisfied till they are as perfect as God."[58]

In 1830, as Finney came to Rochester to capture it for the Lord, a young man known as Joe Smith published the *Book of Mormon* in the nearby village of Palmyra. The family of Joe Smith, like many others who dwelled in Upstate New York, had migrated from New England, specifically from Vermont. Joseph Smith was troubled by the competing claims of the existing religious denominations in the Burned-over District, many of which were now in turmoil because of the controversy over Finney's "new measures." Made anxious by the crop of new religious groups sprouting up, Joseph Smith sought an authoritative answer in golden plates that had been revealed to him, so he said, by an angel. Smith was no Finneyite, and Mormonism was, in many ways, a conservative reaction to the radical religious and social experimentation cultivated by Upstate New Yorkers during the evangelical awakening. The irony was that Mormonism was itself a new religion and that it mirrored its own cultural birthplace. The *Book of Mormon* reflected the eclectic yet powerful religious and social character of the Burned-over District, incorporating, as one of its contemporary critics recognized, "every error and almost every truth discussed in New York for the last ten years."[59]

The followers of the adventist prophet William Miller felt a special urgency during these troubled times. Miller taught that the world would end with the second coming of Christ. Under pressure from his followers to set a specific date, he calculated that those alive in 1844 would witness the event.[60] Although most Upstate New Yorkers did not become Millerites, many did conclude that they were entering a time of testing in which it was important to work for righteousness in preparation for that day when the Kingdom of God would be realized among them. This was *premillennialism*—a belief that, before Christ returned to judge the world, good would triumph over evil for one thousand years. Some Upstaters took up the crusade to reshape the world with such intensity that they were called *ultraists*, a term first applied by conservative critics but later used by social historians to describe those reformers who aimed at the radical reconstruction of self and community. Some enthusiasts withdrew from a sinful world into utopian shelters; others took on the seemingly impossible task of bringing an entire nation into harmony with the moral law of God.

During the first phase of revivals in Upstate New York, the abolition of slavery was not Finney's primary objective. He preached against sin in a general way, urging his hearers to put the works of the devil behind them and to direct their footsteps onto the narrow path of righteousness. His earliest recorded comments regarding the South's "peculiar institution" appear in *Lectures on Revivals of Religion,* published in 1834. Of slavery Finney said, "It is a great national sin. It is a sin of the Church. . . . Let Christians of all denominations meekly, yet firmly, come forth, and pronounce their verdict; let them wash their hands of this thing."[61] Finney attempted to put his antislavery principles into practice at New York City's Chatham Street Chapel (where he preached) by forbidding slaveholders to take communion.

A fair evaluation of Finney must acknowledge his personal animosity toward a system that made one segment of the human race lord over another. His groundbreaking work as an evangelist in Upstate New York did precede the outburst of abolitionist activism that the region witnessed during the Second Great Awakening. He did not inject himself into abolitionist politics, expressing concern about what was called the amalgamation of blacks and whites, and he believed that his most important work was to summon Americans to a great religious revival. By so doing, Finney contended, others were empowered to take up the cause of the slave.[62]

As the third decade of the nineteenth century opened, the nation was— the abolitionist radicals charged—still asleep regarding the crucial question of slavery. It was the age of Jackson, sometimes called the age of the common man. This designation came from the 1828 presidential campaign that pitted Andrew Jackson of Tennessee and the Democrats against John Quincy Adams of Massachusetts and the National Republicans. The Democrats depicted the National Republicans as old-time Federalists. A year after Jackson's victory celebration, in which thousands of his most enthusiastic supporters ran wildly through the White House, bitter debates took place in the U.S. Congress over states' rights and federal power.

Although Jackson was a Southerner and former slaveholder, he gave the following toast on April 13, 1830, at the Jefferson Day Dinner, "Our Union: It *must be* preserved," to which Vice President John C. Calhoun of South Carolina responded, "The Union, next to our liberty, most dear."[63] The debate over federal power broke down, for the most part, along sectional lines. Southerners sought to retain the right to nullify federal laws and seized on tariff, banking, and internal improvement issues as representative of federal impositions that were harmful to them. Lurking in the closet was the most explosive issue of all: slavery. The danger was that it would, when fully and publicly debated, bring sectional tensions to the boiling point.

As we have seen, New Yorkers observed the death of slavery in their state during 1827. Perhaps the inhabitants of Upstate New York, where no gangs of black slaves hoed cotton and where the opening of the Erie Canal promised a bright commercial future, might be forgiven for thinking that slavery was the South's problem. As the Burned-over District advanced from frontier to a more culturally mature and self-sufficient economic unit, regional integration and pride blossomed. Yet the very inland waterway that helped promote economic prosperity by providing Upstate New York farmers and manufacturers with a wider market was also a link to the larger world. It brought in ideas as well as exporting them.

In September 1829, a free black resident of Boston by the name of David Walker published a pamphlet in which he recounted the cruelties of slavery. He summed up by saying, "O Americans! Americans!! I call God—I call angels—I call men, to witness, that your DESTRUCTION *is at hand,* and will be speedily consummated unless you REPENT."[64] Walker's words struck white Southerners as so incendiary that any black person found with the pamphlet was punished severely. Black abolitionist Henry Highland Garnet, who studied at Oneida Institute near Whitesboro (Oneida County) in the mid-1830s, said of Walker's *Appeal,* "It was merely a smooth stone which this David took up, yet it terrified a host of Goliaths."[65] News of Walker's fiery attack upon slavery reached Upstate New York, but how widely his *Appeal* was read cannot be determined.

Most residents of the Burned-over District shuddered at the thought of slave insurrection and looked to other means to resolve the problem of slavery. Chief among these means was the American Colonization Society (ACS), which was organized during 1816 in Washington, D.C. The society proposed the sponsored transport of African Americans to Liberia in West Africa. Although the ACS encouraged a few masters to educate and selectively manumit bondsmen so that they could go to Africa as Christian missionaries, the historical record shows that the organization was far more interested in removing free blacks for the purpose of diminishing economic competition with whites. In the words of historian David B. Davis, the ACS was only a "surrogate for anti-slavery."[66] Those who supported the ACS, like the wealthy Gerrit Smith of Madison County, regardless of their personal antipathy toward slavery, were counted as coconspirators in the black slave's plight by a small, but vocal, group of zealots soon to be known as abolitionists.

To speak of central and western New York State collectively as North Star Country at the end of the 1820s is, of course, to adopt an historical anachronism. Clearly, many individuals felt that slavery was a vice having a pernicious effect on the betterment of the American nation. Perhaps a few individuals believed that something radical ought to be done to expunge the stain of slavery from the country's body politic. Finney had preached the necessity of personal conversion. For those in the Burned-over District who had pledged to seek good and shun evil, it was a small step from thinking in terms of individual regeneration to concluding that there needed to be a national conversion on the question of slavery.

Primed by the revivalists to expect victory in the war against the social manifestations of human depravity, Christians—new converts and reenergized older members alike—expressed optimism about the possibility of American redemption. Slavery, which was perceived as the sin of sins, stood in the way. Finney prepared the ground, but he had not plowed deeply enough to strike at the institutional roots of slavery. Like the tares sown among the wheat in the biblical parable, these roots threatened to choke out the tender shoots of righteousness which, in the abolitionist crusade to come, would symbolize the new and redeemed America. In their frontal assault upon those who believed slavery might gradually disappear, the abolitionists demanded immediate repentance and emancipation. Quaker poet John Greenleaf Whittier explained the basis for this approach of *immediatism,* once one was convinced that slavery was a sin:

> We do not talk of *gradual* abolition, because, as Christians, we find no authority for advocating a *gradual relinquishment of sin.* We say to slaveholders—"Repent NOW—*today*—IMMEDIATELY"; just as we say to the intemperate—"Break off from your vice *at once*—touch not—taste not—handle not—from henceforth forever." . . . Such is our doctrine of immediate, unprocrastinated repentance applied to the *sin of slavery.*[67]

2. The Awakening

*Shortly after David Walker hurled his smooth stone against slavery,
another New Englander struck sharply at what he termed, "the sum of all
villainies." In 1829, William Lloyd Garrison was the twenty-four-year-old
coeditor of a Baltimore-based antislavery newspaper,* Genius of Universal
Emancipation. *The paper was founded in 1821 by Benjamin Lundy, a
Quaker and an advocate of gradual emancipation. The paper became
more radical when Garrison endorsed immediatism. In the issue published on November 13, 1829, Garrison accused Frances Todd, a merchant
from Newburyport, Massachusetts, of allowing one of his ships to transport seventy-five slaves from Baltimore to New Orleans. Todd sued Garrison for libel. While imprisoned in Baltimore, Garrison wrote Todd on
May 13, 1830, "Sir, I owe you no ill-will. My soul weeps over your error. I
denounced your conduct in strong language—but did you not deserve it?
Consult your bible and your heart. I am in prison for denouncing slavery
in a free country! You, who have assisted in oppressing your fellow-
creatures, are permitted to go at large, and to enjoy the fruits of your
crime!—Cui prodest scelus, is fecit."*[1]

News of Garrison's imprisonment spread rapidly. Within weeks
his name was inseparably linked with the antislavery cause.
Arthur Tappan, a New York City merchant and philanthropist,
was angered by the attempt to suppress Garrison. He donated $100
toward the payment of Garrison's fine. During his forty-nine-day
imprisonment, Garrison resolved to dedicate his life to abolishing
slavery. From the Baltimore jail he wrote, "It is my shame that I have
done so little for the people of color. A few white victims must be
sacrificed to open the eyes of this nation, and to show the tyranny of
our own laws. I am willing to be persecuted, imprisoned and bound
for advocating African rights, and I should deserve to be a slave
myself, if I shrunk from that duty."[2]

Garrison returned to New England. In October, he gave a series of anti-slavery lectures. On January 1, 1831, the first issue of Garrison's own newspaper, the Boston-based *Liberator,* appeared.[3] Garrison condemned slavery in the strongest terms and called for immediate, uncompensated, unconditional emancipation. This was at a time when more than two million African Americans were held as chattel property. It was the opening salvo by immediatists, the most radical and uncompromising abolitionist faction.

Like many subsequent white abolitionist leaders, Garrison originally believed that colonization offered a rational remedy to slavery. African Americans strenuously opposed being sent involuntarily to Africa. Garrison heard them; their voices converted him to immediatism. And African Americans apparently approved of Garrison's paper. Most of the first five hundred voluntary subscribers were "colored individuals."[4] Garrison was anxious to elicit the support of the free black community, and he believed he knew why most of its leaders opposed efforts to remove American blacks to the colony of Liberia on the west coast of Africa. "With a few exceptions, the moving and controlling incentives of the friends of African Colonization," he wrote on July 30, 1831, "may be summed up in a single sentence: *they have an antipathy against the blacks.* They do not wish to admit them to an equality. They can tolerate them only as servants and slaves, but never as brethren and friends. They can love and benefit them four thousand miles off, but not at home."[5]

The Southern slaveholders and their allies resented the escalating rhetoric of their challengers. Southerners became more alarmed in August 1831 when a slave named Nat Turner led an insurrection in Southampton County, Virginia, that resulted in the deaths of fifty-seven whites. Though Turner went to the gallows on October 31, 1831, his death did not stem the tide of fear washing over the South. Some slaveholders were quick to associate Garrison with Turner. There is no credible evidence that Turner read a copy of the *Liberator,* and the white abolitionists who centered around Garrison were themselves troubled by the prospect of slave violence. Nevertheless, proponents of the "peculiar institution" of the South as a positive good or, at most, a necessary evil, denounced Garrison and his growing circle of allies for inciting unrest among the slaves.[6] In point of fact, Garrison's reading of the New Testament inspired Christian pacifism or, in the language of the day, *nonresistance.* According to the nonresistance philosophy, slave insurrection was wrong in principle as well as impractical.[7]

Nonviolence was only one aspect of Garrison's philosophy regarding the proper relationship of means to ends in the crusade against slavery. Garrison, like Finney, believed in human agency; that is, in the moral capacity of humans to choose between good and evil. Thus, Garrison held slaveholders accountable for their actions and refused to accept the Southern excuse that slavery had been entailed (inherited) from previous generations. As Finney challenged the old Calvinist notions of predestination and the chained will which led to pessimism about the possible reformation of self and world, so Garrison railed at the idea that the slaveholder was not capable of a radical change of heart. Garrison's principal weapon of attack was nonviolent: *moral suasion* (or persuasion) through the written and spoken word. Though not an ordained minister, he preached as passionately as any evangelist seeking national revival about the question of slavery. Garrison's antislavery letters, essays, and speeches are so imbued with religious language that to strip them of it would have rendered him mute.

Garrison's political views emerged from his religious beliefs. He declared, famously, that the American Constitution was a proslavery document; that abolitionists should not organize political parties, vote, or stand for political office; that the slaveholding South should be cut out like a cancerous growth; that women should participate as equals in abolitionist societies; and that the existing religious denominations were hopelessly mired in hypocrisy with regard to the sin of slavery.[8] Garrison's initial call for immediate emancipation came in language that struck a resonant chord among those who had been prodded by Finney to expect a summons to some form of higher Christian duty.

Copies of the *Liberator* went out to the regional press. One arrived in the office of the *Rochester Observer* in January 1831 during Finney's assault upon the city. Within two months, the *Observer* was won over to Garrisonianism. One of Finney's Rochester converts, young Henry Brewster Stanton, would return to Flour City as an abolitionist lecturer on numerous occasions.[9] Given the absence of instant mass communication in 1831, word of the prophet from the East spread from one convert to another. A profile of the early abolitionists reveals that many of them were young people whose families had migrated to Upstate New York. These youthful recruits, often in their early twenties, were searching for something meaningful to do with their lives. By enlisting in the cause of breaking slavery's stranglehold, they

William Lloyd Garrison (1805–1879). Pictured here with his daughter Fannie, the Boston-based reformer issued a clarion call for immediate, unconditional, and uncompensated emancipation of slaves in January 1831. Garrison's philosophy of nonviolent moral suasion influenced many North Star Country reformers, although, by 1840, a core group of abolitionists in the region gravitated toward the Liberty Party and political action. *Courtesy of the Oneida County Historical Society.*

found their sacred vocation.[10] The call to immediatism was the ultimate retainer from the Lord.

Theodore Dwight Weld's conversion to immediatism illustrates the depth of this commitment. Weld's father was a Presbyterian clergyman from Connecticut who retired to a farm in Fabius township, forty miles southwest of Utica. In 1826, when he was twenty-three years old, Theodore encountered Charles G. Finney when the evangelist was at the height of his powers and was preaching up a storm in Utica. Weld said of Finney, "[there] never was a man whose soul looked out through his face as [his] did." Appalled by Finney's methods, Weld resisted conversion at first, but eventually he, too, confessed his sins and found peace of mind. Theodore then left Hamilton College, where he had been a student since dropping out of Andover Academy in Massachusetts because of emotional and physical exhaustion. During the next year he traveled about the Burned-over District as Finney's lieutenant.[11]

Flushed with enthusiasm, Weld and Finney's other young recruits balked at the idea of pursuing the traditional pedagogical course demanded of candidates for the Presbyterian ministry. It would have required three or four years of seminary training, most likely at a school like Auburn Theological Seminary in Cayuga County. To accommodate these young Finneyites, the Reverend George Washington Gale, Finney's pastor from his Adams period, brought the Oneida Presbytery a proposal to acquire the Hugh White farm. The farm's 114-plus acres was located along the Erie Canal about four miles west of Utica in the village of Whitesboro.[12]

Oneida Academy opened during May 1827 in a converted farmhouse built on the Mohawk River flats bordering Sauquoit Creek. Twenty-seven of Finney's holy band arrived to find that the daily regimen included milking cows as well as studying the Bible and the Latin and Greek classics. Gale's school was chartered as the Oneida Institute of Science and Industry in 1829. It was modeled after educational experiments for poor youth that Phillip Emmanuel von Fellenberg, a Swiss educator and philanthropist, had pioneered in Europe. This manual labor education movement sought to strengthen body and mind.[13]

In 1839, Oneida Institute had to turn away five hundred prospective students for lack of space. Young scholars worked in the fields and shops as well as in the classroom. Theodore Dwight Weld, who was somewhat older than his classmates, was put in charge of the milking crew. Despite periodically flooded fields, cramped facilities, and a chronic shortage of funds, the students remained optimistic. They believed they were engaged in a holy enterprise: the strengthening of body and mind for the spiritual reform of their nation.

How news of Garrison's call for immediate emancipation first reached the students at Oneida Institute is not known. It must have created great excitement because, in July 1832, thirty-five students organized New York State's first antislavery society based on immediatist principles. Those students of the opposite persuasion organized a local auxiliary of the ACS during the next month. The debate was now joined. Earlier that spring, Gale had announced to the school's trustees that he wished to leave the post of principal. He was more a pastor than a theologian and, lacking the dynamic personality of Finney, whom Gale had failed to lure to the faculty, he felt that "the carrying forward of the enterprise might now devolve on someone else."[14] That "someone else" was the Reverend Beriah Green, fresh from the first controversy over immediatism at Western Reserve College in Hudson, Ohio.[15]

Green arrived in Whitesboro to assume leadership of Oneida Institute during August 1833. A native of New England and an alumnus of Middlebury College and Andover Theological Seminary, Green was a professor of sacred literature at Western Reserve when he first took on the mantle of warrior for the black freedom cause. Western Reserve College, which was known among its promoters as the Yale of the West, was located far from the centrifuge of immediatism in New England. It might have escaped the ensuing controversy had a student not brought back copies of the *Liberator* from Boston after the 1831 Christmas recess.

Soon the campus was in an uproar, with trustees, faculty, and students divided into factions of immediatists and colonizationists. On November 5, 1832, Green corresponded with Simeon S. Jocelyn, a white minister of a black congregation in New Haven, Connecticut, and an early convert to Garrisonian abolitionism. Green told him that a "great change" had come over Western Reserve College. Green requested support from the New England Anti-Slavery Society, which had been formed only recently. "We want facts—facts—FACTS," Green implored and added, "We have a great struggle to go through. The strength of public prejudice, as such openly avowed, is awaking."[16]

Green sealed his fate with the conservative trustees on four successive

Sundays in the fall and early winter of 1832. He had used the pulpit of the Western Reserve College chapel to condemn the "loathsome crime of slave-holding." He scorned the colonizationists who thought of themselves as guiltless. At the judgment seat of Christ they would hear the words, "I was a colored man, and you maintained a cruel prejudice against me; enslaved, and you apologized for my oppressor; torn with whips, and you refused to pity me; deprived of the bread of life, and you alleged that expediency required me to submit to starvation; and at length, forced from my native country to a foreign shore, and you assisted in the enterprise."[17] Encouragement came from the East. Garrison applauded Green's sermons and wrote to him, "It now is palpable as the sun in heaven, that the slave holders and the colonization party are united together to suppress the freedom of speech and of the press and even to exclude from the pulpits of our land those who plead for the immediate abolition of slavery."[18]

In April 1833, Green received a letter from the trustees of Oneida Institute inviting him to come to Upstate New York and assume leadership of the school. With the pulpit at Western Reserve closed to him and feeling "unutterable throes in contemplating the condition and prospects of my colored brethren,"[19] Green resolved to commit himself to Oneida Institute—but only if its trustees would allow him to preach abolitionism and would admit students without regard to race.

As May approached, Green wrote to Elizur Wright, Jr., who had already left the Western Reserve faculty, "I am assured that Africa shall lose nothing in the exchange of stations, which I am urged to venture on. I am even assured that the Trustees [of Oneida Institute] will help me in my efforts to 'strike the chains' from colored limbs, etc." Then, hinting at a grand plan, Green confided to Wright that the Upstate New York institution might be transformed into a "school like we talked about."[20]

During the summer of 1833, prior to Green's arrival, some of the advanced students, including Weld and Stanton, left the Oneida Institute to search for a place in which they could plant the abolitionist flag. They went to Pittsburgh and then rafted down the French and Allegheny Rivers to Cincinnati, Ohio, where they enrolled at Lane Seminary, the outpost of revivalism in the West. Frustrated that Lane's faculty had not yet grasped the urgency of the cause, the Oneida boys became Lane rebels. They initiated a debate over immediatism versus colonization.[21] Finding the trustees

Beriah Green (1795–1874). Green was an abolitionist educator and moral theologian who transformed Oneida Institute at Whitesboro into an abolitionist school that was open to white and black alike. He supported the Liberty Party and advanced the comeouter church movement. *Courtesy of the author.*

intractable and the general public hostile, the youthful immediatists again sought a school where revivalism, abolitionism, and a practical theological education could be effectively combined. Led by Weld, forty of them joined the student body of the fledgling Oberlin Institute in Ohio. This was the very school that Finney had gone to in 1835 as a professor of theology. The Oneida boys helped make Oberlin the "hub of Western abolitionism."[22]

The remaining student abolitionists at Oneida Institute welcomed the arrival of Beriah Green. In Green's inaugural address, the new president sketched his vision for the school, one that involved curriculum reform that was designed to do something practical "for dear humanity" by raising up an abolitionist phalanx. A few weeks after hearing that address, a student wrote to William Goodell, an ardent abolitionist who was born in Coventry (Chenango County) and who was publisher of the *Genius of Temperance:*

> Our leader here is President Green, than whom we want no better. His efforts in the cause of the colored man are untiring. He has begun a course of lectures (by request of the students) on slavery and attendant evils, which is listened to with the utmost interest by not only those connected with the Institute but by many from the neighborhood—I am as confident of a final triumph as I am that the Millennium will dawn upon the earth.[23]

Such youthful enthusiasm was what Green wanted, but many more hands would be needed to advance the cause of freedom in central and western New York State.

The reformers who resonated to Garrison's call for immediate, unconditional, and uncompensated emancipation were initially small in number across the Burned-over District. In July 1833, the thirty-five students at Oneida Institute who organized the first local abolitionist society in the state did so only after protracted debate with students who supported the ACS. The student abolitionists found support among a handful of residents of the Whitestown area who issued a circular that proclaimed: "The only proper remedy for the sin of slaveholding must be found in the immediate, full, heartfelt respect of those rights in the invasion of which this monstrous crime consists. Every slave ought immediately and unconditionally to be emancipated."[24] The act of committing themselves to an unpopular cause when there was as yet no statewide or even national organization to support them shows how passionately the youthful immediatists believed in the righteousness of their efforts. Naïveté has its virtues.

Soon, others followed the lead of the Oneida students by banding together for mutual support. The Whitestown (Oneida County) Society organized about one hundred members in April 1834. That month a small group of abolitionists calling themselves the Smithfield Society came together in Peterboro, Gerrit Smith's home town. Another group appeared in Utica during June of 1834. This group, like the Whitestown Society, had a juvenile section. There were more than a dozen local societies prior to the

Oneida Institute, c. 1844. Oneida Institute was located along the Erie Canal, east of Whitesboro. It began as a school for training recruits (from Finney's revivals) for the ministry but, after 1833, it became a hotbed of abolitionism. Under Beriah Green's leadership, it enrolled more African Americans than any other "college" prior to its closing in 1845. *Courtesy of the Oneida County Historical Society at Utica, N.Y.*

formation of the New York Anti-Slavery Society in October 1835. During the following two years, in response to the work of agents from the AASS who toured the Burned-over District, many more local abolitionist societies appeared. It is impossible to determine exactly how many were founded, although one scholar's diligent search of the *Emancipator* and the *Friend of Man* revealed that, except for Chemung, every county in the Burned-over District had at least one abolitionist society by 1839.[25]

The profiles of those friends of freedom who resonated to Garrison's immediatist philosophy of moral suasion are remarkably similar. The activists were born in New England, or in regions such as New York's Burned-over District which were strongly stamped with New England culture. Many of those who formed the abolitionist phalanx were young people who sought their lives' work within the crusade to rid America of the sin of slavery. Some of the young people who had trained for the ministry or who had held teaching as their career goal became full-time agents of the AASS. Others accepted part-time work to supplement the meager stipend the voluntary agencies supplied. Whatever sacrifice these reformers had to make for the greater good of the slave was justified on the grounds that they were participating in a cause much larger than the individual self and more consequential than any other reform and benevolent enterprise. Theodore D. Weld understood this well. The abolitionist crusade, he argued, "not only overshadows all others, but . . . absorbs them into itself. Revivals, moral Reform etc. will remain stationary until the temple is cleansed."[26] Weld's pilgrimage to the shrine of immediatism was one that was replicated by many of the abolitionists who found their sacred vocations in the fight against slavery and who made their marks on North Star Country in the formative years of the crusade.

Weld's biographer, Robert Abzug, said of him, "No abolitionist of the 1830s, save William Lloyd Garrison, became more famous or more notorious. Garrison himself called his comrade, 'the lion hearted, invincible Weld.'"[27] Theodore was born in 1803 to Ludovicus and Elisabeth Weld. The minister's son was energetic and strong-willed, with a burning desire to become somebody, perhaps a great orator. He was exposed to a mother's pietistic ideals at a tender age. Theodore, like many of the converts to immediatism, yearned to be part of something redemptive, for himself as well as for others. He found his calling in 1832 while touring northeastern

Ohio as a lecturer for the Society for the Promotion of Manual Labor in Literary Institutions. Weld visited Hudson where Beriah Green and other abolition-minded faculty won him over to a higher calling: the deliverance of the African American slave.[28] Weld's conversion to immediatism was destined to have as strong an impact on his life as did giving himself over to the Lord under Finney's preaching.

Because of the fervor of young recruits like Weld, abolitionism was becoming the most controversial public issue of the day. It was a topic that people of all social ranks and conditions turned to during informal conversation and during organized rhetorical sparring matches. At public forums in churches and schoolhouses, citizens debated with one another. Some favored colonization as a reasonable solution, arguing that it entailed the least risk to the stability of America's racial and economic status quo. Their opponents asserted that colonization was but a surrogate for slavery by pointing out that slaveholders, who were anxious about the growth of the free black population, supported it.

If Quakers were present, as would have been the case in Farmington and Palmyra (Ontario County settlements), then the call to organize a new antislavery society was more likely to be embraced. Hicksite Quakers believed in the essential quality of all humans, regardless of color. They followed the lead of their namesake, Elias Hicks, who is reputed to have pushed aside a cotton quilt that was offered to him on his death bed because it entailed slave labor. Most of the leaders of the Western New York Anti-Slavery Society were Hicksite Quakers. The Palmyra Anti-Slavery Society grew from 24 to 111 members during one month.[29]

The Quakers had a long tradition of cutting against the grain, but most Upstate New Yorkers who came out for immediatism did so without the support of a dissenting tradition. Individuals who took abolitionism to heart risked censure by family and neighbors. William Jay, a prominent Utica lawyer, wanted his contributions to the AASS to be kept secret out of fear that his reputation would suffer at the hands of antiabolitionists. After a New York City mob rioted during 1834, destroying the property of antislavery advocates and attacking blacks, Jay took a seat on the Executive Committee of the AASS.[30] It was important for individuals who enrolled in the campaign for black freedom to find kindred souls. By coming together in what Frederick Douglass called the antislavery church, individuals received the necessary moral support to transform sentiment into abolitionist action.

The Garrisonians who were centered in and around Boston had formed the New England Anti-Slavery Society in 1832. However, when Beriah Green arrived at Oneida Institute to shepherd the cause of immediatism there was as yet no national society. To take a public stand against slavery in the early 1830s was to invite trouble. The Quaker John G. Whittier, known as "the slave's poet," recalled the risks: "[T]he few abolitionists were everywhere spoken against, their persons threatened, and in some instances a price set on their heads by Southern legislators." So, it must have been with some anxiety that Green left Whitesboro for Philadelphia in December of 1833. Like Whittier, he had been appointed as a delegate to a convention that had been called to establish a national society on immediatist principles. "Pennsylvania," Whittier wrote some forty years later, "was set on the borders of slavery, and it needed small effort of imagination to picture [for] one's self the breaking up of the convention and maltreatment of its members."

When Whittier arrived in Philadelphia, he found about forty of the faithful gathered in preliminary council. Their immediate challenge was not facing overt hostility from Philadelphia's anti-abolitionists but finding someone willing to chair the assembly. A committee visited several prominent Philadelphians known to be friendly to the cause but returned unsuccessful. The following morning, December 4, 1833, sixty-two delegates gathered in the Adelphi Building and chose Beriah Green as president. Whittier recalled that Green, then thirty-seven, was "a fresh-faced, sandy-haired, rather common-looking man, but who had the reputation of an able and eloquent speaker. He had already made himself known to us as a resolute and self-sacrificing abolitionist."[31]

Green was not the lone representative of the Burned-over District. John Frost, the pastor of Whitesboro's First Presbyterian Church and one of Green's staunchest supporters among the trustees of Oneida Institute, attended. William Goodell also came. Garrison headed the delegation from New England. The wealthy merchant Lewis Tappan was prominent among abolitionists from New York City. Ten delegates came from New York State. Nine other states were represented. Of the sixty-two delegates, twenty-one were plainly dressed Quakers, mainly from Pennsylvania. Elizur Wright, Jr., Green's colleague from his Western Reserve days, also participated.

During the days that followed, the delegates drafted a constitution for the AASS, elected permanent officers (Arthur Tappan, brother of Lewis and senior partner in the Tappan mercantile firm, became president), and issued a Declaration of Sentiments. Men dominated the meeting, but several Quaker women, including Lucretia Mott, sat as spectators in the rear of the room. At one point, Mott rose to speak. Most of the men resented this breach of decorum, as political questions were considered their domain. But Green invited Mott forward with the words, "Go on mam, go on; we shall be glad to hear you."[32]

Green closed the convention with what Samuel J. May described as a solemn, sublime, and thrilling speech. (Samuel J. May was a Unitarian clergyman from Boston who later became an important abolitionist in Syracuse.) May testified that Green "proved to be a man in whom there was 'timber' enough to make half a dozen Presidents, if the Convention had needed so many."[33] As the delegates prepared to return to their homes, Green praised them for the harmonious spirit they had demonstrated and warned them that the road ahead would be a long and difficult one. "The chill hoar frost will be upon us," Green told the delegates. "The storm and tempest will rise, and the waves of persecution will dash against our souls. Let us be prepared for the worst."[34]

Back at Oneida Institute, the immediatist cause seemed to be moving in the right direction. Student colonizationists disbanded their auxiliary to the ACS in August 1834. One of Green's most ardent student supporters informed Garrison that Oneida Institute was "every hour becoming more and more an abolition school."[35] The conservatives among the trustees resigned so that, unlike at Western Reserve, Green now had a clear field ahead of him. He was soon using Oneida Institute as a command post from which he and his students carried the abolitionist flag into other parts of Upstate New York. Students fanned out into area churches to preach the immediatist gospel. They attempted to persuade friends and neighbors that it was now time for everyone to come to the aid of those languishing under the yoke of slavery.

The students based their campaign on the principles that had been outlined in the compact drawn up in Philadelphia. The Declaration of Sentiments put forth by the founders of the AASS in December 1833 listed specific means by which the immediatist campaign was to be conducted:

We shall organize anti-slavery societies, if possible, in every city, town, and village in our land.

We shall send forth agents to lift up the voice of remonstrance, of warning, of entreaty and rebuke.

We shall circulate unsparingly and extensively anti-slavery tracts and periodicals.

We shall enlist the pulpit and the press in the cause of the suffering and the dumb.

We shall aim at a purification of the churches from all participation in the guilt of slavery.

We shall encourage the labor of freemen over that of the slaves, by giving a preference to their productions; and,

We shall spare no exertions nor means to bring the whole nation to speedy repentance.[36]

Using this compact, the abolitionists in Upstate New York could build upon the work of Finney and the revivalists of the Second Great Awakening. The reformers would become preachers of repentance. They would seek to awaken the collective conscience of the local community and, in ever-widening concentric circles, the conscience of their county, state, and nation.

This commitment involved the whole self and incorporated more than an attack on the slaveholders. One of the young reformers wrote to James Birney, the former Kentucky slaveholder turned abolitionist:

We see nothing which indicates that our cause is not a *righteous* one—but the character of the opposition is that which always belongs to the *enemies* of Christ. Our business is to *pray* and *preach* and our Master will lead us. We must lean on Him. All is safe in his hands. Who ever expected that this nation could be purged from guilt without painful throes and awful convulsions? Blessed are they who have part in this resurrection. We are now contending not merely for the poor bondmen, but for our own liberty and that of our children and our country and for the liberty of the Gospel.[37]

Of this hope for self-redemption, historian James Brewer Stewart writes, "by dedicating themselves to immediatism, the young reformers performed acts of self-liberation akin to the experience of conversion."[38]

Transatlantic developments in the freedom movement motivated the North Star Country abolitionists all the more. On July 5, 1833, six months after Garrison called for American slaveholders to rid themselves of the sin of slavery, English abolitionists successfully introduced the Emancipation

Act of 1833 (commonly known as the West Indian Act of 1833). The bill took effect on August 1, 1834, and African Americans in Upstate New York celebrated West Indian Emancipation Day until the outbreak of the Civil War. On the first of August, 1838, for example, blacks in Utica gathered in a Methodist chapel. With prayer, hymns, and speeches, they held up the emancipation of the British West Indies as proof of God's favor in the cause "in behalf of bleeding humanity."[39]

Inspired by the success of antislavery activists in the British Parliament, American abolitionists, both black and white, toured Great Britain in search of money and moral support for their own labors.[40] The British prototype made it imperative that American abolitionists devise a practical means of converting fellow citizens to the immediatist credo.

The AASS set up an agency system, as had the New England Anti-Slavery Society's Board of Managers. Paid lecturers were commissioned at $8 per week, plus travel expenses, to broadcast the seeds of immediatism. Because he was already known for his efforts to expose the folly of colonization in the environs of Oneida Institute, Beriah Green received the first commission for central New York State. When Joshua N. Danforth, the permanent agent of the ACS for New York and New England, came to Utica in January 1834, Green took him on in a series of debates. Although Green claimed to have bested Danforth, a group of Uticans who were vexed by Green's attack on the colonization scheme marched through the city, banging on tin pans and blowing horns. They hung Green in effigy, and Utica's Common Council denounced him.[41]

The details of the organizing activities of all the agents who tramped back and forth across the Burned-over District would fill several volumes. Instead, I will highlight the work of those who established the earliest network of local and regional abolitionist societies. Charles Stuart was one of the first agents assigned to Upstate New York. He was a retired captain of the East Indies service and a native of Jamaica who taught at the Utica Academy and served as the school's principal. During vacations, Stuart, a bachelor, traveled the area, talking of temperance and handing out Bibles and religious tracts. In addition to being one of Finney's "holy band," he was young Theodore Dwight Weld's mentor during the formative years of the Burned-over District before he returned to England to assist the British abolition movement.

In the spring of 1834, Stuart sailed back across the Atlantic to take up a commission as a lecturer for the AASS. When he was campaigning against slavery in the British colonies, Stuart was known as *Captain* Charles Stuart; in America, people called him the *Reverend* Charles Stuart. As Stuart's biographer observes, this title substitution symbolizes the "clerical status typical of so many American abolitionists."[42] Older than most antislavery agents, Stuart was noted more for his sincerity and eccentric personal habits than for his speaking abilities. Some thought this quaintly dressed Johnny Appleseed of abolitionism was odd as he tramped around the countryside distributing antislavery tracts.[43]

Stuart lectured around central New York State through the summer of 1834. During August, he spoke and received a tolerant, if not warm, reception in Apulia as well as Franklin, Auburn, and Whitesboro. In September, Stuart found that the trustees of the Baptist church in Buffalo were so afraid of trouble that they closed the church doors to him. On October 1, 1834, he received a formal commission from the AASS to raise funds in the state of New York. Over the winter he labored intensively in the Utica area. He made a special effort to build up the Utica Anti-Slavery Society and convert those who still believed in colonization.

One of Stuart's methods was walking from town to town in Oneida County and "hunting up anti-slavery men" and "ardent friends" of the slave. In April of 1835 he helped organize the Oneida County Anti-Slavery Association at a meeting in Hamilton. He successfully organized an antislavery society in Cazenovia in spite of opposition from the *Cazenovia Whig*. Some places proved to be especially hostile to his message. Stuart was often attacked as a meddling foreigner. In December of 1834, he was the victim of violence while preparing to speak at Winifield, a small community in Herkimer County. As William Lloyd Garrison reported to his wife, "Charles Stuart has been mobbed in the western part of the state of New York. A brick bat struck him on the head, which made him senseless for a time— but as soon as he recovered, he began to plead for the suffering and dumb, until he was persuaded by a clergyman to desist."[44]

William Goodell, who was less flamboyant than Stuart, also made his mark on Upstate New York as an itinerant evangelist for immediatism. Goodell was born in 1792 on the frontier (Chenango County). Raised by his grandmother in Connecticut, he worked in the mercantile business in Providence, Rhode Island, before starting a paper called the *Investigator*. In

1830, the paper merged with the *National Philanthropist,* which was formerly edited by Garrison, to become the *Genius of Temperance.* Goodell carried
on his journalistic efforts by becoming the editor of the *Emancipator,* the
official organ of the national antislavery society.

In the autumn of 1834, Goodell left New York City for Albany to rally
local abolitionists. Next, he brought the immediatist gospel to Utica and
Whitesboro, places that were already friendly to the cause. At Rome he
spoke in the Presbyterian church, which was pastored by the Reverend
Alvelyn Sedgwick, soon to become an agent himself. Goodell visited Hamilton College in Clinton during early October and then met with Gerrit
Smith on his estate in Peterboro. There he joined Beriah Green for a series
of lectures in the Baptist and Presbyterian churches. Both men attended
the first quarterly meeting of the Smithfield Anti-Slavery Society in
Munnsville. From Munnsville, Goodell traveled to Morrisville, Eaton, Nelson, Cazenovia, Canastota, Fayetteville, and Syracuse. He spoke to student
abolitionists at Auburn's Presbyterian Theological Seminary before going
on to Rochester. In Rochester, he met privately with blacks but did not lecture publicly because an impending election had raised the political temperature. Whites in Buffalo, too, gave him a less than enthusiastic reception;
in November, Goodell lectured to African Americans in their own church
before he was allowed to conduct a two-day public meeting. After he visited
Niagara Falls, Goodell took the stage for Warsaw. Now hoarse and unable to
lecture, Goodell retreated before the winds of winter and hastened back
east. He stopped at Perry Center, Brighton, Rochester, Farmington, East
Mendon, and Palmyra, where his message was well received and measures
were taken to establish the Palmyra Anti-Slavery Society. Goodell returned
to New York City in December. During the years that followed he would
have many opportunities to assist the abolitionist cause in North Star
Country. In 1836, he moved to Utica and assumed editorship of the *Friend
of Man,* the abolitionist newspaper of the New York State Anti-Slavery
Society.[45]

There were others who helped spread immediatism across Upstate New
York. The AASS appointed Aaron Judson an agent in 1834. His case is especially interesting because, until his conversion to immediatism, he was one
of the students at Oneida Institute who belonged to the campus colonization society. Convinced that the ACS had deceived its members as to the

true aims of colonization, Judson signed on with the abolitionists and helped form the Oneida County Anti-Slavery Society.

More well-known than Judson was Amos Phelps, a graduate of Yale and Andover, and an ordained Congregational minister who was serving the Pine Street Church in Boston when he was appointed an agent. After he worked in parts of New England and along the Atlantic coast, Phelps concentrated on the Albany area in the spring of 1835. He then moved into central and western New York State. He lectured in Utica, paid his respects to Green in Whitesboro, visited Auburn, and journeyed to LeRoy and Rochester in Monroe County. Despite receiving threats of mob action, Phelps organized a female antislavery society in Rochester. Buffalo refused to give him any platform from which to speak, although, again, he helped form a female antislavery society.[46] On October 12, 1835, Phelps served as midwife to the birth of the Erie Country Anti-Slavery Society. By the time this stalwart of immediatism concluded his tour he had given forty antislavery speeches (in addition to Sunday sermons) in seventeen different communities and helped organize six antislavery societies.[47]

Additional immediatist organizations emerged from the Burned-over District in 1835. By March, in Perry (Genesee County), abolitionists counted a nucleus of 150 members. Twenty-four women set up the Sherburne Ladies Anti-Slavery Society (Chenango County) during the same month. Charles Stuart galvanized abolitionists in Morrisville (Madison County) in April. Abolitionist-minded residents of Union Village organized in July. Oneida Castle (Madison County) witnessed the formation of a society with thirty members in September. After Stuart visited the small community of Russia in Herkimer County, opponents of slavery banded together. Further to the west, in Springville, Erie County abolitionists were sparked by the lectures of Amos Phelps to organize themselves in September.[48]

Theodore Dwight Weld, who was designated, "the most central figure in the anti-slavery agency system of the 1830's, the most successful of the agents,"[49] returned to New York State from Ohio, where his labors had resulted in nearly 100 new antislavery societies. In 1836, he waged a tremendously successful campaign across central New York State. The Utica Anti-Slavery Society added between six hundred and seven hundred members after Weld worked the city in February. The next month he went to Rochester and added more than eight hundred new members to its abolitionist ranks. However, all did not go well in Troy. During May and June, hostile residents forced the cancellation of his lecture series and, on June 11, Weld was nearly killed. His adversaries distributed handbills that warned him to stop. The town crier walked about calling, "All you who are opposed to amalgamation are requested to meet in front of the court house."[50] A mob tried to drag him from the pulpit of Bethel Church. "Stones, pieces of bricks, eggs, cents, sticks, etc. were thrown at me while speaking," according to the orator who once referred to himself as "the most mobbed man in America."[51]

During most of November 1836, Weld stayed in New York and ran a convention that had been called to train new agents for the AASS so that a total of seventy might be sent to labor in the field. The number of seventy came from the account in Luke, chapter 10, where Jesus appointed seventy evangelists "and sent them two and two before his face into every city and place, whither he himself would come."[52] Weld, who already had a reputation as the thunderer of the West, threw himself passionately into the training effort. He spoke for hours on end and stayed up until two and three in the morning. By December 2, when the convention ended, he had lost his voice. Weld was thus forced to abandon his plans to return to the Great West; he remained in New York City to work at the national antislavery office.[53] He lived in a small attic room and tried to mend his overtaxed constitution with regular exercise and the Graham diet. George Storrs, Charles Stewart Renshaw, Henry Bowen, and William Allan also labored in the Burned-over District. Weld helped select them, train them, and, according to Charles Stuart, was "the central luminary around which they all revolved."[54]

Like Weld, Henry Brewster Stanton was a Finney convert, a student at Oneida Institute, and a Lane rebel. Stanton was born in Griswold, Connecticut, moved to Rochester in 1826, worked in the canal office, wrote for the *Monroe Telegraph*, and served as Monroe County's deputy clerk until 1832. Known as an excellent speaker, he lectured in Upstate New York, frequently in the company of Weld or Charles Stuart. Stanton targeted Rochester for particular attention. In 1837, antiabolitionists burned a church he had spoken at in Livingston County. Stanton helped recruit the seventy evangelists, served as the financial secretary of the AASS, and sat on the AASS's executive committee for twelve years. In May 1840, he married Elizabeth Cady. The couple eventually settled in Seneca Falls where Henry practiced law and was elected to the state senate twice (in 1849 and 1851). Elizabeth became one of the founders of the American women's rights crusade.[55]

The financial panic of 1837 caused the national society to cut the agency system, but by then there was hardly a Burned-over District community of note that had escaped one of the traveling lecturers. Amos Phelps, in an effort to bring the wavering Gerrit Smith over to the cause of immediatism, wrote, "The influence of Central and Western New York on the country at large, on any such moral question, is incalculable. The public mind in this section is now in a plastic state. If the friends of God & human rights would come out boldly on the subject in question, the public mind could be gained to the cause of Immediate Emancipation with perfect ease."[56] Earlier that year, the *Emancipator* reported that the AASS had 7,500 members and more than 150 "thorough-going anti-slavery societies."[57] In 1836, New York State had 103 local auxiliaries of the AASS, one-fifth of the total in the nation.[58] Most of these societies were located in North Star Country and were concentrated along the axis of the Erie Canal.

The revivalist and reform culture of Upstate New York provided fertile ground into which the seeds of immediatism could be sown. But the formation of societies based on Garrison's radical call for immediate emancipation did not take place without opposition. For example, in 1835, friends of the slave came together in Onondaga County to discuss what to do. With the goal of organizing a county society, they met at the Baptist church in Syracuse. Anti-abolitionists raised such a ruckus that the group secretly withdrew to the village of Fayetteville, some ten miles to the east.[59] During August of 1835, when Amos Phelps was in Le Roy, "far West, almost to Buffalo," he told his wife that Upstate New York contained "good material to make radicals of," but he also observed, "There is the same negro hatred here, the same political influences, the same love of Colonization, the same Corruption in the Priesthood . . . the same shutting of the eyes to light, the same stopping of the ears to the cry of the suffering and oppressed—in one word, the same every thing that is wicked & hateful to God to contend with here as at the east."[60]

The pioneering abolitionists characterized their endeavors as a righteous crusade. Many went into battle with the notion that the truth concerning the evil of slavery needed only to be proclaimed to be effective. Just as the great revivalist Charles G. Finney had witnessed guilt-stricken sinners falling on their knees in repentance, so did the abolitionists, in their naïveté, expect the slaveholders and their allies to voluntarily dismantle the "peculiar institution" once they had become persuaded of its evil nature.

Reformers within the boundaries of the Burned-over District were predisposed to transform abolitionism into a holy crusade because of the Finneyite legacy. It was to be a bloodless victory and confirmation that Divine Providence was still at work. Historian Lewis Perry has written, "Abolitionism contained an implicit vision of utopia in which man would be rescued from the domination of other men and would respond directly to the governance of God. This vision might never have become problematical if abolition had swiftly succeeded, but such was not the case."[61] As the opening years of the immediatist crusade came to an end, some of the agents of the Garrisonian gospel in Upstate New York saw the need for more organizational muscle. The walls of Jericho had not fallen at the sounding of the solitary trumpets, which took the form of agents working the territory like Methodist circuit riders on behalf of the AASS. It was time to band together at the state level.

In 1835, under the signatures of Beriah Green and Alvan Stewart (a Utica lawyer), a call went out for all friends of the slave in New York State to assemble at Utica, in October, for the purpose of organizing a state society. Green made a special effort to gain the support of Gerrit Smith of nearby Peterboro (Madison County).[62] Though he was well intentioned, Gerrit Smith had not yet climbed aboard the abolitionist bandwagon. As a generous contributor to the treasury of the ACS, he complained about the immediatists who "by violent, bitter and fanatical writing in their publications supporting emancipation, turned public sentiment against colonizationists."[63] In 1834, he wrote in his journal, "I think I cannot join the Antislavery Society as long as the War is kept up between it and the American Colonization Society—a war, however, for which the American Colonization Society is as much to blame as the other Society."[64] Did this portend a wavering on Smith's part? Elizur Wright, Jr., thought so. He thought Smith was "making his last effort to reform the poor old colonization hobby. It is the creation of his imagination he clings to—not the odious reality."[65]

In early 1835, Garrison wrote long letters to Smith, trying to persuade him to give up equivocating, "You *ought* to acknowledge your conversion, if indeed you are converted, to abolition doctrines," Garrison told Smith on February 7, "because you have *publicly* erred in word and deed."[66] Garrison felt perplexed by Smith's habit of condemning slavery as a sin, in language nearly as harsh as his own, but then muting his criticism of slaveholders and colonizationists with softer words about the impracticality of immediate emancipation and the need for addressing one's opponents in the spirit of Christian charity. To illustrate that Smith's chief error was inconsistency, Garrison quoted extensively from Smith's own letters, essays, and speeches, setting the opposing views in parallel columns. "I am offended," the New Englander told the New Yorker, "to see you put an abolition cockade upon your cap, and still wear a colonization uniform: both sides of the combatants must naturally suspect you."[67]

Hoping that Smith had indeed rid himself of the colonization hobby horse, Beriah Green encouraged Smith to come to Utica for the October meeting and to help form a state antislavery society that could unite the existing forty-two local organizations. Having Smith as an ally would be immensely useful to the immediatists.[68] He was a forceful and eloquent speaker and presented a striking appearance on the platform. Contemporaries described him as majestic in personal bearing.

One visitor to Peterboro rhapsodized about the owner of the only mansion in the village: "Tall, magnificently built and magnificently proportioned, his large head superbly set upon his shoulders he might have served as a model for a Greek God in the days when man deified beauty and worshiped it."[69] Though the analogy seems overdrawn, perhaps even pompous, Smith once likened himself to the Greek deity Jupiter when he described his own oratorical powers: "He warms with the subject, especially if opposed, until the climax, his heavy voice rolling forth in ponderous volume and his large frame quivering in every muscle, he stands, like Jupiter, thundering, and shaking with his thunderbolts his throne itself."[70] Jupiter, appropriately enough, was the Greek god who guarded community morals and protected the poor and innocent.

During a reform career that lasted for almost a half century, Smith wrote scores of essays and public letters. Many of these, along with printed versions of his speeches, were published. Curiously, he downplayed his literary abilities, claiming that "in point of rhetorical beauty" he did not rank high as a writer. His only goal was to express himself with clarity and simplici-

Gerrit Smith (1797–1874). Smith was a leading figure in pre–Civil War social reform movements and was Madison County's best-known abolitionist. He converted to immediatist abolitionism in 1835. For the next four decades, he gave liberally to the cause of African American freedom, both from his personal fortune and from his deep commitment to a more egalitarian America. From a portrait, oil on canvas, by Daniel Huntington, 1874. *Courtesy of the Madison County Historical Society.*

ty.[71] By the eve of the Civil War, Smith sported a full beard, which gave him the look we so often associate with John Brown of Harpers Ferry fame. As of 1835, however, Gerrit Smith was sans beard and not thoroughly awakened to immediatist principles. Should the abolitionists win Smith over, they could draw on the purse and the moral stamina of one of Upstate New York's most important residents. They would then be better equipped for their battle to more fully transform the Burned-over District into North Star Country.

3. Into the Storm

By the mid-1830s, the pioneering evangelists of immediatism in the Burned-over District were discovering that white America was not ready for a redemptive awakening on the question of race. Antiabolitionist forces attempted to silence those who so publicly condemned slavery and slavery's allies. The ensuing confrontation engulfed many of the formerly uncommitted individuals who now had to decide where they would stand on the most controversial moral question of their generation. As anti-abolitionist attacks increased, friends of the embryonic endeavor known as immediatism were forced to develop new organizational muscle. This required winning over people like Gerrit Smith who could back up an abolitionist commitment with great wealth. It also required drawing upon the talents and moral passion of many more inhabitants of the region, regardless of race, gender, or class standing.

On October 21, 1835, nearly six hundred antislavery enthusiasts assembled at the Second Presbyterian Church on Bleecker Street in Utica to set up a statewide abolitionist organization. More out of curiosity than conviction, Gerrit Smith, who was en route to Schenectady to visit his father, attended the proceedings. Soon after he had taken his seat, a mob of some three hundred antiabolitionists massed outside. Some of the crowd shouted, "Open the way! Break down the doors! Damn the fanatics! Stop your damn stuff!"[1] This outburst of antiabolitionist violence, which was replicated elsewhere in the North, was evidence of a hardening of the opposition. It also confirmed the immediatists' conviction that they were crusaders in a holy cause.

While the antiabolitionists congregated ominously, Alvan Stewart convened the Utica assembly. He gave a speech about slavery's assault on the "liberty of discussion, of conscience, and the press." A constitution was read and adopted. Lewis Tappan had begun to read a declaration of sentiments when "a large number of persons, in a disorderly and boisterous manner" pushed their way into the church and disrupted the proceedings.[2] The intruders were mostly day laborers, but they had the backing of local elites (bankers, lawyers, merchants, and politicians). These "gentlemen of property and standing" were led by New York congressman and former senator Samuel Beardsley and others who had gathered in the Oneida County courthouse. They had organized the Committee of Twenty-Five in response to the call for the Utica convention. Beardsley was a zealous Jacksonian and defender of other efforts to muzzle abolitionists, efforts which included the seizure of abolitionists' mail and the burning of immediatist newspapers. He represented the commercial and professional interests of Upstate New York who feared that abolitionists were sowing the seeds of public disorder and social revolution.[3]

The interlopers demanded that Alvan Stewart and other prominent abolitionists be turned over to them. As the threat of violence escalated, Gerrit Smith took action: he had heard and seen enough. Smith's "resonant and clear voice" rose above the clamor and confusion. He made an appeal for fairness and free speech, though he declared that he was "no abolitionist."[4] As Smith was insulted by the mob's behavior, he invited the delegates to reassemble in the sanctuary of his Peterboro estate, twenty-seven miles to the southwest of Utica. The delegates dispersed, only to be hounded through the city streets and evicted from their lodgings. About three hundred of them accepted Smith's invitation to reconvene at Peterboro the following day; however, the journey to the village of Peterboro was not without incident. While overnighting in Vernon, some delegates had their carriages damaged and their hotel besieged. Smith led the way to Peterboro over rain-sodden, muddy roads.

By force of circumstance, Gerrit Smith now assumed a prominent role in the deliberations, which resumed on October 22 in Peterboro's Presbyterian church. (The church was built in 1820 and is now the Smithfield Community Center.)[5] Smith believed that no matter how radical their views, the abolitionists had a right to be heard. Of his conversion to immediatism, Smith said, "The enormous and insolent demands of the South, sustained, I am deeply ashamed to say, by craven and mercenary spirits at the North, manifest beyond all dispute, that the question now is not merely,

Presbyterian Church of Smithfield. Now known as the Smithfield Community Center, this structure was built around 1820 and was occupied by Presbyterians until 1870, after which it was purchased by Gerrit Smith for use as an academy and public hall. In 1974, it became a local community center. In 1994, the building was placed on the New York State Historic Register and the National Register of Historic Places. Organizers of the New York State Anti-Slavery Society found refuge here in 1835, after the riot at Utica. *Courtesy of the Madison County Historical Society.*

nor mainly whether the blacks of the South shall remain slaves—but whether the whites at the North shall become slaves also."[6] He later declared that the riot in Utica had been "an instructive providence."[7]

Here was a pattern repeated many times in Upstate New York during the antislavery controversy. Whites who wavered on the question of abolition could be drawn to the support of immediatism if they became convinced that the long arm of slavery was reaching into their personal lives, whether by mob action, economic threat, free speech and free assembly restriction, opposition in churches, or denial of the right to petition the government.

Gerrit Smith's case is exemplary. After witnessing the events in the Bleecker Street church, he wrote to Abraham Cox, secretary of the AASS. He asked that his name be added to the membership roll. He then resigned from the ACS, notifying its secretary that his decision had been motivated by the "recent alarming attacks" on the right to free discussion.[8] Upon hearing of Smith's conversion, Beriah Green wrote to him, "I rejoice to know that your thoughts and heart are so much with the oppressed."[9] Smith's conversion to immediatism made him as central to the abolitionist circles in North Star Country as William Lloyd Garrison was to the New England abolitionists.

Garrison, who had been attacked in Boston on the night of the Utica riot, was elated by the news of abolitionist fortitude in the face of the Utica mob. He wrote, "I am ready to leap joyfully into the air."[10] Of Smith, Garrison now said, "He certainly deserves much credit for the Christian manliness and magnanimity which he manifests in joining our ranks at this perilous crisis. So much for the mob at Utica!"[11]

Before the abolitionists left Peterboro and the hospitality of Gerrit Smith, they completed the task of organizing the New York State Anti-Slavery Society. William Jay of Bedford, in Westchester County, was elected president. Beriah Green became corresponding secretary, and Spencer Kellogg, a Utica businessman, was named treasurer. A nine-member executive committee, chaired by Alvan Stewart, was empowered to manage the society's affairs. In an address to the public, the delegates sought to capitalize on the Utica riot: "The dastardly and ruthless hands, which have attempted to strangle free discussion, have cleared the way before us. Those clamors, in which they have assayed to drown our voices, have roused up myriads of sleepers. Rising from their slumbers, they are demanding the cause of this strange disturbance. Now is the time to speak."[12] The New York State Anti-

Slavery Society set up headquarters in Utica but also held annual meetings in Rochester, Syracuse, and other Upstate New York cities.

The first issue of the society's weekly newspaper, the *Friend of Man,* appeared on June 23, 1836. Using a printing press at Oneida Institute, students turned out this immediatist periodical, although it was edited by William Goodell in nearby Utica. North Star Country abolitionists hoped it would offer an alternative to the New York City–based *Emancipator,* the official organ of the AASS. Stanley Hough, the son of Oneida Institute's superintendent and treasurer, Reuben Hough, became the editor in 1839. The paper folded in 1842, but it was replaced by the *Liberty Press* (1843–1849), the voice of the Liberty Party. The Executive Committee of the New York State Anti-Slavery Society was concerned that the *Friend of Man* was not reaching enough of the abolitionists in the state. So the committee began publishing a monthly paper called the *Anti-Slavery Lecturer* in 1839. Each issue of the paper carried one lengthy essay written by William Goodell; the paper lasted for only twelve issues.[13]

North Star Country abolitionists diversified their activities beyond newspapers as they tried to reach the uncommitted in the years following 1835. The invention of the steam press made it possible to disseminate antislavery writings in far greater quantity, and at less expense, than ever before. Abolitionist pamphlets, circulars, books, and a variety of other printed material flowed in and out of North Star Country. Antislavery almanacs, at six cents per copy, became the stock-in-trade of the traveling agents.

The Executive Committee of the New York State Anti-Slavery Society made up a list of antislavery publications that it recommended as a lending library for each school district. The list included such titles as LaRoy Sunderland's *The Testimony of God Against Slavery,* John Greenleaf Whittier's *Poems,* Lydia Maria Child's *An Appeal in Favor of that Class of Americans Called Africans,* and an account of the mob attack on the abolitionists at Utica entitled, *Enemies of the Constitution Discovered.*[14] Each of the 1,350 homes in Utica received a free, condensed copy of *The Narrative of James Williams,* the story of a runaway who had worked as a slave driver in Alabama.[15]

Abolitionist gatherings frequently began with song. Collections of antislavery songs and hymns met the need for suitable lyrics and melodies. George Washington Clark of Rochester called himself a liberty singer. He put out a small medley of antislavery songs under the title *Liberty Minstrel* in 1844. One composition, "Get off the Track," was sung to the tune of "Old Dan Tucker." It hails the advance of the Emancipation cause and includes this verse:

> Let the ministers and churches
> Leave the sectarian lurches
> Jump on board the car of freedom
> Ere it be too late to need 'em
> Sound the alarm, Pulpits, thunder
> Ere too late you see your blunder.[16]

Clark's other songbook was *The Harp of Freedom*. John G. Whittier and Frederick Douglass provided lyrics for some of the melodies. Abolitionist songs and hymns helped drum up enthusiasm for the cause. "Abolitionists," writes Monroe County historian Shirley Cox Husted, "called each other 'Brother' and 'Sister' and sang abolition hymns with all the fervor of Methodist revivalists."[17]

As important as printed materials were to the abolitionist cause, North Star Country reformers also recognized the value of the spoken word. In an age when many Americans, white and black, were illiterate, the speaker's platform was still an important means of changing public opinion. Because he was endowed with immense wealth, Gerrit Smith had the wherewithal to promulgate his views regarding slavery and other issues through a cascade of circulars, printed essays, and other materials he privately published. However, even without access to the printed word, Smith would have been effective as a reformer because of his rhetorical virtuosity. The African American fugitive and abolitionist Samuel Ringgold Ward, a commanding speaker in his own right, heard Smith for the first time in May of 1838. The Madison County abolitionist was moralizing against "American Negro-hate" at Broadway Temple in New York City in front of a crowd of four thousand. Ward called Smith the "model man" and portrayed his platform presence as follows:

> Standing erect, as he could stand no other way, with his large, manly frame, graceful figure and faultless mannerism, richly but plainly dressed, with a broad collar and black ribbon upon his neck (his invariable costume, whatever be the prevailing fashion), his look, with his broad intellectual face and towering forehead, was enough to charm any one not dead to all sense of the beautiful; and

then, his rich, deep, flexible, musical voice, as of a whisper—a voice to which words were suited, as it was suited to words; but, most of all, the words, thoughts, sentiments, truths and principles, he uttered—rendered me, and thousands more with me, unable to sit or stand in any quietness during his speech . . . To mortal man it is seldom permitted to behold a sight so full of or so radiant with moral power and beauty.[18]

Upstate New York abolitionists of modest means and less oratorical flair than Smith had to scrimp and save to disseminate their views. When Beriah Green collected his abolitionist writings in book form, he was forced to sell the volume by subscription and found only modest success.[19] Like Green, most North Star Country abolitionists labored without sufficient financial resources. The state and national antislavery organizations provided little aid. When the meager funds were depleted, the typical freedom crusader became dependent on the public's generosity. Some of the most self-sacri-ficing abolitionists were female lecturers who found it particularly difficult to garner monetary assistance.

Lucy Newhall Colman challenged slavery with only a token of support from the male-dominated abolitionist societies. She was born in 1817 in Sturbridge, Massachusetts, married at age eighteen, and then moved to Rochester. Her first husband died of consumption. When she was twenty-six, Lucy married again, but when her second husband died after a railroad accident, she was left penniless, with a daughter to raise. Colman took a position at Rochester's school for "colored" students where she was paid less than half the salary of her male predecessor.

Colman left the Universalists, a denomination considered heterodox by most Christians in Upstate New York, because she was a freethinker and they did not measure up to her high abolitionist standard. Instead she became a Spiritualist. Spiritualism exalts the individual's self-worth; this squared with Colman's abolitionist convictions. She conducted an itinerant lectureship by traveling west to Ohio, Michigan, Indiana, and Illinois. In Ohio, she not only encountered a hostile audience, she was in danger of personal harm. The *Ohio Reporter* denounced her as a "woman of weak morals who ignores the commandments of the Bible, uncovering her head and speaking in public. She speaks against the laws of God laid down in the Bible."[20]

Colman persisted under the most adverse conditions. She slept in bug-infested rooms without heat. Not infrequently, she left a lecture hall to find her carriage wheel-less, her horse shorn of mane or tail, and the harness cut. She might have had support from the AASS if her critics hadn't persuaded that national agency to withdraw its offer of financial aid. Frederick Douglass was one of the few male abolitionists to give Colman moral support. He once asked her to aid the daughter of a runaway who had arrived in Rochester. Douglass wanted Colman to take the girl on as a traveling companion and to "initiate her into the ways of advertising and getting up a meeting."[21]

North Star Country abolitionists were typically tradesmen, shopkeepers, ministers, school teachers, lawyers, farmers, laborers, and domestics. "Gentlemen of property and standing" were noticeably absent from the abolitionist ranks.[22] Southern proslavery Democrats vilified the abolitionists as enemies of the republic whose incendiary rhetoric was threatening the economic livelihood of the Democrats. Northern conservatives, Whig and Democrat alike, felt threatened by the prospect of a new America in which distinctions of race and class were to be mitigated. Sometimes, conservative men of means sought out allies among the white poor in an effort to blunt criticism by the antislavery phalanx. Theodore Dwight Weld ran into opposition in Lockport when he attempted to set up the Niagara County Anti-Slavery Society in 1836. A reporter described the antiabolitionists as "*headed* by the first Judge and Sheriff of the County, a Cashier of the Bank, sundry brief lawyers, and *footed* by the liege sons of the bar room, the groggery and the gutter, whose red noses and blood-shot eyes, testified under oath to their warm and *spirited* attachment to the rights of their Southern brethren."[23]

This was an age of martyrs. In a retrospective written in 1863, the *New York Tribune* said this of the antislavery crusade's early years: "Its first battle was for freedom of speech and the press. And, in the face of riots and lynchings, and murders even, and while its meetings were broken up by mobs, and its presses thrown into rivers, and its orators and editors shut up in prisons or shot down at their posts, it fought out this fight during five or six years with a persistency and a courage which have few parallels in the annals of progress and reform."[24] North Star Country abolitionists needed courage in full measure when they encountered hostility close to home.

In 1839, a handful of friends of the antislavery cause met in Skaneateles to advance the work of a local abolitionist society. When opponents threatened bodily harm, they were forced to disband. James Canning Fuller was a Quaker whose home is known to have been an active stop on the Underground Railroad. He placed a notice in the Skaneateles *Columbian* on August 18th thanking "those friends who so kindly and voluntarily offered and perseveringly conducted him to his home, when surrounded by a tumultuous mob Third day evening last; and he sincerely trusts that the mud and missiles [that] were abundantly showered on the occasion may make both himself and friends more determined in the good cause."[25]

Bricks, rotten eggs, tomatoes, and other missiles rained down upon abolitionist speakers—seemingly in proportion to the sharpness of their attacks upon slavery. When abolitionists tried to organize the New York State Anti-Slavery Society in 1835, the oath taken by Congressmen Samuel Beardsley is representative of the depth of antiabolitionist sentiment in segments of the Burned-over District. To the immediatists who asked for permission to use the rooms of an academy in Utica, Beardsley said, "I would rather this building would be razed from its foundation, or be destroyed with fire from Heaven, than be thus contaminated."[26] North Star Country abolitionists directed their anger over slavery against the slaveholders and their Southern apologists, but more often than not the trouble they encountered came from Northerners, sometimes from their own families, friends, and neighbors.

Luther Lee's reform ministry exemplifies the local ferment. In 1838, the youthful Luther signed up as a lecturer for the New York State Anti-Slavery Society. As minister of a thoroughly abolitionist Methodist congregation in Utica, Lee set out to convert others to immediatism. "I soon found the path of an antislavery lecturer not a smooth one," he wrote. "Opposition gathered on every hand, and violence seemed the order of the day."

At a place known as Smith's Pond, Lee spoke in a crowded stone schoolhouse. Halfway through his talk, a drunken mob invaded the meeting, intent on attacking Lee. Fortunately, "a man of great physical power," a blacksmith who was standing in the doorway, came to Lee's defense, although he "was an opposer of abolition in an honest way." To those who managed to get by the blacksmith, Lee shouted,

> Back, you cowardly miscreants! Do you come to disturb me in the exercise of my right of free speech! I am the son of a revolutionary soldier, who fought

through seven bloody years to win this right for me, and do you think I will resign at the clamor of a mob! No, never! When I do it, let my right hand forget its cunning; when I do it, let my tongue cleave to the roof of my mouth; when I do it, let the ashes of that venerable father awake from the dead to reprove a recreant son!

Taken aback by Lee's rhetorical outburst, the crowd silenced. Once more a member of the mob tried to come in one of the windows. At that point, "as large a woman as I ever saw," to use Lee's words, rose up and "sent him [the attacker] reeling from the sill outward, as though he had been but a kitten." Lee resumed his lecture and finished without further incident, though he later discovered that one of the anti-abolitionists had placed a pile of powder at his feet with the object of smoking him out.

Lee had other close calls. Someone shouted, "Shoot him right in his eyes!" when Lee tried to speak inside the Methodist Church at Crane's Corners, in the town of Litchfield (Herkimer County). A gun—one that had been converted into a large syringe—was fired. A mixture of whiskey and lampblack struck Lee. He carried on, confident in his mission, though it was midnight before he could clean himself off. "The devil often overdoes his plans and defeats them," Lee observed. "A quantity of whisky is necessary to get up a mob, but too much spoils it."[27]

Like their male counterparts in the Burned-over District, women with antislavery sentiments organized themselves in an effort to influence public opinion.[28] Women were especially vital in the day-to-day upkeep of local antislavery societies. In many upstate communities, women adapted traditionally female and domestic activities to the needs of the immediatist crusade. They sponsored antislavery fairs and organized sewing circles or church gatherings to discuss slavery. For example, white women set up the Rochester Ladies Anti-Slavery Society (RLASS) in 1835, with Susan Farley Porter as president. The founders of this female abolitionist society were influenced by the evangelical revivals ignited by Charles G. Finney. They were also members of Rochester's growing middle class and, as such, had a vested interest in promoting morality and social stability.

In 1842, a more radical antislavery organization emerged: the Western New York Anti-Slavery Society (WNYASS). Although it included men, the society became an organizational vehicle in which women who were uncomfortable in the more conservative churches and reform societies

Luther Lee (1800–1889). Lee was an abolitionist preacher and Wesleyan Methodist leader. He served the Wesleyan Methodist Church in Syracuse, and his home was a stop on the Underground Railroad. *Courtesy of the Library of Congress.*

could speak out on issues of race, peace, and gender. Most society members were Garrisonians and advocates of moral suasion and nonviolence. They were opposed to party politics. Some helped establish separate abolitionist churches. Rochester's Amy Post, an ally of Frederick Douglass, was active in the Western New York Anti-Slavery Society, along with her husband Isaac.

Historian Nancy A. Hewitt describes the differences between the women who were allied with Susan Farley Porter and those who were allied with Amy Post:

> The officers of RLASS appealed to their affluent neighbors, conformed to community codes of racial and sexual conduct, rejected demands for women's rights, and demonstrated their respectability both privately and publicly. They emphatically contrasted their own efforts with those of their counterparts in WNYASS who wore bloomers, discussed the sexual brutality of slavery in public, demanded sexual equality, and socialized in mixed racial company to the dismay of most of their neighbors.[29]

Distinctions of class and of culture can be seen in the fund-raising fairs sponsored by the two organizations. The women of the WNYASS solicited articles "both useful and ornamental," including "eggs, butter, cheese, cream, turkeys, hams, dried beef, pickles, and fruit."[30] RLASS women tried to appeal to wealthier patrons by offering "finely wrought baby linen, the exquisite seaweed baskets, the drawings, the collection of Irish shells, and the beautiful embroidery."[31]

Women of the WNYASS sponsored the Anti-Slavery Office and Reading Room in Rochester in 1848. They leased a chamber in the central part of the city and furnished it with desks, a table, a showcase, a carpet, and antislavery papers and books. At their fifth annual meeting in December 1848, the women reported, "As this was the only free Reading Room in the city, it was expected that it would become a place of resort, and thus a means of light and usefulness." This was not to be. "The fact that it has been visited by but few," the report conceded, "is sad proof of the little desire for information on the part of the community." The WNYASS blamed the fierce excitement of the 1848 presidential campaign for the public's lack of interest in radical antislavery views. Though they bemoaned the "profligate mendacity, cunning trickery, and bold, bad acts" of electoral politics, the women believed that the 1848 presidential contest had made the antislavery question "*the question* which shall swallow up all minor ones, as the rod

Amy Post (1802–1889). Amy Post and husband, Isaac, were Hicksite Quakers and long active in North Star Country reform causes. Their home at 35 Sophia Street (now N. Plymouth Avenue), Rochester, was an active stop on the Underground Railroad. The Posts were instrumental in encouraging Frederick Douglass to settle in Rochester. *Courtesy of the Rochester Public Library.*

Aaron did the rods of the magicians of Pharaoh in the story of olden time."[32]

Women's groups across Upstate New York held bazaars, fairs, and a variety of antislavery functions to raise funds. They conducted boycotts of slave-produced goods and set up free produce societies in which only products made by voluntary labor were sold. Some of the more bold women took to the lecture circuit on behalf of the slave, and an uncounted number opened their homes to runaways or assisted them with food, clothes, and traveling money. In 1859, the Women's Anti-Slavery Society of Ellington (Chautauqua County) wrote to William Still, the principal agent in the Philadelphia area: "Every year we have sent a box of clothing, bedding, etc., to the aid of the fugitive, and wishing to send it where it would be of the most service, we have it suggested to us, to send to you the box we have at present. You would confer a favor . . . by writing us, . . . whether or not it would be more advantageous to you than some nearer station."[33]

While there is insufficient evidence to make a generalization about the typical abolitionist household in North Star Country, it is very likely that more than a few women took the lead by prodding their husbands to vote for the Liberty Party, beginning with the election of 1840. Lacking the elective franchise, women had to use other means to influence public opinion while they waited for the day they would have access to the ballot box.[34] Women were particularly active in the effort to flood Congress with antislavery appeals. Although the Gag Law of 1836 thwarted this method of influencing Washington politicians, women's experience with organized attempts to sway public sentiment did carry over to their crusade to win the vote a decade later.[35]

The link between abolition and women's rights appears to be especially strong in North Star Country. When the first women's rights convention convened at Seneca Falls (Seneca County) in July 1848, Frederick Douglass was there. He gave an address and stood alone among the men present when the critical moment arrived to support a suffrage resolution. Douglass seconded Elizabeth Cady Stanton's motion that it was the sacred duty of women in the United States to obtain the elective franchise.

At a rally for the cause, held in Rochester during November 1853, Douglass again demonstrated his convictions regarding women's rights. Jermain W. Loguen, the African American preacher from Syracuse, also attended

and was named a vice-president of the convention.[36] New York State Democrats steadfastly held to patriarchal views about the place of women in the
domestic and public realms. They viewed the participation of women in
the freedom crusade as a threat to male control of the home and civic
affairs. North Star Country abolitionists generally supported the reform
of antebellum America's gender hierarchy; a significant number of
them worked for emancipation from the restraints of racial and sexual
domination.[37]

The African American abolitionists who were active in North Star
Country had to combat a double prejudice. Any public hostility toward
antislavery agitators fed upon racial hatred when the speaker was African
American. Samuel R. Ward attracted the attention of Lewis Tappan who
encouraged him to use his oratorical skills as an agent of the AASS. Ward
began to lecture in 1839 and soon came under the direction of the New York
State Anti-Slavery Society. Ordained by the New York Congregational Association, Ward ministered to a white congregation in South Butler (Wayne
County) from 1841 to 1843. Throat trouble compelled him to resign, and for
a while he studied medicine. In 1846, Ward settled in Cortland where he
held a pastorate until 1851 when he moved to Syracuse. Ward was an early
supporter of the Liberty Party. He published the *Impartial Citizen* in two
locations, first in Cortland and later in Syracuse. To raise funds for Ward's
paper, a group of African American women, led by Julia Garnet, Henry H.
Garnet's wife, held an antislavery fair in Syracuse during September of 1849.
The women appealed for support on the grounds that "the press should be
sustained when it boldly and fearlessly advocates our rights."[38]

As an African American and a fugitive, Ward did not need anyone to
convince him to become an abolitionist, no matter the personal risk.
Ward's autobiography first appeared in 1855. In its introduction, he explains
why "the coloured man" was an essential partner in the antislavery enterprise: "I call the expert black cordwainer, blacksmith, or other mechanic or
artisan, the teacher, the lawyer, the doctor, the farmer, or the divine, an anti-
slavery labourer; and in his vocation from day to day, with his hoe, ham-
mer, pen, tongue, or lancet, he is living down the base calumnies of his
heartless adversaries—he is demonstrating his truth and their falsity."
About himself, whether in the pulpit, on the platform, or in the editor's
chair, Ward said, "as a man, a Christian, especially as a *black man,* my

labours must be anti-slavery labours, because mine must be an anti-slavery life."[39]

Proslavery apologists claimed that the "peculiar institution" was justified because slaves were inferior, childlike creatures who were unable to care for themselves. To counter this image, many African Americans in the North stressed the importance of moral probity and self-help on a day-to-day basis. In the 1830s and 1840s, black leaders like Ward espoused racial elevation by way of individual self-improvement. Within the black community, these leaders campaigned for literacy, hard work, temperance, piety, frugality, and respectability. In 1830, Austin Steward was operating a small grocery store in Rochester. He had a license to sell liquor, but he gave up dealing in "ardent spirits" when he became convinced that the abuse of alcohol led to pauperism and crime among his fellow blacks.[40]

In 1852, the Woman's State Temperance Convention organized in Rochester. Frederick Douglass and William Allen, the only black professor at New York Central College, attended. Douglass had been involved in the temperance movement since he arrived in North Star Country, but he drew back after 1853 because the Rochester women with whom he had been working had lost control of the statewide women's organization. Its male counterpart, the Sons of Temperance, stopped granting charters to black branches and was turning away blacks from its predominantly white branches. The Sons of Temperance in Cortland, a white group, had accepted Samuel R. Ward. When the statewide division demanded that Ward be expelled, the local officers, who were members of Ward's all-white congregation, refused. Instead, they gave up the group's charter.[41]

The reluctance of some white reformers to rise above the prejudice in their own ranks precipitated the movement of blacks into their own voluntary associations. This movement included organizing local antislavery societies. For example, in Geneva, African Americans set up the Geneva Colored Anti-Slavery Society in 1836. Horace H. Dawkins served as president, and James W. Duffin was secretary.[42] In 1837, Charles B. Ray visited Geneva as he canvassed Upstate New York to sell subscriptions to the *Colored American*. He reported, "The colored population in this place, number about two hundred and fifty, nearly all of the elder of whom are from the south, brought here by their masters as slaves, and retained in slavery for some time afterwards. They are generally [in comfortable] circumstances, but a plain people, many of them living in their own houses, standing on their own soil." Ray admired Geneva's beautiful setting at the head of Seneca Lake but, he opined, "the people are great aristocrats, and abolition is almost unknown among them; there are a few, however, who profess to be abolitionists, but with five or six exceptions there, abolitionism is not half baked, they need a more thorough going lecturer among them a week, to serve as an oven, to rebake their abolition; the whole people however are as much opposed to slavery as any body."[43] The Geneva Colored Anti-Slavery Society held the goal of forming "a correct public sentiment, on the subject of slavery, and to endeavour by all lawful means to do away with evil, and raise our colored brethren from their state of degradation and misery."[44]

African American abolitionists believed that education enhanced their prospects for self-liberation, yet many a schoolhouse in Upstate New York shut out black children. *Freedom's Journal,* a black newspaper, published this editorial: "Educate our youth, and you remove the moral infection that exists among the lower classes of our people—you elevate the intellect and excite an oppressed and injured people, to honorable and successful endeavors after virtue and competency. This is the whole secret of amelioration."[45]

Rosetta Douglass, the oldest of Frederick Douglass's five children, ran into the roadblock of racism when she tried to attend Miss Lucilia Tracy's Seward Seminary in 1849. Rosetta had qualified to attend by passing the entrance exam, but the nine-year-old girl reported of her first days at school, "I get along pretty well, but father, Miss Tracy does not allow me to go into the room with the other scholars because I am colored."[46] Rosetta's father, not one to shy from the sting of prejudice, confronted the principal and was told that the fault lay with the parents of the other girls. One father had indeed objected, even though Rosetta's classmates did not.[47] In the end, Douglass's daughter was told to gather up her books and pencils and go home.

Although Frederick Douglass found another school for Rosetta, his fight against discrimination in the classroom was not over. In 1849, a committee of Rochester's school board proposed to do away with the "colored school" on the east side of the river and to integrate black children into the schools closest to their residences. Douglass took to the columns of the *North Star* and defended the committee's proposal as an instrument for undercutting "the blind prejudice and haughty contempt with which the colored people are usually treated in this country."[48] Douglass pressed the case for school integration year after year, but Rochester did not actually do away with its "colored schools" until 1857.[49] Schools for blacks, both private and public, developed slowly in Upstate New York before the Civil War. Wherever the schools appeared there was controversy over funding, admission, and curriculum; African American parents persisted. They sought the best available educational opportunities, as Douglass had in Rochester, because they believed that learning would help secure freedom.[50]

Segregated seating and other forms of discrimination existed in most Northern white churches, so forming independent congregations in Upstate New York was another way for African Americans to demonstrate their love of liberty. Some of the earliest of these churches were associated with the independent black denomination known as the African Methodist Episcopal Zion (A.M.E.Z.) Church, which was organized in New York City during 1822.

The oldest existing church structure in Ithaca is St. James A.M.E.Z. Church on Cleveland Avenue (formerly Wheat Avenue). The church achieved state landmark status in 1978 and, in 1982, was placed on the National Register of Historic Places. In the mid-1820s, a group of Ithaca blacks began conducting religious meetings in a building at Green and Geneva Streets. In 1836, the group organized St. James. The original stone meeting house has been greatly altered over the years, although the stone walls and paneled door of the original structure do remain. In 1838, the Reverend Thomas James was the church's pastor and used the church as a stop on the Underground Railroad. Later on, in the 1840s, Jermain Loguen served as pastor to the congregation briefly.[51]

In addition to serving the church in Ithaca, the Reverend James helped establish congregations in Rochester and Syracuse. Jermain Loguen arrived in Syracuse in 1841 and took over as pastor of what has become, in more recent times, the People's A.M.E.Z. Church. Another early black congregation began in Binghamton around 1827: the Trinity A.M.E.Z. Church. Church members incorporated in 1838 but they struggled to find a permanent place of worship. Blacks in Geneva organized the Free Colored Church and were able to use their own building as early as 1834. The Colored

Methodist Society occupied a frame house on Carroll Street in Buffalo; by 1837 the society had joined the African Methodist Episcopal (A.M.E.) Church, a denomination established in 1816 under the leadership of Richard Allen of Philadelphia. In 1839, the Buffalo congregation moved to Vine Street and became known as the Vine Street A.M.E. Church. The towns of Niagara and Lockport also supported black Methodist churches during the height of the abolitionist campaign. In Buffalo, black Baptists organized themselves in the early 1830s. By 1836, the Baptists had begun using a building on Michigan Street. Soon they became known as the Michigan Street Baptist Church.[52]

We have no reliable statistics that can establish the precise number of African Americans who considered themselves church members at the time when abolitionists contested for the soul of the Burned-over District. In 1849, Henry H. Garnet campaigned for a grand convention of black Christians. His purposes: to overcome social caste and sectarianism in black communities and to advance the Gospel among the unchurched. He estimated that New York State held "some sixty or seventy thousand people of color," of which "perhaps thirty thousand" lived west of Albany. Garnet felt that "not more than six thousand" of this number met for religious worship. Because blacks in this area were scattered geographically and discouraged by discrimination from white congregations, too many of them lacked the full enjoyment of Christian privileges. And what were the consequences? Garnet, like Jeremiah of old, was quick to sound the alarm: "Too many suffer their ambition to lead them no where else than to the ballroom, the tippler's retreat, and the gambler's table." "For proof," Garnet argued, "look to Utica, Syracuse, Auburn, Geneva, Buffalo, and especially Rochester."[53]

Using a liberal interpretation of the word "abolitionist," free blacks in the Burned-over District, together with fugitives who put down roots in the region, helped transform the region into North Star Country. By taking responsibility for their own welfare and by working hard, they felt they were part of the emancipation effort even though they were not full-time abolitionists. As they pursued education for their children; supported voluntary associations such as churches, literary societies, and other self-help groups; and remained temperate; they contradicted racist stereotypes. Prejudice, however, was an ever-present reality.

The story of William G. Allen illustrates just how difficult it was for African Americans to break out of the prison to which racist white public opinion confined them. Allen was born in Virginia, about 1820, to a free mulatto mother and a Welshman. He was adopted by a free black family in Fortress Monroe. There he caught the eye of the Reverend William Hall, a New Yorker who ran a school for blacks. In 1839, Hall wrote to Gerrit Smith, urging Smith to sponsor Allen's education in the Empire State. A year later, Smith sent Allen to Beriah Green and to Oneida Institute, along with a letter that described the young man. Allen earned high marks at the institute, both in his studies and for his deportment. He played the flute, assisted the chapel choir, and worked with the school's treasurer. In the summer of 1841, Allen taught at a school that Hiram Wilson established among fugitives who had settled in Canada. He graduated in 1844 with Oneida Institute's last class, then moved to Troy. There he taught school and helped Henry Highland Garnet edit the *National Watchman,* an abolitionist and temperance paper for African Americans.

In 1850, Allen joined the faculty of New York Central College in McGrawville (Cortland County). After Oneida Institute closed, Gerrit Smith and other progressive reformers had turned their attention to the McGrawville college, which was incorporated in December 1848. It opened to students, in September 1849, under the sponsorship of the American Baptist Free Mission Society. Festivities marked the laying of the cornerstone on July 4, 1848. On that day, Elder C. P. Grosvenor, editor of the *Christian Contributor* and president-elect of the college, spoke of the importance of giving women the same educational opportunities that were given to men. He was followed by speakers who decried racism, slavery, and the "War spirit."[54] Like Oneida Institute, New York Central College operated on the manual labor principle.[55]

The Edmondson sisters, Mary and Emily, spent a year at New York Central College. The story of their attempted escape from slavery (via the baycraft Pearl from a Potomac River wharf in Washington, D.C.) was told far and wide on the abolitionist circuit. Of the Edmondson sisters, Miss Keziah King, their primary department teacher wrote:

> These girls have been struggling with many difficulties, endeavoring to get an education. They have been obliged to suspend their studies frequently for months at a time, to earn the money to pay for their board and clothes. It must

be remembered that, like other slave girls, they could neither read nor write at the time they were redeemed. Struggling under all these difficulties, they have acquired the rudiments of a primary education, they can write a legible hand, and have some knowledge of grammar, geography, and arithmetic.[56]

In addition to Gerrit Smith, other abolitionists, such as Frederick Douglass, Samuel Ringgold Ward, William Lloyd Garrison, and Theodore Parker, contributed to the school. Horace Greeley, the famed newspaper reporter and editor of the *New York Tribune,* also sent aid. The college's four-story brick main building was constructed with assistance from the citizens of McGrawville. The school offered both preparatory and collegiate departments. About one-third of the students were female; one of these was Edmonia Lewis, the noted black sculptress.[57]

New York Central College opened with 115 students. By 1856, it had 109 scholars, of whom 18 were African American. Critics derisively called it the "Nigger school." William Allen, who was proficient in both Greek and German, taught language and literature courses at New York Central. His appointment was noteworthy; this was only the second instance of an African American teaching at the college level. Charles L. Reason (the first instance) was already on the faculty, teaching literature, French, and mathematics.[58] In August 1851, Allen wrote to Henry Bibb, a black expatriate who was active among his fellow refugees in Canada West (present-day Ontario, but known as the colony of Upper Canada until 1840): "The college is in a flourishing condition: its doors are open to male and female, black and white. No inequality exists here on account of sex or color. The principles upon which the college is founded are stated in the motto of *Frederick Douglass's Paper*, 'ALL RIGHTS FOR ALL.'"[59]

In 1852, Allen announced that he intended to marry a white student, Mary King, from Fulton (Oswego County). While the couple visited friends in nearby Phillipsville, they received threats from foes of the proposed interracial marriage. King went back to Fulton, and Allen was taken to Syracuse under protective guard. The couple married secretly in New York City on March 30, 1852. The college, which was already on the point of financial collapse, was now the subject of intense ridicule. Allen resigned and took his wife to England, where he wrote a stinging indictment of American racism.[60] Gerrit Smith tried to save the school by purchasing its buildings and part of the farm, but the efforts to keep this radical egalitarian institution afloat faltered. New York Central College closed for good in 1860.[61]

Henry Highland Garnet was another challenger of America's racial conventions. After he escaped from a Maryland plantation in 1824, with his parents, Garnet settled in New York City where he attended the African Free School. Later on, he served as a cabin boy on two voyages to Cuba; during this time, slave hunters broke up the family home. Upon Garnet's return to New York City, Long Island Quakers took him in as an indentured servant for two years. In 1831, he enrolled in New York City's High School for Colored Youth. Soon, however, he departed for Canaan, New Hampshire, and the Noyes Academy, which declared itself ready to admit "colored youth of good character on equal terms with white of like character." Two other black youths, Alexander Crummell and Thomas S. Sidney, accompanied him to the academy.

Crummell relates that the "Democracy of the State could not endure what they called a 'Nigger School' on the soil of New Hampshire." Armed with ninety yoke of oxen, farmers dragged the academy building into a swamp. Then, according to Crummell, he, Sidney, and Garnet heard that Oneida Institute "had opened its doors to colored boys.... Thither we three New York boys at once repaired, and spent three years under the instruction of that Master-thinker and teacher, Rev. Beriah Green."[62]

During the farmers' attack upon the Noyes Academy, Garnet had injured his leg. The injury was serious enough that, on the trip to Upstate New York, Crummell feared for his friend's life. Later, Crummell remarked that Garnet's "early, long continued illness broke up the systematic training of the schools; and so he was never the deep-plodding, laborious student."[63] Nevertheless, Garnet has been remembered for his display of wit and brilliance in public debate while enrolled at Oneida Institute. During a class oration, a heckler threw a squash at him. Garnet retorted, "My good friends, do not be alarmed, it is only a soft pumpkin; some gentleman has thrown away his head and lo! His brains are dashed out."[64]

Garnet graduated from Beriah Green's abolitionist school in 1839 and became pastor of the Liberty Street Presbyterian Church in Troy. In December 1848, he moved back to North Star Country. With fifteen charter members and support from the American Missionary Association, he established a black congregation in Geneva. Henry Bibb once called Geneva "the most aristocratic, pro-slavery hole" he had ever encountered in the North.[65] Garnet saw a need for change and helped the African Americans of Geneva to build Geneva Tabernacle as a place for worship and social gatherings. He also opened a day school and a large Sunday school. During this time, Garnet was residing in Peterboro, where he preached occasionally and drew on the liberality of Gerrit Smith. In the aftermath of the passage of the Fugitive Slave Law, Garnet resigned his AMA commission and, in 1850, he went to Great Britain to lecture on behalf of the Free Produce Association.[66]

Garnet was one of the first African Americans to become active in the American and Foreign Anti-Slavery Society after the division in abolitionist ranks in 1840. He was an outspoken member of the Liberty Party. He fought to obtain voting rights for blacks, harbored fugitives, supported the free produce movement, and was militant enough to believe that African Americans needed to organize their own conventions to debate issues of the day. Black conventions first began, on the state level, in 1840 at Albany. The participants aimed their sharpest arrows at the New York State law that restricted voting rights among black males to those who owned property that was worth $250 or more.[67]

Trouble dogged Garnet throughout his years as an abolitionist activist in North Star Country. In 1848, while en route to Niagara Falls, he was thrown off a train because he sat in a car reserved for whites. The conductor told him, "Colored people cannot be permitted to ride with the whites on this road, for Southern ladies and gentlemen will not tolerate it."[68] Douglass's *North Star* was quick to reprint a report on Garnet's run-in with Northern racism: "Rev. Henry H. Garnet, one of the ablest and most useful clergymen in Troy, was dragged from the cars of the Buffalo and Niagara Railroad on Tuesday last, and so badly bruised that he had to suspend his journey and place himself under the care of a physician.—Reason—His forefathers were stolen from Africa."[69] Regardless of the psychological impact this abuse had on Garnet, he was one of the first African American abolitionists to arrive at the conclusion that the nonviolent approach of the immediatists was an inadequate means of destroying slavery and its evil twin: racism.

By the end of the 1830s, Garrison's philosophy of nonviolence seemed less effective than it had earlier. The killing of clergyman and editor Elijah P. Lovejoy in Alton, Illinois, on a night in November 1837 was key. It was the signal to many antislavery crusaders that they were locked in combat with forces far more obdurate and vicious than they had first expected. There was to be no bloodless regeneration of America. But Garrison held fast to his principles of passive resistance (which he called *nonresistance*) to evil. Though mourning the loss of the brave man who dared to criticize slavery from his newspaper post in St. Louis, Missouri, Boston-based Garrison faulted Lovejoy for relying upon "powder and ball" to defend himself when surrounded by proslavery ruffians.[70] Some North Star Country abolitionists felt differently.

At the urging of Elizur Wright, Jr., and others, Beriah Green accepted the task of composing a fitting eulogy for Lovejoy. Green set aside his responsibilities at Oneida Institute, which were made all the more burdensome by the adverse effects of the financial panic of 1837. He journeyed to New York City to deliver the tribute in a memorial service held at Broadway Tabernacle, the reformist citadel of Lewis and Arthur Tappan. He placed Lovejoy in the book of martyrs, alongside God's faithful witnesses of all ages, and predicted that the editor's death would arouse the indifferent to the claims of the enslaved. He placed the blame for Lovejoy's death upon the "heads of law-abiding, public-spirited, and useful citizens" who were the "instigators and abettors of the intoxicated rabble." Though an advocate of peace principles, Green had not sworn himself to Garrison's absolutist doctrine of nonresistance. Like Lewis Tappan, he, too, concluded that Lovejoy had been justified in planning to defend himself against the Alton rabble. "It was the only point where his rights could be defended," Oneida Institute's president declared. "Abandoned there, they must give place to the yoke of slavery."[71]

Green had traveled down to New York City at the invitation of the officers of the AASS. However, he was now increasingly reluctant to travel outside of North Star Country. Like many Upstate abolitionists, he felt more connected to the New York State Anti-Slavery Society than to the national body. Tensions between the state organization and the national organization derived from many factors: disputes over the allocation and distribution of funds, personality conflicts, disagreements over the place of women in reform movements, and resentment toward Garrisonian agents who canvassed Upstate New York for funds. The strained relations between North Star Country abolitionists and those operating out of New England (as well as those representing Garrison at the national offices in New York City) fractured the immediatist fellowship in 1840.

The precipitating cause materialized a year earlier, in 1839. In a debate over whether women should be allowed to vote in meetings of the AASS, Garrison championed equal rights for women and urged that all abolitionists fight as zealously against the slavery of sex as they did against the slavery of race. Gerrit Smith, William Chaplin, and Alvan Stewart voted in favor of enfranchising women in the national organization, but others with strong ties to the NYSASS voted against the idea. The votes of Beriah Green, Lewis Tappan, and James G. Birney were among the 140 negative votes out of the 320 cast at the meeting. The two-day debate at the 1839 meeting pitted Garrisonian radicals against conservatives who were already upset by Garrison's perfectionist ideals, nonresistance philosophy, criticism of the clergy, and rhetoric about the need for a fundamental transformation of American society. When the convention voted to define members as persons, thereby giving women the right to be voting delegates, the rift deepened between Garrison's supporters and the conservatives aligned with Lewis Tappan and the NYSASS.[72]

A scattering of abolitionists in North Star Country were also disenchanted with the doctrinaire moral suasion philosophy that dominated the AASS. Prior to the fateful meeting of the national body in 1840, Alvan Stewart of Utica had led the push for greater autonomy from the Boston clique surrounding Garrison. Stewart was born in 1790 on a farm in Washington County, New York. He studied law privately at Cherry Valley, in Otsego County. Originally a Democrat, he became a supporter of the Whig Party during its dispute with the Jacksonians over tariffs.[73] Stewart had been so influenced by the religious revivals ignited by Charles G. Finney that, in 1832, he began to speak *for* temperance and *against* slavery. In 1834, he gave up his legal practice to travel throughout the Burned-over District and lecture against the ACS. Although he was elected president of the NYSASS, Stewart did not always receive the approbation of his colleagues. His early call for moving beyond moral suasion and into the political realm met resistance in the circle of reformers centered around Gerrit Smith.

Stewart did find an ally, however, in the person of William Goodell. At the 1839 meeting of the NYSASS, Goodell gave a candid assessment of the challenge abolitionists confronted. Goodell believed that the reformers had operated within a too-restrictive sphere during the first phase of their moral crusade:

They move in circles of the light they have themselves diffused, and forget the dense masses of unpenetrated darkness, at no great distances all around them. There are certain *beaten tracks* of moral, religious and benevolent enterprise, which have been made by successive travelers and voyagers through the middle and eastern states. One of two of those tracks run through the state of New York. On these comparatively comfortable *thoroughfares*, the missionary, the Bible, the Sunday School, the Tract, the Temperance, the Moral Reform, and the Anti-Slavery agents, have successively and successfully passed, and each one had set up landmarks for those who may come after him. A number of promising garden spots have been cleared up, and fenced, and put under tolerable cultivation. Seed has been sown—crops are maturing and must be watched and looked after, and harvested. If any special demonstration or exhibition of our principles is to be made, we naturally look to these *favored sections* for the successful experiment. If our principles are to be carried to the polls, if an array of petitions is to be marshaled, if a certain amount of funds is speedily to be raised, (and these exigencies often occur), all our available forces are put in requisition to traverse over again, hastily, our antislavery thoroughfares, to labor in the fields where we may expect to gather the greatest amount of ripe fruit. And thus it comes to pass that vast sections of the state are scarcely visited at all, or cultivated but inefficiently and at intervals.[74]

Here was a frank admission that the abolitionists had not been able to enlarge their constituency beyond those circles of reform born of the Burned-over District. Despite Goodell's support, Alvan Stewart's advocacy of political action fell upon deaf ears in 1839. Most members of the Executive Committee of the NYSASS were opposed to entering the tawdry business of party politics. Gerrit Smith wrote to Lewis Tappan in March 1840 to complain of infighting among abolitionists: "Poor abolitionists! What ill-tempered fellows they are! How we love to devour one another!"[75]

When delegates to the seventh annual meeting of the AASS gathered in New York City in May 1840, the building volcano finally erupted. The Garrisonians gained control of the convention and elected Abby Kelly to the previously all-male Executive Committee, by a vote of 557 to 451. Lewis Tappan and some thirty other conservatives on "the woman question" then formed a rival organization: the American and Foreign Anti-Slavery Society (AFASS). Many Upstate abolitionists eventually joined this breakaway organization and, in so doing, brought the Burned-over District reform impulse into the AFASS ranks. Although the AFASS eventually foundered and virtually collapsed because of disagreements over whether it should be attached to a third political party, it did provide a forum for abolitionists from North Star Country to escape the ideological tutelage of Garrison and the New Englanders.

Beriah Green did not immediately agree that it was time to break with the Garrisonians. "I cannot think that Bro. Garrison and his co-adjutors are the men to blame. . . . We might as well ascribe the excesses and terrors of the French revolution to . . . such as Danton and Robespierre," he wrote just prior to the breakup. After the schism of 1840, Green wrote to Gerrit Smith, "You know how little sympathy I have with the extravagances of Mr. Garrison. But in my mind he stands Heaven-high above those ministers who early in the controversy threw themselves in the way of Truth and Righteousness. No extravagance is so bad as their inhumanity."[76] Green admired Garrison. The Boston reformer had sacrificed fame and fortune to advance the cause of poor suffering humanity and deserved to be honored, no matter his ideological excesses.

After the division of 1840, Frederick Douglass remained within the Garrisonian fold. In 1843, he participated in the push by the New England Anti-Slavery Convention to send forth lecturers who would organize one hundred conventions. Douglass, together with the corps of speakers on the Hundred Conventions tour, began work in western Vermont and then entered the Empire State. Utica's Alvan Stewart encouraged a boycott of the New England agents. He complained that they preached Garrison's ideas of "no human government," and that by discouraging voting and discouraging the petitioning of government, the agents "actually prolonged the slave's bondage."[77] Douglass was traveling in the company of George Bradburn, a Unitarian minister from Massachusetts, and John A. Collins, a convert to Fourier communitarianism who seemed more interested in promoting his antiproperty views than in speaking against slavery. They arrived in Utica on July 27, 1843, for a proposed three-day convention, but Stewart's blast had soured Upstate abolitionists on the Hundred Conventions tour, and there was a poor turnout. Douglass and Bradburn left the next day; Douglass for Syracuse, and Bradburn for Peterboro and a visit with Gerrit Smith. Collins stayed on to promote communitarianism.

At Syracuse, and elsewhere on his tour of central New York, Douglass encountered something like the adversity with which Upstate New York abolitionists had contended in the early years of their efforts to bring the region into harmony with the goals of the immediatist movement. He later wrote:

> All along the Erie Canal, from Albany to Buffalo, there was evidenced apathy, indifference, aversion, and sometimes a mobocratic spirit. Even Syracuse, afterward the home of the humane Samuel J. May and the scene of the "Jerry Rescue," where Gerrit Smith, Beriah Greene [*sic*], William Goodell, Alvan Stewart, and other able men taught their noblest lessons, would not at that time furnish us with church, market, house, or hall in which to hold our meetings.[78]

Some of Douglass's colleagues thought it best to forsake Syracuse, but Douglass received encouragement from Stephen Smith, with whom he was lodging. Smith's house, Douglass recollected, "stood on the southwest corner of the park, which was well covered with young trees too small to furnish shade or shelter, but better than none."[79] On July 30, a Sunday morning, Douglass made his stand under a small tree on the southeast corner of what is now known as Fayette Park. He began with only five listeners but, when the meeting ended in the afternoon, his audience had grown to "not less than five hundred." That evening, representatives of Syracuse's First Congregational Church, organized in 1838 by abolitionists, visited Douglass and gave him the use of an old wooden building that the congregation had once used. The convention went on there for three more days. Some years later and in a reflective mood, Douglass wrote, "I believe there has been no trouble to find places in Syracuse in which to hold anti-slavery meetings since. I never go there without endeavoring to see that tree, which, like the cause it sheltered, has grown large and strong and imposing."[80]

4. Trouble in God's House

Had Frederick Douglass visited Syracuse a few years later, he would not have had to lecture under a tree. He might have spoken in a church that was built by abolitionist-minded Methodists around 1846. The building where abolitionists were welcomed still stands, facing historic Columbus Circle. An aura of mystery surrounds the red brick structure: Someone chiseled seven human faces into the unfired clay walls of a basement tunnel. Stories persist that the faces were created by fugitives who had been given refuge by the Wesleyan Methodists.[1] Regarded by many as trouble-makers in God's house, these Methodists were willing to risk censure for the sake of their abolitionist commitment. Syracuse's Wesleyan Methodist church was one of the so-called comeouter congregations organized by Christian abolitionists before the Civil War. No issue divided the denominational families of North Star Country more than the debate over slavery.

During the early years of the abolitionist crusade, advocates of black freedom in the Burned-over District discovered that they had two battles to wage. They had to press the case against the slaveholders while attempting to convert white Northerners to the higher standard of immediatism. They needed to carry the crusade into every Northern community, home, and church. Religion had given birth to abolitionism in the Burned-over District, but now abolitionism pitted Christian against Christian. The result: North Star Country church life suffered internal discord with long-lasting consequences.

In 1800, perhaps no more than 10 percent of the American people were church members. In 1809, Yale University's president, Timothy Dwight, bemoaned the public's view of religion. Some Americans saw church people as "dotards and nurses"; others regarded religion as "a system of fraud and trick, imposed by priestcraft for base purposes upon the ignorant multitude."[2]

By the middle of the 1830s, the Second Great Awakening had transformed the country. Church membership had risen dramatically. The three largest popular denominations—the Methodists, the Baptists, and the Presbyterians—accounted for the vast majority of Americans who thought of themselves as Christian and Protestant. In effect, evangelical Christianity was the national religion, despite constitutional provisions prohibiting the establishment of specific religious traditions. The great evangelical denominations contributed to the creation of a national identity and helped hold North and South together prior to the schism over slavery.

Methodism was especially instrumental to forging a sense of intersectional unity. Church historian C. C. Goen has written, "The Methodist Episcopal Church was the most extensive national institution in antebellum America other than the federal government."[3] During the American Revolution, a critic scoffed that there were scarcely enough Methodists to fill a corn crib, but by the time Andrew Jackson was elected in 1828, Methodists were both numerous and widespread. Methodism was popular among common folk because of its simplified doctrines, spirited preaching, and emphasis on personal religious experience. In addition, the Methodists had an efficient organization. Their hierarchical church polity and their mechanism of itinerancy both operated with military-like precision and effectiveness. A Methodist preacher on horseback who was armed with a Bible, a hymnbook, and the Methodist *Book of Discipline* was a formidable weapon in the battle to evangelize and redeem America in the early nineteenth century.[4]

Orange Scott was one of these Methodist evangelists. Born in 1800 to a poor Vermont family, Scott was ordained in 1826. He became presiding elder of Methodist ministers in the Springfield, Massachusetts, area a few years later. But his path to ecclesiastical advancement was cut short when he converted to abolitionism around 1834. Convinced that the ACS was an abomination, Scott threw himself into the immediatist crusade with all of the passion he had previously devoted to revivals. As one of the famous seventy, in 1836 he stumped for the AASS. After the schism of 1840, Scott joined the AFASS. Garrison considered the clergy to be an impediment to immediatism and so washed his hands of organized religion; Orange Scott attempted to reform the church from within. He gave speeches, wrote antislavery articles, and organized caucuses of true abolitionists as a means of leavening the whole loaf of Methodism.[5]

Sculpted face, Wesleyan Methodist Church, Syracuse. This photograph depicts the best-preserved of the seven surviving clay faces that were found on the dug-out wall of the church's basement. Some viewers believe the features represent Frederick Douglass or Jermain Loguen. Solid evidence regarding the faces' creator(s) and the date of origin remains elusive. *Courtesy of Douglas V. Armstrong.*

Scott and his allies hoped to lead their denomination out of the moral quagmire of slavery; obstacles persisted. The Methodist Church was a national institution with strong representation in the South. Many Northern Methodists flinched from condemning their Southern brethren whom they believed had *entailed,* or inherited, slavery through no fault of their own. Methodists of both sections supported colonization and mission work in Africa, surrogates for antislavery sentiment. Antiabolitionists held powerful positions in the episcopal government of the denomination, and they maneuvered to silence Scott and his supporters. At the General Conference of 1836, the bishops' pastoral address declared that the only biblical way to deal with slavery was "to refrain from this agitating subject."[6]

Luther Lee was one Methodist who refused to be muzzled. While he was pastor of Syracuse's Wesleyan Methodist Church, his home was used as a station on the Underground Railroad. The story of Lee's shift to *comeouterism* illustrates how strongly abolitionism dominated the outlook of evangelical Christians once they took a public stand on behalf of God's "suffering humanity."[7] The comeouter movement was based on Revelation 18:4, a passage calling on people to come out of Babylon, and held that Christians should withdraw from impure institutions, such as churches, unwilling to recognize slavery's sinfulness.

Born in 1800 at Schoharie, New York, Lee was alone in the world from the age of thirteen. Largely self-educated, he served as a local Methodist preacher in Plymouth (Chenango County) in 1823 and then in Cayuga County two years later. In 1827, the Genesee Annual Conference of the Methodist Episcopal Church received Lee on a trial basis, appointing him to the Malone Circuit in remote Franklin County. Ordained an elder in 1831, the youthful-looking Lee became a traveling missionary. He battled with Universalists, the occasional Baptist preacher, ordinary skeptics and sinners, and even with Methodists suspicious of his youth. On one occasion, some principal Methodists complained to Lee's ecclesiastical supervisor, Bishop Hedding, that Lee was "too forward and too venturesome for a man of his years." The bishop replied, "You need have no fears for Brother Lee on this subject. I have heard [Universalism] preached upon by our strongest men from St. Lawrence to the Gulf of Mexico, and at the camp meeting in Canton, a year ago, Brother Lee preached upon it by the request of the preachers, and he went beyond any thing I ever heard before. He had enough to overturn all the Universalism in the world."[8]

Championing orthodoxy in contests with the Universalists proved easier than taking up an unpopular cause within Methodism itself. In 1834, Lee began preaching in Fulton (Oswego County). He had not yet enlisted with the abolitionists because, as his autobiography states, "I had received all my information concerning them from the sayings and publications of their enemies, who greatly misrepresented them, and called them incendiaries, and other vile names, such as amalgamationists, negrolovers, etc., and I was ignorant of their real principles, measures, and motives."[9]

Lee answered the abolitionist call at the Methodist General Conference meeting held in Cincinnati during 1836. There he witnessed a vitriolic attack by Southern men upon Orange Scott. Lee joined Scott, and a covey of abolition-minded ministers and laymen, at a gathering of Wesleyans in Utica in early May 1836. Lee lectured on "The Sinfulness of Slave-holding" and was appointed to go to Canada to garner support from the Canada Wesleyan Conference.[10]

Lee returned to Fulton, New York, a changed man, but he kept his counsel on the troublesome question of abolition until the shooting of Elijah Lovejoy in 1837. Then he preached a sermon condemning violence and slavery, and he allied himself with the abolitionists. Lee entered into the denominational fray by debating Methodist leaders who were trying to suppress Scott and Le Roy Sunderland, who was editor of an independent Methodist antislavery paper called *Zion's Watchman*.

In 1838, Lee defended C. K. True of the New York Conference against charges of "contumacy and insubordination" for preaching abolitionism. Though True was convicted and suspended from the Methodist pastorate, Lee did get the opportunity to defend the right of free conscience:

> [I]f this brother must be condemned to an ecclesiastic death for publishing an antislavery tract, for attending an antislavery convention, or for pleading the cause of the enslaved millions of our land, let him die and enjoy a martyr's crown, and let his grave be unknown; and when antislavery shall have triumphed, when the Church shall be purified from the pollution and guilt of slavery, and its foul blot shall be washed from the folds of the stars and stripes, and the chains of slavery shall be stricken from the millions in bonds, then, and not till then, let his monument be erected, and his epitaph written.[11]

But Lee soon had problems of his own. He was charged with causing dissent among Methodists by advocating abolitionism during his tour of

Canada. He now prepared to face his accuser, Jesse T. Peck, in a trial before the Black River Conference. The case was called. Anxious spectators crowded the seats and galleries. Lee was "fearfully roused" and confident that he was in the right, though he was "becoming a little desperate, feeling that the course the authorities and official organs of the Church were pursuing would, if it had not already done it, cripple or destroy [his] usefulness as a Methodist in regular work."[12] Unlike his friend, Brother True, Lee was spared banishment. Several of the Methodist brethren persuaded Peck to drop his complaint for the sake of harmony within the conference.

When the time came to assign stations again, Bishop Morris appointed Lee to a financially strapped congregation in Oswego. Lee was convinced that he was being chastened for his abolitionist views; he declined the assignment and became a traveling lecturer for the NYSASS. He moved his wife and six children to Utica, which already had a Wesleyan antislavery circle and preachers who were sympathetic to the rebels in the local Methodist Quarterly Conference.

Troubles also befell Brother Brown of Auburn, a lay member of the Methodist Church, who went on trial for attending a weekly antislavery prayer meeting. Lee successfully defended Brown against all eight charges save one: "Misrepresentation." Brown was expelled for claiming that the Methodist Church restricted the freedom of the individual conscience. Lee saw the handwriting on the wall. "It looked," he said morosely, "as though the abolitionists would ultimately be crushed out of the Church."[13]

By attempting to silence the abolitionist agitators, the Methodist hierarchy inadvertently opened up the debate about episcopal power versus conference rights. Orange Scott and his allies wanted conference majorities, not bishops, to determine how Methodists were supposed to think and act on moral questions, especially matters as important as the question of slavery. To sidestep episcopal censure, the abolitionists began to work through extraecclesiastical meetings, conventions of the already converted.

When the General Conference of 1840 came round, Scott was there, brandishing his sword against slavery as usual. But the General Conference censured the messenger and the message, and Scott left in a deeply depressed state. In October of that year, he led the formation of the American Wesleyan Anti-Slavery Society. By November of 1842, Scott had seceded from the Methodist Episcopal Church. Luther Lee, together with other abolitionist-minded Methodists, joined the Scottite secession. On May 31, 1843, the Wesleyan Methodist Church was organized at Utica, New York. Lee was appointed president of the new Wesleyan New York Conference and was transferred to Syracuse. There he found "a small band of seceders, but no place of worship."

A group of Syracuse Congregationalists offered shelter to Lee's small flock until he secured a hall. As he wrote in his autobiography, almost four decades later, "My Church was neither numerous nor wealthy, but a truer company of men and women never breathed."[14] In addition to his work in Syracuse, Lee helped organize Wesleyan Methodist congregations at Jamestown and other points in the old Burned-over District territory.

Rochester had its own Wesleyan Methodist group, which Frederick Douglass took notice of, in 1848. He wrote, "In the meeting house of the Wesleyan Methodists amid the many popular and large pro-slavery congregations of this city, a small band of men and women meet to hear the Gospel of Freedom and Love *for all.*"[15]

Soon, the Wesleyan Methodist connection had its own paper, the *True Wesleyan,* and branches in most of the Northern states. Occasionally, entire congregations broke away from episcopal Methodism and joined the abolitionist body. By the end of 1844, the Wesleyans had fifteen thousand members nationwide. Lee was elected president of the General Conference. He moved to New York City where he assumed responsibility for the *True Wesleyan* as well as a semimonthly Sunday-school paper called the *Juvenile Wesleyan.*

In 1852 Lee resigned, returned to Syracuse, and took charge of the congregation of comeouter Methodists that he had organized nine years earlier. This time, the Wesleyans were housed in a red brick structure which is today a landmark of downtown Syracuse.[16]

Ironically, the Methodist Episcopal Church itself split, in 1844. Northern Methodists, perhaps shamed by the constant critique of Scott, Lee, Sunderland, and the other radicals, agreed that they would not elect any slaveholder as bishop. Abolitionists led the campaign to unseat Bishop James O. Andrew of Georgia because he had inherited slaves from his wife's estate. Southern Methodists balked, left the General Conference, and formed the Methodist Episcopal Church, South, which remained a separate entity until

Wesleyan Methodist Church, Syracuse, 1890. Completed in 1847 by a congregation of abolitionists that had organized a few years earlier, Syracuse's Wesleyan Methodist Church is believed to have been a station on the Underground Railroad. Beneath the church are excavated passages or tunnels. At least seven sculpted faces, which are thought to be the work of passengers on the Underground Railroad, have been identified on the passage wall. The clay-formed faces have been removed for treatment and preservation and are exhibited at the Onondaga Historical Association. *Courtesy of the Onondaga Historical Association.*

1939.[17] Orange Scott said of this rending of one of America's great national denominations, "A division of the M. E. Church will hasten the abolition of slavery in our country; it cannot be otherwise. Withdraw all northern support from the abominable system of man stealing, and the traffic in human souls will soon wind up."[18] Scott died in 1847; he was spared the long and painful national struggle that was yet to come.

Like the Methodists, the Presbyterians of Upstate New York also found trouble in God's house as a result of the debate over slavery. Presbyterianism was particularly influential in North Star Country because many New Englanders had migrated to the region after the Revolutionary War. Most of these Yankees with church backgrounds had identified themselves as Congregationalists in New England. In central and western New York State, however, they adopted the Presbyterian form of church polity or governance. This was due to the Plan of Union in 1801, which fostered a hybrid ecclesiastical culture sometimes known as *Presbygationalism.*

To make more efficient use of clerical and material resources, the Presbyterians and Congregationalists agreed to an interdenominational compact whereby Congregationalists who moved into Presbyterian territory took on the Presbyterian identity rather than start rival congregations. Presbyterianism grew at a rapid rate in the Burned-over District, especially among emerging middle-class families who preferred an educated ministry and who looked askance at the enthusiastic preaching of the Methodist revivalists. Although this group clung to the New England model of learned clergy and decorum in worship, Presbyterians and Congregationalists in the district were not immune to perfectionism and millennialism, two theological strains of American Protestantism which encouraged social reform.

Many Presbyterian churches in North Star Country took on a more evangelical character than churches in other sections of the country, especially the South. These New School Presbyterians endorsed the "new measures" in revivalism that Charles G. Finney practiced and were open to cooperation with other Christians. The new school's opponents, the Old School Presbyterians, charged them with doctrinal aberrations and unionistic practices. The question of slavery was close to the core of the debate. Finney, for example, insisted that the surest way to bring about a social good was to work for the moral reform of individuals. He shied away from organized reform movements and emphasized pietistic evangelism.[19]

Despite Finney's reluctance to introduce abolitionism into Presbyterian circles during the time he was active in the Burned-over District, the slavery debate forms a principal chapter in the denominational history of the region.[20] The Synods of Utica, Geneva, and Genesee were so strongly influenced by Finney's revivals that they, along with the Synod of the Western Reserve, were excinded (or put out) by the Presbyterian General Assembly in 1837. Most of the excommunicated ministers and churches in the Burned-over District believed slavery to be incompatible with Christianity. Some of them embraced radical abolitionism. The combination of evangelical zeal and abolitionist convictions was a powerful and troublesome mix. This is best illustrated by examining what transpired when abolitionism was introduced into specific congregations. And there is no better place to start than the First Presbyterian Church of Whitesboro (Oneida County), one of the most historic churches in the Burned-over District.

First Presbyterian began as the United Society of Whitestown in 1794. It belonged to the Oneida Presbytery under the jurisdiction of the Synod of Utica. First Presbyterian's proximity to Oneida Institute made it impossible for the congregation to avoid the abolitionist whirlwind. Beriah Green and his family, institute faculty members, and many of the institute's students worshiped there. The Reverend John Frost, pastor from 1813 to 1833, was a vocal supporter of Oneida Institute. His successor, the Reverend Ira Pettibone, served as one of the school's trustees after Green became president of the school. In 1834, the Oneida Presbytery denounced slavery as "a flagrant violation of human rights; as contrary to the laws of God; and as a crying sin in our land, admitting of no apology."[21] With the October 1835 uproar at Utica's Bleecker Street Presbyterian in mind, the First Presbyterian governing body, known as the Session, affirmed the right of citizens to freely examine and discuss slavery. In December 1835, the Session passed a resolution calling slavery "a sin against God and man."[22] This augured well for Green and for the confirmed abolitionists in Whitesboro.

The climate of free discussion changed again in 1836, when the Reverend David Ogden came to the pulpit of First Presbyterian. Ogden was a graduate of Yale University who had studied at Andover Theological Seminary in Massachusetts. He wrote to the leadership of First Presbyterian about his convictions:

> It is well known that Abolitionism, so called, is agitated with great warmth in your region, and common fame does not put Whitesboro behind in this matter.

Now I cannot conceal it that I am a friend of the American Colonization Society from deep, conscientious conviction, not without much examination. I am an Abolitionist too of the old school, such as New England men have always been. My question here is, would such a sentiment when generally known as it must be, create difficulty or diminution of my influence.[23]

Prior to accepting the offer from First Presbyterian, Ogden visited Whitesboro and met with Beriah Green to discuss their respective views on slavery. "We distinctly understood that we differed," Ogden later wrote. "We parted, however, with mutual expressions of good will."[24] Green had his reservations about having a supporter of the ACS in the pulpit, but he persuaded himself that, with "ever-increasing light," Ogden might become an advocate of the enslaved. Little did he know. Green would later write, "We erred, greatly erred."[25]

For nearly ten months after Ogden arrived in November 1836, he did not use his pulpit to speak about the slavery controversy. Then on July 30, 1837, he delivered a scathing attack on the "fanatical abolitionists" who were, he argued, disrupting churches and communities in the North. Ogden attempted to absolve himself of responsibility for preaching against slavery by noting that no slaveholders sat in the pews before him. "Now I might reason to the day of my death, and whatever theories I might establish, I could not make one of you practically feel that you are guilty of the sin of slaveholding, admitting it to be a sin in every possible case, any more than I could make you confess the guilt of Adam's sin as your own."[26]

Only a few months prior to Ogden's installation, Green had preached a sermon of his own, under the title *Things for Northern Men to Do*. In this sermon, he had castigated Northern Christians who preferred the "peace of the church" to moral rectitude and had argued that the church held "the rusty key" to the dreadful prison in which the slaves, sisters and brothers in Christ, languished.[27] Green had been angered by the complacency of these Northern Christians, and he was further upset by Ogden's attack on the abolitionists. As he wrote to Gerrit Smith, "*Our* people here are uneasy at Mr. Ogden's course [and] have sent him a letter. Last Sab. He gave them a blast, cold and loud, like the North wind. The parish is in a wretched state! It will be, I expect, 'til the cause of the poor slave is admitted to its proper place in the pulpit."[28] Green then penned a series of letters, which were published in the *Friend of Man,* that excoriated Ogden for maintaining "a deceitful peace" in the congregation.

Initially, Ogden refrained from attacking Green publicly, but he wrote the following words in his private journal: "They [the abolitionists] have a poor general in Pres. Green. Like the devil when he tempts men to sin, he puts them into a scrape, but he does not get them out of it." In another journal entry, First Presbyterian's pastor pledged that, just as he had fought Baptists and Universalists in New England, he would not retreat in the face of opposition in Whitesboro: "Now I am fighting these spurious Abolitionists—fanatical ones; or rather, defending the church of God against their wicked machinations." In regard to Green's school, Ogden wrote, "The Oneida Institute is the greatest humbug I know of. Lectures on Nigerology, as Mr. Berry called it, are about all they got." Ogden characterized Green's students as "a parcel of conceited fools," some of whom began their prayers with "O thou head Abolitionist in Heaven!"[29]

Ogden also refrained from openly attacking Oneida Institute. Instead, he found a surrogate within his congregation to do so for him. Charles West was a disgruntled instructor of chemistry who resigned in March 1837 after serving only seven weeks on the faculty of Beriah Green's school. West charged Green with dropping mathematics, bullying students with all the reform fancies of the day, propagating a "leveling system . . . under the banner of abolitionism," and urging students to disrespectfully treat ministers who differed with them. West's diatribe appeared in the *New York Observer*, which was widely read by Presbyterians.[30] Green's school was already in financial trouble because of the Panic of 1837. Not a few of the school's enemies found West's accusations to be a stalking horse for their own dislike of the young abolitionists and their leader.

In turn, Pelatiah Rawson and Reuben Hough, two of Green's supporters, charged West with inspiring "misrepresentations, slanders, and false statements respecting the Oneida Institute, its President and other Teachers and Students."[31] First Presbyterian's Session voted to uphold these accusations against West by a margin of five to three.

Ogden appealed to the Oneida Presbytery on West's behalf. By this time, the rupture within the congregation was so serious that Elder David Foster, one of the voting majority, presented Ogden with the names of fifty-eight members who were prepared to leave the church unless its pastor ceased his efforts to suppress the abolitionists. Ogden accepted most of the resignations, but he tried to obstruct the plan to form a new church on abolitionist principles by denying Hough and Rawson a peaceful dismissal. Now there was no turning back. The dissenters were well on the road to organizing a comeouter congregation.

Eventually, seventy-one communicant members, including most of the elders, left the First Presbyterian Church and put themselves under the leadership of the Reverend Beriah Green. On January 6, 1838, Green wrote to Gerrit Smith, "Today for the first time, the friends of Humanity in this place have had public worship by themselves. Some 70 perhaps of Mr. Ogden's chh. [church], as the fashion is to speak, have obtained letters of dismission to form themselves, if God will, into a new chh. With these, including 6/9ths of the Session, we of the Institute have united. We hope soon to be organized into a chh."[32]

By the middle of 1838, this band of Christian abolitionists had established an independent Congregational church. The Oneida Presbytery refused to recognize the new church or support Oneida Institute. Green, who had been barred from preaching in Presbyterian pulpits and who was incensed that his students could no longer receive aid from Presbyterian sources, became more and more embittered. "I now feel strongly inclined," he wrote to Gerrit Smith, "to transfer from the bands, which ecclesiastically tie me in any way to those ministers, who find it so hard to distinguish a man from a thing."[33] Green became active in the free, or union, church movement, a loose confederation of Christian abolitionists who had been read out of their parent denominations.

While the controversy at First Presbyterian was exacerbated by its proximity to Oneida Institute, the debate about slavery erupted in many North Star Country congregations. Sometimes the winds of ecclesiastical politics blew contrary.

In 1836, abolitionist members of Rochester's First Presbyterian Church left their congregation to form Bethel Free Presbyterian Church. Their actions angered conservative Presbyterians: in 1843, a colony from Brick (Second) Presbyterian Church transferred to Bethel, gained control, and took the congregation back into the Presbytery.[34]

The outcome at Peterboro (Madison County) was quite the opposite because Gerrit Smith led the formation of a free church. David Ogden once grumped that Smith's mistake was falling under the influence of Beriah Green: "If a man is led by Green he must be either an ignorant man, or else one whose blind side is accessible. Green has got around Gerrit Smith by approaching his blind side, and has made him appear ridiculous before the public."[35]

It is true that Green and Smith had a close relationship. Smith served as a trustee of Oneida Institute, gave liberally to its support, and respected its president. The Madison County reformer even named one of his children after Beriah Green.[36] But Smith was fully capable of moving in the come-outer direction on his own.

Although Smith had united with the orthodox Presbyterians in 1826, he remained uneasy with their doctrinal statements. After 1835 and Smith's conversion to immediatism, he voiced sharp criticism of the denomination's reluctance to embrace abolitionism. Peterboro's principal citizen was drawn—by temperament and conviction—into alliances with other Christian abolitionists. In August 1838, he addressed the Christian Union Convention, which met in Syracuse. To those who questioned the wisdom of forming new religious connections when the country was already divided denominationally, Smith responded, "but, now, who that values Christian Liberty and the rights of man, can consent to wear the yoke of the General Assembly of the Presbyterian Church?—or who, that abhors the despotism of popery, does not equally abhor the rival despotism of American Methodism?"[37]

In the fall of 1839, Smith acted on his comeouter principles by purchasing the Congregational church building in Oswego for a new abolitionist church. He selected the pastor, the Reverend S. T. Mills, and paid him. This attempt at nondenominational Christianity did not fare well. Without any distinctive designation, and known only as "The Church of Oswego worshiping on Second St.," the congregation received only a handful of members. In March 1840, a discouraged Mills left Oswego and moved to Ohio.[38]

Gerrit Smith now turned his attention to Madison County, in particular to the Town of Smithfield. He was still a member of the Presbyterian Church of Peterboro, but he busied himself with organizing Christian Union meetings. "I speak against Presbyterian General Assemblies and Methodists conferences," Smith told his ally William Goodell, "as I do against National Whig and Democratic Conventions—as I do against Masonic fraternities. They are all unfit for Christians to belong to—and no one of them is any more a church than any others."[39]

Then, in December 1843, Smith and twenty-seven others left Peterboro's

Presbyterian Church to form an abolitionist congregation. In an early history of the religious denominations of Madison County, Silas E. Persons described the new church: "It was popularly known as 'The Free Church,' though the name which Gerrit Smith chose for it was 'The Church of Peterboro.' For one of his contentions was that Christendom sins by divisions into sects, that there should be but one Church in each city or village, like the primitive Church at Ephesus or Smyrna or Corinth. So he established the Church of Peterboro and expected all Peterboro Christians to recognize it as theirs."[40] With its antislavery stance and its opposition to the use of strong drink, the Church of Peterboro had all the hallmarks of a comeouter community or, in the parlance of the day, a *free church*. Smith described it as "a company of moral reformers."

The Reverend Asa Rand, pastor of the Presbyterian church in Peterboro, kept up a running attack on Smith after the formation of the Church of Peterboro. On September 20, 1845, the two held a debate on the following question: "Is it right to preach on the Sabbath such politics as Gerrit Smith preaches on that day?" Rand accused Smith of common electioneering for the Liberty Party; Smith responded that he was no partisan but that he did have the right to criticize all political parties with respect to their positions on slavery.

The dispute went on for nearly two years, culminating with a hearing before an arbitration board of five members. Smith chose Beriah Green and William Goodell to mediate for him. On September 2, 1847, the arbitrators announced that the whole controversy was so clouded by misunderstandings and invective that no verdict of moral turpitude should be assigned to either Smith or Rand. Smith himself was weary of the battle and, no doubt embarrassed by the spectacle of two Christians at each other's throats, Smith wrote to Rand, "A public parade of the charges would certainly be to the credit of neither of us. . . . My controversy with you is ended. I wish never to hear or speak of it again."[41]

The Church of Peterboro, filled as it was with strong-willed individuals, never did achieve perfect harmony. In 1849, Smith quarreled with the Reverend Hiram P. Crozier. Crozier believed that, outside of the hours of worship on the Christian Sabbath, members could work or engage in recreation in good conscience. Crozier further angered Smith by working—on weekdays—at a Peterboro general store in which liquor was sold.[42]

This Peterboro comeouter story centered on the forceful personality of

Gerrit Smith and its impact on a small community where he was the largest landowner and wealthiest resident. The First Presbyterian Church in Syracuse provides a different, perhaps more typical, illustration of how strife over abolitionism could redraw the ecclesiastical landscape of Presbyterianism in the Burned-over District.

The Syracuse First Presbyterian Church was founded in 1824 and contained many of the town's leading citizens. In 1838, a minority of abolitionist-minded members left to found the First Congregational Church. They held services in a small frame structure where some of the most prominent antislavery radicals, including Smith and Frederick Douglass, came to speak. The church was likened to Boston's famous Faneuil Hall and was called the "Cradle of Liberty." First Congregational developed such a strong antislavery reputation that someone once positioned a cannon outside the building and fired away in hopes of disrupting meetings. The comeouters had their own internal strife regarding how strongly abolitionism should be expressed; First Congregational Church disbanded in 1850. Some members helped establish Park Presbyterian Church (now Park Central Presbyterian Church), which took a moderate position on slavery. Others formed the nucleus of a new Congregational church inside a wooden chapel in 1855. These organizers took the name *Plymouth* in honor of Henry Ward Beecher's famous antislavery church, Plymouth Church of Brooklyn.[43]

Although some abolitionist Presbyterians with comeouter intentions started Congregational churches, the more typical route was nonsectarian community churches. This was the case in Cazenovia (Madison County), where Luther Myrick established the *Union Herald* in May 1836. Myrick, a traveling evangelist from the Finney era, had been ousted from the Presbyterian establishment because he espoused perfectionism and antislavery radicalism. He advocated the formation of the "one union church" free of the exclusive creeds and free of the sin of slavery.[44]

Cazenovia's First Presbyterian Church identified with the more progressive New School Presbyterian wing after the denominational split of 1837, but it refused to take a public stand against slavery. The Session minutes of First Presbyterian contain no entry regarding the controversy over slavery until June 12, 1844. On this date the minutes tell of a visit made by a church committee to a mother and her two daughters who had "connected themselves with another body not recognized by us as a Christian church." The visitors reported that they found the women "entertaining no unkind feelings toward us individually or as a body but that they could not walk with this church on account of their own peculiar views on the Abolition of American Slavery." After First Presbyterian leaders received a written statement that the women had joined the Free Church, and after another futile visit, church leaders voted to "withdraw from them our church fellowship."[45]

Moderate Presbyterians in Upstate New York were particularly embarrassed by an 1841 report that James Richards, president of the Auburn Theological Seminary, owned a slave. The Auburn seminary had long been Oneida Institute's antithesis. Under the leadership of Richards, the seminary had stayed out of the abolitionist controversy (a delicate balancing act, as the seminary was affiliated with New School Presbyterianism). Oneida Institute welcomed youthful enthusiasts who were eager to reform the world and provided them with an abbreviated theological education. Auburn, in cooperation with Hamilton College, the Presbyterian institution at Clinton, retained the rigid seven-year course necessary for ordination. Between 1831 and 1843, not one of the seminary's 231 graduates entered into professional abolition work. Of the 107 students listed as not graduating during that same period, only one became an antislavery agent.[46] The abolition controversy seemed to pass Auburn by; that is, until the scandal of 1841. Richards was then seventy-four years old and in the final years of his tenure as seminary president.

On June 23, 1841, Richards's troubles flared up at a meeting in the First Methodist Church of Auburn. The meeting had been called to discuss slavery. Elon Galusha presided. William Goodell and Beriah Green were there. Richards was not present, although sixteen representatives of the Auburn seminary did attend. As a group, the delegates (fifty-seven of whom were Presbyterians) condemned "slaveholding by professing Christians" and called for an investigation into missionary and other benevolent societies to see if they were receiving funds from "slaveholding ministers and churches, or appoint slaveholders, or those who approve of slaveholding, as missionaries, and agents."[47] A discussion regarding the morality of minimal slaveholding followed. Green, who was already under fire in Presbyterian circles for his abolitionist transformation of Oneida Institute, rose to the attack. He claimed that there was a professor of theology and seminary president somewhere in the North who "in sustaining the relation of a master, was worse than the rankest southern slaveholder." Goodell followed with a caustic blast: *"It is a lie to call such a man a Professor of Theology! A Professor of Theology! Why he sets all theology, and God himself at naught, and much more to the same effect."* [48]

After the evening session, the Reverend John Frost, a former pastor of the First Presbyterian Church of Whitesboro who was then stationed at Waterville, learned the identity of the "nominal" slaveholder. It was none other than the distinguished and much-respected James Richards. Frost went to see Richards the next morning. He was told that the seminary's president did indeed own a slave, an elderly woman. Around 1808, this woman had asked Richards to purchase her. She had done so because emancipation in New Jersey had not included slaves over forty years of age—the state feared the former slaves would become burdens to the state. When Richards moved to Auburn, she remained legally bound to him but stayed in New Jersey. Frost reported, "Whether he did right or not, he would not say."[49] Abolitionists judged Richards to be a hypocrite and called for right-minded Christians to leave Presbyterianism's ranks.

Although Congregationalists were less well entrenched in the orthodox religious establishment of North Star Country than the Presbyterians, they also witnessed defections to the comeouter movement. In 1841, the African American clergyman Samuel Ringgold Ward became the pastor to white Congregationalists in South Butler (Wayne County). He immediately set to work persuading church members that denominationalism was sectarianism in collusion with the antidemocratic forces that undergirded the institution of slavery. To those who tried to keep discussion of slavery outside church circles, Ward said,

> When urged, as it frequently is, that it is no part of the business of the Church, or her benevolent handmaids, to speak against existing social and political evils, abolitionists remind brethren of the firm lodgment which the evils connected with and inseparable from slavery have in the Church; so that, as the gentle and gifted Birney hath it, "the American Church is the bulwark of slavery: so that, as the amiable Barnes saith, 'there is no power out of the Church that could sustain slavery a twelvemonth, if the Church should turn her artillery against it.'"[50]

Like Congregationalists, Baptists stressed the autonomy of the local assembly of believers. The lack of an ecclesiastical hierarchy allowed local

Baptist churches in North Star Country to join the abolitionist crusade without interference from external judicatories. However, in many communities, Baptists did not speak with one voice on slavery.

Antislavery agitation among Baptists began in New England and was carried into central and western New York State by Yankee migrants. Baptists were generally of the poorer class; many of them lived as farmers and dwellers of crossroads towns. The Freewill Baptists and the Free Communion Baptists were both opposed to strict Calvinist doctrine. They united in 1841 to form one abolitionist church fellowship. One year later, their leaders formed the Freewill Baptist Anti-Slavery Society.

Other Baptists, who were sometimes referred to as regular Baptists, also moved into the abolitionist ranks. Elon Galusha from Connecticut was their John the Baptist, holding aloft the banner of enthusiastic religion and abolitionism and calling on Baptists to meet a high test of fellowship. Some Baptists resented the efforts of the abolitionist phalanx to interject the slavery question into local churches, thereby disrupting Baptist harmony. Despite this resentment, Baptists of various persuasions met in New York City in 1840 to form the National Baptist Anti-Slavery Convention. But most Baptist societies shunned the abolitionists, and Galusha was rejected as a delegate to the Triennial Convention. He led a group that started its own missionary organization, the American Baptist Free Missionary Society, in 1843. Even though Galusha's troops failed to convert a plurality of Baptists to immediatism, they did function as a catalyst.[51]

In 1845, Northern representatives to the Home Mission Society balked at commissioning John Busheyhead as a missionary. Busheyhead was an Alabamian who wanted to work among Native Americans; his impediment was that he owned slaves. Proslavery Baptists took Busheyhead's rejection personally and, in 1845, they organized the Southern Baptist Convention at Augusta, Georgia. Northern Baptists set up their own missionary body, called the American Baptist Missionary Union, but did not create their own convention until 1907.[52]

In response to their lack of hierarchical church structure, the Baptists created voluntary associations to support important endeavors such as missions and education. The Hamilton Literary and Theological Institution, as Colgate University was known from 1833 to 1846, was one place where Baptists worked together outside of the local congregation. (The school was incorporated in 1819 and sponsored by the Baptist Education Society). College leaders were eager to maintain good relations with Baptists everywhere, including those in the South, so they tried to keep the abolitionist controversy away from campus. On three separate occasions (in 1834, 1837, and 1841), the faculty took action to disband groups of student abolitionists.[53] The *Baptist Register* blasted the idea of discussing abolitionism on the campus of the theological institution in Hamilton: "Let the decrepitude of the Oneida Institute, and the heresy which reigns in Oberlin, bid them beware how they seek to make our own Seminary a school for reformers."[54] In 1842, the faculty voted to keep publications of the AASS on closed shelves in the library.

Shutting down discussion of the great question of the day was difficult to do—especially in the heart of central New York State where abolitionist stalwarts like Gerrit Smith lived. In 1837, Isaac K. Brownson, a student abolitionist, recorded this entry in his diary: "a brother of high standing from Maryland" used the chapel to put on "a burlesque of Mr. Gerrit Smith's lecture on abolition given recently in the village." Brownson thought the lampooning of Smith could have taken place only if it had received "favor in high places." He was pleased to see that it "met with general indignation & pity" among the students. Isaac Brownson visited Peterboro shortly thereafter and took tea at the Smith residence. The talk, of course, was "chiefly connected with abolition of Slavery."[55]

Student abolitionists never fared well at this school, which was called Madison University after 1846 and Colgate University after 1890. George Gavin Ritchie was expelled in 1847 for publishing material in the first issue of the *Hamilton Student* that offended the faculty. Ritchie's crime: he called the failure of New York State voters to grant suffrage to black males in an 1846 election "a disgrace to the state of New York."[56]

With the Hamilton school in the hands of conservatives, antislavery Baptists sought to make their mark elsewhere in North Star Country. In 1841, one group came from Vermont and founded Clinton Seminary in the village of Clinton. The seminary emphasized manual labor and was, according to a report in the *Liberty Press*, "free from the odious system of caste." Alvan Stewart visited the institution in January of 1843 and found seven African American students being treated "with perfect kindness and equality."[57] When Oneida Institute fell upon hard times because of its radical reputation, it was offered for sale. In 1844, the Freewill Baptists purchased the school's buildings and grounds (only six acres remained), with the intention of expanding it and offering theological courses. An alumnus of Oneida Institute, who was then working among refugees in Canada, gave his blessing to the Freewill Baptist venture: "The school will be open to candidates for the ministry of all denominations and of ALL COLORS free of a slaveocratic cast. Here young men looking forward to the work of the ministry, can study theology without having the font out of which they drink polluted with a slaveholding spirit. Whitestown Seminary is the only school of a high order in this state, that is conducted upon the anti-slavery principle."[58] Whitestown Seminary, the new venture, lasted until 1884. Thereafter, the buildings were modified to accommodate a textile factory.[59] Antislavery Baptists were also instrumental in founding New York Central College in McGrawville (Cortland County). It was chartered in 1849 by the American Baptist Free Missionary Society and was open to all, regardless of gender or race.[60]

The high-water mark of antislavery church secessions in North Star Country can be located in the mid-1840s. Historian Douglas Strong identified 317 comeouter congregations in New York State by 1845. A few others formed after 1845 from preexisting abolitionist cells. The forty-five counties north and west of the Catskills—a region that Strong calls upper New York—contained nearly all the comeouter churches. Out of the 708 towns in upper New York, 261 had at least one abolition church or a significant element of church-based abolitionism.[61]

Comeouter churches clustered along an axis formed by the Erie Canal as it ran from the Mohawk Valley to the Niagara frontier. In addition to the ones in Syracuse, Whitesboro, Peterboro, and Cazenovia, antislavery comeouter churches sprang up in Alder Creek, Canastota, Hamilton, Moravia, Preble, Penn Yan, Sherburne, and many other places in North Star Country. All across Upstate New York, abolitionists exited their denominations in obedience to their interpretation of the Biblical injunction found in Rev. 18:4, "Come out from her, my people, that ye receive not of her plagues" [KJV].

In 1843, William Goodell resigned as editor of the *Friend of Man*. He left Utica for Honeoye, a village in the hill country south of Rochester. He served the local comeouter church as a preacher, without ordination, for nine years. Goodell also started a paper called the *Christian Investigator* that promoted his comeouter philosophy under the banner "Pro-slavery, or Apparently Neutral Churches, are Anti-Christian."[62]

Goodell, Luther Myrick, Gerrit Smith, and the other promoters of the one union church idea hoped that all abolitionist-minded Christians would free themselves of denominational constraints. However, most comeouters in Upstate New York reverted to such denomination-based antislavery churches as the Wesleyan Methodist Connection, the Franckean Evangelical Lutheran Synod, the Freewill Baptists, the American Baptist Free Missionary Society, and the Free Presbyterian Church.[63] Those churches that persisted independently of denominational affiliation kept only small memberships until the Civil War. Once emancipation came, most of these free churches, which had been born of the struggle over abolitionism, folded.

As historian John R. McKivigan argues, the comeouter sect phenomenon was "motivated by anti-clerical and perfectionisitic religious beliefs as well as the desire to protest the churches' complicity with slavery."[64] Christian perfectionism found fertile ground in North Star Country because of the revivalist culture that remained in the Burned-over District. Comeouterism was only one expression of this impulse. The other, less conventional expression was troublesome to mainstream Christians because it rejected orthodox doctrine and social convention. Even Christian abolitionists, including those who led the comeouter movement, found this radical perfectionist impulse irritating because of the public's tendency to connect abolitionism with anything theologically heterodox or socially unacceptable. Conservative critics of comeouterism argued that the abolitionist spirit supplied fringe religious movements with new members.

Some Christian perfectionists did leave orthodox churches for unconventional groups such as the Millerites, the Spiritualists, or the Pantheists.[65] Others took the utopian route. Whitney R. Cross has written a classic study of enthusiastic religion in the Burned-over District. He chronicled a rich variety of utopian groups, including those that followed dietary regimens designed to purge body and soul. Cross thought that the community John Humphrey Noyes established at Sherrill (Oneida County) was "veritably the keystone in the arch of Burned-over District history, demonstrating the connection between the enthusiasms of the right and those of the left."[66]

The Oneida Community began in Putney, Vermont, during the early 1840s. In 1848, it was reestablished in central New York near the Oneida Indian Reservation at Oneida Depot (now Sherrill). Today, the Oneida Community is recognized as one of the most unusual fruits to develop on the tree of religious perfectionism. "The Oneida members," Cross tells us, "thought of themselves as saints, purified by repeated, intense religious experiences and disciplined by prolonged search for true righteousness."[67] Free of such social conventions as individual property ownership, law, and marriage, Oneida Community members engaged, instead, in economic communalism, mutual criticism (a form of social monitoring), and complex marriage (a type of marital communism).

Most Upstate New Yorkers were shocked by what they thought were free love practices and dismissed Noyes and his followers as crackpots. For a long time, proslavery apologists had assaulted immediatism on the grounds that it was fundamentally anarchistic, a threat to the basic institutions of American life, including marriage and the family. The apologists tried to convince the public that abolitionists kept company with heretics and social radicals, including free-thought advocates, students of utopian Robert Dale Owen, feminists such as Abby Kelly, and misguided religious prophets like Noyes. By the late 1830s, even some of the more conservative abolitionists became concerned that the immediatist crusade was, in the words of historian James Brewer Stewart, "being overrun by dreamers and cranks."[68]

Beriah Green disparaged these attempts to foster guilt by association among Christians. He pointed out that John Humphrey Noyes was no abolitionist, having withdrawn, as he had, from worldly affairs. The Oneida Community was situated only a dozen miles west of Oneida Institute and Green did not want his institute to suffer, which it would if ignorance could put all Christian reformers in the same tub. He did what he could to educate his students about the dangers of a religious ultraism that so feared worldly pollution that it ignored the suffering slave.

Slaves did not have the option of retreating into makeshift utopias.[69] The perfectionist logic of Noyes and his fellow utopians went something like this: Create the sinless community and universal emancipation must follow. If a decade of struggle had taught North Star Country abolitionists any lesson, it was that the tree of slavery and all it symbolized was deeply rooted in the soil of American culture. The struggle to topple it would be long and difficult.

The folly of radical Christian utopianism came home to many North Star Country reformers in the person of John A. Collins. This thirty-year-old disciple of Garrison had discovered the horrid life led by the white working classes and the poor while he was on a fund-raising mission to England in 1840. He concluded that slavery was not simply a matter of color but a form of labor deeply mired in unjust economic systems. When he returned to the United States in 1841, Collins launched a personal campaign to expose the root of all social ills, including war, slavery, and intemperance: property ownership.

In 1843, Collins decided to test his socialist beliefs. He purchased a 350-acre farm three miles outside Skaneateles (Onondaga County) and proposed a "Hunt for Harmony." Collins invited others to help him build a community free from the tyranny of organized religion and from the government. Members were to own everything in common, give up their children to the community, become vegetarian, and practice the cold-water therapy. Divorce bore no social or religious stigma. Collins's manifesto renounced all creeds: "Believe what you may," he told his followers, "but act as well as you can."[70]

The Hunt for Harmony began with ninety-one members, but their number soon dwindled as the idealists disagreed about whose perfectionist ideas should be practiced. E. L. Hatch visited the collective and reported, "There was not much of the home feeling there. Everyone seemed to be setting an example, and trying to bring others to it."[71] Only eight months after it began, the "No-God, No-Government, No-Money, No-Meat, No-Salt and Pepper" utopia collapsed. Collins blamed the "impracticable, inexperienced, self-sufficient, gaseous class of mind"[72] exhibited by the unruly communists, and he underwent a metamorphosis. Disillusioned with religious utopianism, he set out for California to find gold. There, according to one of Garrison's loyalists, he became a brazen-faced businessman.[73]

Upstate New York abolitionists cultivated the comeouter spirit, but they leaned more toward pragmatic reform than did the Garrisonian radicals like Collins. Only a minority drifted into communal experiments in which everything came under question.[74] Despite their own perfectionist tendencies, most Christian abolitionists in North Star Country cherished associational ties and therefore reorganized into new religious denominations like the Wesleyan Methodist Church that Luther Lee joined. Even the union church associations, of which there were several dozen nationwide, attracted only moderate interest among the non-Garrisonians in the region.

This discussion of how the slavery debate caused trouble in the white churches of North Star Country ought not to mask a related and important issue—the persistence of the "Negro pew." Freestanding black churches dotted the landscape during the decades when white abolitionists sought to cleanse themselves and their coreligionists from slavery's stain. The persistence of these separate Christian fellowships demonstrated that the work of Christian abolitionists was but half done when abolitionists formed come-outer congregations. As long as black and white Christians were distanced from each other by the sin of racism, the goal of a single fellowship remained elusive. Witness the challenge Beriah Green set before fellow abolitionists at the second annual meeting of the AASS in 1834: "If the gospel cannot destroy the cords of *caste* in this country, why go to attempt it in Hindostan?—Perhaps some shrewd Brahmin may find out, that Christianity is not able to make an American believer receive his brother as his own mother's son. And he will say to your missionary, 'Go home and break the cords of caste in your own CHURCHES, before you come here to make the Brahmin and the Soodra mingle together in the charities of life.'"[75]

Henry Highland Garnet, when he was one of the African American students at Oneida Institute, addressed the seventh anniversary meeting of the AASS in 1840. He, too, spoke to the issue of racism within America's churches: "Colored men have been with you in this labor. We are with you still, and will be with you forever. We even hope to worship in the earthly temples of our Lord."[76]

It is difficult to make generalizations about how abolitionists—white or black—might have been treated in any specific congregation. Now and then, fellow Christians were their fiercest opponents. When Theodore Dwight Weld went to speak at Third Presbyterian in Rochester, he discovered a spirit of hostility both daunting and discouraging. Mary Mathews, a Finney convert from 1830 and a local abolitionist, reported:

> Oh! how dear brother Weld is treated—we had a small riot here in the old Third Church. If it had been any other lecturer and in any other house I could have borne it, but to see a crowd in that house . . . hissing and insulting Mr.

Weld, it was more than I could endure. And Christians here had so much religion that they could not feel for the poor slave. Mr. Weld said he had been mobbed and had all kinds of trials, but he never had any which drunk up his spirits and broke his heart like the treatment he received from his old friends here.[77]

For a man who was once struck on the head with a stone during an antislavery rally in Ohio, this is a telling admission. Weld no doubt appreciated the warmer reception he received from the Utica Presbyterians in 1836: "I lectured for the eleventh time in the Bleecker Street Church tonight—great crowd. The Lord is with us—truth *tells*. Mob dead, buried, and rotten."[78]

The majority of North Star Country Christians were neither openly hostile to abolitionists nor widely enthusiastic. Most did not welcome troublemakers in their churches, but did not go out of their way to hunt them down or join attacks upon them. Nevertheless, the denominational officials who were charged with keeping good order within their respective associations often found the abolitionists vexatious and difficult. The Reverend Samuel J. May believed that the relationship between organized religion and antislavery was more complex than either the latter's defenders or detractors would acknowledge. When recording his recollections of the antislavery conflict in the years after the Civil War, May said:

Very much the larger portions of our antislavery host were recruited from the churches of all denominations, though some persons who made no pretensions to a religious character rendered us signal services. It ought also to be stated that more of the antislavery lecturers, agents, and devoted laborers had been of the *ministerial* profession than of any other of the callings of men, in proportion to the number of each. Still, it cannot be denied that the most formidable opposition we had to contend against was that which was made by the ministers and churches and ecclesiastical authorities.[79]

As a Unitarian, May belonged to a religious fellowship that was shunned by others and judged to be heterodox. Despite this, "for the sake of humanity" (a catch-phrase of his) he was willing to cooperate with anyone, irrespective of denomination, who had the welfare of African Americans at heart. He found divisions within the House of the Lord especially painful and sought to work with evangelical abolitionists as well as with their orthodox opponents.

"New measures" revivalism in the Burned-over District did release

Christians from the lethargy of gloomy Calvinism and unleash a whirlwind of reform zeal. But Charles G. Finney's assault on the doctrine of total depravity did not imply that he believed humans capable of constituting heaven on earth.[80] When abolitionists in North Star Country turned to politics after 1840, they did so because they saw the limitations of moral suasion and the doctrine of perfectionism. For almost a decade, freedom's champions had tested moral suasion within their nation's great denominational structures and within their local congregations. The outcome had been disheartening. But what about the country's other fundamental institutions: the Whig and Democratic political parties? As we will see, the troubles in God's house were mirrored in the turbid waters of electoral politics as abolitionists of North Star Country stepped out of their churches.

5. Bible Politics

On March 4, 1837, Martin Van Buren became the eighth president of the United States. "I must go into the Presidential chair," the native of Kinderhook, New York, vowed, "the inflexible and uncompromising opponent of every attempt on the part of Congress to abolish slavery in the District of Columbia against the wishes of the slaveholding States, and also with a determination equally decided to resist the slightest interference with it in the states where it exists."[1] As heir to the political legacy of Andrew Jackson, Van Buren and the Democrats abhorred the abolitionists. The anti-Democratic coalition, which was known as the Whig Party, had held no national convention in the presidential campaign of 1836. The party put up only regional candidates—Daniel Webster, William H. Harrison, and Hugh L. White—to appeal to the East, West, and South, respectively, and attempted to throw the election into the House of Representatives.[2] America's two-party system was off to a shaky start.

Whigs and Democrats became better organized by the 1840 election, the first national contest in which abolitionists participated under their own banner: the Liberty Party. The Liberty Party, which was born in Upstate New York's Burned-over District, embodied the abolitionist spirit of comeouterism. The party tried to redeem party politics with a single-issue reform coalition of voters. As historian Lawrence J. Friedman points out, leaders of this third-party effort envisioned, "a national venture in Bible politics," albeit a short-lived one. Once the nation had been infused with "the moral antislavery posture" favored by North Star Country abolitionists, the party leaders were prepared to exit politics, which was for them a realm of tarnished virtue.[3] As we shall see, however, American party politics, like quicksand, trapped many of the moral suasionists. Getting out—without compromise of principle—would prove to be difficult.

William Lloyd Garrison and his disciples contended that all political activities, from voting to holding public office, were tantamount to a compact with the devil, at least until there was a thorough regeneration of the electorate. Laws regulating human behavior were ill-founded attempts to enforce moral duty through the threat of sanction. This invariably compromised the good. In its most utopian and, as historian Lewis Perry has argued, most anarchist expression, the Garrisonian position was essentially a "no human government" philosophy.[4] When Garrison was asked to choose the lesser evil in the presidential campaign of 1836 (Van Buren or Webster), Garrison responded, "No—no—vote for an honest and upright man, even if you vote alone, or do not vote at all. 'Let the dead bury their dead.' "[5]

Garrison's antipathy toward direct political action upset abolitionists who had come to recognize both the ineffectiveness and limitations of moral suasion. Elizur Wright, Jr., wrote to Beriah Green in October 1837, "Garrison is doing us more mischief than his neck is worth. The wind of perfectionism has blown off the roof of his judgment, which was already somewhat started by indiscreet praise. . . . I have no more hope of help from him in the future, than I have from the inmates of Bedlam in general."[6]

In the absence of their own political party, some abolitionists in Upstate New York began to question the existing candidates regarding their positions on such issues as the annexation of Texas, the "gag resolution" of 1836, slavery in the District of Columbia, and the elective franchise for black males. During March of 1838, the *Friend of Man* editorialized that the ballot box was "an element of reformation which God has put into the hands of the abolitionists." Beriah Green wrote to Gerrit Smith in October of that year: "I am well convinced that God, the God of the Oppressed, calls us into the field of Politics; and we must obey. I enter without any very great reluctance, as I am clear on the point of duty. And Politics is with us a Sacred Concern."[7] The fusion of religion and politics was to become one of the most distinctive aspects of the abolition crusade in North Star Country.

Merely questioning Whig and Democrat candidates did not prove productive, as politicians said one thing when they were courting votes and did another once they were elected. So, North Star Country abolitionists took another half-step into the morally ambiguous realm of politics. When no suitable candidate appeared on a ballot, abolitionists vowed to write in the name of someone they approved of, or to scatter their votes among the least reprehensible aspirants. To those who complained that this was an empty gesture, Green replied, "Count them anything but lost. Scattered they may be; but lost they cannot [be]. . . . They will point you out as the standard bearers in the sacramental host of God's elect."[8]

A group who felt the scattering tactic was ineffective put together a "Freeman's ticket" in central New York. The ticket was composed of independent nominations; it attracted little support. Green thought he knew why and wrote to Gerrit Smith in November 1838, "How much have we done for the ten years past to elevate politics to their proper place?. . . We have treated politics too much as a smutty concern, with which our clean hands had nothing to do."[9]

Just how ill-prepared the abolitionists were for grappling with Green's Science of Civil Government became apparent in January 1839, at the meeting of the New York State Anti-Slavery Society's Executive Committee. When Alvan Stewart suggested the formation of an abolitionist political party, Gerrit Smith countered that, "*Caucus & party* management [are] necessarily at war with vital religion." According to William Goodell, Stewart's proposition could only be acted upon after there was "*some grand reform* in the management of a political party." In the end, the committee recommended that no antislavery party be formed.[10]

Alvan Stewart was not a man to be easily deflected. The Utica lawyer had given up his practice in 1835 to devote himself more intensely to abolitionism. Historian Richard H. Sewell has characterized Stewart as "a witty, companionable man, casual in manner and dress," and yet "an imposing figure—tall, dark, and muscular" who "blended immense learning with mordant humor in ways in which juries and, later, antislavery assembles found marvelously effective." "But," Sewell adds, "he had a violent, vindictive side as well, which made ridicule his stock-in-trade and laced his discussion of slavery with bloody metaphor."[11]

As an early convert to antislavery constitutionalism, Stewart argued, "If we ever strike a political blow for the slave we must go deep."[12] In 1838, at the annual meeting of the AASS, he made a case for employing the federal constitution in the fight against slavery. Although he failed to get the two-thirds of the votes that he needed, he wrote to his wife, "I have argued my constitutional argument for two days. Mr. William Jay, Mr. Birney, Mr. Leavitt . . . and many others came down upon me like a thunder shower. . . . The vote was finally taken and there was 47 for me and 37 against me, 10 majority—*immense victory*."[13]

Ironically, Stewart's early advocacy of political involvement gained momentum from the infamous speech that Henry Clay gave on the floor of the United States Senate. Clay was the most likely of the Whigs to become a candidate for president in 1840. The Kentuckian said he was "no friend of slavery," but he described abolitionism as "[no] imaginary danger" and said that he had been moved to speak out against "their mad and fatal course" because "those ultra-Abolitionists have ceased to employ the instruments of reason and persuasion, have made their cause political, and have appealed to the ballot box."[14] Clay's attack convinced others that Stewart was correct to believe that the Whigs offered little hope for antislavery advocates and could, at best, be expected to nominate some "milk & water or a vainglorious nominal abolitionist."[15]

Myron Holley of Rochester now rallied to Stewart's call for political action. Clay's antiabolitionist speech, Elizur Wright, Jr., recalled, "struck at the foundation not only of [Holley's] politics but of his religion."[16] Holley was an early advocate of separate antislavery nominations and, by the summer of 1839, he was prepared to take another step. He started publishing the *Rochester Freeman* and sold his farm to support the paper.

Holley knew something about the world of politics. He had worked for the Anti-Masonic Movement, served a term in the New York State Assembly, and been treasurer of the Erie Canal Commission. In an address he gave on July 4, 1839, at Perry (Wyoming County), Holley argued that religious convictions should be institutionalized "in the civil government, in legislation, in the administration of justice, in the ballot box, as well as in the temple of God. . . . Abolitionists should . . . purify political life, at present the most potent source of social control."[17]

Holley and Stewart were among the approximately five hundred abolitionists from twelve Northern states who met in Albany, on July 31, 1839, to discuss the growing controversy over pursuing political means. The convention brought together politically minded abolitionists and the rigidly moral suasionist Garrisonians. Stewart presided over three sweltering days of debate. The end result: the delegates approved the policy of voting for only those candidates who pledged themselves to immediate abolition. Stewart and Holley left the convention disappointed by the attendees' failure to embrace separate nominations for president and vice president. But Garrison and his allies were so distressed by the talk of politics that they filed a formal protest.

The gulf between advocates of an antislavery party in North Star Country and the New Englanders widened further when Garrison sent Henry C. Wright, one of his Boston lieutenants, to central and western New York to suppress the embryonic movement toward political organization. Of his opponents, Wright wanted to know how they expected "to make an antislavery Congress out of pro-slavery materials."[18] The problem with Wright's case for the old moral suasionist point of view was that it had been ensnared in a tangled web of Garrisonian ideas.

Upstate New York abolitionists were already ridiculing Garrison's philosophy as the no-human-government theory because the Boston-based reformer's perfectionist ideology discounted all political arrangements (short of the establishment of the Kingdom of God on earth). "For his skepticism about politics as the vehicle of moral reform and his spiritual vision of an unselfish, loving society," writes Garrison's biographer Henry Mayer, "party-minded managers and aspirants scorned him as an anarchist."[19] As to the Garrisonian position that the North should rid itself of slavery by cutting the South out of the Union, Beriah Green responded that this would leave the slaves to the mercy of their masters. Green did not care to be identified with disunionism and wrote to Gerrit Smith, "Bro. H. C. Wright's doctrines on these subjects I would be very sorry for my children to embrace."[20]

To counter the Garrisonian loyalists, a small number of abolitionists met on September 28, 1839, in Rochester, to nominate antislavery candidates for the New York State Assembly. Myron Holley successfully engineered a resolution that called upon the AASS to put forward presidential and vice presidential candidates who were solid on the slavery question. Holley then went to Cleveland in late October for a special convention that had been called to deal with the controversy raised by the political insurgents within abolition circles. He found that most of the four hundred delegates were not prepared to support independent nominations in the presidential elections of 1840. When Holley returned to North Star Country, he learned that several counties in the old Burned-over District were already nominating independent candidates for local and state offices. Oswego County abolitionists took the lead by organizing as an antislavery party.

Distinct antislavery tickets appeared in a number of other states. Even in Massachusetts, Holley's ideas made a few prominent converts. These converts included Elizur Wright, Jr., who was in Boston at the time and who was disgruntled about how the women's rights question had replaced political abolition as the chief concern of the Garrisonians. Joshua Leavitt, who was editor of the *Emancipator* (the official organ of the AASS) and a member of the society's executive committee, soon joined Holley in calling for independent nominations. Although these developments hardly demonstrated a groundswell of support in his direction, Holley called a convention in order to nominate independent antislavery candidates for the upcoming national election.

Over five hundred abolitionists met on November 13–14, 1839, at Warsaw (Genesee County), New York. This group nominated James G. Birney for president and Francis J. LeMoyne, of Pennsylvania, for vice president. The introduction of James Gillespie Birney's name into this narrative may come as a surprise to those readers who are familiar with his background. He was neither a native New Yorker nor an heir to the Yankee cultural tradition that had been brought to the Burned-over District from New England. He was, by birth, a Kentuckian and, until June 1834, a slaveholder. Yet, he has been called one of New York State's top five abolitionist leaders, and abolitionists of the region came to think of him as one of their own.[21] Birney was the ideal Liberty Party candidate, a reformed slaveholder whose conversion to immediatism epitomized the redemptive power of evangelicalism. His biographical profile shows him to be precisely what North Star Country abolitionists wanted for their experiment with Bible politics.

Birney was left motherless at the age of three, and he learned to question the legitimacy of slavery from his father, a man who advocated state emancipation. The younger Birney graduated from Princeton University in 1810, was admitted to the bar in 1814, and began to practice law in Danville, Kentucky. He became a slaveholder through marriage: Birney and his wife lived in Alabama for a number of years as fixtures in the planter aristocracy. After a crop failure in 1821 as well as a string of gambling losses, Birney settled in Huntsville and resumed his law practice.

In 1826, he converted to Presbyterianism and, like many of those in New York's Burned-over District who took up the cause of the enslaved, he began to examine the connection between personal religious values and the victims of the "peculiar institution." In 1828, Birney confided to his diary, "It [is] hard to tell what one's duty [is] toward the poor creatures; but I have made up my mind to one thing . . . I will not allow them to be treated brutally."[22]

As an outspoken opponent of the Jacksonian slavery policy, Birney soon found that Southern whites did not share his view of slavery's corrupting influence. Twice they turned back Birney's constitutional efforts to stop the import of slaves into Alabama. In July 1832, Birney put his property up for sale, with the intention of moving to Illinois, but Ralph R. Gurley of the ACS pressed him to become a permanent agent for Alabama, Mississippi, Louisiana, and the territory of Arkansas.

Birney agonized over what to do. He was convinced that Christian slave-holders in the valley of the Tennessee would embrace the opportunity to "put their slaves in a way of final emancipation, with the view of sending them to Liberia." Nevertheless, he worried about the impact that becoming an agent would have on his family and on his professional life.[23] Birney accepted a commission in August of 1832. He labored mightily on behalf of colonization until April 1834 when he traveled to Lane Theological Seminary in Cincinnati to visit Theodore Dwight Weld. Weld, along with his classmates, was then engaged in the struggle to convert the school to immediatism.

By the time Birney arrived at Lane he had been instrumental in setting up the Kentucky Society for the Gradual Relief of the State from Slavery. Weld wanted more from Birney: He wrote to Birney that the colonization society meant to "crush the free colored man and put far off the day of emancipation."[24] In May of 1834, Birney resigned from his positions with the ACS and the Kentucky society.

Throughout that summer and early fall, Weld kept pressing Birney to stay his ground and expose the proslavery sentiment in Kentucky's church-es. "Determined to hazard the consequences," Birney helped form the Kentucky Anti-Slavery Society in March 1835. Gerrit Smith sent a $50 check to Birney, to be used as he wished to promote immediate emancipation.[25] Birney planned to publish a newspaper called the *Philanthropist and Advocate of Immediate Emancipation* in Danville. A mob came close to destroying the printing press he had intended to use. When Weld urged him to move to southern Ohio, Birney did so, in October 1835, reestablishing both his family and his newspaper in Cincinnati.

Southern Ohio, however, had its own share of antiabolitionist hotheads. They heckled and egged Birney when he spoke against colonization, and they destroyed the office of his printer. To compound Birney's problems, he was indicted in 1837 for harboring an escaped slave named Matilda.[26]

Birney spent the early summer of 1837 lecturing in Upstate New York. He stayed with Gerrit Smith at Peterboro and came to admire the man. "Wherever we go," Birney informed Lewis Tappan in July, "I find that he is greatly respected. The people every where have been anxious and keen to hear him."[27] Encouraged by the support he had received in North Star Country, Birney sold his Ohio house, moved to New York City, and became a corresponding secretary for the AASS.

Henry B. Stanton, who was one of the two existing corresponding secretaries (along with Elizur Wright, Jr.), wrote to Birney in early August and tried to rid him of any doubts about the wisdom of this new venture. Stanton stressed the support that Birney had among many prominent abolitionists in the Garrisonian faction as well as among those, like Gerrit Smith, who belonged to what Stanton called "the prudent party." To clinch his case, Stanton wrote, "Half the moral power of the nation lies within 24 hours easy ride (mostly steam boat) of New York City. There the fulcrum must be placed by which we are to overturn the nation."[28]

Given the upward road Birney traveled from slaveholder to abolitionist, we can readily understand why Myron Holley and the other political abolitionists who met in Warsaw during November 1839 wanted him to head their presidential ticket. When Birney received news of the nomination, he responded that, although he supported the concept of independent nominations, he did not believe that abolitionists were sufficiently united to make a presidential bid feasible.[29]

Francis J. LeMoyne was a physician and, at the time of his nomination, head of the Pennsylvania Anti-Slavery Society. He was even more pessimistic than Birney and told him that Warsaw efforts to draft them into "party excitement" would have disastrous consequences. "Then the bright standard of Emancipation, which has hitherto been raised aloft and nailed fast to the high and holy pinnacle of right,—would be lowered by un-hallowed hands, blurred and smutted at the demand of time serving politicians."[30]

Despite the qualms of Birney and LeMoyne, Myron Holley forged ahead with his proposal for a separate abolition ticket. He now had a weighty ally: Gerrit Smith. In January 1840, Smith and Holly advocated independent nominations at an ad hoc convention of six hundred to seven hundred abolitionists assembling in Arcade (Wyoming County). Smith attempted to head off potential charges of inconsistency (he had been sour toward polit-ical means up until then): "What should I have been, at the present time, had I resolved unalterably, a dozen years ago, on maintaining a consistency between my past and future conduct? I should have been a rum-drinking colonizationist—and I leave it to any sober man of color to say whether I could be a much worse thing."[31]

William Lloyd Garrison was not impressed by the switch from moral suasion to political activism that was taking place in North Star Country. He accused the advocates of the new political party of base motives. As he wrote in the *Liberator,* "It is evident that there is, in the western part of New York, a small but talented body of restless, ambitious men, who are deter-mined to get up a third party, come what may—in the hope, doubtless, of being lifted by it into office."[32]

A disappointingly small number of abolitionists showed up in Albany on April 1, 1840, for what was to be the Liberty Party's first national conven-tion. Organizers blamed the poor turnout on snow-clogged roads. Gerrit Smith was ill at home in Peterboro. Of the 121 delegates, 104 were from New York State. Alvan Stewart presided over what Garrison's loyalists began call-ing the April Fools convention. For two days, debate ebbed and flowed. In the end, with more than one-third of the delegates abstaining, Holley's motion for independent candidates passed. James G. Birney was nominated again for president, and Thomas Earle was nominated for vice president.[33]

Back in New York City, Birney got word of the slate. This time he accept-ed what he had so firmly rejected less than five months before. He wrote in his diary, "Joshua Leavitt returned last night and . . . gave me news of the Albany Convention—they decided on Independent nominations by a vote of 44 to 33. . . . I wrote to him [Earle] entreating him to accept the nomination on the ground that the political movement was the only one that can now save the abolition party from dissolution and from being lost in the Whig and V. Buren parties."[34]

The Albany convention adjourned without giving a name to the new antislavery party. Gerrit Smith had written of "the great 'Liberty party'" in a letter sent to William Goodell, editor of the *Friend of Man,* in February 1840. However, it was not until 1841 that the new organization formally adopted the label.[35] Beriah Green, like a number of veteran upstate abolitionists, had been ambivalent about the third-party movement. He confessed to Smith in March 1840, "How to maintain in the common form a Human rights party without involving ourselves in the same evils, as now stare so frightfully upon us from the ranks of the existing parties—that is the problem, which demands for its solution more wisdom than most men are gifted with."[36] Despite his misgivings, Green attended the Albany meeting and supported the new party. He believed that the best way to avoid sinking into the moral miasma of American politics was to think of the party as temporary and to erect only one plank of its platform: immediate emancipation. The Liberty Party must be the grand *one idea* party.

William Goodell grumped that Garrison and his crowd of "non-resistants and whole-Whig-ticket abolitionists" planned to take over the AASS at the next national convention.[37] Although the women question is said to have triggered the 1840 schism in the national body, the walkout by Goodell, Tappan, and the other anti-Garrisonians can be understood against the backdrop of the movement into political activity which was centered in North Star Country. After the fracture of the AASS, ardent advocates of political involvement managed to position the new AFASS behind the Liberty Party and its presidential candidate, James G. Birney.[38]

The Liberty Party represented a form of political comeouterism. Liberty voters stood for the immediate end of slavery, a higher goal than the mere suppression of its expansion via the unorganized territory out West. In addition, the architects of this unique combination of political means and moral idealism talked of building an egalitarian society all across America, one in which blacks and whites enjoyed equal opportunity and protection under the law.

How this society was supposed to come about was a much-discussed and disputed subject. Most Liberty Party activists viewed their mission as one of goading Whigs and Democrats to take the higher ground; others mused about what would be needed if, by some miracle at the ballot box, they were given the power to govern. The likelihood of an abolitionist political takeover was never a realistic outcome. Instead, Liberty Party theorists pressed hard for lesser victories such as the abolition of slavery in the District of Columbia. Abolition there was, for them, among the constitutional prerogatives of the federal government. When reduced to its philosophical core, the Liberty Party was a reincarnation of the revivalist ethos that had been cultivated by Charles G. Finney in the Burned-over District. Finney taught reformers to isolate sin, preach repentance, and expect miracles. He preached deliverance from the slavery of sin. The Liberty Party enthusiasts, epitomized by James G. Birney, preached deliverance from the sin of slavery.

Unfortunately, Liberty Party leaders launched their single-issue political undertaking at a time when abolitionism was giving way to antislavery sectionalism. Within the debate over how to bring new territory into the Union, Northern politicians pushed the free-soil doctrine, but at a price. Now the objective was not to eradicate slavery everywhere but to contain the expansion of the South's congressional political power by keeping slavery where it was. This limited goal undercut the support for the Liberty Party.

White Northern voters viewed this redefinition of the antislavery crusade as less threatening to their economic welfare than the Liberty Party's vision of a racially egalitarian America. Although the Liberty Party's attempt to infuse American politics with biblical moralism eventually ran out of steam, the party's supporters kept the sin of slavery on the national agenda and carried the torch for a more racially egalitarian America when the major political parties sought to ignore the issue.

When *one-ideaism* was pitted against the political appeal of the Democrats and Whigs, it had limited success because voters wanted to know how Birney, and the party he represented, stood on issues other than slavery. For example, the Reverend Hiram H. Kellogg, a Presbyterian minister from Clinton, wrote to Birney to report that while visiting Wampsville (Madison County) Kellogg had been told, by several sources, that Birney had violated the sanctity of the Sabbath: Birney had taken a train from Utica to Wampsville and then hired a "conveyance" to Peterboro. Kellogg also wrote that he had little knowledge of Birney's views on the Sabbath question, but he presumed that the Liberty Party's standard bearer was a consistent Christian, consistent with the practices "of your Presbyterian and Cong'nl brethren" at least, and would not have violated the Lord's day of rest without good reason.[39] There is no record of Birney's response to this strict Sabbatarian, but Kellogg's inquiry portended the difficulties ahead for those who used only one plank in the Liberty Party's platform.

Birney's candidacy did find a pocket of supporters in the leadership of the Wesleyan Methodist Church, which historian Douglas M. Strong calls the "first specifically abolitionist denomination." Although Strong acknowledges that "the Liberty Party was not a church, and the Wesleyan Methodist Connection was not a political party," he concludes that "the Wesleyans often operated politically as an extension of the Liberty Party, and the 'Liberty men' used the tactics and arguments of an evangelical perfectionist religious group."[40] "Vote as you pray, and pray as your vote," argued Liberty Party zealots. This infusion of religious rhetoric into Liberty Party campaigns helped to transfigure the antislavery impulse in North Star Country into Bible politics. It also drew a gibe from Garrison, who complained that the Liberty Party was being overrun with ministers.[41]

The righteousness debate saturated Liberty Party political thinking. In July 1840, the *Friend of Man* published an extra edition that contrasted the high morality of Birney with Martin Van Buren's "obsequious subservience to the wishes of the slaveholders." Having consigned the Democratic standard bearer to ignominy, the Liberty Party paper reminded potential voters that William Henry Harrison, the Whig candidate, had told Virginia Whigs to say that he was "sound to the core" on the subject of slavery.[42]

Election day came, and Harrison won, in part because the Whigs successfully portrayed themselves as the party of political rectitude and Christian virtue, and the Democrats as irreligious and morally repugnant.[43] Birney and Earle garnered only 7,059 votes out of the millions cast nationwide, or about one-tenth of the voters who, according to one estimate, belonged to the antislavery societies.[44] New York State provided about 2,800 of those party votes, most in North Star Country, a dismal showing for the abolitionists. Gerrit Smith was particularly embarrassed by the "Whig whirlwind" which carried off many Madison County voters who had supported his abolitionist ticket in the 1839 local and state elections. If friends of the slave could be so fickle in what was one of the hotbeds of North Star Country abolitionism, then it was time to revisit the old question of ends and means.

In the wake of the Whig triumph, Beriah Green, among others, decided that the Liberty Party's design was flawed. "I abhor the notion of making Abolition exclusively a matter of chattel principle slavery," he told Smith in June 1841.[45] Green understood that voters, even abolitionist ones, wanted to ballot on other issues such as banking, tariffs and trade, land policy, and internal improvements like canals and railroads. Gerrit Smith was not so sure. In 1843, he said, "Let us be content with the Liberty party as it is. Let us believe, that a party which is true to the essential interests of man, may safely be trusted with his minor interests also."[46] Green also believed that the Liberty Party should take a stand against discriminatory practices in the North. It irritated him that prominent Liberty Party activists, who had the means to do so, did not send their sons to his hard-pressed Whitesboro institution.[47]

Had more sons of white abolitionists enrolled at Oneida Institute, they would have encountered several African American students who had become vocal supporters of the Liberty Party. Henry Highland Garnet was one of those students. He had been graduated in 1839 and become the pastor of Liberty Street Presbyterian Church in Troy. In late April 1840, Garnet and other African Americans met at the Baptist church in Albany where, thirteen years earlier, Nathaniel Paul had delivered his stirring address that celebrated the end of slavery in New York State. This time the topic was the Birney-Earle slate. Despite the existing law that required citizens to own at least $250 worth of property to be eligible to vote, the convention urged blacks to vote the Liberty Party line and become more politically active in order to "hasten the consummation of our disenthralment from partial and actual bondage."[48] Garnet remained loyal to the Liberty Party after the 1840 election and was pleased when the party's central nominating committee expanded to included three African Americans: Theodore S. Wright, John J. Zuille, and Charles B. Ray.[49]

At the same time, African Americans were beginning to organize themselves independently of the white-dominated abolitionist factions. The black convention movement started at the local and state levels. Its purpose was to discuss how African Americans could empower themselves in the changing political climate. When white abolitionists met, even at Liberty Party gatherings, African American abolitionist voices were muted. But in the black-led conventions that Henry Highland Garnet started attending in the early 1840s, African Americans set the agenda and took to the podium free of white paternalism.

Garnet's most memorable speaking opportunity came in Buffalo in August 1843 when he spoke before the first national convention of "colored men."[50] Fifty-eight delegates, thirty-six of whom were from New York State, attended. Garnet, who called himself "the first colored man that ever attached his name"[51] to the Liberty Party, rocked the assembly on August 16 with his now famous "Address to the Slaves of the United States of America." He described Denmark Vesey's 1822 insurrection as a "blast of the trumpet of freedom." He called Nat Turner "noble and brave." He summoned the slaves to "RESISTANCE! RESISTANCE! RESISTANCE!" "It is an old and true saying," Garnet thundered, "if hereditary bondsmen would be free, they must themselves strike the blow."[52]

Frederick Douglass, who was still under the influence of Garrison's non-resistance doctrine, construed Garnet's speech as a call to violence and sharply criticized it in a speech of his own. Aided by William Wells Brown and Amos G. Beman, Douglass successfully persuaded the convention to reject Garnet's address. Garnet responded by calling Garrison's philosophy "ridiculous." Emotions were still running high when the issue of endorsing the Liberty Party's 1844 ticket came up. In the end, the convention gave the Liberty Party an overwhelming vote of confidence. There were two dissenters: Frederick Douglass and Charles Remond.[53] The former was still a lecturer for the AASS and, therefore, committed to nonviolent and apolitical moral suasion. The latter was a loyal Garrisonian whom the AASS sent to the first World Anti-Slavery Convention in 1840, as one of its four official delegates.

In the charged atmosphere precipitated by Garnet's remarks, Liberty Party activists met again in Buffalo, shortly after the 1843 National Convention of Colored Men adjourned. Samuel R. Ward opened the convention with prayer. The Liberty Party faithful invited African Americans to join their new party and they condemned racial discrimination as well as slavery. When the two-day meeting adjourned on August 31, Garnet and Henry Bibb (another escapee from the South) took to the field to promote their

1844 election nominees: James G. Birney for president and Thomas Morris for vice president.

Beriah Green contributed to the cause by writing a campaign biography of Birney in which he pointed out that the former Kentucky slaveholder had voluntarily and at his own expense raised all the slaves he inherited from his father to the dignity of free people, a laudable example of demonstrating principle through practice. The *Liberty Press,* the official organ of the Liberty Party, urged every voter in the land to read Green's account of the life of Birney before going to the polls.[54]

The 1844 election turned on the issue of slavery as no election had before. Harrison, the Whig victor in 1840, had died of pneumonia after one month in office. Vice President John Tyler became chief executive by default, the first such occurrence in American history. Tyler was a Virginian who championed states' rights but opposed Jackson and Van Buren in the nullification debates when John C. Calhoun had argued that the Southern states could constitutionally invalidate federal laws. Despite Tyler's Southern orientation and states' rights politics, Whigs liked his soft money policy and advocacy of internal improvements. So they harnessed him with Harrison in 1840.

Since assuming the Oval Office after Harrison's death, Tyler had vetoed Whig-sponsored bills and, most ominously, showed his proslavery colors by reintroducing the question of Texas annexation. In 1837, the United States government had recognized the Republic of Texas but had refused to annex it. Now Tyler reopened the explosive issue of what to do with the territory gained in the conflict with Mexico.[55]

The Texas question divided abolitionists and conservatives in Upstate New York. Samuel J. May, of Syracuse's Church of the Messiah, hit a nerve when he condemned the conflict with Mexico as "unjustifiable war" and preached against the Texas annexation. Some of his parishioners and neighbors accused him of "introducing politics into the Sacred Desk."[56]

The Liberty Party's 1844 platform opposed the extension of slavery but did not specifically address the question of the annexation of Texas. In all the noise about stopping the spread of slavery, the trumpet of immediate emancipation, which had been the hallmark of the Liberty Party four years earlier, sounded less loudly. Democrats nominated James K. Polk, former governor of Tennessee. Many considered Polk a dark horse candidate because his Whig rival was the well-known Henry Clay, who had retired from the Senate in 1842. The problem with Clay, as Liberty Party activists continually pointed out, was that he was hard to skewer in debate. He claimed that he was not for the annexation of Texas *and* said that he was not opposed to it.

Abolitionists griped about Clay's "slippery tactics." Liberty Party optimists were convinced that sound antislavery voters would not be taken in by Clay, and they predicted that Birney and Morris might get as many as 160,000 votes in 1844. When the returns were totaled, the antislavery ticket had amassed only 65,608 votes nationally. Ironically, Birney's candidacy took away enough ballots from Clay in New York State to tip the electoral count toward Polk, the least acceptable candidate according to those in abolitionist circles. In February 1845, Polk signed a joint congressional resolution to annex Texas, which came into the Union the following December as a slave state.

Liberty Party leaders now redoubled their efforts to find a candidate with broader appeal, someone who was less likely to be perceived as a political extremist. Gerrit Smith thought that William H. Seward, the recently defeated Whig governor of New York, might accept the challenge, although Seward had sided with Clay in 1844. To those abolitionists who resented Seward's apostasy, Smith responded, "Have patience with him and the thousands of Whigs, who sincerely believed that they were aiding the cause of the slaves, when they were casting their votes for Henry Clay."[57]

Antislavery forces rallied a bit in August 1846 when David Wilmot, a Democratic congressman from Pennsylvania, attached an antislavery amendment to a bill that would appropriate $2 million to acquire additional territory from Mexico. However, the Senate rejected the House bill and Congress went on to pass one without Wilmot's proviso that prohibited slavery. In 1848, the New York State legislature reaffirmed its support for the Wilmot proviso but, as Frederick Douglass declared in New York City on May 9, 1848, the proviso turned out to be merely a "little protuberance on American politics" and was by now quite "flattened out."[58]

Although Douglass had moved to Rochester in 1847 and was publishing the *North Star* to the displeasure of the Garrisonians, he was not yet fully in harmony with the political conviction of Upstate New York abolitionists. In 1842, Douglass said to those who had gathered to observe the tenth anniversary of the Massachusetts Anti-Slavery Society, "Then, again, look at the root of this third party [Liberty Party]. Those who were active once in the cause, and began to find out that it led to more sacrifice than they wanted to make, got it up when they found their plans to put down the old Society [Garrison's AASS] failed."[59]

When Douglass traveled to London in 1846, he lectured to an estimated twenty-five hundred to three thousand people, who crowded "almost to the point of suffocation" into Finsbury Chapel. During a three-hour address, Douglass made it clear where his allegiance lay. "There are two classes of abolitionists in the United States," he informed the British, "one takes the ground that slavery is a creature of the law, that it must, be proceeded against as such; and they have formed themselves into what is called, 'The liberty party.' There is another class—that with which I am particularly associated, and they take the ground that our energies should be devoted to the purifying of the moral sentiment of the country."[60] Despite being a Garrisonian on philosophical grounds, Douglass did find much of value in the work of those who fashioned the Liberty Party. He praised the actions of Gerrit Smith and William Goodell in calling for divorcing slaveholders from the church.[61] Was America's most prominent black abolitionist signaling his annoyance with the rigid apolitical stance of William Lloyd Garrison?

Garrison called the Constitution a proslavery document and condemned it as a "A COVENANT WITH DEATH, AN AGREEMENT WITH HELL."[62] In 1854, at a Massachusetts Anti-Slavery Society picnic in Framingham, he held aloft a copy of the U.S. Constitution and burned it. With apocalyptic fervor, Garrison spoke of the Constitution's "parchment lies," in a most striking demonstration of his views regarding the compromise struck by the framers of America's most important political document.[63] Upstate New York abolitionists had to find a way to redeem the Constitution as a basis for entering the realm of electoral politics. They needed a legal foundation upon which they could enter the fray with the Whigs and Democrats over the legitimacy of slavery and its expansion.

William Goodell was one of the first American abolitionists to recognize this need. In 1844, he published his massive book *Views of American Constitutional Law in Its Bearing upon American Slavery*. To claim that the Constitution "can secure *general liberty* and at the same time guarantee *local slavery,* or even compromise or permit its existence, is," Goodell wrote, "to

affirm the greatest of moral absurdities, to deny self-evident truths, to falsi-
fy human history."[64] Goodell read the Constitution with a lens focused on
the egalitarian thrust of the preamble and the liberalizing philosophy of its
authors. Garrison pointed to clauses such as Article 4 which gave masters
the right to recover runaway slaves and, more crucially, Article 1. Here the
slaveholding states were favored by being allowed to count three-fifths of
their slave populations when determining representation in the House of
Representatives.

Liberty Party supporters highlighted the intentions of the framers and
drew encouragement from others who emphasized the egalitarian rhetoric
of the Declaration of Independence. In their campaign literature, party
leaders also made reference to *The Unconstitutionality of Slavery.* This book
was written in 1845 by Lysander Spooner, an eccentric Boston lawyer who,
like Goodell, found an antislavery argument in the political ideals and high
intentions of the Constitution's framers.[65]

Hoping to win over some Liberty Party men, the AASS scheduled a
debate between Gerrit Smith and Charles C. Burleigh, a staunch Garrisonian, for January 31, 1850, in Syracuse. Douglass, a vice president of the convention, sided with Burleigh's advocacy of the Garrisonian position, where-
as Samuel R. Ward spoke on behalf of Smith's advocacy of antislavery
constitutionalism. At one point, Douglass said, "There has been a great deal
of assumption on the part of the Liberty party. To say that the constitution
is Anti-Slavery, is an assumption against an overwhelming array of testimony, and against the Constitution itself."[66] However, it was not long before
Douglass changed course. The change took place after the passage of the
Compromise of 1850, which included the dreaded Fugitive Slave Law. Pro-
voked by the federalization of the runaway question, Douglass arrived at
the point where Liberty Party activists began.

Douglass's move toward antislavery constitutionalism signaled how far
he had come since he had been sheltered under Garrison's wing in New
England. Garrison found no legitimate basis for the black freedom cause in
a document that had been drafted by Thomas Jefferson, who was himself a
slaveholder. But Douglass redeemed it.

In one of his most memorable speeches—the Fourth of July address
delivered in Rochester on July 5, 1852—Douglass asked, "What to the Slave
is the Fourth of July?" He snatched hope out of the pit of despair with an

affirmation of the Constitution: "In *that* instrument I hold there is neither warrant, license, nor sanction of the hateful thing [slavery]; but, interpreted as it ought to be interpreted, the Constitution is a GLORIOUS LIBERTY DOCUMENT."[67] The five hundred to six hundred people had paid twelve cents each to listen to the nation's most famous black orator. They felt they had received good value for their money and subscribed for seven hundred copies of his address on the spot.

When Douglass first settled in Upstate New York in 1847, there was more confusion than confidence in the ranks of political abolitionists. Except for a few local elections, Liberty Party candidates had all gone down to defeat. William Goodell, James Jackson, William Chaplin, and James G. Birney renewed talk of going beyond *one-ideaism*. The broad-platform partisans received support from Beriah Green, who had written to Gerrit Smith in 1846, "If the L. Party is too ignorant to understand the duties of Am. citizens, it is unworthy of the name and influence of a national party. . . . If the shabby one-idea-ism, which is made so much of in various quarters is all it has to boast," Green fairly shouted, "it is poor indeed."[68] In a lengthy letter that Green wrote to James G. Birney, Green urged political abolitionists to enlarge their mission: "For I insist upon it, that we are now an essential part of the Government;—have just the same responsibilities in Kind to *honor*, as if the *visible* scepter were placed in our hands."[69]

Birney's thoughts were already moving in this direction. He had twice been the losing standard bearer of the Liberty Party. In April 1846, he warned, "Unless we join other interests to the cause of Anti-Slavery, it is in vain for us to expect the progress that we have made. Indeed if we fail to incorporate in our party-creed, that which interests the majority, as much as the sufferings of the slave interests the conscientious, we shall only make such advances as will alarm the timid and discourage even the boldest among us."[70] Birney admitted that the Liberty men were in "party-array"; that is to say, divided on the strategy necessary for victory. He pushed for a broader platform in order to keep abolitionists from defecting to the Whigs and the "Loco Foco" faction of the Democrats in New York State.[71]

Gerrit Smith soon came on board, although Alvan Stewart opposed any change of course. So did prominent Liberty Party men in Ohio and Michigan who wished to preserve the party's single-issue identity and who were wary of the growing convergence of antislavery and sectionalism.

In an effort to draw away New York State's third-party voters, some Whig leaders offered to support an equal suffrage amendment to the state constitution. Gerrit Smith and the Liberty Party founders had long advocated the removal of the $250 property qualification that kept the number of voting black males to a minuscule number. Democrats opposed lowering the qualification, which had been supported by none other than Martin Van Buren when it had been introduced in 1821. The Equal Suffrage to Colored Persons question went before New York State delegates at a special June 1846 convention. In a November referendum it went before the voters who defeated it by a margin of three to one. The defeat could be partially attributed to Whig operatives who voted against the referendum in spite of earlier promises to work with the Liberty Party black suffrage advocates.

Henry Bradley, the Liberty Party candidate for New York State's governor, received only 12,844 votes, about 3.2 percent. After analyzing electoral returns, historians Alan M. Kraut and Phyllis F. Field concluded that "after seven years of strenuous effort," the Liberty Party had attracted "only about 15 per cent (12,844 of 85,406) of the individuals who agreed with them on the topic of black suffrage."[72] This state of affairs undercut the power of Liberty Party purists who hoped to perpetuate Bible politics in the face of defections to the Whig party and criticism from those disenchanted with the one-idea platform.

William Goodell met with the other broad platform advocates at Macedon Lock in June 1847. They came away opposed to slavery and against "the withholding of suffrage from permanent resident citizens on the ground of birth, parentage, race, color, or avocation." To the chagrin of Liberty Party traditionalists, the broad platformers took stands on nearly twenty reform questions, including contentious matters like the elimination of legalized monopolies (the postal service, for example), the eradication of secret societies, the promotion of free trade, the dismantling of the army and navy, and the distribution of public lands. Had Bible politics run amok? One Liberty Party editor, Wesley Bailey, thought so. He wrote to Gerrit Smith, "I dispise [sic] the craven spirit of that man who will not vote the fetters of the slave off unless he can at the same time 'vote himself a farm'!"[73]

The Macedon Lock delegates nominated Gerrit Smith for president and Elihu Burritt (later replaced by Charles C. Foote) for vice president. They called themselves the Liberty League. Once again, abolitionists from the

Burned-over District put themselves in the eye of the storm. Liberty Party men from Maine to Michigan—and most especially Ohio—dubbed the Upstate New York abolitionists the "Macedon Lock-Smiths" and began to look more seriously at other options as the 1848 elections approached.

Some abolitionists, like the Liberty Leaguers, sought to reshape the Liberty Party so that it could embrace a cornucopia of reform. At the same time, others attempted to widen its appeal by moving closer to the "conscience," or antislavery, Whigs who opposed admitting Texas to the Union as a slave state and who opposed the war with Mexico. The Liberty League (or universal reform faction) and the regular Liberty men came together in Buffalo for a two-day meeting during October 1847. Representing about one-third of the delegates, Goodell, Smith, and their allies did not have enough strength to prevail over those who wished to maintain the one-idea thrust of the party. Among the latter were such stalwarts as Lewis Tappan, Henry B. Stanton, and Joshua Leavitt. They nominated John P. Hale for president and Leicester King, of Ohio, for vice president.[74] This was not the end of political maneuvering and confusion in North Star Country. The events of the second week of August 1848 would demonstrate that.

Once again the setting was Buffalo. Thousands of delegates and onlookers from every Northern state—and three Southern ones—swarmed over Buffalo on a hot summer day that would turn out to be the founding convention of the Free Soil Party. Antislavery Whigs, or Conscience Whigs, and centrist Whigs, including Henry Clay, attended. The dissident faction of Van Buren Democrats, called Barnburners in New York State, also came.[75] There were Liberty Party men and a host of attendees with special interests such as cheap postage and land reform. Because of the unwieldy size of the assembly, a Committee of Conference directed the affairs from the Universalist meetinghouse while the crowd waited in a huge tent in a nearby park.

By the morning of the second day, the Buffalo conclave had a platform, which historian John Sewell notes, "offered something for everyone."[76] When the delegates left Buffalo they also had a ticket: Martin Van Buren (of New York) for president, and Charles Frances Adams (of Massachusetts) for vice president. Fearing Southern domination of his own party, Van Buren, heretofore known as the original Northern man with Southern principles, had bolted from the Democrats. Earlier, the Democrats had nominated Lewis Cass for president, under the banner of "popular sovereignty."

Liberty Party representatives were mollified by the presence of Charles Francis Adams on the ticket. He was the son of John Quincy Adams, whom abolitionists remembered affectionately as "Old Man Eloquent" for his courageous 1836 attack on the gag resolution in the House of Representatives and for his efforts to release the Africans who had mutinied on the Spanish ship *Amistad* in 1841.

Joshua Leavitt moved to make Van Buren's nomination unanimous after a straw ballot gave Van Buren 244 votes and John P. Hale (of New Hampshire) only 183. As veterans of the creation of the Liberty Party looked on, Leavitt pronounced the benediction of Bible politics as it had been originally conceived in North Star Country. The Liberty Party, he said, is "not dead, but TRANSLATED."[77] It had been translated into the Free Soil Party.

The Free Soil Party platform that was adopted in Buffalo opposed the extension of slavery, advocated homestead legislation, and called for the elimination of slavery in the District of Columbia. But it failed to call for the end of slavery in the Southern states. Beriah Green, who had been too ill to journey to Buffalo, was furious when he received news of what had transpired at the convention. He termed the new Free Soil Party "wholesale apostasy" and became so disgusted with the bad fruit of popular democracy that he drifted into an idiosyncratic political philosophy that promoted rule by the wise—a kind of divinely instructed oligarchy.[78]

Gerrit Smith favored Van Buren, as Van Buren would be the political spoiler to the two dominant parties, but Smith would not vote for him. "I can vote for no man for President of the United States," he said, "who is not an abolitionist; for no man, who votes for slaveholders; or for those who do; for no man, whose understanding and heart would not prompt him to use the office, to the utmost, for the abolition of slavery."[79] Instead, Smith and William Goodell carried on their work with the Liberty League, which now functioned almost like a fourth party. This group's members accused Free Soilers of being more concerned with stopping the expansion of slavery than with its abolition. According to the Liberty League, abolitionism was giving way to her weaker sister, political antislavery. In this respect, at least, the Liberty League members agreed with Garrison: Political compromise had tarnished the grand moral crusade. As Garrison's biographer Henry Mayer points out, "To consider slavery bad policy because it threatened the dignity and ambition of white workers was a different matter from considering slavery a sin because it infringed upon the freedom God granted every soul."[80]

African Americans faced a discomfiting choice with regard to the Free Soil Party. The Barnburner Democrats of New York State who had joined the Free Soil coalition had helped block the extension of the vote to blacks at the state constitutional convention in 1846. They equated *free* labor with *white* labor.[81] Samuel R. Ward, who was still a confirmed Liberty Party activist, condemned the Free Soil movement as hostile to African American interests and inimical to the goal of immediate emancipation. He asserted that Free Soilers were "as ready to rob black men of their rights" as the Barnburner faction had been in the debate over giving the vote to African Americans.[82]

Frederick Douglass adopted a pragmatic policy. Though Free Soilers were officially silent on the question of black rights, and not a few of them harbored racialist sentiment, Douglass felt that the Free Soilers had a chance of actually gaining control of the federal government. Like Douglass, most old Liberty Party men convinced themselves that the Free Soil platform contained enough Liberty Party wood to stand on. As historian Richard Sewell wrote, "A surprising number of Liberty men, however, ate crow as if it were quail and enthusiastically touted Van Buren's newly discovered virtues."[83]

In the 1848 elections, the Free Soil Party did acquire five seats in Congress but did not carry a single state. It finished second in New York State, where it defeated the Hunker Democrats but lost to the Whigs. Nationally, Martin Van Buren lost to Whig candidate Zachary Taylor, the Mexican War hero. Frederick Douglass wrote an essay titled, "What Good Has the Free Soil Movement Done?" which was published in the *North Star* in 1849:

> Much in many ways but not every way. It has for once rallied a large number of the people of the North in apparent hostility to the whole system of American slavery; it has subjected this vile abomination to wide-spread exposure; it has rebuked and humbled quite a number of corrupt and cringing politicians, by driving them to change their positions on this subject, and driven them from

office. It has awakened the whole south to a sense of danger, and perhaps has checked the proud and arrogant pretensions of the slaveholder with respect to the extension of slavery. So far so good.[84]

After the emergence of the Free Soil coalition, Bible politics in North Star Country declined. Gerrit Smith and the Liberty League were left with the *Liberty Party Paper*, a weekly that was edited and published by John Thomas in Syracuse, but little else. The prospects for antislavery gains in the next general election did not look promising, even for the Free Soilers in New York State. The Barnburners defected from the coalition forged at Buffalo and rejoined the Democratic fold in 1850. From then on, the Free Soil Party was essentially moribund. The Seward and Filmore Whig factions were at war with each other in the Empire State. Aided by influential Thurlow Weed, Seward led Northern Whigs in opposition to the Compromise of 1850, thereby alienating Whig conservatives and driving many of them into the arms of the Democrats.[85]

Antislavery advocates were demoralized. The public seemed weary of abolitionist rectitude. Millard Filmore was now president, having assumed the office after the death of Taylor in July 1850. He promoted the Compromise of 1850, which included the Fugitive Slave Law, as "a final settlement of the dangerous and exciting subjects which they embraced."[86]

The Fugitive Slave Law of 1850 settled nothing. Historian Henry Mayer rightly argues that it was "not so much a remedy for the South's chronic runaway problem as it was a deliberate condemnation of the abolitionist agitation that had unsettled traditional politics."[87] The politics of compromise prevailed in the nation's capital. Now the contest was not about right and wrong, and certainly not about black rights. It was about how to control the hotheads in both the North and the South and how to cool the flames of sectional disunionism.

The proponents of the Compromise of 1850 were personified by Daniel Webster of Massachusetts, who hoped to keep the peace by promoting the federal statute as a Union-saving measure. But the new law had the opposite effect. The new regulation empowered special federal commissioners to issue warrants for the arrest of runaways. While affidavits given by the claimants were sufficient proof of ownership, freedom-seekers were denied the right of trial by jury. Their testimony was not admitted as evidence, though claimants could introduce two witnesses. To add insult to injury, the commissioners were paid $10 when they decided in favor of the slave catchers, but only $5 when they ruled that the alleged fugitive had a right to go free.

Federal marshals had the authority to ask the general public for help with recapturing runaways. Failure to comply could cost a bystander $1,000 and imprisonment for up to six months. Even nonabolitionists in North Star Country saw this stipulation as an odious violation of the right of conscience.

In October of 1850, incensed by the enactment of the Fugitive Slave Law, Frederick Douglass traveled to Boston to speak on behalf of a "horror-stricken and suffering people." Along the way he met terrified blacks who were fleeing to Canada, although winter approached. He even had a close call himself. Although English friends had purchased Douglass's freedom for $750 in British gold, and although he had a bill of sale, this meant little to the slave catchers. Douglass told his Boston audience, "While in Rochester, at my residence, a short time since, I was very agreeably surprised and alarmed on learning that a party of these man-hunters had really come to that place for the purpose of conveying my body, yes, carrying these flesh and bones back to the master from which [I] had escaped."[88] Had the potential kidnappers laid their hands on him, Douglass wrote in his autobiographical *Life and Times,* there would have been "blows to take as well as blows to give."[89]

By December of 1850, Douglass was back in Rochester. On Sunday evenings, he delivered a series of lectures (in Corinthian Hall) that attacked the Fugitive Slave Law. "While this nation is guilty of the enslavement of three millions of innocent men and women," Douglass intoned, "it is as idle to think of having a sound and lasting peace, as it is to think there is no God, to take cognizance of the affairs of men."[90]

As long as slavery existed and fugitives resolved to die rather than to return to captivity, there would be no peace in the streets of Rochester—or in any other North Star Country city—despite what politicians said or did. The nation had rejected Bible politics. The passage of the Fugitive Slave Law foreshadowed a long and difficult struggle for the decade of the 1850s. North Star Country was being drawn deeper into the national maelstrom.

6. The Turbulent 1850s

Powerful political forces conspired to uproot the tree of liberty during the 1850s. During this stormy decade, North Star Country champions of black liberation discovered that their struggle was tightly ensnared in a thicket of national conflicts, beginning with the turmoil over slavery's expansion into the territories and the passage of the Fugitive Slave Law. The controversies over Harriet Beecher Stowe's Uncle Tom's Cabin, *the Kansas-Nebraska Act, and the Dred Scott decision added to the turbulence. Whether they wanted it or not, Upstate New York abolitionists were being drawn into the national maelstrom. The stage upon which they were destined to play out their moral crusade was now larger and more Byzantine than it had been in the formative years of the immediatist campaign, when faith in an America redeemed and cleansed was strong in the old Burned-over District.*

While congressmen in Washington wrangled over the Compromise of 1850, friends of the freedom cause prepared to obstruct enforcement of the new Fugitive Slave Law. In August of 1850, less than a month before the federal statute was enacted, Gerrit Smith called a protest meeting in the name of the New York State Vigilance Committee. He invited "such persons as have escaped from slavery, and those who are resolved to stand by them."[1] This meeting signaled an escalation of tactics used by North Star Country abolitionists. Supporters of the cause were about to be asked to challenge federal authorities in a very public way.

Smith and his allies selected Cazenovia (Madison County) as the site for "A jubilee proclaimed over our pilfered and plundered property!!!" as a Southern newspaper angrily referred to it. The *Madison County Whig* ridiculed Smith's overture, asserting that only "a few idle women and children" frequented abolitionist meetings. "The tender of our hospitalities," grumped the *Whig*, "is therefore unauthorized."[2]

Undaunted by the threat of rejection, convention planners went ahead. The General Agent of the New York State Anti-Slavery Society, William Chaplin, was scheduled to make a dramatic appearance in the company of fugitives whom he intended to spirit away from Washington, D.C. But on August 8, 1850, Chaplin was arrested in Rockville, Maryland. He was charged with aiding the escape of two slaves who were owned by Robert Toombs and Alexander H. Stephens, prominent Georgia congressmen. Chaplin's imprisonment dramatized the risks abolitionists now faced and outraged the Cazenovia Convention participants.[3]

As the convention began on August 21, 1850, about fifty fugitives, as well as former fugitives, were present at the Free Congregational Church. Jermain Loguen was there. Frederick Douglass traveled from Rochester to chair the proceedings. The Edmonson sisters, Mary and Emily, ages 17 and 15, were featured guests. The girls, whose bid for freedom upon the *Pearl* had caused a storm of controversy three years earlier, sang, "I hear the voice of Lovejoy on Alton's Bloody Plains."[4] Upwards of two thousand attended the two-day convention, which was the nation's largest protest against the impending Fugitive Slave Act.

In a bold move that was meant to encourage those still held as chattel, the assembly endorsed "A Letter to the American Slave from those who have fled from American Slavery." The militant tone of the communiqué was exceptional. "For you are prisoners of war, in an enemy's country—of a war, too, that is unrivaled for its injustice, cruelty, meanness—and therefore, by all the rules of war, you have the fullest liberty to plunder, burn, kill, as you have occasion to do to promote your escape."[5] Small wonder that Cazenovia's other churches refused to let the convention use their facilities when it became clear—on the first day—that the Free Congregational Church could not accommodate everyone. Grace Wilson, a widow, former schoolteacher, Liberty Party supporter, and member of the Cazenovia Ladies Anti-Slavery Society, offered her apple orchard as an alternative.[6]

The abolitionists reconvened in Grace Wilson's orchard at 9 A.M. on August 22nd. It was a day to thrill and inspire all friends of the fugitive as well as the fugitives themselves. Douglass spoke. Resolutions urging the boycott of products produced by slave labor and of political candidates

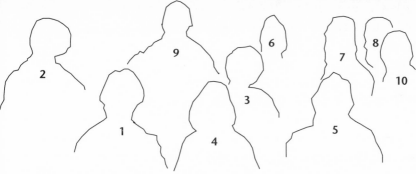

Cazenovia Convention, August 22, 1850. From a daguerreotype taken by Ezra Greenleaf Weld. Convention participants are gathered in Grace Wilson's apple orchard on the second day of the convention, which had been called to protest the Fugitive Slave Law of 1850. *Courtesy of the Madison County Historical Society and Hugh C. Humphreys.*

1. Frederick Douglass
2. Mary Edmonson
3. Emily Edmonson
4. Theodosia Gilbert
5. Joseph Hathaway (prob.)

6. George W. Clark
7. Samuel J. May
8. Charles B. Ray
9. Gerrit Smith
10. James Caleb Jackson

unwilling to embrace abolitionist principles were debated. The crowd donated liberally to the purchase of a silver pitcher in honor of William Chaplin, the incarcerated rescuer. Chaplin's fiancé, Theodosia Gilbert, sat at the front of the assembly.

Sometime in the early afternoon, Ezra Greenleaf Weld, a Cazenovia daguerreotypist and brother of Theodore D. Weld, set up his equipment and captured the orchard scene in one of the most famous and historical daguerreotypes ever made. Gerrit Smith stands, with arm outstretched, flanked by the Edmonson sisters who were dressed alike. Frederick Douglass sits in front of Smith, next to Ms. Gilbert. Samuel J. May, George W. Clark, the abolitionist composer and singer, Charles B. Ray, co-convener of the convention and editor of the *Colored American,* and James Caleb Jackson, the abolitionist "preacher of healthful living" who advocated hydropathic care, have all been positively identified in the image.[7]

The press's reaction to the convention was hostile. In his *North Star,* Frederick Douglass wrote that the "letter" (or address) from the fugitives would "cause a howl to go up from all the bloodhounds of our land."[8] He was correct. Northern papers depicted the Cazenovia meeting as a gathering of fanatics. The *Buffalo Morning Express* called Smith a "Madman and knave." The *Syracuse Daily Journal* described the convention as a "gathering of a few monomaniacs" who used "their labored efforts to out-do each other in the loudest brayings, and the most extravagant resolutions." Predictably, Southern newspapers were filled with invective and ridicule. The *Federal Union* of Milledgeville, Georgia, editorialized, "A meeting more fanatical in its proceedings and more diabolical in its character and tendencies, we venture to say was never held out of Pandemonium."[9] In a sense, the antiabolitionist press did capture the gravity of the Cazenovia Convention accurately: Friends of the fugitive in North Star Country were now prepared for a showdown with proslavery forces, including federal authorities, if necessary.

Soon after the passage of the Fugitive Slave Law, abolitionists in Syracuse formed a biracial vigilance committee. The thirteen members pledged to protect any fugitive who entered the city. W. H. Burleigh wrote to Gerrit Smith, "It would be almost certain death to a slave-catcher to appear, on his infernal mission, in our streets. No fugitive can be taken from our midst."[10] Approximately five hundred people attended a protest meeting in Syracuse

5000 Men & Women
WANTED,
To attend the Meetings in

Canastota, *Wednesday, Oct. 23d, 10 a. m.*

Cazenovia, *Friday, Oct. 25th,* "

Hamilton, *Wednesday, Oct. 30th,* "

Peterboro, *Friday, Nov. 1st,* "

None but *real* Men and Women are wanted. The sham Men and Women, who can stick to the Whig and Democratic parties, are not wanted. These parties made the accursed law, under which oppressors and kidnappers are now chasing down the poor among us, to make slaves of them. Hence, there is no hope of good from persons, who can stick to these Devil-prompted parties.

We want such men and women to attend these Meetings, as would rather suffer imprisonment and death than tolerate the execution of this man-stealing law. We want such, as would be glad to see William L. Chaplin, now lying in a Maryland prison on account of his merciful feelings to the enslaved, made Governor of the State of New-York. We want, in a word, such noble men and women, as used to gather under the banners of the good old Liberty Party.

Let us, then, get together again to speak the truth, and to sing the truth. Those were good times, when we came together to hear warm-hearted speeches for the slave, and to hear Otis Simmons' daughters, and Rhoda Klinck, and Miss Cook, &c. &c., sing

" *Come join the Abolitionists.*"

" *What mean ye, that ye bruise and bind !*"

" *The Yankee Girl.*"

" *There's a good time coming, boys.*"

October 10, 1850.

Abolitionist broadside. Subsequent to the Cazenovia Fugitive Slave Convention, North Star Country abolitionists rallied their supporters in a series of protest meetings designed to condemn the Fugitive Slave Law signed by President Millard Fillmore on September 18, 1850. Here is a broadside that was inserted in the *Madison County Whig* of October 23, 1850, calling for "noble men and women" to gather under the "banners of the good old Liberty Party" and reminding the public that William L. Chaplin, the general agent of the New York State Anti-Slavery Society, was still imprisoned on the charge of aiding runaways. *Courtesy of Hugh C. Humphreys.*

on October 4, 1850. Although he was a Democrat and no abolitionist, Mayor Alfred H. Hovey declared, "Come what will of political organizations, and fall where I may, I am with you." Samuel R. Ward delivered a blistering attack on the slave catchers. But it was Jermain Loguen's speech that "uncapped the volcano."[11]

Loguen was living and preaching in Troy, New York, when the great debate over the Compromise of 1850 began. As soon as it looked like Southerners would get federal assistance for recapturing runaways, Loguen returned to Syracuse, a place he knew to have many friends of the fugitive. Although he was urged by some to seek refuge in Canada, Loguen decided to stay and fight the new law. In a speech ringing with defiance, Loguen told the protesters at the October rally:

> What is life to me if I am to be a slave in Tennessee? My neighbors! I have lived with you many years, and you know me. My home is here, and my children were born here. I am bound to Syracuse by pecuniary interests, and social and family bonds. . . . I don't respect this law—I don't fear it—I won't obey it! It outlaws me, and I outlaw it, and the men who attempt to enforce it on me. I place the governmental officials on the ground that they place me. I will not live a slave, and if force is employed to re-enslave me, I shall make preparations to meet the crisis as becomes a man.[12]

Loguen's defiance of the Fugitive Slave Law was partly generated by his conviction that Syracuse was "no mean city."[13] When push came to shove, Loguen believed, the abolitionists of North Star Country would meet the challenge. But bravado is only bravado until the day comes when bold deeds back up bold words. That day was not far off.

Northern politicians were anxious to appease the Southern hotheads who now threatened secession; they saw things otherwise. Senator Daniel Webster of Massachusetts campaigned throughout the North on behalf of the Compromise of 1850. He came to Syracuse in May of 1851. Standing on a small balcony of Frazee Hall (later known as the Courier Building), and overlooking the yard in front of the city hall, Webster thundered, "Depend upon it, the law will be executed in all the great cities, here in Syracuse; in the midst of the next Anti-Slavery Convention, if the occasion shall arise; then we shall see what becomes of their lives and sacred honor."[14] Samuel J. May dubbed Webster's words "a rehash of his infamous speech in Congress on the 7th of March, 1850." May described the crowd's reaction: "Indigna-

Jermain W. Loguen (c.1812–1872). A fugitive from slavery himself, Loguen boldly championed freedom's cause during his many years as a preacher and Underground Railroad operative in Syracuse. An ordained clergyman of the A.M.E.Z. Church, Loguen participated in the Jerry Rescue and, after the Civil War, supported educational and missionary work among the freed people of the South. *Courtesy of the Onondaga Historical Association.*

tion flashed from many eyes in that assembly, and one might almost hear the gritting of teeth in defiance of the threat."[15]

On October 1, 1851, Syracuse's hotels and boarding houses were fully booked. Thousands of visitors thronged the Onondaga County Agricultural Society Fair in the Hanover Square area. Liberty Party faithful were holding a convention at the Congregational church. Around noon, the bell of the Presbyterian church rang. Within minutes, every church bell in Syracuse—except the Episcopalian one—tolled the alarm. Out-of-town guests, who were puzzled by the resulting cacophony of sound, doubtless wondered whether it meant disaster or something less ominous.

Samuel J. May, who was at home eating lunch, and the other members of Syracuse's Vigilance Committee knew that the bells signaled the arrival of slave catchers in town. The hour for action had arrived. A large crowd gathered in front of the Townsend Block Building, at the corner of Water and Clinton Streets, where the office of United States Commissioner Joseph F. Sabine was located. As others joined the rush to the center of Syracuse, they wondered who it was that the slave hunters sought.

One member of Syracuse's black community, young Lucy Watson, was ironing at home when the alarm sounded. She had started the trip downtown when a man called out to her, "Tell your people there's a fugitive arrested."[16]

The quarry turned out to be William ("Jerry") Henry, an escaped slave from Missouri who was born in Buncombe County, North Carolina, in either 1811 or 1812. We know little of Jerry's physical appearance. Contemporaries took note of his red hair; May described him as an "athletic Mulatto."[17]

On the morning of October 1, 1850, Jerry was working in the cooperage shop of Frederic Morrell in the First Ward. A marshal presented Jerry with a warrant that accused him of theft. Handcuffed and thrown into a hack, Jerry was taken to the office of Commissioner Joseph F. Sabine. Only there was he told that he was being apprehended as a fugitive slave. When news of Jerry's seizure reached the Liberty Party delegates, they immediately adjourned and rushed to his hearing. As many as possible pressed into Sabine's office, where twenty-one marshals and deputies guarded the handcuffed fugitive. The government's representatives had already begun to argue their case based on the Fugitive Slave Law of 1850. Leonard Gibbs and

Gerrit Smith acted as Jerry's legal counsel. James Lear, the agent of Jerry's purported owner, sat next to Jerry with his pistols tucked into his trousers. As he started to testify, Jerry's supporters began to hiss and boo. They created so much noise that Sabine, over Smith's protests, decided to adjourn the proceedings for half an hour in order to find a larger room. It was now around 2:30 P.M.

Perhaps by prearrangement, the abolitionists and their allies now took matters into their own hands. Some of them hoisted Jerry over their heads and propelled him toward the door and down the stairs; others pressed the marshals and deputies against the office walls. Jerry was hurt as he fell down the stairs, but he recovered enough to struggle, still cuffed, down Water Street. A black barber and dyer named Prince Jackson ran interference, but the authorities recaptured Jerry on the Lock Street Bridge. They put him in leg irons and took him to the Police Office, which was located in the Journal Building of "the Raynor" Block (facing Clinton Square).

By now Jerry was so agitated that the police asked that the Reverend Samuel J. May come and calm him down. May did so by persuading Jerry that an attempt to rescue him would be made later that evening. Outside the police station, Samuel Ringgold Ward and others addressed a growing crowd of protestors, telling them that Jerry would not be abandoned and could well be freed as a result of the upcoming hearing.[18] Sabine had scheduled Jerry's case to be continued at 5:30 P.M. It was now a little after 3:00 P.M.

In the late afternoon, Ward, Smith, May, Loguen, and twenty-four other men met at Dr. Hiram Hoyt's office on South Warren Street to plan a course of action. Meanwhile, County Sheriff William C. Gardner tried to prevent civil disorder by calling out the National Guard, Syracuse's Citizens Corps, and the Washington Artillery. But Colonel Origen Vanderburgh of the 51st National Guard Regiment persuaded Lieutenant Pendergast not to move the guard out of the armory. Charles A. Wheaton, a local hardware dealer, argued that troops would be prosecuted if they marched under the orders of the sheriff. The Citizens Corps also disbanded, and the Washington Artillery was the only show of force now available to authorities. The artillery did appear later, but placed just one cannon at the corner of City Hall Park and fired ten blank shots, thereby dispersing the crowd and opening a path for Jerry's friends.

As they began to debate a course of action, Jerry's potential rescuers were unaware that their chances for success had been enhanced by the stand-down of the military. Gerrit Smith is reported to have counseled those convened in Hoyt's office: "It is not unlikely the Commissioner will release Jerry if the examination is suffered to proceed—but the moral effect of such an acquittal will be as nothing to a bold and forcible rescue. A forcible rescue will demonstrate the strength of public opinion against the possible legality of slavery and this Fugitive Slave Law in particular. It will honor Syracuse and be a powerful example everywhere."[19]

Some of the abolitionists were reluctant to engage in a rescue by forcible means because of their long-standing nonresistance principles. May was one of those whose Garrisonian ideals still discountenanced violence. May suggested, however, that a rescue could be conceived of as an act of self-sacrifice—if the abolitionists avoided injuring the marshals and were not motivated by hatred. As the potential rescuers left Dr. Hoyt's office, May said, "If any one is to be injured in this fray, I hope it may be one of our own party."[20] Jermain Loguen took a more strident position: "If white men won't fight, let fugitives and black men smite down Marshals and Commissioners—any body who holds Jerry—and rescue him or perish."[21]

If we can judge them by their actions, many of the people who roamed the city and periodically stoned the police station during the afternoon and early evening of October 1 favored Loguen's bolder position. As day gave way to night, an estimated two to three thousand people were gathered outside the station where Jerry was being held.[22] Sabine reopened the hearing at 5:30 P.M. Due to the ruckus put up by protestors, he adjourned an hour and a half later, with the intent of resuming at 8:00 A.M. the next morning. Jerry was now placed in a back room of the police station.

Stones continued to pelt the building. Around 8:00 P.M. the cry of "NOW!" was heard. Picking up clubs, iron bars, and axes which had been stacked outside of Wheaton's hardware store, a band of men, some with burnt cork smeared on their faces, rushed the building. Doors and windows were smashed. The gas-jet lamps of the front office went out. A stone knocked down one of the deputies. Within minutes, the rescuers had forced their way into the police station. Marshal Fitch stood guard behind the door of the inner room in which Jerry was being kept. With cries of "old Oswego is coming!" the rescuers charged the door with a ten-foot pine

Jerry Rescue Memorial, Syracuse. As a result of a community-wide campaign that was spearheaded by Chester Whiteside, a retired African American city fireman, this memorial was dedicated on August 10, 1990. It stands on the west end of Clinton Square, in downtown Syracuse, a stone's throw from the site of the original Jerry Rescue building. Sharon BuMann sculpted the statue. The three figures represent William "Jerry" Henry, Jermain Loguen, and Samuel J. May. *Courtesy of the author.*

beam. Just then, Fitch stepped out of the back room and fired two shots at the mob. Someone smashed his arm with a club, and he jumped out of a second-story window.

The abolitionists now had their prize. They carried Jerry out through the front door and paraded him through the streets—to the hurrahs of others. Sixteen-year-old Lucy Watson recalled that, soon after she returned to her home on Irving Street, William Thompson rapped on the door. What followed was high drama:

> And he says, "I've got Jerry." Then my sister Frances got out and my sister and I made a queen's chair like the children make with their hands and we carried him into the house that way, Thomson steadying him.
>
> We lived in the basement. When we got him there Jerry was awfully frightened. His face was bleeding and his hands shackled. He explained his bruises in this way: When the crowd broke open the door the officer was so frightened that he put Jerry in front of him to protect himself until he got to the door, then slipped away. Jerry got a stone in the forehead before the crowd appreciated that they had him.
>
> We started to get the shackles off. We worked a good while with a hammer and flatiron, and finally broke them. Mrs. Mahala Robbins and I buried them in the garden, for we knew it was high treason if we were discovered.
>
> Then we tried to get someone to file off the handcuffs. We finally got Peter Lilly, the blacksmith, after we had been there twice, to come and do it. He was an Abolitionist and he was so excited when he found that we had Jerry that he could scarcely file them.
>
> Then we put some women's clothes on Jerry and took him into the back yard and boosted him over the back fence, and that was the last we saw of him.[23]

Disguised in a dress, hood, and shawl, Jerry took refuge for four days at the home of an unlikely ally: a proslavery Democrat named Caleb (or "Cale") Davis who lived at Genesee and Orange Streets.

Davis was described as "a butcher of rough exterior and great physical strength" and a hothead who "never met the sweet-tempered Samuel May in public without reviling him."[24] As was characteristic of those who demonstrated for Jerry's release, Davis resented the intrusion of outsiders and had a strong sense of fair play. After receiving medical care and food, Jerry was secreted in the bottom of Davis's meat wagon. He was given a gun, covered with sacking, and, on Davis's weekly drive out of the city to buy beef, driven northward. Davis headed toward Cicero on the Plank Road. Earlier, he had taken the same route and bribed the toll keeper to delay any pursuers.

During the next few days, Jerry was passed from abolitionist to abolitionist, from Brewerton to Mexico, where he was harbored by Orson Ames, whose house still stands.[25] Then it was on to Oswego where, with the aide of Sidney Clarke, he boarded a British schooner bound for Kingston, Canada, and freedom. The Sidney Clarke farmstead was located in Scriba on the outskirts of Oswego. Clarke's son, John Jackson Clarke, wrote a short memoir in 1931:

> As it would never do for one of father's abolitionistic [sic] proclivities to be seen convoying a negro toward the wharf, strategy had to be employed. Just after dark, daddy accompanied the fugitive to a point where the houses of the city proper commenced, near the corner of Tenth and Oneida streets, and started ahead, bearing a heavy hickory cane, whose iron ferule made a resonant whack on the sidewalk and enabled the negro to follow at a discreet distance. Northward on Tenth to Bridge street, thence straight down and across the river to Water Street, which was traversed to a point near the vessel's side, where the famous fugitive was stowed away, provided with food and a small sum of money. In due time a few neatly written lines were received from some point in Canada, reporting his safe arrival.[26]

Jerry sent a letter from Kingston, thanking his rescuers. He farmed until he succumbed to tuberculosis and died on October 8, 1853. His final resting place may be Cataraqui Cemetery in Kingston.[27]

The "Jerry Rescue" received widespread comment in the national press. Syracuse's renown as a bastion of antislavery sentiment grew stronger. Southerners, of course, condemned the actions of the rescuers. Many conservative Northern editorialists described the forcible rescue as unwarranted and unwise. Northerners who were skittish about the danger of fueling sectional tensions decried those who flaunted the Fugitive Slave Act.

Four years passed between the Compromise of 1850 and the Kansas-Nebraska Act of 1854, which nullified the prohibition of slavery's expansion into those territories gained by the Louisiana Purchase north of latitude 36°-30' ft. During that time, 160 fugitives came before federal tribunals and were returned to their owners or were taken back to the South without due process of law. Although nine fugitives were rescued from federal custody, the rescue of Jerry has been described as "the most dramatic and influential early instance of resistance."[28] After the passage of the Kansas-Nebraska Act, white Northerners did become more supportive of efforts to thwart the Fugitive Slave Act. But back in 1851, the abolitionists of Syracuse had dared to do what abolitionists in few other Northern cities had attempted.

The group of Jerry rescuers contained a disproportionate number of commercial and professional people. Of the fifty-two male participants, 68 percent belonged to this class. At least twelve of the fifty-two known rescuers were African Americans, among whom were Prince Jackson, Samuel R. Ward, Jermain W. Loguen, Peter Hallenbeck, William Gray, Enoch Reed, John Lyles, William Thompson, and James Baker.[29] Less than two weeks after the tumultuous events of October 1, abolitionists met in Syracuse to applaud the actions of the rescuers. Samuel J. May argued that they had not violated any law but had instead vindicated the natural rights of man by setting aside an "unnatural, cruel edict."[30] President Fillmore told James R. Lawrence, United States attorney for western New York, that the "supremacy of the laws must be maintained, at every hazard and at every sacrifice."[31] In a gesture of defiance, the Vigilance Committee sent Fillmore a box containing the shackles that Jerry had worn. Unfortunately, the president's zeal to see violators of the Fugitive Slave Law prosecuted was not tempered by this gift.

Federal Judge Alfred Conkling of Auburn issued arrest warrants for the rescuers. By October 15, five men had been apprehended. Other warrants and arrests followed. Some of the rescuers feared that charges of treason would be leveled against them. At the preliminary hearing conducted in Auburn, eight of the rescuers were charged with violating section seven of the Fugitive Slave Law. This section provided punishment for individuals who "knowingly and willingly obstruct, hinder, or prevent" the capture of an escaped slave.

Bail was set at $2,000 for the white defendants, and at $500 for the black defendants. William Henry Seward posted bail for the blacks, and several Syracuse citizens did so for the whites. On November 5, 1851, a federal grand jury in Buffalo indicted another five persons for having "engaged in the Syracuse riots."[32] As Samuel J. May wrote to William Lloyd Garrison on November 23, 1851, as of that date "twenty-five persons have been indicted, twelve of them colored men, all but three of whom have escaped to

Canada . . . and four of the white men have also gone thither."[33] The trial of the rescuers was moved from Auburn to Buffalo, then to Albany, where Enoch Reed, a black laborer, was convicted of violating the Fugitive Slave Law of 1793.

In an ironic twist, the issue of the 1850 Fugitive Slave Law's constitutionality was sidestepped within the government's case against Enoch Reed. Because Jerry was not technically the property of the Missourian McReynolds (having been sold *in absentia* after his escape), the government could not prosecute Reed under the provisions of the Fugitive Slave Law of 1850. Instead, they charged Jerry with resisting a federal officer who was discharging official duties under the Fugitive Slave Law of 1793. The jury convicted Reed on this lesser count, but he died of consumption during the appeal process.

In the case of Ira Cobb, the jury became hung: eight for acquittal and four for conviction. Cobb was a white mason who may have been most instrumental in gaining access to Jerry on the evening of the rescue. The cases of the other Jerry Rescue defendants ended in hung juries or acquittal.[34] Despite a concerted effort and the expenditure of nearly $50,000, federal prosecutors did not successfully punish anyone for violating the Fugitive Slave Law of 1850. Abolitionist protests of the trials made it clear that the Jerry Rescue was a defining moment in North Star Country's fight against slavery.

The leaders in Jerry's deliverance countered with their own lawsuits. They charged James Lear (McReynolds's agent) with attempted kidnapping, but he died before the case came to trial. They then charged U.S. Deputy Marshall Henry W. Allen with violating the 1840 state personal liberty law.[35]

Allen came to trial on June 21, 1852, before Justice R. P. Marvin of the state supreme court in Syracuse. The abolitionists turned the two-day trial into a debate about the constitutionality of the Fugitive Slave Law. Gerrit Smith spoke for the prosecution. He gave a long speech in which he declared, "If an execution is put into the hands of the sheriff, for the purpose of having him levy on hogs, he may take it for granted, that all is right—for he knows that hogs are property. But if a process is put into his hands, for the purpose of having him treat a human being as property, and reduce that human being to slavery, then he is bound to pause, and to enquire, whether the law for that process can possibly be a Constitutional, valid law."[36] Judge Marvin directed the jury to bring in a verdict of not guilty.

On each October 1st until the Civil War, and intermittently thereafter, abolitionists used the occasion of the "Jerry Rescue" anniversary to tout the region's humanitarian and liberal spirit and to call for renewed vigor in the ongoing struggle for a more equitable society. Abolitionists held the first Jerry Rescue celebration on October 1, 1852. Five thousand people attended and heard William Lloyd Garrison, Frederick Douglass, Gerrit Smith, Lucy Stone, Lucretia Mott, and others condemn the odious fugitive law.[37] Some conservative Syracuse residents attempted to disrupt the celebration by closing all public facilities to participants. In response, John Wilkinson, owner of the Syracuse Railroad, opened the company's engine house, a 150-foot rotunda, to the abolitionists and their supporters.

On October 1, 1853, shortly after the end of the Jerry trials, Samuel J. May arranged for another celebration. He gave a speech in which he declared that no law had been broken, because no law protecting slavery could exist; no slave had escaped because no such thing as a slave could exist. "Can a man be turned into a horse or a stone?" he exclaimed. "Can immortality be merchandise?"[38] In 1867, at seventy years of age, May would recall his involvement in the resistance to the Fugitive Slave Law: "I have not lived long enough yet, to be ashamed of anything I said, or did, for the Rescue of Jerry."[39]

Jermain Loguen's wife and friends had prevailed upon him to seek asylum in Canada. He was accused of assaulting a marshal during the melee of the rescue, and he felt particularly vulnerable. Loguen traveled to the city of St. Catharines, in southeastern Ontario. From there he wrote to New York Governor Washington Hunt on December 2, 1851. He did not deny being present in Syracuse during the Jerry Rescue, but he contradicted the claim that he had engaged in any violent act and pointed to the injustice enshrined in the Fugitive Slave Law.

> It was ordered by an all-wise Providence, that watches over the falling sparrow and numbers the very hairs of our head, that I should visit again this glorious land of refuge about the time some of my fellow-sufferers in freedom's cause were being arrested at Syracuse; but be it known that I am not here, sheltered under the protecting aegis of her Majesty's powerful Government, as a felon or a fugitive from justice—for I have committed no crime—but the fiendish machinations of the merciless slave-hunters, and their equally guilty, but infi-

nitely meaner and more contemptible Northern abettors (officials and non-officials), with the fear of flagrant injustice, have driven [me] to these shores.[40]

Loguen wanted Governor Hunt's guarantee that Loguen would not be prosecuted as a fugitive slave if he voluntarily returned to Syracuse to rejoin his wife and four children. Loguen was willing to stand trial "for rescuing Jerry, and that *alone*."[41] The governor ignored the request. Nevertheless, Jermain returned to Syracuse in the spring of 1852 and resumed his labors as Superintendent of the Underground Railroad. Apart from his desire to rejoin his wife, Caroline, and his children, his decision to come back was based on his confidence in the depth of antislavery feeling in central New York State.

The Jerry Rescue may have been North Star Country's proudest moment, but it was not the only occasion on which freedom's allies triumphed and a captive was set free. In the public uproar over what happened on October 1, 1851, some Syracuse residents recalled a daring recue from a dozen years earlier—one that set the stage for later acts of resistance.

In October 1839, Mr. and Mrs. John Davenport of Mississippi booked rooms in the Syracuse House, the best hotel Syracuse had to offer. They brought a young servant girl, named Harriet Powell, with them. She was said to be "as richly dressed as her mistress."[42] Beneath the fancy clothes, however, there beat a heart in distress. Sensing that something was wrong, a black waiter named Tom Leonard spoke privately with Harriet. He convinced her to attempt escape, although she feared being "sold South" should she be recaptured. Leonard got word to local abolitionists who acted with dispatch. On October 7th, John R. Owen, a marble merchant, and William M. Clarke, a deputy county clerk, cloaked Harriet in a man's coat and hat. They spirited her away in a carriage, which had been supplied by a DeWitt farmer named Nottingham, to the mansion of Gerrit Smith in Madison County.

Elizabeth Cady (Stanton), then twenty-four, was staying in Peterboro that October. Gerrit Smith, her older cousin, invited her to come up to the third story of the Smith house and into a large room in which sat "a beautiful quadroon girl, about eighteen years of age." Gerrit addressed the girl, "Harriet, I have brought all my young cousins to see you. I want you to make good abolitionists of them by telling them the history of your life—what you have seen and suffered in slavery."[43]

Elizabeth and the others sat transfixed for two hours as Harriet recounted her story, including how she was separated from her family and sold in a New Orleans slave market when she was but fourteen. Smith filled in details about the rescue in Syracuse: how Harriet had been taking care of the Davenport baby while they were attending a farewell party; how Harriet had managed to escape by saying she had to run an errand; and how she had been brought to Peterboro. When twilight of that night arrived, Harriet was dressed as a Quakeress and placed in a carriage. She was escorted north toward Lake Ontario. Elizabeth Cady, the future women's rights activist, said of the encounter: "We all wept together as we talked, and, when Cousin Gerrit returned to summon us away, we needed no further education to make us earnest abolitionists."[44]

The Davenports offered a $200 reward for Harriet's recapture. Mr. Davenport boasted that his slave was worth at least $2,500. In a notice that appeared in the local press, Davenport made the claim that Harriet's elderly mother would die of heartache should her daughter be lost to her. The handbill contained a detailed description of Harriet's physical appearance and clothing.[45] Davenport and the marshals from Syracuse arrived at Smith's residence only eighteen hours after Harriet's departure. They were given permission to search the house and grounds, and invited to stay at the house and dine. Elizabeth Cady recalled,

> The master was evidently a gentleman, for, on Mr. Smith's assurance that Harriet was not there, he made no search, feeling that they could not do so without appearing to doubt his word. He was evidently surprised to find an abolitionist so courteous and affable, and it was interesting to hear them in conversation, at dinner, calmly discussing the problem of slavery, while public sentiment was at white heat on the question. They shook hands warmly at parting and expressed an equal interest in the final adjustment of that national difficulty.[46]

Later, Smith would write an open letter, which was published in the New York *Tribune*, to Davenport in which he told the Southerner (and the world) of his part in the rescue of Harriet Powell, whom Smith reported was "now a free woman, safe under the shadow of the British throne."[47]

Although Harriet's rescue proved that North Star Country abolitionists were prepared to defy the law when necessary, the stakes were much higher after 1850 as slaveholders then had the support of federal authorities. Frederick Douglass understood this when he came to the aid of participants in the famous Christiana slave riot.

In September 1851, slaves of Maryland farmer Edward Gorsuch took refuge in the house of William Parker (an escapee himself) near the Quaker village of Christiana in southeastern Pennsylvania. Violence erupted, shots were fired, and Gorsuch was killed. His son was wounded. President Fillmore sent a company of U.S. Marines to accompany the posse of Philadelphia policemen. Parker and thirty-eight others were arrested. They were charged with treason and with resisting the Fugitive Slave Law. Parker escaped on the Underground Railroad; he traveled with two other members of the accused. They got as far as Rochester where they found shelter with a boyhood friend of Parker's, Frederick Douglass.

As Douglass recalls in his autobiography: "The work of getting these men safely to Canada was a delicate one. They were not only fugitives from slavery but charged with murder, and officers were in pursuit of them. There was no time for delay. I could not look upon them as murderers. To me, they were heroic defenders of the just rights of man against manstealers and murderers. So I fed them, and sheltered them in my house."[48] With the telegraph wires hot with news of the riot, it was important for Douglass to act with dispatch.

He sent Julia Griffiths, an English woman who had come to America to help Douglass edit the *North Star,* to a landing three miles away on the Genesee River. Her assignment was to ascertain if a steamer could take the fugitives to a port in Canada. That very night, Douglass put Parker and the other men in his "Democratic carriage" and took them to the boat. "I remained on board till the order to haul in the gangplank was given," Douglass recalled in his third autobiography. "I shook hands with my friends, received from Parker the revolver that fell from the hand of Gorsuch when he died . . . and returned to my home with a sense of relief which I cannot stop here to describe."

Some three decades after the events recounted here, Douglass wrote, "The affair, at Christiana, and the Jerry rescue at Syracuse, inflicted fatal wounds on the fugitive slave bill. It became thereafter almost a dead letter, for slaveholders found that not only did it fail to put them in possession of their slaves, but that the attempt to enforce it brought odium upon themselves and weakened the slave system."[49]

Douglass was correct. Slave captors who came into North Star Country during the 1850s encountered a regional spirit that was hostile to their odious intentions. For example, in 1858, Napoleon B. Van Tuyl was convicted of kidnapping two black freemen and attempting to sell them into slavery. This strange case began in November 1857 when Van Tuyl, a clerk in a Geneva dry goods store, abducted Daniel Prue and John Hite. He employed the ruse that he was going to find them employment at a hotel in Columbus, Ohio. His true intentions were to take them to Cincinnati, cross the Ohio River, and sell them into slavery.

Prue escaped and found work at a livery stable in Columbus. Hite was eventually sold to a Kentucky slaveholder. Petitions circulated around Geneva that asked New York Governor John A. King to commission agents to recover Hite. Claven Walker went to Kentucky, obtained Hite's freedom, and pursued Van Tuyl, who was eventually returned to Ontario County to stand trial. Although his only conviction was for inveigling, Van Tuyl was considered a disgrace to his family and community. Hite's fate is unknown; Daniel Prue lived out his days in Geneva on a military pension that he earned from serving in a black regiment during the Civil War.[50]

The willingness of North Star Country abolitionists to oppose the recapture of runaways did not mean that African Americans, fugitive or not, rested easy during the troubled 1850s. The bloodhound bill, as it was called, alarmed the African American households of North Star Country. Free blacks who feared false accusations of being runaways now looked more closely at the option of going to Canada. Fugitives, some of whom had been living in Upstate New York without much trouble for years, realized that it was time to take the last leg of the journey to freedom.

In many respects, Canada, and more specifically central and western Ontario, became an extension of North Star Country. As Henry Bibb reported from Canada via the *Voice of the Fugitive* on November 5, 1851, "the road is doing better business this fall than usual. The Fugitive Slave Law has given it more vitality, more activity, more passengers and more opposition which invariably accelerates business."[51] And Frederick Douglass wrote about the effect of this cruel enactment:

> Fugitive slaves who had lived for many years safely and securely in western New York and elsewhere, some of whom had by industry and economy saved money and bought little homes for themselves and their children, were suddenly alarmed and compelled to flee to Canada for safety as from an enemy's land—a doomed city—and take up a dismal march to a new abode, empty-handed,

among strangers. My old friend Ward, of whom I have just now spoken, found it necessary to give up the contest and flee to Canada, and thousands followed his example.[52]

Douglass had only to look at Rochester to see the impact of the new law. The Reverend Horace H. Hawkins of Rochester's Abyssinian Baptist Church—also known as the Third Baptist Church (African)—led an exodus to Canada that included almost all of the members of his congregation.[53]

Now that slave captors had been encouraged by the federal government to prowl northern communities for alleged runaways, African Americans in Upstate New York became more vocal in their own defense. Rochester's black community organized a vigilance committee at a meeting held on October 13, 1851.

The meeting took place in the A.M.E.Z. church at 40 Favor Street. It was presided over by J. P. Morris, a skilled barber and agent of Rochester's school board who had been assigned to look after the city's "colored schools." William Cooper Nell acted as secretary. Nell had come to Rochester in 1847 to serve as publisher of Douglass's *North Star.* Although he was a Garrisonian loyalist, he introduced resolutions that called upon blacks to be on their guard. "The tocsin of alarm," he warned, "[is] now being sounded in the City of Rochester presaging the Hunting of Men in the Valley of the Genesee."[54] In Nell's mind, any commissioner who dared to capture those who had been guided by the North Star into Rochester and to deliver them to the Fugitive Slave Law was no better than Judas Iscariot. After the attendees swore to be eternally vigilant, the meeting adjourned with the agreement that the air would resound with "the signal word" should slave hunters come to town.

Frederick Douglass echoed the sentiments of fugitives and their allies when he declared, "The only way to make the Fugitive Slave Law a dead letter is to make half a dozen or more dead kidnappers."[55] Samuel Ringgold Ward argued that the Fugitive Slave Law gave black Americans "the right of Revolution."[56]

The 1852 publication of an attack upon slavery that was titled, *Uncle Tom's Cabin; or, Life Among the Lowly,* occurred in the midst of the public furor over the Fugitive Slave Law. Harriet Beecher Stowe's emotionally powerful account of the horrors of slavery helped sensitize many Northern whites to the plight of runaways. It also raised the temperature of the public debate over the South's "peculiar institution."

The account was first issued in forty installments by the *National Era*, a popular antislavery paper published by L. P. Noble, a one-time resident of Fayetteville (Onondaga County). After Stowe's work came out in book form, the "novel" sold more than three hundred thousand copies in its first year. Some thought that Mrs. Stowe had used Frederick Douglass as the model for her chief character, a pious slave named Tom, although the Baptist preacher Josiah Henson was a more likely candidate among contemporaries.[57] In the summer of 1851, Stowe had written to Douglass and asked him to lend authenticity to her sketches. But Douglass's experience in Maryland hardly qualified him to give the perspective of a laborer in the cotton fields.[58]

Douglass found *Uncle Tom's Cabin* to be "a work of marvelous depth and power." "Nothing," he later wrote, "could have better suited the moral and humane requirements of the hour. Its effect was amazing, instantaneous, and universal."

Shortly before Stowe departed for England (British admirers of her novel planned to give her a sum of money for the freedom cause), she asked Douglass to come to her house in Andover, Massachusetts. There she sounded him out on what to do with the funds. She had an industrial school in mind. "What I thought of as best," Douglass remembered, "was rather a series of workshops, where colored people could learn some of the handicrafts, learn to work in iron, wood, and leather, and where a plain English education could also be taught."

Douglass wrote a long letter for Mrs. Stowe to carry to London. The letter emphasized the educational needs of African Americans. He was disappointed when the author of *Uncle Tom's Cabin* failed to render assistance upon her return. Douglass, who had defended Stowe against accusations of using the British funds for her own purposes, felt "great disappointment."[59]

Douglass was not the only person who was dissatisfied with Stowe's literary creation. Harriet Tubman, of whom I will have more to say in the next chapter, felt that no novel, however well-intentioned, could capture the pain and suffering of the enslaved. In *Scenes in the Life of Harriet Tubman,* Sarah Bradford reports Tubman's reaction to hearing that a stage version of *Uncle Tom's Cabin* was playing in Philadelphia in the early 1850s.

Tubman refused to attend and told Bradford, "I've heard *Uncle Tom's Cabin* read, and I tell you Mrs. Stowe's pen hasn't begun to paint what slavery is as I have seen it in the far South."[60]

Of course, Southern slaveholders felt that Stowe's book drew a false picture of their way of life and they considered Stowe to be a tool of the radical abolitionists. The controversy sparked by *Uncle Tom's Cabin,* coming on the heels of the Fugitive Slave Law, kept abolitionist circles in North Star Country in an agitated state during the 1850s.

Yet another troublesome issue of the decade centered around the question of emigration. New York State Governor Washington Hunt promoted colonization, advocating state and federal aid for the effort. Several black leaders, notably Martin R. Delany and James T. Holly, blew the emigrationist trumpet. But Frederick Douglass boycotted the National Emigration Convention of the Colored People, which took place in Cleveland in 1854. The talk there was of going to Central America and South America. Douglass held back because he felt, "We are Americans. We are not aliens. We are a component part of the nation. Though in only some of the States, are we an acknowledged necessary part of the 'ruling element,' we have no disposition, to renounce our nationality."[61] Others shared Douglass's mistrust of the emigration movement. In response to a federal initiative that would promote emigration to Central America or South America, Gerrit Smith reminded its sponsors that any such program must be voluntary and "be couched in words that would [not] offend the black, or invade their self-respect."[62]

The debate over emigration and colonization intensified in the wake of the Kansas-Nebraska Act's passage in 1854. This legislation allowed settlers in the northern lands between Iowa and the Rocky Mountains to decide the question of slavery under the principle of popular sovereignty. In effect, the act repealed the Missouri Compromise. Frederick Douglass implored "companies of emigrants from the free states . . . to possess the goodly land." He wanted an army of one thousand families to move from the black communities of the North to Kansas. He argued, "The true antidote . . . for *black slaves* is an enlightened body of black freemen."[63] Not many went. Historian David W. Blight, cognizant of how deep antiblack sentiment ran among Free Soilers, observes, "This was Douglass at his most impractical. At times he needed to throw his dreams out to his readers, to envision the world as he wished it to be, and the excitement over Kansas and the Republicans seemed to offer a brief interlude when dreams were possible."[64]

Some North Star Country abolitionists were drawn away from Upstate New York by their desire to stop the expansion of Southern power. These abolitionists were motivated by humanitarian principles rather than a hunger for new homesteads. They ventured to the Kansas Territory as an expression of the abolitionist spirit that had been fired in the crucible of Upstate New York's old Burned-over District a generation earlier. These freedom fighters, mostly young men, rekindled the zeal for the black freedom crusade and the willingness to sacrifice that had been typical of the abolitionist evangelists at Oneida Institute and elsewhere in parts of central and western New York State during the 1830s. For example, in 1857, Jared P. Barnes, age 23, left Onondaga County for "Bloody Kansas," where he joined the 4th Kansas Militia in its fight against proslavery Missourians. The Syracuse Kansas Company proposed the purchase of 160 acres of Kansas land and set up a colony there. In September 1856, a large rally for presidential candidate John C. Frémont was held close to the Barnes family farm at Betts Corners, near Lysander (Onondaga County). Speakers condemned the spread of slavery. A glee club sang "Ho! for the Kansas Plains."[65] Central New Yorkers sent money, clothing, and bedding out to Kansas to aid Free Soilers like the Barnes family. Gerrit Smith himself gave liberally to the cause.

Smith pursued the politics of righteousness in the 1850s, despite the defection of some abolitionists to the major political parties. He did so in the face of clear evidence that sectional loyalties governed the solidification of political alliances. In 1853, Smith ran for Congress on an independent ticket, with support from antislavery Whigs, Democrats, Free Democrats, and voting abolitionists. Smith garnered 8,049 votes in the 22nd New York District of Oswego and Madison Counties, and he won. (One of Smith's most enthusiastic allies termed his election "the sequel to *Uncle Tom's Cabin*.")[66] Garrison's *Liberator* declared, "The election of Gerrit Smith as Representative to Congress ... is among the most extraordinary political events of this most extraordinary age."[67]

Smith bought a house in Washington, D.C., and hired carpenters to renovate it. He entertained politicians of all persuasions and made speeches in Congress about temperance and slavery. Smith voted against the Kansas-Nebraska Act, but he cut his term short by resigning on August 7, 1854. Abolitionist friends expressed regret; Smith's excuse was the "pressure of my far too extensive private business."[68]

Friends and admirers attempted to explain Smith's sudden departure on other grounds. In 1878, Octavius Brooks Frothingham published a biography, which was approved by Smith's family, in which he wrote:

> Here was a simple-hearted bible-Christian going where Christianity was a worldly institution, and the bible a sealed book; an independent going where the party politician alone was regarded. . . . He never drank, and he was to be the associate of men who tippled at all hours of day and night. He never smoked or chewed tobacco, and he was about to live among people who thought the air unfit to breathe until it was thick with the fumes of cigars, and in whose opinion the indispensable article of furniture was the spittoon. He went to bed with the chickens and rose with the birds, and he was to pass months in a city where day began in the afternoon, and reached the meridian at midnight. The man of prayer is sent down to the metropolis of profanity; the free soul to the stronghold of slavery; the child of the Spirit to the arena of gladiators.[69]

Despite Smith's distaste for the nation's political culture, he joined William Goodell and Lewis Tappan as they organized the American Abolition Society in 1856. Its members thought of their organization as the "revival of primitive abolitionism."[70] Frederick Douglass and James McCune Smith showed interest. The new party launched the *Radical Abolitionist* newspaper and nominated Gerrit Smith for president in 1856.[71]

Still unshaken in his hostility toward political action, William Lloyd Garrison mocked the idea that abolitionists should be nominating candidates for the presidency and vice presidency of the United States. "Can any thing more ludicrous than this be found inside or outside of the Utica Insane Asylum," he wrote Samuel J. May. "It is really sad to see so good a man as Gerrit Smith befooled in this manner."[72] Most Americans were more concerned with sectional hostilities than with the egalitarian idealism behind the architects of the American Abolition Society. By the end of 1858, the always-minuscule party was moribund.[73] Radicals on both sides of the slavery question laid out their swords, anticipating the day when political rhetoric would not be enough to turn back the winds of war. William Henry Seward, now a member of the United States Senate, was speaking of an "irrepressible conflict."[74]

Back in 1850, Seward had invoked "a higher law than the Constitution" to keep slavery out of the territories during the great Senate debate over Henry Clay's compromise proposals.[75] In 1854, Seward and other anti-Kansas-Nebraska Whigs joined the radical abolitionists, both black and white, who condemned the Kansas bill. Free Soilers and Northern Democrats joined Northern Whigs in the search for a political vehicle to break the existing juggernaut. There was talk of organizing a new party. On March 20, 1854, anti-Kansas-Nebraska Whigs and Democrats met to discuss a political alternative in Ripon, Wisconsin. This place is generally given the honor of being the birthplace of the Republican Party, although the name *Republican* was adopted on July 6, 1854, at a fusionist meeting in Jackson, Michigan. Other places, including Exeter, New Hampshire, claim the honor of being the cradle of the Republican Party.[76] North Star Country is generally not among them, but the region may well have contained the seeds of the new party.

General Amos P. Granger of Syracuse is said to have written and offered resolutions at the Auburn Whig Convention of 1853 which contained the rudiments of the Republican political philosophy. The notion of a new party may have originated one year earlier from a discussion underneath a great tree at the Syracuse home of Vivus W. Smith. Present were Smith, Horace Greeley, and Thurlow Weed, William Henry Seward's political ally.[77]

Whatever the actual birthplace of the Republican Party nationally, New York State's Republican organization emerged in the context of Whig factionalism and competition from the Know-Nothings (so-called because members, if asked, were supposed to deny knowledge of the political movement's existence or purpose). The Know-Nothings, or the "Native American" party, fed upon anti-Catholic and anti-immigrant sentiment in the early 1850s. To the consternation of the antislavery Whigs, Upstate New York had strong pockets of Know-Nothing voters. The anti-Seward Whigs, conservatives loyal to Millard Fillmore and dubbed the "Silver Grays" because of their leader Francis Granger's silvery mane, periodically made overtures to Know-Nothing partisans and to an extreme bloc of the Hunker Democrats now called the Hard Shells.

After the passage of the Kansas-Nebraska Act, antislavery advocates sought to create a fusion party out of all those opposed to the extension of slavery. Rudiments of the Republican Party emerged in New York State during the fall of 1855, about one year later than a similar effort in Wisconsin.[78] A fully functioning New York State Republican Party did not appear until the summer of 1856. By then, the state's Whig Party had broken up, with its losses going to the Know-Nothings and to the Republicans. Myron H. Clark, the last Whig governor of New York State, wrote to Seward on October 1, 1855:

> We have turned over a new leaf, in the political history of our State; and not only so, have commenced a new chapter. This point has been reached sooner than was anticipated a year ago. The Kansas and kindred outrages, together with the Know Nothing furor has had the effect to break up and scatter into fragments all the old political parties, while the same influences will effect a union of the honest and true men of all parties in opposition to both.[79]

Republican candidate John C. Frémont lost to Democrat James Buchanan in the 1856 national election, despite strong support for him in North Star Country and in the Northern states generally. Republicans soundly defeated Democrats in the heart of the old Burned-over District. Democratic operative Horatio Seymour informed William L. Marcy, "In central and western New York we were swept away by the popular feeling. In Oneida county we put our best speakers and most active men into the field, but the majority against us is nearly five thousand."[80]

Democrats did better in the eastern and southern parts of New York State, especially in the Irish wards of New York and Kings Counties. Millard Fillmore, candidate of the American (Know-Nothing) Party ran third in New York State in the presidential vote of 1856; thereafter the Know-Nothing frenzy dissipated. Free Soilers, and most voters who had supported the Liberty Party prior to its breakup, joined the Republican coalition.[81]

Gerrit Smith came late to endorsing the Republican Party. In 1858, he ran for governor of New York State on the People's State ticket. He espoused temperance and black freedom but polled only five thousand votes, an indication of how many of his old allies were now marching under the Republican banner.[82] Smith, ever the maverick, did not endorse the Republicans until after the Civil War began, but most North Star Country reformers already viewed the Republican Party as the best vehicle available for carrying forward the crusade for black freedom. David A. Ogden, not to be confused with Beriah Green's old nemesis David L. Ogden, understood something of the passion that most Northerners exhibited in their embrace of the Republicans. He grumped, "They would not reason or hardly think, but the Republican party moved forward in solo column like the crusaders of old excited, fanatical, abusive, & irresistible."[83]

Public excitement escalated after James Buchanan's inaugural address of March 4, 1857. In it, he lent support to the much-contested doctrine of "popular sovereignty" in the territories, but allowed that the Supreme Court should decide its constitutionality. Two days later, Chief Justice Taney, in a barely audible voice, read the majority's decision in the *Dred Scott v. Sanford* case. The Court ruled that Dred Scott, a slave who had been taken from Missouri to Illinois (a free state) and then to the Wisconsin territory, did not have the right to sue for his freedom because no black of slave ancestry could be a citizen. Six of the nine justices also ruled that the Missouri Compromise was unconstitutional, arguing that Congress had no power to keep slavery out of a territory.

These decisions outraged abolitionists throughout North Star Country. From his self-imposed isolation, Beriah Green spoke out to denounce the suffocating falsehoods of the Dred Scott decision as judicial lies proceeding from the "bloodless" lips of Taney.[84] Frederick Douglass condemned the Dred Scott ruling in a New York City speech before the AASS on May 11, 1857. "You will readily ask me how I am affected by this devilish decision—this judicial incarnation of wolfishness! My answer is, and no thanks to the slaveholding wing of the Supreme Court, my hopes were never brighter than now. I have no fear that the National Conscience will be put to sleep by such an open, glaring, and scandalous tissue of lies as that decision is, and has been, over and over, shown to be."[85]

The Dred Scott decision, Douglass's defiant reaction notwithstanding, cast a pall over African Americans everywhere. Chief Justice Taney's comment meant blacks had no rights that whites needed to respect. This confirmed the pessimism of the emigrationists. Throughout the turbulent 1850s, because slavery's defenders seemed to have the upper hand, African Americans, both fugitive and free, moved across the forty-ninth parallel to seek asylum in the British North American Provinces.

Most refugees from American slavery and racism settled in Canada West, which is present-day Ontario. Perhaps forty thousand fugitives crossed into Canada in the three decades before the American Civil War. Slavery had been abolished in Canada by the Emancipation Act of 1833, and runaways could not be extradited to the United States for "self-theft." Blacks in Canada could vote, own property, serve on juries, attend common schools, and establish their own churches and businesses. From the perspective of freedom seekers who passed through Upstate New York, Canada West was an extension of North Star Country.[86]

Samuel Ringgold Ward was known as a fearless opponent of the American spirit of caste and not as a man who would run from a fight. But he crossed over the forty-ninth parallel after the Jerry Rescue. Ward's sojourn in Canada West gave him the opportunity to survey conditions there and it put him in touch with others from North Star Country who had taken asylum under the British flag.

Ward and his family left Syracuse for the Canadian provinces in early October 1851. On October 16, he wrote to Henry Bibb from Beauharnois, Canada West, announcing his arrival. Bibb himself was an escapee (from Kentucky) and a leader in the Canadian black settlements. Ward's letter appeared in Bibb's *Voice of the Fugitive:*

> I am, like yourself, a refugee. President Fillmore has issued orders for the "arrest of all, without distinction of persons, who were engaged in, or directly or indirectly aided in, or encouraged" the rescue of poor Jerry. I am so much afraid that his Excellency's order would include me, and that trial would be conviction, and as the President has been kind enough to designate treason as the crime committed, I so much suspect that conviction would be suspension, that I have determined to let "catching" precede any other step. To insure this, I have come to Canada, and I am now on my way from Montreal to your part of the province, making, or intending to make, Toronto my head-quarters for the winter. In the spring I may be a candidate for hoeing in your garden.[87]

Ward made ends meet somehow, without having to put hoe in hand. He settled in Toronto and soon applied pen and voice to his old trade of abolitionist editor. He was quick to condemn racial discrimination wherever he encountered it. As Ward wrote to Bibb, "The boast of Englishmen, of their freedom from social negrophobia, is about as empty as the Yankee boast of democracy. In all this, I repeat, I am not at all disappointed; and I believe that a universal agitation, by the press and the tongue, in church and at the polls, will rid our beloved adopted country of this infernal curse. God forgive me when I shall refuse or neglect to do my humble part in this agitation!"[88]

Ward's move to Canada West brought him into contact with other abolitionists who had been schooled in the crucible of reform within Upstate New York. Hiram Wilson was a graduate of Oneida Institute, one of the Lane Rebels who left to study at Oberlin College, and a member of the abolitionist army known as the Seventy (those who planted the standard of immediatism after the formation of the AASS). During the early 1840s, Wilson moved to Canada West, where he worked among the fugitive colonies and helped to found schools. In 1842, with support from the American Missionary Association, Wilson helped to establish the British-American Institute at Dawn. The institute was a manual labor school for black children and adults, situated on three hundred acres. And it managed to fulfill its mission well, until discord over finances and management erupted. In 1850, Wilson left the school and the settlement and moved to St. Catharines. There he assisted Jermain Loguen when Loguen sought asylum after the Jerry Rescue.

In 1853, Ward made a six-week, 565-mile tour of the southwestern part of Canada West for the Anti-Slavery Society of Canada. Hiram Wilson hosted him at St. Catharines and introduced him to abolitionist and temperance allies as well as "gentlemen of prominence" in the region. Ward noted, with satisfaction and pride, "Our people in St. Catharines are not the poorest in the town, by a good deal. Many of them own little houses and lots, and enjoy a comfortable maintenance."[89]

Ward, unlike Loguen, decided to stay on in Canada after the furor over the Jerry Rescue died down. He maintained that American abolitionists should offer greater support for black Canadian settlements, in order to undercut the efforts to push African Americans toward Liberia. Ward boasted of the potential for Canada to become the "great moral lighthouse for the black people" north of the forty-ninth parallel.[90] He did his part to promote the image of an open and free society in Canada West by acting as an agent of the Anti-Slavery Society of Canada, which was founded in Toronto in 1851.

In March of 1853, Ward announced the publication of a second black newspaper in Canada West. The *Provincial Freeman* was published weekly in Toronto, although the first issue came from Windsor. Supporters of Henry Bibb's *Voice of the Fugitive* thought a second black newspaper in Canada West to be unnecessary, but Ward argued that the size of the black population now under the rule of British law made it useful to have "a family newspaper, uncommitted to any clique, sect or party."[91] Much of the work that went into producing the *Provincial Freeman* fell to others while Ward traveled to Britain in 1853 and spent two years raising funds for the fugitives that the Anti-Slavery Society of Canada aided. While in England, Ward published *Autobiography of a Fugitive Negro: His Anti-Slavery Labours in the United States, Canada and England*, which contains lengthy sections about Ward's reform career in North Star Country. It is an invaluable resource for understanding how black abolitionists helped reshape the culture of Upstate New York in its postrevivalist phase by providing a link to the fugitive settlements in Canada.[92]

Like Ward, William Wells Brown considered Canada West an extension of North Star Country. Brown was born around 1814 in Kentucky, escaped in 1834, made his way north, and found work on a Lake Erie steamboat. He helped fugitives who were fleeing to Canada, and in 1836 he settled in Buffalo. Active in the WNYASS, Brown took part in the National Convention of Colored Citizens which was held in Buffalo in 1843. In 1847, he moved to Boston, served as a lecturer for the Massachusetts Anti-Slavery Society, and published the narrative of his life. It sold five thousand copies in less than a year. Brown went to Great Britain in 1849 and stayed there during the controversy over the Fugitive Slave Law, lecturing and writing the novel *Clotel*. British abolitionists purchased his freedom in 1854.[93]

In the fall of 1861, Brown visited St. Catharines, a place he described as "the principal depot for fugitives slaves who escape by way of New York, Philadelphia, Harrisburg, and Buffalo." Only ten miles from the American side of the Niagara River, St. Catharines boasted a black population of nearly eight hundred. Brown was impressed with what he saw:

> THE COLORED SETTLEMENT. The colored settlement is a hamlet, situated on the outskirts of the village, and contains about 100 houses, 40 of which lie on North Street, the Broadway of the place. The houses are chiefly cottages, with from 3 to 6 rooms, and on lots of land of nearly a quarter an acre each. Most of the dwellings are wood-colored, only a few of them having been painted or whitewashed. Each family has a good garden, well-filled with vegetables, ducks, chickens, and a pig-pen, with at least one fat grunter getting ready for Christmas. The houses, with the lots upon which they stand, are worth upon an average of $500 each. Some of them have devoted a small part of the garden to the growth of the tobacco plant, which seems to do well. Entering North Street

at the lower end, I was struck with surprise at the great number of children in the street. On passing a gate, I inquired for Mr. ——; and a good-looking woman coming out of her door, informed me, and in return said, "Stranger here, I spose." "Yes, madam," I replied. "Come from behind the sun?" continued she. I replied I had. "Den as you is light and well dressed, I speck you is yer marster's son, ain't yer?" "No, I am my uncle's son,"[94] I said. "Well," she continued, "dat is strange—I never heard of any one being dar uncle's son before, but heaps of 'em who comes out here is dar marster's sons. De war makes good times now for our people, while de white folks is fightin', de colored people can run away. Heaps of 'em comes along now."

The houses in the settlement are all owned by their occupants, and from inquiry I learned that the people generally were free from debt. Out of the eight hundred in St. Catharines, about seven hundred of them are fugitive slaves. I met one old lady who escaped at the advanced age of eighty-five years—she is now *one hundred and four.*

Among them I found seventeen carpenters, four blacksmiths, six coopers, and five shoemakers. Two omnibuses and two hacks are driven by colored men. Not long since, a slave run away from Virginia, came here, and settled down; a few months after, his master "broke down," cheated his creditors, escaped to Canada, came and settled by the side of his former chattel. Their families borrow and lend now, upon terms of perfect equality.

SUNDAY AT THE SETTLEMENT. They have two churches, both on North Street, and in the centre of the settlement. In the morning I listened to a good discourse from Anthony Burns, formerly the chattel of Col. Suttle of Virginia, and made somewhat noted by being returned under the Fugitive Slave Law from Boston, in 1854. His congregation is not large. The Methodists have a very commodious church, finely finished, and have about 250 members. In the afternoon I listened to one of the "locals," the pastor being absent; in the evening I was invited to occupy the pulpit, and did so. Perfect order was observed all day on Sunday. Indeed, the settlement made a very neat and clean appearance. Taking an early walk, I found that during the previous night the street had been swept, and every door-yard looked as clean as a pin. Even the pigs that had been a little noisy on Saturday, seemed to understand that it was Sunday, and behaved themselves accordingly. The people appeared at church well dressed, many of them coming ten miles from the country.

The different styles of dress and the Southern look of some of the bonnets, contrasted strangely with the turban, the scuttle, the scoop, the glengarrie, and the jaunty Scotch cap, that I have seen upon the heads of the ladies of Toronto, the previous Sunday. Nevertheless, no matter how much out of fashion, these coverings were always clean and neat. The Methodists have a large Sabbath School, and there are several benevolent societies among the women; the only name of them that I learned, was the "Harrywines of Jerico." This village is the home of Hiram Wilson, long known as the fugitive's friend. I called at his residence, but he was from home—probably on some errand of mercy.[95]

Had Brown visited St. Catharines a few years earlier, he might have met the most famous helper of the fugitives who found their way to Canada. Indeed, some of the people she rescued and guided may have been among those that Brown met in 1861. Her name was Harriet Tubman. By listening to her story, and the stories of other Underground Railroad agents and conductors who were active in central and western New York State, one can better understand how the region earned the reputation of a place where fugitives were welcomed, harbored for a while, and then sent along freedom's road to Canada.

7. Moses and Her People

I do not know if the atmospheric conditions are such that, on a cloudless night, the North Star can be seen more clearly from the vantage point of Upstate New York than elsewhere north of the Mason-Dixon Line.[1] However, one does not have to dig deeply into the historical record to discover that the geographic location of the old Burned-over District made it one of the most heavily trafficked routes for fugitives who were using the North Star to guide them on the route to freedom. Canada, which was called the Promised Land, lay to the north and west of Upstate New York; Pennsylvania, where many friends of the fugitive lived, especially among the Quakers, lay to the south.[2]

Southerners accused Garrison and his allies of "running off" thousands of slaves each year. The abolitionists, eager to dispel the myth of the contented slave, probably inflated the number of escapees.[3] William C. Nell, who helped Douglass publish the *North Star,* was quick to claim the fugitives as abolitionist victories. "Abolitionists," he wrote in 1848, "are sometimes asked how many slaves they have emancipated. If the comparison between their labors and those of the Colonization Society is wanted, it may not be amiss to mention that since 1816 there have not been more than 6,000 transported to Africa, while Anti-Slavery has forwarded to Canada, by the Car of Freedom, near 20,000."[4] Whatever the volume of traffic on the "highway to heaven" or "the liberty line," which was more widely known as the Underground Railroad, Upstate New York served as a major escape route. Syracuse was home to Jermain Loguen, whom the *Weekly Anglo-African* newspaper called the Underground Railroad King.[5] Harriet Tubman was known as the Moses of her people. She was perhaps the most famous of the Underground Railroad conductors, and she made her home in

Auburn after 1857. The Burned-over District was well-positioned to receive runaways, harbor them for a while, and then pass them on to Canada.[6]

During the 1890s, William H. Siebert was gathering information about Underground Railroad operations in New York State for what became *The Underground Railway from Slavery to Freedom* (1898). At that time, there was yet alive a dwindling number of contemporaries of those who had actively helped runaways who came into North Star Country. For example, Carlton Rice, a close friend of Gerrit Smith, responded to Siebert's query with details regarding Smith's work as the station agent at Peterboro. "I remember," the elderly Rice wrote, from his home in Hamilton, "this R.R. organization was quite extensive and by it many slaves obtained their liberty."[7] Unfortunately, present-day researchers no longer have access to eyewitnesses such as Rice, and the search for reliable primary sources can be frustrating. However, there has been a revival of interest in the Underground Railroad in the last decade. The interest was stimulated by the enactment of Public Law 101-628 in 1990 (at the federal level), which required the National Park Service to conduct a study of the Underground Railroad and how best to commemorate it.[8] In addition, the New York State Freedom Trail Act of 1997 has sparked a renewal of interest in documenting and preserving the history of the Underground Railroad in all regions of the state.[9]

Sorting fact from fiction is a difficult task in any account of the Underground Railroad. So strong is the romance and drama of poorly clad runaways being hidden in alcoves and secreted behind trap doors that many houses between the borders of Pennsylvania and Canada are touted as having been stations. Regional lore celebrates stories of runaways taking refuge in barn lofts, caves, dry cisterns, tunnels, church basements, attic hideaways, crawl spaces under loose floorboards, and in assorted "hidey holes." The oral tradition has to be tested against archival materials. Carol Kammen reminds us of the pitfalls that come with doing research on the Underground Railroad: "About no other local topic, except possibly the weather, are there more legends, more hearsay or more dubious claims; about no other topic is there more to question."[10] Nevertheless, there is enough evidence from a wide variety of sources, including the testimony of some who were themselves fugitives, to demonstrate that Upstate New York deserves to be called North Star Country in a very real sense.[11]

The cast-iron roadside historical markers that were placed by the New

York State Education Department in the 1930s are now beginning to rust and show signs of neglect. Contemporary travelers can still find a few that tell of the connection of an Upstate New York building, perhaps an old house or church, with the Underground Railroad. One of these markers stands in the front yard of a home at Seneca Falls (Seneca County) and reads, "The Cobblestone or Ferry Farm, known during the Civil War as a station on the so-called Underground Railway. The trail of slaves to Canada was broken by bringing them across the lake from Union Springs, which was an ardent abolition Quaker village."[12] The Salisbury-Pratt homestead on Route 281, at Cold Brook Road in Cortland County, merited a sign from the education department in 1932. The marker reads: "Used before the Civil War as an 'Underground Station' where Oren Cravath sheltered and aided fugitive slaves on way to Canada." Cravath's son remembered that his father sent fugitives on to Syracuse and to the home of Horace White, a director of the New York Central Railroad, who provided them with tickets to take trains to Canada.[13]

In some places, roadside sign posts are all that remain to remind us of the location of an Underground Railroad site. This is the case with the marker honoring Catherine Harris. Harris was a free black woman who harbored runaways inside a blind attic in her house at the settlement known as Africa, in Jamestown.[14] The physical artifacts from which historians can reconstruct the story of the fugitive flight to freedom are fast disappearing. We tear down; we remodel; we rebuild. In 1964, while demolishing the Richards house in Skaneateles, workmen discovered a secret cubbyhole behind a second-floor closet. It contained a wool blanket and a vial of poison.[15] Those runaways who feared recapture more than death were known to have resorted to poison. But the discovery of a secret room or mysterious tunnel does not provide the kind of hard evidence necessary to confirm a link with the Underground Railroad. The historian must move cautiously across a landscape that is so rich in history when the subject is a secretive network designed to aid freedom-seekers whose legacy is not in physical landmarks but in personal courage and heroism.

Any telling of the story behind Freedom's Train must acknowledge that slaves ran away from their masters, or attempted to do so, long before there was a network of safe houses and abolitionists ready to assist. Some of the earliest runaway arrivals in the Upstate New York region found refuge among Native American peoples such as the Senecas and Onondagas, when New York was still under British colonial rule. Others sought asylum with the French in Canada. In 1705, afraid that runaways would provide the French and the Indians with military information, the New York State assembly decreed that any African American slave found, without a pass, more than forty miles north of Albany was subject to the death penalty.[16]

We do know that fugitives came into central and western New York State and were given aid prior to the inauguration of the abolitionist movement. Austin Steward tells us that, about the time of the collapse of the Carthage Bridge in Rochester (1820), a slave known to him only as Ellen was captured within the city. She was arrested under the provisions of the Fugitive Slave Act of 1793, brought before Judge Moses Chapin, put in custody, and escorted back to her owner by a company of the "Light Horse." Although Ellen had her friends, they were powerless to prevent the authorities from returning her to the South.[17]

In another escaped slave story that Steward relates, the outcome was quite different. Two bounty hunters came from Kentucky to Rochester to claim a black man known as Doctor Davis. "When it became generally known that Davis was arrested, and about to be tried," Steward remembered, "the excitement grew intense among all classes; but more particularly among the colored people." They crowded into the courtroom, distracted the officers, and hustled Davis out, in disguise. Davis tried to get to Buffalo on a packet boat, but he was recognized and cut his own throat with a pocket razor as authorities struggled to drag him off. The Kentuckian bounty hunters assumed that Davis was going to die and left Rochester. Instead, friends removed him to a place of safety, nursed him back to health, and helped him escape to Canada. Of Davis's fate, Steward added, "I have often heard from him during his residence in that country, where no slaves exist and he has done well, having quite an extensive practice in medicine, and lives in the quiet enjoyment of that liberty which he struggled so hard to obtain and came so near losing; yet, to this day he prefers death to Slavery."[18]

Mapping Underground Railroad lines in North Star Country is an imaginative enterprise because the available evidence is fragmentary and elusive. Nevertheless, it is believed that fugitives entered the Burned-over District by one of two principle routes. One route came from the east, along the

Erie Canal. The other route came up out of Pennsylvania and into New York's Southern Tier.[19]

The eastern route began down in Philadelphia, passed up through New York City, and then up along the Hudson River valley. Fugitives then traveled west along the Erie Canal and into the Mohawk River valley where they were sometimes directed to Whitesboro. Some students at Oneida Institute hid runaways in their dormitory rooms. Beriah Green took fugitives into his home. Before long, some Whitesboro residents began complaining that there were too many "strange" blacks around the village.[20]

On the route up from Pennsylvania, Elmira (Chemung County) played an important role as a forwarding station because of John W. Jones. After escaping from a plantation in Leesburg, Virginia, Jones came to Elmira in 1844. One historian has estimated that one thousand fugitives passed through Elmira between 1840 and 1860. Jones was chief station master from 1850 until the Civil War. He directly assisted hundreds of escapees, harboring more than thirty in his home at one time.[21] When the Northern Central Railroad began operations in 1850, it linked Elmira with the Niagara frontier via a transfer to the New York Central at Canandaigua. Jones could then send fugitives further north on the iron rails.

Perhaps it was a real depot, then, that Jones referred to in an 1860 letter he sent to William Still, the famous black agent and leader of Philadelphia's Vigilance Committee: "FRIEND WM. STILL:—All six came safe to this place. The two men came last night, about twelve o'clock; the man and the woman stopped at the depot, and went east on the next train, about eighteen miles, and did not get back til to-night, so that the two went this morning, and the four went this evening. 'O, old master don't cry for me, For I am going to Canada where colored men are free.'"[22]

Still kept a detailed record of passengers that he sent further north, a record that was published in 1872. In October of 1856, Jermain Loguen, signing himself "Agent of the Underground Rail Road," wrote to Still about a woman (Emeline Chapman, but using a pseudonym here) who had arrived at his house in Syracuse and wanted information about her husband and children:

> DEAR FRIEND STILL:—I write you for Mrs. Susan Bell, who was at your city some time in September last. She is from Washington city. She left her dear little children behind (two children). She is stopping in our city, and wants to

John W. Jones (1817–1900). Jones was born a slave in Loudon County, Virginia, but escaped in 1844 and settled in Elmira (Chemung County) where he became sexton of the First Baptist Church. Jones aided as many as eight hundred fugitives during his nine years as an agent of the Underground Railroad. He also had charge of the burial of Confederate prisoners who died in Elmira's Civil War prison. *Courtesy of the Chemung County Historical Society.*

hear from her children very much indeed. She wishes to know if you have heard from Mr. Biglow, of Washington city. She will remain here until she can hear from you. She feels very anxious about her children, I will assure you. I should have written before this, but I have been from home much of the time since she came to our city. She wants to know if Mr. Biglow has heard anything about her husband. If you have not written Mr. Biglow, she wishes you would. She sends her love to you and your dear family. She says that you were all kind to her, and she does not forget it. You will direct your letter to me, dear brother, and I will see that she gets it.[23]

William Still provided invaluable assistance to many of the freedom-seekers who were transferred into the care of North Star Country abolitionists.

Elmira was not the only community in the Southern Tier where runaways received a helping hand. In Owego, a house that was built around 1806 stands at the corner of Front and Ross Streets (351 Front Street). Fugitives who came up the Susquehanna River, which reaches its nothernmost point at Owego before making a bend eastward, sought shelter in this safe house. They entered this house, which was owned by Judge Farrington, via a tunnel approximately four hundred feet long, which led from the river's edge.[24] Another Underground Railroad stop can be found at Fairview Manor, in Big Flats, along Route 352 in Chemung County. Built by Clark Winans in 1812, the house has a fireplace with a removable fieldstone base. The base conceals the entrance to an underground cave outside the foundation, a place where fugitives could, and did, hide.[25]

The Cyrus Gates mansion is a Greek Revival structure on Nanticoke Road in the town of Maine (Broome County). It looks today much as it did when Gates outfitted a large room in his attic to harbor runaways. (One of the fugitives he assisted was Margaret Cruzer; she stayed to work for the Gates family and is buried in the family cemetery.) Unlike the Gates house, the Mecklenburg house is gone. Formerly, it belonged to an old Quaker settlement in the town of Hector (Schuyler County). It had twenty-three rooms, two of which were concealed under the main house. William Carmen, a devout Quaker, hid fugitives under the kitchen at the back of the house until it was safe to pass them on to another station.[26]

As fugitives made their way closer to the heart of the Burned-over District, they encountered others ready to help them. Louis Beers of Tompkins County hid runaways on his farm; they used secret rooms over a kitchen addition and hid in his barn. Members of the Presbyterian Church in Hornellsville (Steuben County) opened their homes to runaways. Marcus F. Lucas, an ex-slave and barber, took charge of the Corning section of Freedom's Train. His obituary read, "By disposition he was very gentle. But he was courageous too, and did not hesitate to give his escaping fellow-Negroes the hand he thought that they deserved."[27] In the Tompkins County village of Ithaca, St. James A.M.E.Z. Church was a well-frequented stop. Many fugitives found refuge in the basement of the church as well as in the homes of members and their pastor, Thomas James.[28]

The Reverend Samuel R. Ward actively assisted runaways during his pastorates in central New York. Of one freedom-seeker who braved the snow and the cold to find safety in Canada, Ward said, "Liberty was before him, and for it he could defy the frost."[29] Ward also visited Gerrit Smith frequently in Madison County, and he forwarded fugitives to Smith's Peterboro estate where they were secreted on the third floor of the mansion. At the Central New York Anti-Slavery Convention in 1839, Smith called upon abolitionists to give direct aid and comfort to fugitives.[30] Smith fed and clothed runaways and hosted some for long periods of time. Several former slaves decided to settle in Peterboro where they joined other African Americans associated with the Smith household and farm.

In 1841, Malvina ("Viney") Russell came to Peterboro with her parents and her four siblings. Gerrit Smith had purchased all of them from Samuel Worthington of Mississippi. Viney's mother, Harriet, had once been owned by Ann Carroll Fitzhugh (who married Gerrit Smith in 1822), back when the Fitzhugh family lived in Maryland. Smith commissioned James Canning Fuller, a Quaker abolitionist from Skaneateles, to go to Harrodsburg Springs, Kentucky, where the Worthington family spent the summers. Fuller's assignment was to purchase Harriet, her husband Samuel, and their five children. On August 7, 1841, a contract was signed for $3,500. On August 25, Smith wrote to Worthington to inform him that Harriet and her three daughters had arrived the previous Sunday evening "all in good health, save the baby—& that she is recovering from a bowel complaint." Harriet's husband Samuel and the two boys were expected in three to four weeks. Always the abolitionist, Smith counseled Worthington: "I wish you were as thoroughly persuaded, as Mrs. Smith and I am, of the inexpediency and sinfulness of slavery. Should you wash your hands of that stain, the conspicuous and influential example would tell much for the antislavery cause. Allow one, dear Sir, to ask you, in all the kindness of my heart, whether it is right to reduce immortal beings to property—whether it is wise and sane to live and die a slaveholder."[31]

On October 1, 1841, Gerrit and Ann Smith addressed a letter to Samuel and Harriet Russell outlining the arrangements that had been made for them and their family in Peterboro. I quote the letter in its entirety, for it reveals much about the relationship of the Smiths to the Russells.

Peterboro Oct. 1 1841

Samuel & Harriet Russell

Dear friends,

We have purchased your liberty and that of your five children, and paid $3500. In addition, we have paid several hundred dollars to defray your traveling expenses and those of the dear friend James C. Fuller; who went for you. We now consent to let you occupy until 1st April next without rent the small white house opposite Mr. Schofield's. The few articles of clothing which we let you have and of furniture which consist of beds, bedding, table, chairs etc etc—we give you. We also give you ten dollars in money. And now we say to you that this little outfit is all in the way of property, which you are to expect from us. For the means of your subsistence hereafter you are to look under God to your own industry & frugality & prudence. Our advice is that Samuel should seek employment immediately in one of the large towns in this vicinity—and that the two oldest girls be put into families where they will be fed & clothed & educated without any expense to yourselves. We beg you to be very industrious—and to lay up as much as you can of your earnings, so that you may in the course of four or five years be able to buy a little home for yourselves. But above all, we beg you to seek the salvation of your own and your children's souls, and to lay up treasures in Heaven.

Your friends
Gerrit Smith
Ann C. Smith

Gerrit appended a note that Samuel could use when meeting prospective employers. The recommendation praised the former slave as a man of "very-high character" who was both "honest & industrious." Given Samuel's experience as the head waiter and steward in the Worthington household, Smith recommended him for employment "as a coachman or as the head waiter in a private family or public house."[32]

Samuel sought employment in Syracuse. Mary, one of the older daughters, traveled to Michigan to live with James G. Birney and his second wife, Elizabeth Fitzhugh, sister of Gerrit Smith's wife. Another one of the Russell girls, Emily, found a home in the Smith mansion.[33] When the last Russell boy was born, Gerrit Smith suggested that he be named Freeborn; instead, the Russells named him Gerrit Smith Russell, after their benefactor.

After the death of their father, Samuel, in 1857, and the death of their mother, in 1886, Malvina kept house for her brother, William. Thereafter, she moved into the Smith mansion and served as personal nurse to Mrs. Gerrit Smith Miller, wife of grandson Gerrit Smith Miller, who occupied the house until it was destroyed by fire in 1936. In *The Borough of Peter* by Raymond P. Ernenwein, one can find a photograph of Malvina Russell.[34] She sits on the back stoop of the shiplap-sided mansion. She is shaded by a large climbing vine, symbolic of the shelter she found when she was brought to Gerrit Smith's house as a small child.

A year after the Russells came to Peterboro, a visitor from Jamaica wrote about Gerrit Smith's hospitality: "That home of yours is a snare to a stranger. You throw around it such an atmosphere of affection that the wight [human being] must be heartless, as well as luckless that does not fall in love there—at least with yourself and family."[35] Several of the black families who settled in Peterboro ended up working for the Smith and Miller families, either in the house or on the farm, for more than three generations.[36]

The Sage of Peterboro, as Smith came to be called, received many letters asking for assistance. Abolitionists wrote to him with the intent of forwarding refugees from the South to Madison County. Southerners with uneasy consciences, and some who were simply anxious to rid themselves of "troublesome property," corresponded with Smith. Ezekiel Birdseye of Newport, Tennessee, badgered Smith for money so that Birdseye could purchase the freedom of slaves and send them north. In one instance, Smith sent $450 to Birdseye.[37] Samuel R. Ward sought Smith's assistance after the Supreme Court ruled—in *Prigg v. Pennsylvania* (1842)—that states had no power

Malvina ("Viney") Russell (1840–1925). Viney is shown on the back stoop of the Smith-Miller mansion. She was a babe in arms when Gerrit Smith purchased her family's freedom in 1841. The family was purchased from a Mississippi slaveholder to whom they had been sold by one of Smith's wife's relatives. Malvina lived in Peterboro for the rest of her life and did domestic work for the Smith and Smith-Miller families. *Courtesy of the Madison County Historical Society.*

over cases arising from the Fugitive Slave Act of 1793. Believing that all was now made easier for kidnappers, Ward wrote from South Butler to ask for help with disposing of his property and a horse said to be worth $70. This disposition would allow him to move to Keystono, Canada.[38]

In a most peculiar affair, Congressman John T. Mason of Virginia saw a report in a Utica newspaper about four slaves who had run away from him and stopped at Smith's home on their way to Canada. Curious to know, Mason wrote to ask Smith why slaves, whom he claimed not to have abused, stole away. On the back of Mason's letter, Smith scribbled, "They fled because they feared Mason's financial status might force their being sold."[39] In November 1842, Mason wrote to Smith again, asking where a letter might reach an aged former slave, Dorsey Ambush, who had escaped seven years earlier. Mason pledged to free Dorsey upon Dorsey's return, saying that he was sorry to lose an old friend. Dorsey distrusted Mason and decided to remain in Canada until Mason sent manumission papers. Frustrated, Mason resolved to have no further contact with his former slave.[40] The runaway, whose full name was Clement Dorsey Ambush, wrote to Smith in June 1843, asking for advice and referring to a letter he had received from Mason.[41]

In May 1844, Jesse Walton, a slaveholder from Augusta, Georgia, wrote to Smith and reminded him of a letter Walton had sent in 1838, a letter in which Walton had sought the abolitionist's assistance. The Southerner wished to free his slaves and had entrusted the original letter to a Quaker silversmith to carry to Smith. However, the silversmith had been intercepted and a $500 reward had then been posted for the capture of Walton. By 1844, Walton, who was still determined to cut his losses, contacted Smith directly. Perhaps as a means of getting Smith's attention, Walton mentioned that he shared the Upstate New Yorker's interest in the dietary regimen touted by Sylvester Graham and that he had not eaten "flesh meat" in six years.[42]

When Smith was ready to direct fugitives to their next stop, he had several options. Sometimes Smith entrusted freedom-seekers to the care of Dr. Alexander Ross of Toronto, Canada. Other times, he forwarded them to Oswego and to other points on Lake Ontario from which boats departed for Canada.

Oswego County was a lively place of abolitionist activity and contained several important stops on the Underground Railroad. John B. Edwards, Smith's business agent in Oswego, kept his employer informed about local Underground Railroad activity and aided in runaways' safe passage and employment. On July 20, 1852, he wrote to Smith, "I was not before aware that you were expecting 40 to 50 colored people from New Orleans. I will do the best I can to get them employment." Edwards added, "The fugitive slave, Dorsey, came to me today with your letter. I have put him aboard of a vessel bound for Canada and gave him $1.00."[43] On March 19, 1860, Edwards informed Smith, "The young colored man that was at your house last week arrived at my house last evening, I shall keep him a few days to recuperate."[44]

Oswego's profugitive climate was due to the presence of abolitionists—in the municipality and the county—such as Orson Ames, Asa Wing, James C. Jackson, Edwin W. Clarke, and Tudor E. Grant.[45] Grant, a leader of the African American community, listed his birthplace as Maryland in the federal census of 1850, but in the 1855 New York State census, he gave his birthplace as Westchester County, New York. Perhaps this was a reflection of the precautions African Americans in North Star Country took after the passage of the Fugitive Slave Law in 1850.[46] Favored with a lakeside location, Oswego provided ready access to Canada and to freedom. The same was true of other communities along Lake Ontario. Captain Horatio N. Throop lived in a cobblestone house at Pultneyville (Wayne County) and commanded a steamer, *Express*, from 1839 to 1842. When a conductor brought runaways to him, Throop responded to the conductor's declaration of "I have some passengers for you" with the code "My boat runs for passengers."[47]

Gerrit Smith could also forward fugitives to Jermain Loguen in Syracuse. Onondaga County, as fellow Underground Railroad agent Eber M. Pettit testified, had the reputation of being "the great central depot of the institution in this State" because of the work of Jermain Loguen and his supporters. "He is respected," Pettit wrote, "and beloved by all classes in Syracuse, where he has lived many years, and no other man could have done so much for the U. G. R. R. as he did."[48]

Loguen reciprocated in kind through a letter to the public, which was placed in *Frederick Douglass' Paper*, on June 8, 1855. Of those in Syracuse and vicinity who gave aid and comfort to runaways, he said, "When such as these leave their warm beds in the coldest nights of a winter like the past, to lead these shivering and stricken ones to the Underground Railroad Depot, where I and my family are found, I am encouraged to believe that the prowling man-hunter better not dwell in or pass incog [sic] through our blessed little city."

Loguen then tempered his warm words with an admonition. Friends of the slave had to do more than deliver captives from whips and chains. "Who, then, in and about Syracuse will take into their shops and on their farms our coloured youth, and discipline and educate them to the industry and arts of life, as white children are educated?" Loguen acknowledged that "the schools and many churches in Syracuse are thrown open to us and our children," but he called for more—for open access to the mechanical and agricultural fields and for opportunities for both boys and girls to learn a suitable trade. All those willing to assist were asked to leave their names "with Abner Bates, or at Wynkoop & Bro. Bookstore, or at the office of the Mayor of this city."[49] Loguen's letter asked central New Yorkers to go the extra mile; how they responded to the continuing presence of African Americans in their midst would speak volumes about their moral convictions.

Loguen, having been a fugitive himself, knew how desperately runaways needed a place to rest as they made the long trek to freedom. Born around 1813 in Davidson County, Tennessee, Loguen escaped during 1834 by stealing a horse named Rock and making his way to Canada. After farming for a few years, Loguen moved to Rochester in 1837. There he worked as a hotel waiter until he enrolled at Oneida Institute. While studying at the institute under Beriah Green's guidance, Loguen started a Sunday school for African American children in nearby Utica. He married Caroline Storum of Busti, New York, in 1840. A year later they moved to Syracuse, where they found a black population of around two hundred in a community of approximately seven thousand.

Loguen taught school and became a licensed preacher of the A.M.E.Z. Church, serving congregations in Syracuse, Bath, Ithaca, and Troy. However, his vocation was as much abolitionist activist as it was preacher of the Gospel. When the flow of fugitives through Syracuse grew too large for Samuel J. May to handle by himself, he asked Loguen for assistance. (May was the Unitarian clergyman and Garrisonian who had come from New

England in 1845 to serve Syracuse's Church of the Messiah.) May, who was known as the gentle humanitarian, served as the principal agent of the Syracuse station until Loguen took on the role.[50]

Almost from the day he arrived in Syracuse, Loguen had been helping runaways. He worked full-time as general agent of Syracuse's Fugitive Aid Society beginning in 1857. His home at 293 East Genesee Street served as the official Underground Railroad station for the city. Notices appeared in the local press which advertised his agency:

> FUGITIVE AID SOCIETY.—A large and interesting quarterly meeting of the Executive Committee of this Society was held last Friday, at their rooms. The President, Rev. S. J. May, in the Chair. The report of the General Agent, Rev. J. W. Loguen, in regard to the Underground Railroad and its working at present, was cheering and encouraging. This road was never doing a better business than at this time. All wishing to take stock in this valuable and mysterious Railroad will do well by calling on the Agent or some other members of the Society soon. The stock is rising.[51]

Loguen placed letters in the Syracuse newspapers, seeking employment for fugitives in area shops and farms. In 1859, thirty of the fugitives for whom Loguen had found jobs chose to express their appreciation by donating money to the Fugitive Aid Society and by giving personal gifts to Loguen and his wife, Caroline. (The gifts included a butter knife and an engraved sugar spoon.)

Money, food, clothing, and other forms of assistance came not only from local abolitionists but from sources outside the city. The Irish Ladies Antislavery Society (Great Britain) sent Loguen $72.79 in February of 1859.[52] Loguen published his calling card in the local newspapers:

> TO THE FRIENDS OF HUMANITY:—The entire care of the Fugitives who may stop at Syracuse, for comfort and assistance, having been devolved upon me by the Fugitive Aid Society, I hereby give notice that I shall devote myself assiduously to the duties I have undertaken to discharge. I must depend for the support of my family, and of the operations I am to conduct, upon the liberality of the friends of freedom. I shall gratefully receive money, clothes and provisions.—I will make faithful use of the same, and will report semi-annually (in *Frederick Douglass' Paper,* and the Syracuse *Standard* and *Journal,*) the amounts that I have received, and of the numbers of Fugitives that I have sheltered, and have found homes for. Meanwhile, and at all times, my accounts will be open for the inspection of any friends of the cause. Syracuse, Sept. 17, 1857.[53]

Samuel J. May (1797–1871). A Garrisonian disciple and Unitarian clergyman, Samuel J. May settled in Syracuse during 1845 and championed nonviolent abolitionism. He gave support to freedom-seekers fleeing slavery, participated in the rescue of William "Jerry" Henry, and was active in many reform movements both before and after the Civil War. *Courtesy of the Onondaga Historical Association.*

In 1859, Loguen provided some details of how he and Caroline helped fugitives for publication in *Douglass' Monthly:*

> The slaves come to us with their frostbitten feet, and then we go to work to get them healed. Sometimes we have to keep them for weeks and months—we have two mothers, with a child each, to care for with us at present. Their husbands were sold, and they made their escape and came to us some months ago. We have a father that has just got to us with his little daughter about three years old; its mother was taken from it, and the father then ran away with the child, so that man thieves could not get it. We are caring for them too at present. It takes about all the time of myself and family to see after their wants; I mean the fugitives. We have so much to do in the night that some nights we get little or no sleep. They often come sick, and must be cared for forthwith.[54]

Frederick Douglass has left an interesting testimonial to the sacrifices made by the Loguen family. In 1857, Douglass was returning to Rochester by train and stopped in Syracuse. He had barely disembarked when he encountered a group of nine fugitives who wanted to known where "one Mr. Loguen" resided.

> The writer had some curiosity to see how these weary travelers, without money, and without friends, could be received by the family aroused from sweet sleep, at this late hour of a stormy night. We had scarcely struck the door when the manly voice of Loguen reached our ear. He knew the meaning of the rap, and sung out "hold on." A light was struck in a moment, the door opened and the whole company, the writer included, were invited in. Candles were lighted in different parts of the house, fires kindled, and the whole company made perfectly at home. The reception was a whole souled and manly one, worthy of the noble reputation of Brother Loguen, and showed that he remembers his brethren in bonds as bound with them.[55]

One of the most poignant accounts of Loguen's efforts to aid fugitives comes to us from a letter written by L. D. Mansfield, a professor at Auburn Theological Seminary. Mansfield wrote to William Still on December 15, 1856:

> DEAR BRO. STILL:—A very pleasant circumstance has brought you to mind, and I am always happy to be reminded of you, and of the very agreeable, though brief acquaintance which we made at Philadelphia two years since. Last Thursday evening, while at my weekly prayer meeting, our exercises were interrupted by the appearance of Bro. Loguen, of Syracuse, who had come on with Mrs. Harris in search of her husband, whom he had sent to my care three weeks

before. I told Bro. L. that no such man had been at my house, and I knew nothing of him. But I dismissed the meeting and went with him immediately to the African Church, where the colored brethren were holding a meeting. Bro. L. looked through the door, and the first person whom he saw was Harris. He was called out, when Loguen said, in a rather reproving and exciting tone, 'What are you doing here; didn't I tell you to be off to Canada? Don't you know they are after you? Come get your hat, and come with us, we'll take care of you.' The poor fellow was by this time thoroughly frightened, and really thought he had been pursued. We conducted him still under the impression that he was pursued and that we were conducting him to a place of safety, or were going to box him up to send him to Canada. Bro. L. opened the door of the parlor, and introduced him; but he was so frightened that he did not know his wife at first, until she called him James, when they had a very joyful meeting. She is now a servant in my family, and he has work, and doing well, and boards with her. We shall do all we can for them, and teach them to read and write, and endeavor to place them in a condition to take care of themselves. Loguen had a fine meeting in my Tabernacle last night, and made a good collection for the cause of the fugitives.[56]

Loguen is said to have helped fifteen hundred fugitives during his years as superintendent of Syracuse's Underground Railroad station.

Due in no small part to Loguen's labors, Syracuse became known as the most openly abolitionist city in the nation. Some even called it "the Canada of the United States."[57] Caroline Loguen's services to those traveling on the Emancipation Train ought not to be overlooked. While her husband worked in the public eye, Caroline aided fugitives in a private way, opening her home to them, caring for their personal needs, and offering them food and a place to rest.

Rochester and Monroe County, Frederick Douglass's operational center, held many friends of the fugitive.[58] When Wilbur H. Siebert compiled his pioneering history of the Underground Railroad, which was published in 1898, he still had access to individuals who were personally familiar with its operations, or who were but one generation removed. In his book, Siebert included a "Directory of the Names of Underground Railroad Operators" and organized the 3,200 entries by state and county. Of the twenty counties that Siebert surveyed in New York State, Monroe County had thirty-six names of activists; Wyoming County, its nearest rival, had thirteen.[59]

The city of Rochester was critical to Monroe County's concentration of abolitionist support. The city's first antislavery society was organized in 1838. Lindley Mott Moore, the Quaker teacher, was its first president. Frederick Douglass attributed the growth of abolitionist sentiment in Rochester to the labors of Myron Holley. Holley, as was discussed earlier, was one of the founders of the Liberty Party and the publisher of the *Rochester Freeman*. Holley died in 1843, four years before Douglass settled in Rochester.

Although Douglass was technically beyond the reach of slave catchers (his freedom had been purchased in 1846), he put himself at risk by opening his home at No. 4 Alexander Street (later 297 Alexander, just west of East Avenue) to fugitives. Historian William McFeely writes that for most slaves, "The route to liberation led due north, and Frederick Douglass chose the richest image of the resolute, hopeful trek of runaways to freedom when he named his new anti-slavery newspaper, *North Star*."[60]

Douglass's ability to shelter fugitives improved in 1852 when he purchased a farm about two miles outside Rochester's center. McFeely writes of Douglass's new residence at the South Avenue address, near present-day Highland Park: "The farm's roadway connected with the dirt road leading into the city from the southeast, and soon the Douglass place became a reliable stop for fugitive slaves making their way to Canada. There, in the house or the barn, runaways could spend their last night in the slaveholding United States or wait to be taken by wagon down-town after dark, to be hidden in E. C. William's sail loft or Isaac Post's barn on Sophia Street."[61] While Douglass was critical to the Underground Railroad in Rochester, he did not work alone. In his third and last autobiography, Douglass wrote,

> The underground railroad had many branches, but that one with which I was connected had its main stations in Baltimore, Wilmington, Philadelphia, New York, Albany, Syracuse, Rochester, and St. Catharines (Canada). It is not necessary to tell who were the principal agents in Baltimore; Thomas Garret was the agent in Wilmington; Melloe McKim, William Still, Robert Purvis, Edward M. Davis and others, did the work in Philadelphia; David Ruggles, Isaac T. Hopper, Napolian, and others, in New York City; the Misses Mott and Stephen Myers were forwarders from Albany; Revs. Samuel J. May and J. W. Loguen were the agents in Syracuse; and J. P. Morris and myself received and dispatched passengers from Rochester to Canada, where they were received by Rev. Hiram Wilson. When a party arrived in Rochester it was the business of Mr. Morris and myself to raise funds with which to pay their passage to St. Catharines, and it is due to truth to state that we seldom called in vain upon whig or democrat for

help. Men were better than their theology, and truer to humanity than to their politics, or their offices.[62]

No fugitives were recaptured in the Flour City during the period that Douglass was a station master.

Curiously, William Still made no mention of Douglass in his 800-page account of the Underground Railroad, a classic which was published in 1872. In 1893, Douglass wrote to William H. Siebert to say that Still "omitted to mention my name in his book, as one of the Conductors on the Underground Railroad" because Douglass had criticized Still for "his conduct in taking from the fugitives who passed through his hands."[63]

The couple who had helped persuade Douglass to remove to Upstate New York—Isaac Post, a Quaker druggist, and his wife, Amy—provided a helping hand to many refugees at their Plymouth Avenue home in Rochester. Amy Post recalled that "the most we ever had at one time was twelve." She estimated that 150 fugitives passed through Rochester each year. Amy Post testified, "Many a time I have gone out to the barn after dark with a basket of food and frightened men crept out of the hay to take it."[64] In a retrospective account of the Underground Railroad, Amy Post wrote of the heroism and constant help rendered to fugitives by the African Americans living in Rochester: "They were always ready to fight for a fugitive slave, and, if they failed to rescue one here, they would form a company of stalwart men and follow the party, spy out where they were stopping for the night, and, generally finding the watchman asleep, they only failed once to return in triumph with their rescued brother or sister."[65]

Douglass also had assistance from Jacob P. Morris, an operator of several barber shops, and from William S. Falls, the production foreman for the *Daily Democrat.*[66] It is said that fugitives were taken to the foot of Buell Street and put on English steamboats bound for the Queen's dominion. When the ships were three miles out on Lake Ontario, they would hoist the British flag, a symbol that all on board were now beyond the reach of the American slave catchers.

Other Rochester sites were associated with the Underground Railroad: the A.M.E.Z. Church at 42 Favor Street, where Douglass began publishing the *North Star* in 1847; George Avery's store at 12 Buffalo Street (now Main Street); and the barn of Samuel D. Porter on South Fitzhugh Street. Porter served as the secretary of Rochester's Anti-Slavery Society and was the Liberty Party candidate for mayor.[67] The house of portrait painter Grove S. Gilbert at 40 Grieg Street near Clarissa, the Clark house on Monroe Avenue, the Hargous house at 52 Main Street, and the Isaac Moore house at 1496 Culver Road, are all said to have had Underground Railroad connections.

William C. Bloss, a temperance advocate, promoter of the free school law, and editor of the *Rights of Man,* was a well-known station master in the Rochester area. Bloss's son, Joseph Blossom Bloss, in recalling his boyhood, described runaways that arrived in the night, were fed and clothed, and were then taken on to another safe house. On one occasion, the elder Bloss led young Joseph to the woodshed on their property at East Avenue. There hid an escaped woman awaiting safe passage to Canada. William Bloss asked his young son to lay his fingers on the deep whip-welts in the woman's back and said, "I am subject to a fine of $1,000 and an imprisonment of six months for giving this woman a crust of bread, a cup of water—for not arresting her, or for in any way aiding her to escape from her master. But I shall disobey this law, and when there is another law like this in the land, do you disobey it."[68]

The Thomas Warrant homestead, on East Henrietta Road beside the Barge Canal, also belonged to a network of safe houses in the Rochester area. Warrant was a coppersmith, farmer, and devout Baptist. At night he would hide runaways under a wagonload of hay and drive them to stations near Lake Ontario.[69]

Some fugitives stayed out at Frederick Douglass's house on the outskirts of Rochester (off present-day South Avenue). If he wanted to forward them to someone in town, he would send a note to that person by means of one of his children. "Two weary people here; need transportation in the morning." Sometimes the missive bore the initials D.F., which was "a perfunctory effort at disguise," says Douglass's biographer McFeely.[70] About his involvement with Freedom's Train in Rochester, Douglass himself said:

> On one occasion I had eleven fugitives at the same time under my roof, and it was necessary for them to remain with me until I could collect sufficient money to get them to Canada. It was the largest number I ever had at any one time, and I had some difficulty in providing so many with food and shelter, but, as may well be imagined, they were not very fastidious in either direction, and were well content with very plain food, and a strip of carpet on the floor for a bed, or a place on the straw in the barn.[71]

AFRICAN CHURCH,
ROCHESTER, NY.

A.M.E.Z. Church, Rochester. Organized by the Reverend Thomas James in the early 1830s, the congregation that built this structure on Favor Street welcomed abolitionist lecturers and runaways seeking shelter. Frederick Douglass published the *North Star* in the church's basement for a brief time. *Courtesy of the Rochester Public Library.*

Fugitives also made their way directly to the offices of the *North Star* in the Talman Building on Buffalo Street. Early morning arrivals could be found sitting on the steps until opening time. A present-day historic marker in front of the Reynolds Arcade on Main Street (formerly Buffalo Street) calls attention to the location of Douglass's offices in downtown Rochester.[72]

While Douglass was routing runaways from Rochester north to the shores of Lake Ontario, station masters in the southwestern corner of the state used the far western section of the Underground Railroad, sending fugitives toward the Niagara River for passage to Canada. One such station master was Eber M. Pettit.

Pettit was a descendent of French Huguenots who had suffered persecution in Europe on religious grounds. He headed rescue efforts that were made from his farm near Versailles, in Cattaraugus County. In 1868, the *Fredonia Censor* began to publish a series of articles in which Pettit recounted how he, in concert with other friends of the fugitive, helped runaways. Willard McKinsty, president of Fredonia's Historical Society, obtained Pettit's permission to compile the sketches into a small volume in 1879. The volume is dedicated to Frederick Douglass, who acknowledged the honor by writing, "The author of this book is well remembered by me as one of those who were true and faithful in the days that tried men's souls."[73]

Pettit's serialized remembrances were originally published in the *Censor* under the pen name of Conductor. In one of the articles, he tells of visiting Attica (Wyoming County) and meeting Charles O. Shepard, who showed him a box fitted inside a gardener's market wagon. A Mr. Barbour of Onondaga County had, but a few days earlier, rescued a woman named Statie and her daughter, Lila, by secreting them under straw in the box and then spiriting them away from Virginia. Pettit describes how Barbour managed to get his charges into North Star Country:

> When out of sight of settlements, they sometimes went out and picked berries, and when safe to do so they walked about in the night. He stopped at taverns or farm houses, leaving the wagon in the barn. The wagon was what is called in that country a "Jersey wagon," having six posts and covered with oil cloth. When inquired of as to the contents of the box he said he had been peddling clocks, and was going home to York State, and as he drove a splendid team his word was taken without examination.[74]

Shepard then took mother and child to Attica. Soon, slave catchers showed up. Attica's postmaster warned the Southerners that recapture would come at high cost because a crowd that was sympathetic to the fugitives had gathered in the village. Rebuffed, the slave hunters "mounted their horses and rode silently out of town, the people making no demonstration until they were on the bridge, when a shout, a cheer, three times three, seemed to put new life into their horses, and they were soon out of sight."[75]

Buffalo and the Niagara frontier area deserve additional comment in this sampling of Freedom's Train in North Star Country. Efforts to identify, document, and mark Underground Railroad sites along the Niagara River have been stimulated by state and federal initiatives to develop freedom trails.[76]

One of the key figures in the region was William Wells Brown; he ran a rescue operation out of Buffalo. After escaping slavery in Missouri around 1840, Brown dedicated himself to helping others find freedom. In 1842, over a period of seven months, he personally conducted sixty-nine fugitives to freedom in Canada. In 1843, he visited the Canadian settlement at Malden where he found seventeen individuals whom he had assisted on the Underground Railroad.[77]

Many of the Buffalo stories about fugitives center on the Michigan Street Baptist Church, a historic structure that was built about 1845. For much of the twentieth century, it was known as the Michigan Avenue Baptist Church. Cubbyholes in its basement may have been used as hiding places. The church also played a key role in black communal protest when abolitionists such as William Wells Brown and Frederick Douglass spoke in Buffalo.[78]

Some freedom-seekers crossed over the Niagara River at Buffalo and found refuge in present-day Ontario. Ontario's Niagara Economic and Tourism Corporation has developed a freedom trail to celebrate the African-Canadian connection to the Underground Railroad.[79] Others chose to risk a stay in Buffalo.

On October 1, 1847, two Kentuckians arrived in Buffalo. They were searching for Christopher Webb, a fugitive who was then working as a waiter at the Gothic Hall Saloon. While threatening to kill anyone who interfered, the two seized Webb, with the intent of taking him back into slavery. Webb managed to escape, and his would-be captors were charged with false imprisonment. Now it was their turn to flee. Pursued by the deputy sheriff

Michigan Street Baptist Church (formerly Michigan Avenue Baptist Church), Buffalo. Built in c. 1845 by an African American congregation, this structure is now listed on the National Register of Historic Places. Governor George Pataki signed the New York State Freedom Trail Act at this church in 1997. *Courtesy of Buffalo and Erie County Historical Society.*

and, as Buffalo's *Commercial Advertiser* observed, "people of various hues," the Southerners absconded. The incident, as was reported in the *Daily Courier,* "caused much excitement for a while, especially among our colored citizens and abolitionists."[80]

The term *Underground Railroad* was a figurative reference to the loosely organized network of people willing to shelter and aid runaways. Some fugitives who passed through North Star Country used the iron rails in a literal way. They were helped by Horace White of Syracuse, one of the directors of the New York Central Railroad. Some years after White's death, his son, Andrew D. White, divulged the following story to Siebert:

> I met an old "abolitionist" of Syracuse, who said to me that he had often come to my father's house, rattled at the windows, informed my father of the passes he needed for fugitive slaves, received them through the window, and then

departed, nobody else being the wiser. On my asking my mother, who survived my father several years, about it, she said, "Yes, such things frequently occurred, and your father, if he was satisfied of the genuineness of the request, always wrote off the passes and handed them out, asking no questions."[81]

Andrew D. White, who was to become Cornell University's first president in 1866, shared his father's profugitive sentiments. The younger White applauded William "Jerry" Henry's rescuers.

Many more friends of the fugitive existed throughout North Star Country than I have focused on here. Some, like Jermain Loguen, were well-known abolitionists who conducted their Underground Railroad activity openly. Others did so entirely in secret. We may never identify everyone who provided a helping hand; however, one name is so frequently attached to Freedom's Train that it has become symbolic of the entire enterprise of aiding runaways.

Harriet Tubman did not settle in Upstate New York until 1857, but she had been escorting fugitives through the area since her own escape years earlier. She is now remembered as North Star Country's most notable conductor.

Harriet was born in Dorchester County, Maryland, around 1820. She spent her childhood years on plantations near Bucktown, not far from present-day Cambridge, Maryland. Known first as Araminta Ross, she was one of the eleven children born to Benjamin Ross and Harriet (Greene) Ross. When Harriet was about thirteen she was working as a field hand. An overseer, in an attempt to stop another slave from escaping, threw a two-pound iron weight that struck her on the head. As a consequence, the woman who was later called Black Moses suffered from narcolepsy, a kind of stupor or lethargy which would come on unpredictably for the rest of her life. During conversation or work, she would fall asleep, then awaken and resume her activity. The blow from the weight left a permanent indentation in Harriet's skull, which was visible many years later.

Despite this injury, Harriet developed a strong physique. Less than five feet tall but with a muscular build, she excelled at physical labor and often performed astonishing feats of strength. Her father was a timber inspector who was responsible for cutting and hauling lumber to Baltimore's shipyards. On occasion, Harriet helped him with this work, and she could cut half a cord of wood in one day.

In 1844, she married a free black man named John Tubman. Some sources claim that she was forced into marriage, but historian Earl Conrad argues that, because of her injury, Harriet was not "considered a breeder type."[82] Conrad speculates that she was therefore allowed to choose a free black as her husband. She and John Tubman had no children.

When Harriet learned that she was in danger of being sold, in 1849, she decided to escape north toward Pennsylvania and freedom. It was too perilous to divulge her intentions to her family, so she sang one of the old spirituals. Her farewell song was long remembered in the slave quarters. Like many of the spirituals, it bore a double meaning:

> When dat ar old chariot comes,
>   I'm gwine to lebe you,
> I'm boun' for de promised land,
> Frien's, Im qwine to lebe you.
> I'm sorry, frien's, to lebe you,
>   Farewell! Oh, farewell!
> But I'll meet you in de mornin',
> When you reach de promised land;
>   On de oder side of Jordan,
> For I'm boun' for de promised land.[83]

Knowing little about the geography of the promised land, Tubman did what so many others had done: she followed the North Star. Taking advantage of the inlets and waterways, the thick brush and tangled grasses, Harriet made her way up the Eastern Shore of Maryland, along the Chesapeake. At one point, a white woman who knew of Harriet's desire to be free helped her by directing her to Wilmington, Delaware.

Once Harriet was in Wilmington, she sought out the famous Quaker agent Thomas Garret. Although he operated a shoe shop, he devoted much of his time to assisting fugitives. Garret forwarded her to Philadelphia, where she found work. In later years, Garret often helped Harriet to bring slaves up out of the House of Bondage. Garret described one of these transactions in a letter to J. Miller McKim, a fellow abolitionist, which was written on December 29, 1854: "We made arrangements last night, and sent away Harriet Tubman, with six men and one woman to Allen Agnew's, to be forwarded across the country to the city. Harriet, and one of the men had worn their shoes off their feet, and I gave them two dollars to help fit them out, and directed a carriage to be hired at my expense, to take them out, but do not yet know the expense."[84] One wonders how many pairs of shoes Tubman wore out during the decade or so that she served as America's most celebrated conductor on the Underground Railroad.

Tubman is credited with as many as nineteen trips into slavery's domain, and with bringing out an estimated three hundred individuals. She made eleven of these trips between 1850 and 1857, using St. Catharines (Canada) as a place of rest and refuge between her raids upon the South. In 1850, she brought out her sister and one of her brothers, as well as others. In 1851, she managed to get as far south as the Bucktown area, only to discover that her husband had married another woman and had no desire to leave. In December of the same year, she brought out a group of eleven slaves, including another one of her brothers and his wife.

Harriet's modus operandi was a silent invasion of the South, a quick gathering of her "passengers," and a quiet withdrawal that did not alarm the authorities. Often, she appeared mysteriously, in the dark of night, at the door of slave cabins along Maryland's Eastern Shore. Word of her impending arrival would spread on the slave grapevine, and bands of trembling fugitives would await their deliverer. No exact map can be made of her routes of invasion and retreat, although after gathering up her railroad passengers, her first destination was often Wilmington or the Quaker settlements of southeastern Pennsylvania. She appeared to have an intuitive sense of where to find food and shelter on her long perilous journeys. Often, her only guide was the North Star.

Tubman's motto was "Keep Going." Crying infants were given opium to make them fall asleep. Adults carried children in baskets. When her charges complained of being tired or hungry, the Moses of Her Race—to use the inscription on the highway historical marker at the Harriet Tubman Home in Auburn—said, "If you want a taste of freedom, Keep Going." A natural navigator, with an almost mystical ability to read the landscape, Harriet deeply trusted in the providence of God. She prayed for divine guidance and had visions and dreams in which portents of future events came to her. She addressed her God on intimate terms, calling her conversations "chats" with the Lord.

Tubman herself was fearless. She carried a pistol for those times when reluctant and petrified fugitives needed to be "encouraged" to continue putting one foot ahead of the other. William Still, who knew her well, has left us a fascinating word portrait of this remarkable woman:

> The idea of being captured by slave-hunters or slave-holders, seemed never to enter her mind. She was apparently proof against all adversaries. While she thus manifested such utter personal indifference, she was much more watchful with regard to those she was piloting. Half of her time, she had the appearance of one asleep, and would actually sit down by the road-side and go fast asleep when on her errands of mercy through the South, yet she would not suffer one of her party to whimper once, about "giving out and going back," however wearied they might be from hard travel day and night. She had a very short and pointed rule of law of her own, which implied death to any who talked of giving out and going back. Thus, in an emergency she would give all to understand that "times were very critical and therefore no foolishness would be indulged on the road."[85]

There is no evidence that Harriet ever used the gun she carried, although she was fully capable of doing so and saw little value in Garrison's doctrine of nonresistance.

Tubman brought fugitives to Gerrit Smith's mansion in Peterboro, to Jermain Loguen's home in Syracuse, and to Rochester.[86] She operated at a time when the penalty for aiding and abetting runaways was severe. As she said of the Fugitive Slave Law, "After that, I wouldn't trust Uncle Sam wid my people no longer, but I brought 'em all clar off to Canada."[87] Angered by Tubman's audacity, and troubled by the loss of valuable "property," Southerners offered rewards for her capture which totaled nearly $40,000.

On November 29, 1856, William E. Abbott, who was treasurer of Syracuse's Fugitive Aid Society (organized in January 1856) wrote a letter to Maria Porter of Rochester. In it is a reference to Moses and those who aided her in getting her "children" safely to Canada:

> The woman who accompanies the party on their way to Freedom is well known to us for her untiring devotion to the cause of the enslaved. She *is* herself an escaped bondswoman and this the second company that she has brought forth out of the land of servitude at great risk to herself. It has been our custom to forward all directly on to the Bridge. But now our funds fail us & we are obliged to send them forward to the different halfway houses that are on their route.[88]

Tubman sometimes entered Canada, where slavery had been abolished in 1833, by traveling over the famous suspension bridge. The bridge was designed for carriage and pedestrian traffic and was built in 1848 to connect Niagara Falls, New York, with Niagara Falls, Canada West. In 1855, it was replaced with a two-level railway suspension bridge.[89] The trains that crossed the bridge, which was located near the site of the present-day Whirlpool Bridge, afforded runaways transportation for the last segment of their flight from the slave hunters. Midway across, the fugitives could see the Promised Land on the other side. They would sing, "I'm on the way to Canada, That cold and dreary land, De sad effects of slavery, I can't no longer stand." But they knew that they were not truly safe until they reached the center of the bridge. When they finally set foot on Queen Victoria's soil, Harriet would tell them that now they could "shake de lion's paw," meaning that they were now under the protection of British law.[90]

In 1857, when Harriet was still conducting the Underground Railroad, William Henry Seward aided her and her parents to settle in Auburn (Cayuga County). Seward offered the elder Tubmans a small plot of ground off South Street, about one and one-half miles from his own home, on easy terms. The Seward compound at 33 South Street reputedly sheltered many fugitives who were sometimes hidden by Seward's wife, Frances, in the upper level of the family carriage port.[91]

William Henry Seward served two terms as Whig governor of New York State (1839–1843). Seward signed important legislation protecting the rights of African Americans; an 1840 act guaranteed a jury trial for alleged runaways, and an 1841 bill gave all children, regardless of race, access to public education. He also waged a number of legal battles with Southern governors by seeking to block the extradition of runaways.[92] Seward's interest in Harriet Tubman and her work persisted long after the Civil War.

Tubman actively aided fugitives until the eve of the Civil War. In April 1860, Harriet participated in the spectacular rescue of Charles Nalle in Troy. Nalle was a runaway who had been arrested under the Fugitive Slave Law of 1850. He was waiting in the office of U.S. Commissioner Miles Beach, and he was about to be returned to Virginia, when a crowd gathered outside. William Henry, a black grocer and member of Troy's Vigilance Committee, shouted, "There is a fugitive slave in that office!"

Tubman was visiting a cousin in Troy while on her way to an abolitionist meeting in Boston. She heard the ruckus, pushed through the mob and into the office, and caused a disturbance by blocking the stairs. In the ensuing confusion, Nalle's rescuers managed to get him down to the Hudson River and into a skiff. Nalle was recaptured at West Troy across the river. But Tubman and Nalle's other supporters soon arrived on a ferry. They stormed the building where Nalle was held. Nalle's captors struck him on the head, he fell unconscious, and Tubman helped carry him to safety. Nalle was taken to the town of Niskaynua, outside Schenectady, where he remained in hiding. One month later, fifty-one citizens of Troy purchased Nalle's freedom for $650.[93]

In the summer of 1868, the South was divided into military districts under martial law, and traffic on the Underground Railroad had ended. Frederick Douglass, who was still living in Rochester, took pen in hand to write a promotional piece for a soon-to-be-published book about Harriet Tubman. The story of this illiterate woman, who was already being called the Moses of her people, was being assembled by Sarah Bradford of Geneva, New York. Bradford was the sister of Samuel Miles Hopkins, a professor at Auburn Theological Seminary. She had met Harriet's parents while she was visiting in Auburn and had helped them write to Union Army officers about Tubman's Civil War activities as spy, scout, and nurse.[94]

Harriet told her story to Bradford, who published the interviews in 1869 under the title, *Scenes in the Life of Harriet Tubman*. The intention was to raise funds which would pay off the mortgage on Tubman's parents' seven-acre farm.[95] Upon reading Tubman's "biography," Frederick Douglass was generous in his comments:

> I am glad to know that the story of your eventful life has been written. . . . You ask for what you do not need when you call upon me for a word of commendation. I need such words from you far more than you can need them from me, especially where your superior labors and devotion to the cause of the lately enslaved of our land are known as I know them. The difference between us is very marked. Most that I have done and suffered in the service of our cause has been in public, and I have received much encouragement at every step of the way. You on the other hand have labored in a private way. I have wrought in the day—you in the night. I have had the applause of the crowd and the satisfaction that comes of being approved by the multitude, while the most that you have done has been witnessed by the few trembling, scarred, foot-sore bondsmen and women, whom you have led out of the house of bondage. . . . The midnight sky and silent stars have been the witnesses of your devotion to freedom and of your heroism. . . .[96]

Harriet Tubman (c.1820–1913). The Moses of her people is shawled and seated among friends and admirers, some of whom may have been residents of the brick structure pictured here. It housed elderly African American men and was known as John Brown Hall. *Courtesy of Pauline Copes Johnson, a great-grandniece of Harriet Tubman Davis.*

Tubman did not consider her work done once she had finished bringing fugitives out of the South. After Harriet and her aging parents settled in Auburn, some of the people whom she had helped to free came to live near her. When they became infirm and elderly, none of the homes for the aged in Auburn would admit them. Moved by their plight and that of other elderly blacks in the community, Tubman dreamed of establishing an agricultural cooperative that could support them, using additional property she had purchased in 1895. She converted two structures, one wood frame and one brick, into dwellings. The ten-room brick building—not to be confused with the existing brick house at the front of the Harriet Tubman historic site—was set back from South Street, in the orchard. It is believed to have been a residence for men and was probably constructed sometime in the 1870s.[97]

The Harriet Tubman Home, as some took to calling both dwellings, was dependent upon charitable contributions. It was not a large endeavor; in 1903, ten years before Tubman's death, the home had only a handful of residents and had to be reorganized under the custodianship of the A.M.E.Z. Church. But Tubman's concern for the elderly had considerable symbolic significance as an extension of the work she had done on the Underground Railroad. Her own understanding of its importance to the cause of freedom is suggested by the name she gave the brick building: John Brown Hall.[98] Tubman's acclamation of John Brown introduces us to one of the most impassioned opponents of slavery to pass across North Star Country's stage.

8. John Brown's Body

John Brown did not want his wife to be present when he met what he called his public death, but abolitionist friends persuaded her to travel to Virginia, once the date of his execution was set. On December 2, 1859, the day the "Ol' Man" was hanged for treason at Charles Town, Mary was at Harpers Ferry. That evening, authorities brought her husband's body to Harpers Ferry in a "plain decent" walnut coffin. It was moved under guard to prevent any attempts to steal it or mutilate it. On December 3rd, Mary Brown began the six-hundred-mile journey back to the rugged north country of the Adirondacks. She sat on a train bound for Baltimore, her husband's casket in a baggage car.[1]

When Mary saw her husband during their last visit, he told her of his wish to be buried at home in the shadows of the Adirondack high peaks. John Brown loved the mountains, particularly in autumn, and drove through them in a long buckboard wagon, often in a frock coat and tails.[2] Mary's husband had gone away many times during their marriage of more than a quarter century, usually on ill-fated business ventures. Then, as 1859 drew closer, he left for good in search of his own destiny. Now her husband would wander no more.

Today, visitors to the John Brown farm at North Elba (a few miles south of Lake Placid) pay their respects to the abolitionist and his sons at a small cemetery near the cabin that the family once occupied.[3] Although North Elba lies outside of the region we have defined as North Star Country, the story of how John Brown's body ended up in an Essex County grave reveals much about the development of the abolitionist movement in Upstate New York. The story also involves personalities that are central to our account, notably Gerrit Smith and Frederick Douglass. One clue to the mystery of

Brown's connection with North Star Country can be found in the events of December 8th, the day the internment took place.

On a clear, frigid morning, men dug a burial pit at the base of a large granite boulder. White Face Mountain, one of the tallest peaks in the Adirondacks, served as a solemn backdrop. Around 1:00 P.M., the coffin that held Brown's body was set on a table outside the still-unfinished cabin and nailed shut. The Reverend Joshua Young, a Unitarian from Burlington, Vermont, recited these words of St. Paul: "I have fought the good fight; I have finished my course; I have kept the faith." (Young later lost his church because he presided at Brown's funeral.) The white abolitionists J. Miller McKim and Wendell Phillips made speeches. Phillips intoned, "John Brown has loosened the roots of the slave system; it only breathes,—it does not live,—hereafter."[4] Then the African American Epps family stepped forward from the crowd of two hundred mourners. Lyman Epps led the singing of an old hymn, a Brown favorite:

> Blow Ye the Trumpet Blow,
> the gladly solemn sound,
> let all the nations know,
> to earth's remotest bound,
> the year of Jubilee has come.[5]

The martyr of Harpers Ferry had been friend and neighbor to the African Americans living in the Adirondacks for the better part of a decade. Brown helped blacks in the North Elba area to fell trees, build cabins, plant, and harvest. He preached to them on the Sabbath, enabled them to obtain pure-bred livestock, and bought barrels of pork and flour for them when they were near starvation. Brown hired Thomas Jefferson when he needed a teamster, and he employed a fugitive by the name of Cyrus, a runaway from Florida, to work on his own farm in the town of North Elba. A black housekeeper helped Mary with the care of her home and large family.[6] It was the presence of African Americans such as Lyman Epps[7] in colonies like Timbuctoo (Essex County) and Blacksville (near the present Loon Lake in Franklin County) that drew John Brown to the Adirondacks.

Brown first visited the black settlements in 1848. At that time he was a wool broker for the firm of Perkins & Brown at its eastern office in Springfield, Massachusetts. Ten black families comprised the Timbuctoo colony, which was located near West Keene. The black farmers, who had forty acres

John Brown's grave at North Elba, c. 1897. Brown purchased land from Gerrit Smith and moved his family into the Adirondack wilderness in 1849. Here he lived among, and aided, recipients of Smith's effort to move African Americans onto their own farms. *Courtesy of the Library of Congress.*

each, were housed in shanties "built of logs with flat roofs out of which little stove pipes protruded at varying angles." Brown would later write to his father, "There are a number of good colored families on the ground; most of whom I visited. I can think of no place where I think I would sooner go, all things considered than to live with those poor despised Africans to try, & encourage them; & show them a little so far as I am capable how to manage. You need not be surprised if at some future time I should do so." Brown wrote to his son about his desire "to get some colored men of the right stamp for colonists."[8]

In 1849, one of the black farmers at Timbuctoo informed Henry H. Garnet, "I have been here eight months, and I like the land and the country well. There is no better land for grain. We get from 25 to 50 bushels of oats to the acre. New land is the best for oats, and for potatoes and turnips; of the two last articles we get from 200 to 400 to the acre.—The farmers here get 46 cents per bushel, cash in hand, for their oats. I have seen Mr. J. B., of Springfield, Mass., and he says that he will move here in the Spring, and will give us a start if we will try and help ourselves."[9]

The blacks who were trying to eke out a living on the forested and rocky soil of the Adirondacks had been placed there by Gerrit Smith. Smith met Brown for the first time on April 8, 1848, when Brown came to Peterboro to learn more about the philanthropist's plan to do something practical in the name of abolitionism. Brown had heard about Smith's offer, announced on August 1, 1846, to give parcels of land in the Adirondacks to blacks. From these blacks, Brown intended to recruit volunteers for a bold plan he was already working on. When meeting Smith, Brown said, "I am something of a pioneer; I grew up among the woods and wild Indians of Ohio and am used to the climate and the way of life that your colony find so trying. I will take one of your farms myself, clear it up and plant it, and show my colored neighbors how such work should be done; will give them work as I have occasion, look after them in all needful ways and be a kind of father to them."[10]

Gerrit Smith had many passions and the wealth with which to indulge those passions. His father, Peter Smith, had made a fortune trading furs and speculating in land. Eventually, Peter Smith owned nearly one quarter of a million acres. The elder Smith, whose temperament was somewhat unstable, entrusted Gerrit with the management of the family's landholdings when Gerrit was in his early twenties. During the depression that was triggered by the Panic of 1837, the Smith empire suffered, but Gerrit promised himself—and perhaps his God—that when he had paid off all his debts he would give away farms to the poor.

Although his own extensive landholdings seemed to be at odds with anti-land-monopoly rhetoric, Smith advocated the redistribution of land, especially because the ownership of land was a step toward gaining the right to vote. As a confirmed agrarian, Smith believed that true virtue was derived from working the soil. In a speech given in Syracuse on January 20, 1848, Smith complained, "Often, within the last few years, has my heart ached, when I have heard abolitionists speak contemptuously of land-reform. They know not what it is of which they speak contemptuously. They know not that it is one of the most effective anti-slavery measures—most effective, not only to overthrow present slavery, but to prevent, and make impossible, its resuscitation and repetition."[11]

Illustrative of his point, the abolitionist gave away parcels of land to the deserving poor. He initially shrank from limiting the grants to the black poor, because he did not want to put a "bounty on color." In the end, he restricted the recipients to African American males between the ages of twenty-one and sixty who were not "in easy circumstances as to property" or land, and who were not drunkards. Smith hoped to enable the black farmers to vote by helping them amass property that was valued at $250 or more.[12]

Most of the forty-acre parcels to be conveyed were located in Delaware, Essex, Franklin, Fulton, Hamilton, Madison, Oneida, and Ulster Counties; most of the proposed recipients were recruited from downstate, especially New York City and environs. Some, however, did come from Upstate New York. An elderly black woman recalled during the 1940s, "Gerrit Smith gave ten or twelve Negroes, living in Ithaca during his time, twenty or thirty acres of land in Essex County so they could vote. They just had to keep the taxes paid. I don't remember the names of all the Negroes so favored, but I do know that my grandfather, Titus Brum, and Henry Moore who lived on South Plain Street, were among them."[13]

Smith sought the assistance of African American leaders with selecting grantees. He asked Charles B. Ray, J. McCune Smith, and Theodore S. Wright to draw up lists of worthy beneficiaries. All three lived in New York City. Ray and Wright were clergymen; Smith had a degree in medicine. Smith hoped to get the names of 1,985 colonists. In September of 1846, Gerrit Smith announced that two thousand parcels were ready for distribution. Most were located in Franklin and Essex Counties.

Elated with the prospect of owning land, African Americans held public meetings to thank their benefactor. A "convention of Gerrit Smith's grantees" met in Ithaca during February 1847. At the National Convention of Colored People, which was held in October 1848 at Troy, delegates drew up a statement that thanked Smith for his proposed gift of 120,000 acres of land and urged fellow blacks to take up farming "as the surest road to respectability and influence."[14] Austin Steward of Rochester also advocated the resettlement of blacks on the open land as a means of delivering them from the miseries of urban life where they were made "hewers of wood and drawers of water."[15]

In their exhilaration over the prospect of poor blacks from the cities becoming self-supporting farmers, Smith's admirers may not have adequately considered the speculative nature of trying to plant and harvest on marginal acreage. There were start-up costs—tools, seed, oxen, and horses—none of which Smith provided, and few of Smith's grantees had agricultural skills. Around the time that John Brown was surveying conditions in the vicinity of North Elba, an experiment took place in the heart of North Star Country which demonstrated the drawbacks of these abolitionist-sponsored agricultural settlements.

Stephen A. Myers was the black journalist from Albany who founded the *Northern Star and Freeman's Advocate.* He also established the Florence Farming and Lumber Association for a black farming community that was projected to be established on land that Smith was giving away in the vicinity of Florence (Oneida County). On December 22, 1848, the *North Star* reprinted an article from the *Colored Farmer,* giving details about the proposed settlement: "It is twenty-two miles from the village of Rome, where the railroad depot lays, 23 miles from the Erie Canal, 12 miles from the village of Constantia, and 2 miles from the village of Florence, which is a pleasant village, having three churches, a school house and several stores. The town of Florence is a favorite town of Mr. G. Smith."[16]

Smith issued a public disclaimer that, of the approximately eighteen thousand acres he had once owned in the town of Florence, only a few hundred "of very moderate fertility" remained.[17] Henry Bibb labeled the Florence venture "humbug" and said, "I have every reason to believe it to be a cunning trick of an unprincipled clique, whose chief object is to build up themselves on the benevolence of our anti-slavery friends."[18] The Florence Farming and Lumber Association eventually dissolved, without fulfilling the agrarian dream of Stephen Myers. Its prospects were not helped by Frederick Douglass's report of having heard "from various sources, as to the wildness of the country, the infertility of the lands, the distance and the difficulties of the way to market, and the entire absence of water power." He also said, "there is much to discourage emigration to that place, as a suitable one for establishing a flourishing and influential town."[19]

Frederick Douglass was barely settled in Rochester when Smith donated forty acres to him, although the two men had not yet met. Smith wrote on December 8, 1847:

> Conformably to my purpose of giving to 3000 colored inhabitants of this State the principal share of my lands, which are fit for farming, I made out 2000 deeds last year: I am now busy, with my clerks, in making out the remaining

1000. Inasmuch as you and Mr. Nell have become inhabitants of this State, I feel at liberty to convey a parcel of land to each of you. Herewith are the deeds. I wish that the land was in less rigorous clime; but it is smooth and arable, and not wanting in fertility. Forty acres—that is, a quarter of the same lot of which I have conveyed a quarter each to yourself and Mr. Nell,—I have given to Mr. C. L. Remond. The remaining quarter will probably be conveyed to Mr. W. W. Brown, who has also become an inhabitant of this State. One of the contiguous lots I have divided amongst four fugitive slaves, viz: Henry Bibb, and the three brothers, Lewis, Milton, and Cyrus Clark.[20]

Douglass was delighted with Smith's altruism and used the *North Star* to promote the land giveaway:

Advantage should be at once taken of this generous and magnificent donation, on the part of Gerrit Smith, to colored residents in the State of New York. To prevent it from becoming a curse, and to make it what it should be—a blessing, such as will cheer the heart of the generous donor, the land ought to be immediately occupied. The sharp axe of the sable-armed pioneer should be at once uplifted over the soil of Franklin and Essex counties, and the noise of falling trees proclaim the glorious dawn of civilization throughout their borders. Let the work be commenced at once. The day has come. The spring is near at hand. Seed-time is near; and what a man soweth that shall he reap.

Companies of tens and of twenties should be formed, and the woods at once invaded. There should be as little delay as possible about this. We should hail with delight the news of the arrival in those regions of the first pioneers, and record their names to be handed down, and read with grateful admiration by future generations. Come, brethren, let it not be said, that a people who, under the lash, could level the forests of Virginia, Maryland, and the whole Southern States, that their oppressors might reap the reward, lack the energy and manly ambition to clear lands for themselves. Let us make those who declare us incapable of taking care of ourselves, slanderers before all the people.[21]

Smith's hope of creating a cadre of thousands of virtuous black farmers did not materialize. In November 1848, he wrote to Charles B. Ray, informing him that twenty or thirty families had been settled on their farms, a far cry from the numbers Smith had anticipated.[22] With limited agricultural skills for dealing with the short growing season and poor soils, grantees struggled to achieve economic independence. Except for a few fleeces, they had little to sell, and stock had to be wintered from early November to mid-May.

Mapping the black colonies of North Star Country proved difficult, even when the settlers were moving in. Jermain Loguen checked out the lands in Essex and Franklin Counties during a seven-week exploratory trip in 1848. Though he found the farms "as good land as any man can need," some suited for tillage and others valuable for timber, Loguen reported that "a high-handed game had been played upon many of our colored brethren." So-called pilots were swindling grantees out of the best land, leaving the prospective black farmer with "a very undesirable spot—perhaps a mountain peak or an irrecoverable swamp." Loguen's advice was to go "in the company of tried friends" who could read and write, and to learn how to recognize the axe marks on trees, which were known as blazes, that were left by the surveyors.[23] A. C. Van Epps wrote to Smith in 1851, complaining that, without surveys, the bounds and corners mentioned in the deeds were difficult to locate.[24] John Brown worked "early and late" to survey the lost boundaries and attempt to sort out the legal tangles. It was during these visits among the black settlers, to whom he preached on Sabbath afternoons in a small church not far from Timbuctoo, that the fierce abolitionist and sometime wool trader talked to them about toppling slavery.

Brown initially purchased two small farms from Smith for $1 per acre, using, in the main, donations from those who backed his cause. Plagued by lawsuits, the wool-dealing firm of Perkins & Brown had proven to be a financial liability, and Brown was a poor man with a large family. He managed to pay off Smith in November of 1849. The Browns initially rented a two-room cabin that was known as the Flanders' house, on the road from Keene to Lake Placid.

During June 1849, two or three weeks after the Browns moved in, Richard Henry Dana, Jr., of Boston, a lawyer and author of *Two Years Before the Mast*, became lost in the Adirondack woods. He took refuge with the Browns and gives us this colorful account of the visit:

> The place belonged to a man named Brown, originally from Berkshire in Massachusetts, a thin sinewy, hard-favored, clear-headed, honest-minded man, who had spent all his days as a frontier farmer. On conversing with him, we found him well informed on most subjects, especially in the natural sciences. He had books, and had evidently made a diligent use of them. Having acquired some property, he was able to keep a good farm, and had confessedly the best cattle and best farming utensils for miles around. His wife looked superior to the poor place they lived in, which was a cabin, with only four rooms. She appeared to be out of health. He seemed to have an unlimited family of children, from a

cheerful nice healthy woman of twenty or so, and a full sized red-haired son, who seemed to be foreman of the farm, through every grade of boy and girl to a couple that could hardly speak plain. . . . June 29, Friday—After breakfast, started for home. . . . We stopped at the Browns' cabin on our way, and took affectionate leave of the family that had shown us so much kindness. We found them at breakfast, in the patriarchal style. Mr. and Mrs. Brown and their large family of children with the hired men and women, including three negroes, all at the table together. Their meal was neat, substantial, and wholesome.[25]

Daughter Ruth Brown remembered how confining the rented house was. Her father said, "It is small; but the main thing is, *all* keep good-natured."[26] In his narrative, Dana might have added that Brown's hair and beard were already greying, and that his nearly five-foot, eleven-inch frame was beginning to stoop, giving him the prematurely old look that was remarked on by Frederick Douglass and others. Having only experienced the Adirondacks of early summer, Dana could not have known how dreary, cold, and inaccessible North Elba was over the long winters.

Brown was away from home, on business in Springfield, Massachusetts, when the Fugitive Slave Law was enacted. He wrote to his wife that the new law would make more abolitionists than would years of lecturing. He urged his "coloured friends to trust in God and keep their powder dry."[27] Forty-five African Americans joined Brown's newly formed United States League of Gileadites and pledged to resist the slave catchers, with force if necessary. When Brown was yet at North Elba, he had urged the settlers to prepare to protect the fugitives in their midst, including his farmhand Cyrus. "Our faithful boy, Cyrus," Ruth Brown wrote years later, "was one of that class and it aroused our feelings so that we would *all* have defended him, if the women folks had had to resort to *hot water*. Father said, 'Their cup of iniquity is almost full.'"[28]

In the early 1850s, Brown tried farming back in Ohio. In 1854 he purchased an additional 160 acres in the Adirondacks from Smith, making Brown's total holdings 244 acres.[29] In June of 1855, Brown returned to North Elba. The fiery abolitionist moved his large family into an unplastered four-room house that had been built by Henry Thompson, Ruth's husband, on the farmstead to which John Brown's body would be brought in 1859. Now out of the wool business and at home in the isolation of the far reaches of the Adirondacks, Brown turned his full attention to the battle ahead. The Old Man, as Douglass nicknamed Brown, had visions of a grand assault upon slavery from the depth of the Alleghenies. He had chosen a strategic place, known as Harpers Ferry, where there was a federal arsenal. He might have gone south to Virginia in 1855, but he had urgent business out in the West. In the Kansas territory, a group of abolitionists who sympathized with the Free Soil movement were at war with proslavery forces.

During late June of 1855, in Syracuse, supporters of the Kansas Aid movement met with kindred spirits at a three-day convention of the Radical Abolitionist Party. The Radical Abolitionists, some of whom were ex-Liberty Party stalwarts, considered slavery an "unsurpassed crime" and believed that the federal government had the power to abolish slavery in the states and territories. Gerrit Smith, William Goodell, Lewis Tappan, S. S. Jocelyn, W. E. Whiting, James McCune Smith, George Whipple, and Frederick Douglass signed the "address" of the convention, thereby affirming the aggressive antislavery constitutionalism which could be used to justify abolitionist participation in the conflict over popular sovereignty and slavery.

John Brown attended the Syracuse conclave on its last day. Using a fiery speech, he solicited funds to purchase arms for himself and his sons so that they could repel "Satan and his legions" out in Kansas. Frederick Douglass bolstered the arms proposal, but other Upstate New York abolitionists, notably Samuel J. May, hesitated. For him, and others, guns, violence, and abolitionism still constituted an unholy trinity.[30]

By October 1855, John Brown was out in Kansas among his boys, five of whom were lodged near Osawatomie. When proslavery border ruffians from Missouri swarmed into Lawrence, Brown led a counterattack on one of their settlements, an encampment along the Pottawatomie River. Five men of the slave-state faction died at Pottawatomie; they were hacked to death with broadswords. Frederick Douglass commented, "The horrors wrought by his iron hand cannot be contemplated without a shudder, but it is the shudder which one feels at the execution of a murderer. . . . To call out a murderer at midnight and without note or warning, judge or jury, run him through with a sword, was a terrible remedy for a terrible malady."[31]

Free-state partisans and their opponents clashed again at Osawatomie in August 1856. Merritt Anthony, Susan B. Anthony's brother, hosted John Brown in his cabin on the evening before the abolitionist's small force set out to punish slaveholders. The Anthonys assumed that Merritt had been killed at Osawatomie but, after the raid, a letter from Merritt appeared in Rochester's *Daily Democrat,* a Free Soil paper. Susan wrote to her brother:

> Your letter is in today's *Democrat,* and the *Evening Advertiser* says there is "another letter from our dear brother in this morning's 'Shrieker for Freedom.'" The tirade is headed 'Bleeding Kansas.' The *Advertiser, Union* and *American* all ridicule the reports from Kansas, and even say your letters are gotten up in the Democrat office for political effect. I tell you, Merritt, we have 'border ruffians' here at home—a little more refined in their way of outraging and torturing the lovers of freedom, but no less fiendish.[32]

Joseph H. Morey, another Free Soiler from Rochester, was captured at Osawatomie, taken to Kansas City, put on a boat, and told to go back East. Dr. John Doy, a hydropathic physician from Rochester, and William W. Bloss, son of the Hon. William Clough Bloss, were also among the "Jay-hawkers" who clashed with proslavery ruffians out in Kansas. Bloss was wounded; Doy was arrested for "Negro stealing" and sentenced, in 1859, to five years in prison.[33] For Upstate New York abolitionists like these Free Soilers, John Brown's actions in Kansas were entirely in keeping with the spirit of North Star Country.

When Brown returned from Kansas, he was more convinced than ever that he was God's providential instrument. He went to Boston in January 1857 to seek financial assistance and meet with Gerrit Smith, Thomas Wentworth Higginson, George L. Stearns (a mill owner from Medford, Massachusetts), Reverend Theodore Parker (a noted Boston divine), Dr. Samuel G. Howe (the husband of Julia Ward Howe, who wrote "The Battle Hymn of the Republic"), and Franklin B. Sanborn (a Massachusetts educator and abolitionist). As a group, they had been dubbed the "Secret Six," but each of these men had actively supported the emigrants who had gone to Kansas and might reasonably be enlisted to support an even bolder enterprise.[34]

During the summer of 1857, Brown was back again in the Kansas Territory but found little to do because the free-state settlers appeared to have the upper hand. The Old Man now focused on a direct assault on slavery's domain. He quartered his band of Kansas fighters at Springdale, Iowa, and came back East in 1858 to generate more financial support. Gerrit Smith was receptive to Brown's visit. On January 22, 1858, Smith wrote to Sanborn (another member of the Secret Six) about helping Brown and reported that

Brown had alluded to a bold plan of action that he wished to discuss with his Eastern allies: "The topography of Missouri is unfavorable. *Would that a spur of the Alleghany extended from the east to the west borders of the State!*"[35]

Gerrit Smith was not the only North Star Country abolitionist that Brown sounded out. Beginning in late January of 1858, Brown stayed with Frederick Douglass in Rochester for several weeks. Douglass had first encountered Brown in 1847 at Springfield, Massachusetts, after having heard Brown's name from Henry Highland Garnet and Jermain Loguen. "In speaking of him," Douglass recalled, "their voices would drop to a whisper, and what they said of him made me very eager to see and to know him."[36] In his *Life and Times,* Douglass left us this vivid portrait of Brown drawn from that first encounter:

> In person he was lean, strong, and sinewy, of the best New England mold, built for times of trouble and fitted to grapple with the flintiest hardships. Clad in plain American woolen, shod in boots of cowhide leather, and wearing a cravat of the same substantial material, under six feet high, less than 150 pounds in weight, aged about fifty, he presented a figure straight and symmetrical as a mountain pine. His bearing was singularly impressive. His head was not large, but compact and high. His hair was coarse, strong, slightly gray, and closely trimmed, and grew low on his forehead. His face was smoothly shaved, and revealed a strong, square mouth, supported by a broad and prominent chin. His eyes were bluish-grey, and in conversation they were full of light and fire. When on the street, he moved with a long, springing race-horse step, absorbed by his own reflections, neither seeking nor shunning observation.[37]

Douglass noted that the parlor of Brown's modest house in Springfield lacked furniture. Brown had decided to keep it empty so that he might have funds to aid freedom-seekers.

In keeping with his character, John Brown insisted on paying board when he lodged with Douglass in January and February of 1858. Douglass charged him $3 per week. While residing with Douglass and his family, Brown labored on a constitution for the provisional government he planned to institute after he had taken his men into the mountains of Virginia. "His whole time and thought were given to this subject," Douglass recalled. "It was the first thing in the morning and the last thing at night, till I confess it began to be something of a bore to me."[38] Brown spoke of a plan to capture Harpers Ferry, although Douglass took the talk as mere speculation.

Gerrit Smith mansion. This mansion was built between 1804 and 1806 by Peter Smith and extensively remodeled by his son, Gerrit, and by Gerrit Smith Miller. The Smith house in Peterboro (Madison County) harbored many a fugitive and stood witness to the manifold reform interests of its occupants. The structure was originally situated on an estate of thirty acres. It burned down in 1936, probably as a result of a malfunctioning furnace. *Courtesy of the Madison County Historical Society.*

One day, Brown asked Douglass for two smooth-surfaced boards. Using a pair of dividers, he scratched out a sketch of the fortifications he would require when he went below the Mason Dixon Line. "I was less interested in these drawings than my children were," Douglass wrote many years later, "but they showed that the old man had an eye to the means as well as to the end, and was giving his best thought to the work he was about to take in hand."[39] Sarah, one of Brown's daughters, recalled that her father often diagrammed and explained his plans to family members, and some of the black colonists, while sitting in the North Elba cabin. Her father tried in vain to recruit Lyman Epps. Like Douglass, Epps may have thought the Old Man's scheme to be too risky and impractical.[40]

While boarding in Rochester, Brown also busied himself with writing letters to Gerrit Smith and his other Eastern friends. Smith had been generous to Brown during the troubles in Kansas, once writing to him, "We must not shrink from fighting for Liberty—and if Federal troops fight against her, we must fight against them."[41] Brown invited the Secret Six members to meet him at Smith's home in Peterboro and discuss, as he said to Thomas Wentworth Higginson, "Rail Road business on a *somewhat extended scale*"[42] Higginson did not attend the Peterboro conference, nor did Stearns, but Franklin B. Sanborn was there. He arrived early in the evening of February 22, 1858.

After dinner, Sanborn, Brown, Smith, and Edwin Morton, a tutor in the Smith household, went up to Morton's room on the third floor of the mansion. By a small fireplace, Brown outlined his plans to "beat up a slave quarter," presented the constitution he had written, discussed establishing a mountain fortress in Virginia, and appealed for funds. The talks renewed the next day. Sanborn later disclosed, "as usually happened when he had time enough, Captain Brown began to prevail over the objections of his friends." In the late afternoon, with the sun setting over the snowy hills, Sanborn and Smith walked in the woods and fields for an hour. Meanwhile, Brown stayed in the mansion, by the fire, discussing theology with Charles Stuart, the Jamaican-born abolitionist and pioneering antislavery lecturer in Upstate New York, who had arrived on one of his many visits to Peterboro. Sanborn remembered, "Mr. Smith restated in his eloquent way the daring propositions of Brown, whose import he understood fully; and then said in substance: 'You see how it is; our dear old friend has made up his mind to this course, and cannot be turned from it. We cannot give him to die alone; we must support him.'"[43]

Although Brown may not have specified Harpers Ferry as his intended point of attack, it is difficult to believe that the general thrust and import of his remarks could have eluded Smith and the others during the enclave in Peterboro. Whatever the exact nature of the conversations regarding the Virginia plan, Osawatomie Brown, as he was now known, was confident that he would receive support from his host. He wrote to his wife, Mary, "Mr. Smith and family go *all* lengths with me."[44]

Smith's own views on the matter are revealed in a letter he wrote, on March 25, 1858, to the Ohio abolitionist Joshua R. Giddings: "The slave will be delivered by the shedding of blood—and the signs are multiplying that his deliverance is at hand."[45] On July 26, 1858, Smith communicated with Sanborn: "I have great faith in the wisdom, integrity, and bravery of Captain Brown. For several years I have frequently given him money toward sustaining him in his contests with the slave-power. Whenever he shall embark in another of these contests, I shall again stand ready to help him; and I will begin with giving him a hundred dollars. I do not wish to know Captain Brown's plans; I hope he will keep them to himself."[46]

Brown expected to begin his campaign the following spring. In the meantime, he went to Boston to meet with the members of the Secret Six who had not been able to come to Peterboro. He was also anxious to acquire the support of black abolitionists.

In March 1858, he was in Philadelphia, talking with black leaders, including Douglass, Garnet, and William Still. He also met with Jermain Loguen and James N. Gloucester in New York City. Loguen had "whole heartedly" given his support to Brown's plan. In early April, Loguen accompanied Brown to Chatham, Ontario, where they met with Harriet Tubman.

Brown wanted Tubman to recruit soldiers for him from among the thousands of fugitives living in Canada West. Later, he called her "the most of a man, naturally, that I ever met with." Tubman, who urged Brown to strike against slavery on the 4th of July, impressed the Old Man as "the most abundant material, and of the right quality, in this quarter, beyond all doubt." "Harriet Tubman hooked on his whole team at once," Brown affirmed, once again using the masculine pronoun.[47]

Brown gathered up his band of freedom fighters from Iowa and brought them to Chatham where a convention, disguised as a meeting to organize a black Masonic lodge, opened on May 8, 1858. Twelve whites (including Brown) and thirty-four blacks attended. Brown had invited Jermain Loguen to come up from Syracuse, but Loguen did not attend. He wrote to Brown from Syracuse on May 6:

My dear Friend & Bro—

I have your last letter from Canada. I was glad to learn that you & your brave men had got on to Chatham. I have see[n] our man Gray, & find it with him as I feared we should—that he was not ready yet. I do not think he will go to war soon—others that would go have not the money to get there with. And I have conclud[ed] to let them all rest for the present. Have you got Isaac Williams with you or not? Have you got Harriet Tubman of St. Catherines? Let me hear from you soon or whenever you can. As I think I cannot get to Chatham, I should like much to see you & your men before you go to the mountains. My wife & all unite in wishing you all the great success in your *Glorious undertaken.* May the *Lord* be with you is our prayer.[48]

Loguen closed his letter with, "Your friend in the cause." Loguen was nominated for president of Brown's proposed provisional government during the Chatham meeting, but his name was withdrawn when someone announced that Loguen would not serve if elected. Brown would later grouse that Loguen was "too fat" to meet the challenges to come.[49]

Frederick Douglass did not participate in the Chatham convention, but Shields Green was there. A fugitive from South Carolina who sometimes called himself Emperor, Green first met Brown at Douglass's home. Green was a clothes cleaner and presser in Rochester who was living with the Douglass family prior to the Chatham meeting and endorsed Brown's plans for black liberation wholeheartedly.[50] The Chatham convention adopted Brown's "Provisional Constitution and Ordinances for the People of the United States." Brown envisioned his own judiciary and congress.

On May 24, 1858, Gerrit Smith gave the keynote address at the American Peace Society gathering in Boston. His theme: "Peace Better Than War." While in Boston, Smith and the Secret Six (except Higginson) met and talked with Brown at the Revere House. They urged him to delay his plan of operations for a year, return to Kansas, and allow them time to raise more money. Brown seems to have taken their advice. He went back out to Kansas in June, and he remained there most of the following winter. In one daring exploit, he brought eleven slaves out of Missouri and escorted them safely to Canada.

When the spring of 1859 arrived, John Brown came back east. He was accompanied by Osborne Perry Anderson, one of the African Americans who would eventually fight alongside Brown at Harpers Ferry. Brown had recruited the young printer's devil at the Chatham convention.

In April, Brown and Anderson visited Smith in Peterboro. Edwin Morton was one of those present; he reported that Smith gave Brown $400 and was so moved by the Old Man's speeches that he said, "If I were asked to point out—I will say it in his presence—to point out the man in all this world I think most truly a Christian, I would point to John Brown."[51] Brown was not altogether happy with his prominent supporters, thinking some of them too cautious. In a note left by Higginson, we read, "G. S. [Gerrit Smith] He knew to be a timid man. G. L. S. [George L. Stearns] & T. P. [Theodore Parker] he did not think abounded in courage."[52]

Brown rented a place known as the Kennedy farm, about five miles from Harpers Ferry, in Maryland, to be his base of operations. Sometime in September of 1859, approximately three weeks before the raid on Harpers Ferry, Brown wrote to Frederick Douglass and asked him to come down to Chambersburg, Pennsylvania. Brown told Douglass that he had mining tools and other supplies stored at Chambersburg, which was located about twenty miles from Harpers Ferry. In addition, Brown and John H. Kagi, secretary of Brown's provisional government, wanted to meet with Douglass. Douglass came and brought Shields Green with him, as well as funds to aid Brown's cause.

The four men met at a stone quarry near Chambersburg. Brown was using the name John Smith and had fishing tackle in hand to throw off suspicion. There, among the rocks, he divulged a plan to capture the federal armory at Harpers Ferry. Douglass argued that an attack on the federal government was too risky, but he was outmatched by Brown's stubbornness. After almost two days of intense debate, the four men prepared to part company. Brown said, "Come with me, Douglass; I will defend you with my life. I want you for a special purpose. When I strike, the bees will begin to swarm, and I shall want you to help hive them."[53]

Shields Green decided to follow Brown, saying, "I b'lieve I'll go wid de ole man." Douglass held back. "My discretion or my cowardice," he later wrote, "made me proof against the dear old man's eloquence—perhaps it was something of both which determined my course."[54] One wonders how Jermain Loguen would have responded if Brown had asked him directly to join in the assault upon Harpers Ferry. On May 17, 1859, Brown had written to Loguen, "I will just whisper in your private ear that I have no doubt you will soon have a call from God to minister at a different location."[55] Perhaps the call did not come, or if it did, perhaps Loguen had reservations that were similar to those of Douglass. Neither man went to Harpers Ferry. According to several sources, Harriet Tubman wanted to go but could not because of illness.[56]

Shields Green was a member of Brown's "Army of Liberation" when it attacked the United States Armory and Arsenal on the night of October 16, 1859. Green and the other raiders marched across the bridge that spans the Potomac River on a quiet Sunday night. The battle that Brown had dreamed of and thought of for so long had begun. Ironically, the first man killed was Hayward Sheppard, a free black porter at the railroad depot.

Government troops, commanded by Brevet Colonel Robert E. Lee and Lieutenant J. E. B. Stuart, soon overpowered Brown and his raiders. Of the 22 men (17 white and 5 black) in Brown's raiding force, 10 were killed, 7 escaped, and 5, including the Old Man, were captured.

The trial at Charles Town centered on charges of murder, treason, and fomenting slave insurrection. Brown rejected his lawyer's attempt to enter a plea of insanity. As he walked from his cell to meet his "public death," the Old Man handed this message to a bystander: "I John Brown am now quite *certain* that the crimes of this *guilty land: will* never be purged *away;* but with Blood. I had *as I now think: vainly* flattered myself that without *very much* bloodshed; it might be done."[57]

News of Brown's attempt to invade the lower valley of Virginia shocked the nation. When Douglass heard the report of what had happened at Harpers Ferry, he was in Philadelphia, delivering a lecture in National Hall on the topic of Self-Made Men. Douglass remembered, "The announcement came upon us with the startling effect of an earthquake."[58] He digressed to speak of Harpers Ferry and was applauded for calling Brown's actions justified. Fearful that he would be arrested as an accomplice, Douglass left Philadelphia for a "more Northern latitude." Before doing so, he asked his assistant, the German-born Ottilia Assing, to send a message to the telegraph operator in Rochester. The telegram warned Lewis Douglass, his oldest son, to "secure" any incriminating evidence, including the relevant correspondence and Brown's constitution, both of which were in Douglass's high desk.[59]

Douglass returned safely to Rochester, went on to Canada, and then made a trip to the British Isles. Governor Henry A. Wise of Virginia sought to indict Douglass and paid a detective $100 a month to track him down. John E. Cook, one of Brown's captured insurgents, accused Douglass of failing to deliver weapons and men as promised. The charges were false but, from the safety of Canada West, Douglass wrote a long letter—to be published in Rochester's *Democrat and American*—that praised Brown and explained his own actions:

> I may be asked why I did not join John Brown—the noble old hero whose one right hand had shaken the foundation of the American Union, and whose ghost will haunt the bed-chambers of all the born and unborn slaveholders of Virginia through all their generations, filling them with alarm and consternation. My answer to this has already been given, at least impliedly given—"The tools to those who can use them!" Let every man work for the abolition of slavery in his own way. I would help all and hinder none.[60]

Evidence that linked Douglass to Brown was found in the Old Man's carpetbag at the time of his capture. Douglass was in London when John Brown was hanged, but Susan B. Anthony, Parker Pillsbury, and a few others held a vigil and memorial service at Rochester's City Hall. George W. Clark sang, and a collection was taken to aid Brown's family. Black Americans hailed Brown as a martyr and celebrated his life and death long after he went resolutely to the gallows.[61]

Brown's carpetbag also contained letters and documents that implicated Gerrit Smith. Authorities found a canceled bank draft which had been written from Smith to Brown, in the amount of $100. It had been drawn on a bank in Albany and was dated August 22, 1859. Hugh Forbes and John E. Cook publicly named Smith as a coconspirator.[62] Democratic newspapers in the North, including the *Rochester Union and Advertiser,* called Smith a traitor. Rumors spread that Smith intended to flee to Canada. Smith placed armed guards around his Peterboro mansion. Any parcels sent to the household were cautiously opened to guard against injury by explosives (what Octavius Brooks Frothingham, Smith's friend and biographer, described as "those infernal machines").[63]

With the exception of Thomas Wentworth Higginson, who braved the public outcry against Brown's supporters, Smith had to face the firestorm of post–Harpers Ferry criticism alone. The Reverend Theodore Parker was in Italy, dying of tuberculosis. Sanborn, Howe, and Stearns fled to Canada; Morton, who was privy to the meetings with Brown at Peterboro, went to England. Highly agitated and fearful of arrest, Smith destroyed evidence that linked him to the Secret Six and to Brown. Smith's son-in-law, Colonel Charles D. Miller, went to the home of John Brown, Jr., in Ohio, to locate incriminating materials. Miller recalled being told by Brown's son that

Smith "was in a very distressed state of mind, fearing that the Government would pounce on him and ruin him, and he wished to destroy every vestige of evidence in my hands that could be made use of against him."[64]

Gerrit Smith was indeed a troubled man. A reporter from the *New York Herald*, which printed documents disclosing Smith's association with Brown, wrote, "[The raid] has not only impaired his health, but is likely to seriously affect his excitable and illy-balanced mind. . . . His calm, dignified, impressive bearing has given place to a hasty, nervous agitation, as though some great fear was constantly before his imagination."[65] Smith slept and ate irregularly. He talked about going to Virginia where he could join in John Brown's fate. In the parlance of the nineteenth century, Smith was said to be suffering from a state of exaltation of the mind. He showed symptoms of neuralgia, dropsy, and dyspepsia. With his feet so swollen that he was forced to wear moccasins, Peterboro's most famous citizen suffered a nervous breakdown.[66] Afraid that he might commit suicide, family members and friends took him to the New York State Lunatic Asylum in Utica on November 7, 1859 (five days after John Brown was sentenced). A pall of fear and anxiety now fell over the Smith mansion, heretofore a place of great liveliness, noted for the hospitality of its owner.[67]

The asylum, which is now the Mohawk Valley Psychiatric Center, was chartered in 1836, opened in 1843, and held more than five hundred patients in 1859. Dr. John Perdue Gray kept case notes on Smith. Gray believed that the Harpers Ferry shock had triggered an emotional breakdown because Smith's general physical health had been weakened by a bout with typhoid, in 1857, and by "aggravated dyspepsia." Gray prescribed a special diet and rest. Smith was diagnosed as suffering from acute mania. He failed to recognize his friends and had periods of "wildness." Smith was discharged from the asylum on December 29, 1859, and urged to avoid all forms of stress.

News of Smith's admission to the insane asylum reached Brown in prison. On Mary Brown's last visit with the Old Man in the Charles Town jail, the following occurred:

> Mrs. Brown then spoke of Gerrit Smith and asked if her husband had heard of the affliction that had visited him. Brown answered, "Yes I have read something about it."
>
> "Do you know that he is now in Utica?" said Mrs. Brown.

John Brown (1800–1859) during the 1850s. John Brown became acquainted with Upstate New York abolitionists in the late 1840s. Gerrit Smith, Jermain Loguen, and Harriet Tubman, among others, knew of his plans to do something bold to bring down the "peculiar institution." *Courtesy of the Library of Congress.*

"Yes I have been so informed; he was a good friend and I exceedingly regret his misfortune. How is he, have you heard lately?"

"Yes, I heard direct from him a few days ago. He was thought to be improving."

"I am really glad to hear it," replied Brown.[68]

In an effort to besmirch Smith and the Republicans, the New Democratic Vigilant Association (a political arm of the Democrats) accused Smith of having prior knowledge of Brown's raid. Smith sued for $50,000 damages. The matter was settled out of court, but Smith's reputation suffered. He continued to deny that he knew of Brown's intentions to strike at Harpers Ferry.

In 1865 Smith sued the *Chicago Tribune* for libel after it charged that he had feigned insanity to avoid being prosecuted. The *Tribune* had said, "on the arrest of Brown, his tender hearted financial patron became insane, fled from the wrath of Buchanan and the slaveholders who then ruled the Government, took refuge in a lunatic asylum and remained there until Lincoln was inaugurated."[69] There was a quasi-retraction, Smith published a long manifesto denying any direct knowledge of Brown's plans, and Frederick Douglass came to Smith's defense with a letter that declared, "Captain Brown never told me that you knew anything of guns or other weapons."[70]

Historians have echoed the accusation that Smith feigned insanity or, more charitably, that he was frightened "out of his wits," as biographer Ralph Harlow puts it, by the possibility that he would share Brown's fate.[71] The best—and most recent—interpretation of the evidence, using Gray's case notes and an understanding of modern psychological theory, has concluded that "the stress which Smith felt following Harpers Ferry had triggered a psychological episode that required hospitalization for what today would be called a bipolar disorder."[72] It is difficult to conceive of a situation where a sane man, who could have headed for Canada (less than a day's travel away) with some of the other conspirators, would choose to remain in an insane asylum with the social stigma then attached to mental illness.

No matter how we interpret Smith's behavior after Brown was captured, it is clear that public exposure of Smith's connections with the Old Man caused the Peterboro abolitionist great pain. In 1872, Franklin B. Sanborn (one of the Secret Six) quietly asked Smith to set the record straight. Smith demurred: "I am not competent to advise in the case. When the Harper's

Ferry affair occurred, I was sick, and my brain somewhat diseased. That affair excited and shocked me, and a few weeks after I was taken to a lunatic asylum. From that day to this, I have had but a hazy view of dear John Brown's great work."[73]

While Gerrit Smith was struggling to maintain his emotional balance in the aftermath of John Brown's arrest, the Reverend Samuel J. May, still the peace man, pondered what the attack meant for the country as a whole. May first heard of the outcome of the Harpers Ferry raid as he was returning from Europe in November 1859. The steamer stopped at Halifax, Nova Scotia, where May learned the news: "I felt at once," May later wrote, "that it was 'the beginning of the end' of our conflict with slavery."[74] Emboldened by the escalating spirit of sectionalism, the South's partisans, May noted, "rudely treated and grossly insulted" abolitionists in Boston, Buffalo, Rochester, and other places. Of Brown's forthcoming execution and the national furor over the Harpers Ferry incident, May wrote in his diary: "I apprehend it is but the beginning of sorrow, the pattering of the rain before the hurricane."[75]

In Syracuse, Rochester, and elsewhere in North Star Country, abolitionists and their allies planned memorial services for the day of John Brown's execution: December 2, 1859. On December 1, the *New York Times* printed the following text, in a column titled "Sympathy for the Condemned": "The Wesleyan Methodists in Syracuse, N.Y., have appointed a prayer-meeting at their Chapel, on Friday morning, at 6 o'clock, for the purpose of offering up prayer for John Brown, who is to be executed on that day. All Christians in that city are invited to attend this meeting."[76] Hoping to thwart an outbreak of violence, May attended the gathering in Syracuse. At 6:30 in the evening, the bells of City Hall tolled out the age of John Brown, striking once for each of his fifty-nine years. At first, the assembled mourners stood silently, but during the service that followed they transformed the event into a war demonstration. May managed to sublimate their anger in a resolution that urged Congress to call a national convention to abolish slavery. "It was a noble gesture," writes historian W. Freeman Galpin, "but that was all."[77]

Due to the efforts of Susan B. Anthony, about three hundred people gathered at Corinthian Hall in Rochester for a meeting of mourning and eulogy. Anthony presided. In her diary she records that "not one man of prominence in religion or politics will publicly identify himself with the John Brown meeting."[78] Fearing mob violence, the meeting's organizers charged fifty cents for admission. Parker Pillsbury, a white Garrisonian, and the Reverend Abram Pryn, a Free Church minister, both spoke.

Now John Brown's body "lies moulderin' in the grave," to borrow a phrase from the song that Yankee soldiers sang as they finished the work he had begun. Guarded by the majestic sentinels of Tahawas and Whiteface, the Old Man's bones lie in ground that has become part of the history of North Star Country by virtue of Brown's connections to abolitionists in Upstate New York.[79] Despite his often ghost-like presence in the region, John Brown left his mark upon those advocates of freedom who called North Star Country home. The Old Man made a deep impression upon all who met him, whatever they thought of his actions during the autumn of 1859 and of the issue he brought forth: When is it right to use violence in a just cause? Brown acted upon impulses long dormant in the abolitionist crusade, forcing others to confront the connection between strong words and strong deeds.

Frederick Douglass tells us that, after his first visit with Brown, something changed. Although he was still a moral suasionist in the Garrisonian mold, Douglass described himself as "less hopeful of its [slavery's] peaceful abolition. My utterances became more and more tinged by the color of this man's strong impressions."[80]

The raid upon Harpers Ferry caused abolitionists to rethink their positions on the use of violent means. William Lloyd Garrison spoke of peace in his eulogy of Brown, reaffirming the principles of nonresistance. He appealed to the "doctrine of the inviolability of human life" and reminded his listeners that he had "labored unremittingly to effect the peaceful abolition of slavery by an appeal to the reason and conscience of the slaveholder." Yet even Garrison was so affected by what Brown had done and hoped to do, that he was prepared to say, "success to every slave insurrection at the South, and in every slave country."[81]

After the closing of his beloved Oneida Institute, Beriah Green had gone into isolation and subsequent despair over the failures of the Liberty Party. But after Harpers Ferry, Green felt a rush of hope. Green congratulated Wendell Phillips for participating in Brown's memorial service at North Elba, "From my obscure corner, I cannot well help joining the myriad host in the heart bursting exclamation, Servant of God, well done! . . . you have identified yourself with a great soul—a true Hero—a genuine Son of Humanity."[82]

In the aftermath of Harpers Ferry, the public was quick to associate the abolitionists, despite their longstanding protestations to the contrary, with violence. The *New York Times* of October 20, 1859, was filled with dispatches and intelligence regarding what one correspondent called, "the insane undertaking of the insurgents." Many Americans believed that the assault upon Harpers Ferry represented more than a tactical blow to slavery that had been delivered by a small band of misguided zealots led by Captain Brown, late of the Kansas wars. To most Southerners and many Northerners, the fanatics who attacked the Armory with sword and pistol were acting out the violent rhetoric of Northern abolitionists.

The *Times* made much of the discovery of 1,500 pikes with large blades in Brown's possession. But equally damning were the contents of that carpetbag: letters from Douglass and Smith. This was confirmation enough that the abolitionists of North Star Country were prepared to wage warfare upon the South and to divide the nation in the process. To make its case, the *Times* reprinted a letter that Smith had written to John Thomas, chairman of the Jerry Rescue committee, on August 27, 1859.

In 1859, Thomas had invited Smith to deliver the commemorative address at the approaching anniversary of the deliverance of Jerry. As Smith had done each year since 1851, he declined. He still believed that the rescue of Jerry was "a great and glorious event" that had been demanded of the abolitionists as a demonstration of their own humanity. He had frequently boasted that Jerry had been snatched from the evil grasp of slavery without bloodshed. However, in the late summer of 1859, less than two months before Harpers Ferry, Gerrit Smith, who had flirted with violence from time to time, at least rhetorically, came close to the precipice.

"It is perhaps," Smith wrote Thomas, "too late to bring Slavery to an end by peaceable means—too late to vote it down. *For many years I have feared, and published my fears, that it must go out in blood.*"[83] The *Times* editorialized that Smith's words to the Jerry rescuers of Syracuse "will be read with interest, as a prophecy, if nothing more, of the outbreak at Harpers Ferry."[84]

Of the lesson of the hour given at Harpers Ferry, Wendell Phillips said, "Insurrection of thought always preceded the insurrection of arms. The last twenty years have been insurrection of thought. We seem to be entering on a new phase of the great moral American struggle."[85]

William Henry Seward did not belong to the Secret Six, nor is there evidence that John Brown wished to involve him. But in the furor over John Brown's raid at Harpers Ferry, abolition's enemies remembered Seward's speech about "the irrepressible conflict," a speech he had given in Rochester, on October 25, 1858. The New York *Herald* thought that Seward should replace Brown on the scaffold at Charles Town and it called the senator the "arch agitator who is responsible for this insurrection."[86]

A lengthy article in the *Washington Constitution* drew the curtain of guilt down upon Seward by linking his "irrepressible conflict" doctrine to the abolitionists of the Burned-over District, and then to John Brown. The editorial asserted that Seward had inspired "the fanatical and reckless religious abolitionists [who] felt that a new impulse had been given to their unholy cause." They became more confident, more insolent, and more determined to wage war upon the South. "The number actually engaged in the insurrectionary movement at Harpers Ferry," the *Constitution* maintained, "is no indication of its extent or even the parties involved in the outrage." The same paper implicated Gerrit Smith by reprinting two of his letters to John Brown in which Peterboro's leading abolitionist, surely one of the most well-known "*religious* abolitionists" of the North, commended the freedom fighter and urged him on in his "Kansas work."[87] In Richmond, Governor Wise of Virginia gave a speech in which he condemned Smith by name and boasted, "If any one should smuggle off Gerrit Smith some night, and bring him to me, I would read him a moral lecture, and then send him home."[88]

Frederick Douglass called John Brown's actions "the logical result of slaveholding persecutions." While still a slave in Maryland, young Frederick had stood his ground, fought, and defeated the slave driver (Covey) in a battle that was the turning point of his life. Douglass understood, more so than any of his white abolitionist colleagues, that slavery was an institution built upon violence and maintained by the fear of violence.

Southerners did not, by and large, rest uneasy in their beds as long as the abolitionist movement restricted itself to the use of rhetorical condemnations of the sin of slavery. But when John Brown—as Nat Turner and Denmark Vesey had done before him—invoked the doctrine of righteous violence as premise for a just war, the South gathered itself, like a poisonous snake, ready to strike back. Douglass knew instinctively that John Brown's body symbolized that something had gone wrong, deeply wrong, in the soul of America. He wrote of the Old Man, "His corpse was given up to his woe-stricken widow, and she assisted by anti-slavery friends, caused it to be borne to North Elba, Essex County, N.Y., and there his dust reposes amid the silent, solemn, and snowy grandeurs of the Adirondacks. This raid upon Harpers Ferry was as the last straw to the camel's back. What in the tone of Southern sentiment had been fierce before, became furious and uncontrollable now."[89]

9. Battlefields and Home Fronts

"The storm has broken upon us," nineteen-year-old Caroline Richards of Canandaigua wrote in her diary on April 15, 1861. "President Lincoln has issued a call for 75,000 men and many are volunteering to go all around us. How strange and awful it seems." In May of that year, Caroline and her schoolgirl friends went down to the trains to see the soldier boys off. The girls gave flowers to the young volunteers from Canandaigua and neighboring towns; they received buttons cut from the boys' coats in return. It was a gay time: martial music, flags flying, and the boys singing, "It is sweet, Oh, 'tis sweet, for one's country to die." But the older women were already at work, cutting up garments and scraping lint to make bandages for the soldiers. Caroline confided to her diary, "it will not seem so grand if we hear they are dead on the battlefield, far from home."[1]

Hundreds of New York State communities, large and small, were caught up in the tumult of patriotism and passion during the early months of the contest with the South, a contest that John Brown's assault on Harpers Ferry had helped to excite. President Abraham Lincoln's call for volunteers found a ready response among those who were eager to thump the rebellious Confederates. Most believed the battle would be short, with victory assured.

Henry Conklin of Herkimer County was a hardscrabble farmer with a wife and three small sons. He held out until October 22, 1861, when a pro-Union demonstration took place in the town of Ohio. "At this meeting the wants of the government were so vividly portrayed," Conklin recalled many years later, "that I forgot all about my family, listening to the patriotic speeches, and when the opportunity came, I with others walked up and enlisted." The new recruits "talked it all up about going off to war" on their way home that night. They called each other "comrade," and they steeled themselves to tell their families. For the last half mile, Conklin walked alone and nearly repented signing the enlistment papers. "But it was too late now, so I made the best of it and began to harden myself to what must come sooner or later, and that was a soldier's adieu. When I told my wife what I had done she did not scold me, but the silent tears trickled down her face as she looked at the little boys who stood gazing at us in wonderment."[2]

Conklin's wait for his soldier's adieu was not long. On November 13, he was mustered at Prospect Depot. Within a few days, he traveled by train to Rome where he joined the Mohawk Rangers, under the command of Colonel O. B. Pierce.[3]

On April 13, 1861, the day Fort Sumter was surrendered, a South Carolina Piedmont farmer named David Golightly Harris wrote in his journal: "This notorious little battle will have a tendency to bring out the other states, and show the Black Republicans that the South will fight."[4] The South fought because the Yankees were coming. "Lincoln may bring his 75,000 troops against us," said Confederate Vice President Alexander Stephens. "We fight for our homes, our fathers and mothers, our wives, brothers, sisters, sons and daughters! . . . We can call out a million of peoples if need be, and when they are cut down we can call another, and still another."[5]

In 1862, Harris got his orders to join in the defense of homeland and honor and, like Henry Conklin of Upstate New York, he prepared himself for an uncertain fate. Harris's journal entry for March 21: "Hoping that all will go well with me while in the army and at home with my family. Something has to be done, and I should do my part. The military life will be a new life for me, as I have never been in the ranks in my life, and scarcely know a word of command. If I go, I hope my wife will be reconciled to it. Parting with my family will be worse than meeting the yankees."[6]

When Yank first met Reb in the early months of the Civil War, there was little talk of abolition and slavery. "The sum of all Villainies" was of less importance than restoring the Union. Lincoln did not intend to make the conflict with the Confederates a war to end slavery—an abolitionist war would make him lose popular support in the North and in border states, such as Kentucky, Missouri, and Maryland. Former President James Buchanan's dictum, "Touch the question of slavery seriously, and the Union is from that moment dissolved," was the prevailing sentiment in the South as well as the fear of many in the North.[7]

In Rochester, on June 16, 1861, Frederick Douglass took the podium to challenge the limited goals of the federal government. Describing the conflict that was then under way as the "American Apocalypse," he demanded that "not a slave should be left a slave in the returning footprints of the American army gone to put down this slaveholding rebellion. Sound policy, not less than humanity, demands the instant liberation of every slave in the rebel states."[8]

Gerrit Smith likewise chafed at Lincoln's reluctance to put an end to slavery. Smith criticized Lincoln for listening to proslavery elements in the North, and he ridiculed the notion that the North owed the Rebels any constitutional obligations. Smith made the following journal entry on May 18, 1861: "The war will be short. It will establish Government beyond all hope of present and future traitors to overthrow it. It will free the slave; and then the North and South, freed forever from the only cause of their mutual alienation, will grow up together into that 'more perfect union' for which the Fathers ordained the constitution."[9]

Not everyone shared Smith's belief that the war would transform America. Beriah Green, who was as disgruntled as ever with the lack of principled righteousness among America's leaders, adopted an anti-Unionist position on the grounds that Lincoln's government was as treasonous as that of the Confederacy. Garrison's *Liberator* aired Green's angry letter on April 19, 1861, alongside announcements that the Civil War had begun, Fort Sumter had been captured, troops had been mustered, and "The North United at Last." "Traitor throttles traitor," Green had written to Garrison. Perhaps, Oneida Institute's old champion went on, the "Potsherds of the earth striving with each other" would "blindly clear the way for something essentially other than now obtrudes its ghastliness upon our loathing thoughts."

Garrison described Green as an esteemed friend but he urged the friends of freedom to support Lincoln. He called for a clean break with the South: "Let 'the covenant with death and the agreement with hell' be . . . annulled."[10]

Green complained to Gerrit Smith that none of the "Friends of Humanity" could be found who shared his view that the federal government was no government. When he was pressured to support the war effort, Green responded, "What are ten thousand Fort Sumters to one poor Baby reduced to chattelship?"

Smith urged him to set aside his differences with the Republicans until the rebellion had been put down. Beriah countered, "I am not a war-man" and once pointedly refused to "get up" an audience for a pro-Union speaker.[11]

Most Upstate New Yorkers rallied round the federal government, but the war was not to be the short one that Smith had prophesied. New York State's allotment of the initial 75,000 troops had been 13,000 men; in a rush of patriotic enthusiasm, the legislature in Albany authorized the enrollment of 30,000. New York City and Elmira were named as the principal mobilization points. Later, Albany also became an important staging area where men and boys from central and western New York State prepared themselves for the fight ahead. After the Union armies took heavy casualties at the first Battle of Bull Run in July 1861—fought near Manassas Junction, Virginia, just twenty-five miles from Washington—the call went out for more troops.

In the North, the popular sentiment that favored armed conflict with the South was growing. Prior to the attack upon Fort Sumter, Wide-Awakes Clubs had been organized in North Star Country to rouse the public mind to the danger that the slave oligarchy posed to the Union.

While many Northerners "reposed in wonted security," Auburn's leaders made early preparations to raise a militia and, by December 1860, had placed a supervisory committee in charge of recruitment. Local historian Henry Hall claimed that the "honor remains to Auburn of being the fore-most of the cities of this patriotic state to announce the impending danger of the country, and call for the raising of troops."[12] Doubtless there were a few Republicans in Auburn, not to mention Democrats, who held a skeptical outlook and viewed the Wide-Awakers as alarmists. But, once the popular enthusiasm for repulsing the Southern threat to the Union's peace and stability—and not incidently to the prosperity of the North—gained a head of steam, dissident voices were muted by loud patriotic choruses.[13] Nevertheless, the question of what the fight was about was troubling.

Newton Martin Curtis answered Lincoln's call for 75,000 volunteers after the loss of Fort Sumter. He did so with the certainty that he, and the other soldiers who made up the 16th New York Infantry, was marching off to preserve the Union. The underlying cause of the conflict, Curtis believed, was not slavery but sectional differences which were rooted in debates over economic policies that dated back at least as far as the Tariff Act of 1828.[14]

Historians argue that the North and the South developed distinct and different identities after the American Revolution. North Star Country abolitionists recognized the economic and cultural results of sectionalism, yet they saw the Civil War, fundamentally, as a conflict over the morality of slavery, and they urged full support of the war effort.

Although he was a longtime supporter of the American Peace Society, Gerrit Smith was ready to put down traitors when the issue was slavery. On May 18, 1861, he wrote, "For, although the passions, prejudices, and perverseness of men beget many forms of insanity, Southern slavery only is capable of driving millions to the made work of violently overthrowing a government whose partiality toward them and indulgence of them are the only wrong it has done."[15] Frederick Douglass welcomed conflict with the slaveholders and assumed the role of war propagandist with enthusiasm. "We earnestly desire to see the South humbled," he wrote in May 1861.[16]

North Star Country also contained its share of dissenters. They were upset by the call to arms, and they blamed abolitionists and other "agitators" for bringing about the national conflict. In November 1861, Frederick Douglass came to Syracuse to lecture. He found the following handbill posted:

NIGGER FRED IS COMING!
This Reviler of the Constitution, and author of
"Death in the Pot!"
and who once in this city called George Washington a
THIEF, RASCAL AND TRAITOR!
is advertised to lecture on "Slavery" again on Thursday and Friday evenings of this week, at Wieting Hall!

Shall his vile sentiments again be tolerated in this community by a constitutional-liberty loving people? Or shall we give him a WARM reception at this time, for his insolence, as he deserves? Rally, then, one and all, and DRIVE HIM FROM OUR CITY! Down on the arch-fugitive to Europe, who is not only a COWARD, but a TRAITOR to his country! RALLY FREEMEN!

Admission, 10 cents.[17]

When Douglass rose to speak at Wieting Hall, a special police force of seventy, and a cadre of military cadets, stood guard with fixed bayonets. The police arrested a boy with rotten eggs and stones in his pockets, and the crisis passed.

Earlier in January 1861, the outcome had been different. The AASS had tried to meet in Syracuse's Convention Hall. A hostile crowd gathered, threw eggs, broke benches, and hooted down the Reverend Samuel J. May when he tried to speak. The abolitionists retreated to the home of Dr. R. W. Pease and held their meeting.

The next morning, they found Convention Hall to be in control of the rioters and so closed their business. The following evening, the mob celebrated their "onslaught upon popular liberty," to use May's words, by marching to Hanover Square. They carried banners that said "Abolitionism No Longer in Syracuse," "The Jerry Rescuers Played Out," "Freedom of Speech, But Not Treason," and "The Rights of the South Must Be Protected." Once they arrived at the square, the antiabolitionists burned two effigies:, one labeled Susan B. Anthony and the other, Samuel J. May. "The effigies were burned up," May later wrote, "but not the great realities for which we were contending."[18]

Despite the rancor of the peace-at-any-cost element in New York State, the North's most populous and wealthy state had contributed 448,000 soldiers and sailors to the Union effort by the time Generals Grant and Lee met at Appomattox courthouse in 1865 and the Southern cause was clearly lost. One of every six soldiers who wore the Union blue hailed from New York State. Most of them were young men with the full promise of life ahead of them. Seventy percent of the 2.3 million soldiers in the United State Army were under the age of twenty-three.[19]

North Star Country did more than its fair share of bearing the burden of conflict. Upstate men and boys fought in every major battle, and thousands of them never saw family and friends again. Approximately 53,000 New Yorkers died as a result of taking up arms against the Rebels. In 1865, the population of New York State was 48,958 less than it had been in 1860.

The first Northern officer to be killed in battle was Colonel Elmer Ephraim Ellsworth of Mechanicville, New York. Later, Empire State soldiers would use "Remember Ellsworth" as a battle cry, drawing inspiration from the memory of one of their own who had been shot dead when he tried to remove the Confederate flag from the roof of a Virginia tavern.[20]

Thoughts of dying in the woods, somewhere south of the Mason-Dixon

Line, were easily pushed to the back of their minds when the volunteers from North Star Country were first mustered. Some were only three-month men, and their ears still rang with the hurrahs and shouts of acclaim from fellow citizens who were eager to see them off.

At Alfred University, a Seventh-Day Baptist school in Allegany County, the entire senior class enlisted in the 23rd Regiment of New York Volunteers. Abigail Allen recalled,

> The moving meeting in the chapel the day that our boys were to leave can never be forgotten by anyone who was present. It was crowded to over flowing by citizens and students so that there was hardly standing room. The eleven members of the graduating class were called upon to state their reasons for leaving their studies and all peaceful pursuits for the turmoil and uncertainty of war. Every heart was stirred especially when two of them said "We give our all—our lives—and never expect to return." And so it proved, for these two came back only in their coffins and that within a year.[21]

Towns and villages across North Star Country erected liberty poles, called out their bands, and, with banners flying nearly as high as the patriotic rhetoric, sent their men and boys off to war.

Patriotism and duty were the bywords of the day, and they were hard to ignore when martial music filled the air and one's comrades were joining up. On May 3, 1861, four companies of the 74th Militia left Buffalo for mobilization at Elmira. Six more followed about one week later. One day after the assault upon Fort Sumter, at a get-out-the-troops rally in Buffalo, ex-President Millard Fillmore had said, "We have reached a crisis in the history of this country when no man, however humble his rank or limited his influence, has a right to stand neutral. Civil war has been inaugurated, and we must meet it. Our government calls for aid, and we must give it."[22]

Buffalo set up a Union Defense Committee, city churches gathered collections for the departing soldiers, and women dedicated sewing circles to the making of blankets and bandages. Fillmore captained a company of elderly citizens who called themselves the Union Continentals and dressed in Revolutionary War uniforms. The old men performed escort duty for the boys from Buffalo who went off to form the 21st New York Voluntary Infantry Regiment, a regiment which was to suffer heavy losses in the battle at Manassas Junction (Second Bull Run) in August of 1862. After their arrival at Elmira, the recruits from Buffalo had little time for military drill before being sent on. Of the early days of the war, a county historian wrote, "Sometimes the need for men at the front was so desperate that whole companies were sworn aboard the south bound trains at Elmira. Sometimes men went to war in cattle cars."[23]

One unique unit to assemble in Elmira during the summer of 1861 was the 50th New York Voluntary Regiment. The 50th was composed of canal boatmen and construction workers from Upstate New York, and they had been recruited by the eminent New York civil engineer Charles B. Stuart. The 50th proved to be invaluable when pontoon bridges were needed by Union forces who were fighting on Virginia's swampy peninsula.[24]

The first volunteers to rendezvous at Elmira belonged to the 24th New York Voluntary Infantry Regiment. Company K was made up of men and boys from Oswego and Jefferson Counties. One of their number was Newton Rounds.

On May 26, 1861, Newton wrote to his sister Elmina about the journey he had made by train from Belleville to Rome to Geneva, by steamboat on Seneca Lake to Watkins Glen, and then to Elmira via the Chemung Canal. It was dark, rainy, and cold when the troops arrived in Elmira. The troops spent their first night in the Presbyterian church, "with a blanket which we rolled about us and slept as best we could amidst so much noise and confusion on the soft side of the boards of the floor." The earliest arrivals had been quartered in a barrel factory, but Rounds and his compatriots arrived to find that twenty wooden barracks, each of which could hold a company of eighty men, had been erected along the river. The barracks stood about one mile from the heart of Elmira, which was then a village of about ten thousand. Although he was unschooled in the military arts and awaiting his private's light gray uniform, Newton was assigned guard duty. He paced his beat with musket and bayonet, feeling "considerable like a soldier."[25] Newton's pay was all of $11 per month.

Of camp food, Newton told his sister, "Are pretty well satisfied in that respect. About 800 eat at the tables in one building here. The cooking is done by means of a steam engine and on a large scale. We get now and then some milk and eggs etc. and all we want at that. Have know[n] some of the boys to eat from 12 to 15 eggs at a meal."[26] It was advisable for these greenhorns to stock up. Soldiers often marched and fought on empty stomachs. In 1864, the daily rations for a Union army man (measured in ounces) were beef (20), flour (18), dry beans (2.6), green coffee (1.6), sugar (2.4), salt (.64), and lesser quantities of pepper, yeast powder, soap, candles, and vinegar.[27] These amounts were not always available, and many times rations were spoiled or delayed. Except for a "hard cold," Newton judged his health to be "good," although lots of the boys were "sorely vexed with diarrhea." Like the others, he was anxious to get into active service. Newton Rounds saw more fighting than he wanted at the battle of Second Bull Run on August 30, 1862, where he was mortally wounded. David Hamer, another volunteer from Ellisberg and the Sandy Creek area, recalled that so many of the 24th had been killed, lost by sickness, or discharged that "the regimental quarters would hold the whole brigade and then some" after the Federals pulled back to Washington.[28]

Orderly Sergeant David Hamer survived his tour of duty and was discharged in the fall of 1863 and returned to the town of Boylston. Twelve men of Company G did not survive. They missed the welcoming home banquet that the citizens of Sandy Creek had arranged. The train from Utica was late to arrive, and hungry celebrants wanted to eat the roast pig without waiting for the remnant of returning soldiers. A farmer named Stevens, who had donated the pig, protested, "I roasted that pig for the soldiers, and if they don't have it I'll take the pig home." Neighbors kept the pig and chicken pies warm until evening when the surviving twenty-two men of Company G finally arrived "looking a bit worse for wear but happy."[29]

Hamer and his comrades had good reason to be happy. They had beaten the odds and escaped the angel of death. They were changed men, however, having come to know the sound and smell of death. Hamer recalled that when the "mantle of night" settled over the carnage at Gainsville, during the battle of Second Bull Run, he could hear "the groans of the wounded and their piteous cries for water and care. Their moans and the clear notes of the whip-poor-will mingled together, making strange music."[30]

An old man named Sheppard came up the road along which the surviving members of the 24th regiment from Oswego had camped after the Union defeat. The old man asked Hamer if he knew the Sheppard boys and where to find them. "I told him I knew them well and that we left both at Bull Run," Hamer reported. "I shall never forget the expression he made and the agonizing look he wore. 'Oh, my God,' he exclaimed, 'They are all I have got in the world, and now they are gone.'"[31]

Who else from North Star Country heeded the call to rally 'round the

Union flag? In response to the federal government's call for an additional 300,000 men in July 1862, Governor Morgan sounded the patriotic appeal to every fireside in the state: "Let the glorious example of the Revolutionary period be our emulation."

J. A. Mowris signed up with the 117th regiment as a member of what was popularly known as the Fourth Oneida. Among his comrades, he found "the athletic lumberman; the youthful yeoman, legal heir to many a paternal acre; the staid mechanic; the punctual operative; the tidy clerk; the bank accountant; and not least, the oft-hidden son of sage Mother Hamilton."[32] Mowris served as regimental surgeon and discovered that men of all classes and backgrounds bled alike, including those students who had dutifully left their studies at Hamilton College in Clinton.

Hermon Clarke was another one of the recruits in the 117th New York Volunteer Infantry. By following his story one can learn much about how extraordinary events captured ordinary Upstaters in the fiery crucible of the Civil War.

Clarke was a twenty-four-year-old farm boy and general store clerk from an area near Waterville (Oneida County). He left home on August 4, 1862, to join the Fourth Oneida at Camp Huntington, on the western edge of Rome. Five feet and nine inches tall, with grey eyes and dark hair, Hermon weighed in at 132 pounds. Fortified with an oyster lunch at Waterville's International Saloon and with a speech and a prayer from L. Wayhurst, principal of the local academy, Clarke set off on the greatest adventure of his life. Seventy-two of the letters he wrote home have survived the vagaries of time. They give us an intimate view of how one soldier from North Star Country attempted to keep in touch with the home front while he was on the battlefield.

By October, the 117th was at Fort Ripley, one of the many fortifications that defended Washington, and the nights were getting cold. Hermon was pulling guard duty and making up lists of things his family should send him. "In the first place, I want my wrappers and two pairs of cheap colored drawers and a pair of lined gloves. In the line of provisions, most anything that will keep, for instance, dried beef, dried apples, ginger cookies, etc. A bottle of pain killer would be good to have these cold damp nights, and a package of mustard and some cheese would be best of all. It costs 20¢ per pound here."[33]

When Hermon's box arrived, he reported that it was in A-1 condition, no broken bottles of honey or strawberry preserves to ruin everything else. "I tell you," he wrote Silas Clarke, his father, on November 9th from Fort Ripley, "we had a good supper last night of victuals that were clean and didn't smell of greasy, smoky camp kettles. I ate until I wasn't hungry. I didn't stop because the meat was rank or because I found a worm in the bread, but ate without fear of finding anything of the kind."[34] Hermon's subsequent letters requested the tangibles that every soldier clung to as confirmation that the folks at home still cared, items such as a good pair of boots and a winter vest. Army life apparently agreed with him. By March 1863, he reported that he weighed 164 pounds, a gain of 32 pounds since leaving Waterville. Hermon sent a photograph home to prove that he was as well as could be expected.[35]

By June 1863, the Oneida "boys in blue" were at Camp Haskins, Virginia, still untested in battle but close enough now to the war-weary countryside to see the human and physical wreckage. The 117th feigned a march toward Richmond, hoping to draw Lee's forces away from Gettysburg. A great many men returned to Camp Haskins sick with the fever. In August, the 117th was on the sandy waste of Folly Island, engaged in the effort to take Fort Wagner. Herman's regiment escaped the carnage, but shells fell too close for comfort.

Hermon's father was a conservative Democrat. By November 1863, Silas's soldier son had grown impatient with the nay-saying of the Peace Democrats, including his father. He wrote Silas,

> I expect to hear soon of a great victory in New York, either Democratic or Republican—I don't care which. I have become disgusted with politics. Just as long as people [in the] North pay attention to that, just so long will the war last, and I should think they would see it. It seems that they are all afraid our army will be increased to a sufficient force to close the war and end the suffering of hundreds of soldiers by so doing.[36]

Herman discounted his father's speculation that only Republican soldiers had been furloughed to go home and vote for the administration ticket. On December 7, 1863, he wrote, "The past six months have made a great change politically in the Army. Men who a year ago were bitterly against the [Lincoln] Administration have failed to find even sympathy, much [less] encouragement from the Administration."[37]

Herman Clarke's growing resentment fed on the failure of Northern

Democrats to support the war effort. They actively discouraged volunteers and were implicated in the New York City draft riots of July 1863. Embarrassed by Union reversals, and frustrated by Copperhead denunciations of its war policies, the Lincoln administration pushed for a draft.

In March 1863, the Enrollment and Conscription Act passed in Congress. Those who were wealthy enough could escape the draft by paying a $300 "commutation" fee or by hiring a substitute. The poor understood what this meant for them. In the slums and shanty towns, tough talk targeted the enrollment officers and clerks. When the drawings began, jeering crowds assembled, egged on by Democratic politicians. Anti-draft, anti-black speakers inflamed whites whose latent racial hatred erupted in riots. Mobs roamed the streets, looting property and assaulting blacks. Rioters burned the Colored Orphan Asylum at Fifth Avenue and 43rd Street, and they lynched William Jones, who made the mistake of going out early in the morning to find a loaf of bread for breakfast.[38]

Dr. Benjamin A. Fordyce of Scipio (Cayuga County) was in New York City during the draft riots. He was an assistant surgeon with the 160th New York State Volunteers. Fordyce ventured out onto the streets during the demonstrations and barely escaped the brickbats and clubs himself. Of the protestors, the upstate doctor informed his wife, "They are [the] hardest lot of low mean Irish that any person can conceive of. They look as if rioting, stealing, arson and Murder would be but idle pastimes and pleasing amusements."[39]

Frederick Douglass was in Philadelphia, at Camp William Penn, helping to recruit black troops when the rioting broke out. On the advice of a friend, he steered clear of the area where protestors still controlled the streets, as he made his way back to Rochester via New York City. Later, he wrote, "There is perhaps no darker chapter in the whole history of the war than this cowardly and bloody uprising in July, 1863. For three days and nights New York was in the hands of a ferocious mob, and there was not sufficient power in the government of the country or of the city itself to stay the hand of violence and the effusion of blood."

Douglass viewed the mob, which "dashed out the brains of young children against the lampposts" and "forced colored men, women and children to seek concealment in cellars or garrets," as "part of the rebel force, without the rebel uniform." He chastised Horatio Seymour, the Democratic governor of New York, who had been elected in 1862, for addressing the anti-draft protestors as "My friends."[40]

Antiblack violence also broke out in Buffalo. With its concentration of Irish, Buffalo had a vocal Democratic element that opposed turning the conflict with the South into an abolition war. At around the same time that the four-day riot in New York City was ignited by opposition to the National Conscription Act, Irish laborers attacked blacks, who were seen as competition for jobs, on Buffalo's docks. Sergeant George Tipping, an Irish immigrant to Buffalo, was away fighting with Corcoran's Irish Legion in the Union Army when he heard of the troubles at home. He wrote his wife, "Well Catharine there is a lively time in Old Buffalo by all accounts That is with the nigers and the Irish the News is here that there is a regular Rebellion on docks in Buffalo and the Darkey Some of them were Killed."[41]

The midsummer carnage in New York City, and the outbreak of antiblack violence in Buffalo, underscored the old debate about the meaning and purpose of the Civil War. The "peace-at-any-cost" politicians blamed the abolitionists for stirring the pot of sectionalism. Most white soldiers from the North, including those from New York's old Burned-over District, left kith and kin to stop Southern aggression, not to free the slaves. This was in keeping with Lincoln's policy in 1862.

In a reply to an editorial written by Horace Greeley of the *New York Tribune* on the aims of the war, Lincoln declared: "My paramount object in this struggle *is* to save the Union, and is *not* either to save or to destroy slavery. If I could save the Union without freeing *any* slaves I would do it; if I could save it by freeing *all* the slaves I would do it; and if I could do it by freeing some and leaving others alone, I would also do that."[42] This political doublespeak troubled North Star Country abolitionists, but they soon had reason for renewed confidence in the president.

In July, Lincoln informed his cabinet, including Secretary of State William Henry Seward, that he would on January 1, 1863, declare "all persons held as slaves within any state . . ., wherein the constitutional authority of the United States shall not then be practically recognized, . . . forever . . . free."[43] Seward urged the president to delay informing the public of his intentions until the Union armies had a battlefield victory. After the Battle of Antietam (Sharpsburg) in September, Americans of all persuasions learned that, on the first day of 1863, the war to restore the Union would also become a war to end slavery.

In anticipation of the historic moment, Frederick Douglass spoke at the Favor Street A.M.E.Z. Church in Rochester on December 28, 1862. "This is scarcely a day for prose. It is a day for poetry and song, a new song. These cloudless skies, this balmy air, this brilliant sunshine (making December as pleasant as May) are in harmony with the glorious morning of liberty about to dawn upon us." But Douglass cautioned that the work of abolitionism was not done. Proslavery doughfaces in the North, he warned, would use the Emancipation Proclamation as reason "to inflame the ancient prejudice against the negro."[44] Douglass waited in Boston at Tremont Temple, along with a large crowd of the friends of freedom that included William Wells Brown, for news of what he called "the trump of jubilee." Messengers stationed between the platform of Tremont Temple and the telegraph office passed the word on, "It is coming! It is on the wires!!" The assembly erupted in celebration. A black preacher led in the singing of "Sound the loud timbrel o'er Egypt's dark sea, Jehovah hath triumphed, his people are free."[45]

Later, North Star Country's most eloquent black abolitionist gave the Emancipation Proclamation a more critical examination. He observed that, by freeing the slaves only in those parts of the Confederacy that were not yet under Union control, the proclamation had been "apparently inspired by the low motive of military necessity." Nevertheless, Douglass viewed the first of January, 1863, as "the turning-point in the conflict between freedom and slavery. A death-blow was given to the slaveholding rebellion."[46] Biographer William S. McFeely writes, "Frederick Douglass all but snatched the Emancipation Proclamation from Abraham Lincoln's hands to make of its flat rhetoric a sharpened call for freedom and equality."[47]

Upstate New York soldiers who were out on the battlefield echoed Douglass's interpretation of Lincoln's move. Thomas Ward Osborn, a line officer from the Watertown area, was encamped before Fredericksburg (Virginia) in January 1861. "I think," the Union artilleryman wrote to his brother, "the President's Emancipation Proclamation precludes the possibility of any settlement except by absolute subjugation, and even that carried to the last extremity."[48] On the very day the Emancipation Proclamation took effect, Osborn had written, "If we lose in this war, the country is lost and if we win it is saved. There is no middle ground."[49]

Lincoln hoped that his emancipation decision would create enough consternation and chaos behind Confederate lines to give his generals a tactical advantage. Lee's victory at Second Bull Run, and the invasion of Maryland by the Army of Northern Virginia, caused Lincoln's critics to call for the removal of the overly cautious General McClellan. Lincoln did so in February 1863, and he replaced him with Ambrose Burnside. Caroline Richards of Canandaigua—together with her society of girls who were working for the aid of the soldiers—wrote McClellan a letter of support on February 13. They expressed admiration for his leadership from Rich Mountain to Antietam and for his calm courage on the battlefield. They pledged to pray that the general would be restored to lead his men "to victory in the sacred name of the Union and Constitution."[50] About a week later, McClellan replied, thanking Caroline and her friends: "Such sentiments on the part of those whose brothers have served with me in the field are more grateful to me than anything else can be."[51]

Caroline had no brothers, but scores of her friends and acquaintances had gone to war. Many of the male teachers and pupils of the Canandaigua Academy had enlisted at the recruiting tent pitched in the village square. Caroline and her friend Abbie Clark had their ambrotypes taken "for two young braves going to war." In May 1863, she reported that her society had, in a year's time, made "133 pairs of drawers, 101 shirts, 4 pairs socks for soldiers, and 54 garments for the families of soldiers."

Her diary's next entry, for July 4, 1863, contained a somber report: "The terrible battle of Gettysburg brings to Canandaigua sad news of our soldier boys of the 126th Regiment. Colonel Sherrill was instantly killed, also Captains Wheeler and Herendeen, Henry Wilson and Henry P. Cook. Captain Richardson was wounded." Captain Charlie Wheeler's body was sent back home and buried with military honors from the Canandaigua's Congregational church on July 26. "It was," Caroline wrote, "the saddest funeral and the only one of a soldier that I ever attended. I hope it will be the last. He was killed at Gettysburg, July 3, by a sharpshooter's bullet. He was a very bright young man, graduate of Yale college and was practicing law."[52]

In August of 1863, Canandaigua sent Dr. W. Fitch Cheney and seven assistants to Gettysburg to help the United States Sanitary Commission (USSC) care for the sick and wounded. Caroline called it "a blessed work."[53] Organized by civilians in June 1861, the USSC was a quasi-governmental organization in which those on the homefront could participate, vicariously at least, in the effort to put down proslavery forces. North Star Country women actively supported the USSC. Some assisted in the collection of medical supplies at the local level; others assumed leadership roles in the USSC bureaucracy, thereby capitalizing upon their experience in traditional female benevolence work and expanding the role of women in the public sphere.[54]

The state of New York had eighty-seven regiments and batteries in position at the Battle of Gettysburg. Among them was the 149th Regiment of the New York State Volunteers from Onondaga County. The regiment's silk flag was fringed with yellow and bore the thirty-four stars that represented the United States of America. In 1906 the veterans of the Grand Army of the Republic donated it to the county clerk's office, where it remained in a wood and glass case, so fragile that if taken out and unfurled it would fall apart.

On the third day of the Battle of Gettysburg, eighty-eight bullets were shot through that flag during the fighting that took place under the command of Brigadier General George S. Greene, in defense of the eastern slope of Culp's Hill. When the flag's staff was severed and the emblem of the 149th fell, Sergeant William Lilly climbed over a dirt wall and, on his hands and knees with bullets flying all about, dragged the flag to safety. He lashed the staff together using splints from a cracker box and leather straps from a knapsack, and he held it aloft. Lilly died in a Tennessee battle, but the flag was brought back to Syracuse by his surviving comrades. Civil War veterans saw to it that likenesses of the flag and of William Lilly were sculpted into bronze monuments in Syracuse's Clinton Square and at Gettysburg.[55]

Rochester, too, had its Gettysburg heroes. Colonel Patrick O'Rourke served with the 140th New York and was assigned to defend Little Round Top. O'Rourke was a native of Cavan County, Ireland, who had been apprenticed to a Flour City mason before he attended West Point, from which he graduated in 1861 at the top of his class. The 140th New York found itself in the thick of the fight on July 2, 1863. O'Rourke fell, mortally wounded, and was numbered among the one hundred men from the 104th that were killed or wounded in the Union attempt to hold Little Round Top. His widow had his body brought back to Rochester for burial in Holy Sepulcher Cemetery; she never remarried. In 1889, the surviving members of the 140th commissioned a granite monument and bronze marker to be placed at the spot where O'Rourke fell at Gettysburg.[56] After three deadly days at Gettysburg, the Army of the Potomac claimed victory. But the price had been high: 51,000 Union casualties. When North Star Country dwellers read the long lists of the dead in their newspapers, something of the magnitude of the war's cost came home to them.

Black Americans were willing to share in the fighting and the dying, if the conflict became something more than a white man's war. Jermain Loguen was serving an A.M.E.Z. congregation in Binghamton when the Civil War began. He recruited a company of African Americans known as Loguen's Guards. State officials in Albany prohibited them from enlisting.[57] In April 1861, African Americans who were eager to fight attended a "war meeting" held at Loguen's Zion Church in Syracuse. On April 23, the *Syracuse Journal* reported that "They resolved to stand by the Stars and Stripes to the death. Between 30 and 40 brave men formed themselves into a company, and many more are ready to join. They are going to offer their services to the governor of the state."[58] A few weeks later, the *Syracuse Courier* remarked, "A company of colored volunteers has been raised in Syracuse, 82 strong. An Albany company contains 95 members. Should the governor accept them, the Rev. Mr. Loguen intends going to Canada and bringing down two regiments of fugitives from St. Catherine's [*sic*] and one from Montreal, which are already raised."[59]

After the Emancipation Proclamation, black leaders redoubled their efforts to make the federal government allow "sable arms" to help abolish slavery. Governor John A. Andrew of Massachusetts was authorized to raise a regiment of black volunteers. He asked Boston's George L. Stearns, who was one of the Secret Six supporters of John Brown, to spearhead the recruitment campaign. Stearns sought the aid of Douglass in filling the ranks of what was to become the 54th Regiment of the Massachusetts Voluntary Infantry.[60]

On March 2, 1863, Douglass wrote a stirring appeal for volunteers entitled, "Men of Color, To Arms," which appeared in his paper and was widely copied in the leading newspapers. He regretted that the state of New York had not been the first to call for black soldiers, but he argued that all who answered his appeal could "get at the throat of treason through the State of Massachusetts." Douglass urged eligible free black males to join the fight. "The iron gate of our prison stands half open. One gallant rush from the North will fling it open, while four millions of our brothers and sisters shall march out into liberty." He invoked the memory of Denmark Vesey of Charleston and Nat Turner of Southampton, and recalled Shields Green and John Anthony Copeland, who "followed the noble John Brown."[61] Already, Douglass informed his readers, the first regiment was being mustered at Camp Readville on the outskirts of Boston.

The 54th Massachusetts was the vanguard of approximately 180,000 black troops who served in the Civil War—85 percent of those who were eligible to fight. Of all the black troops raised in the United States, 4,125 belonged to regiments raised in New York State, and 5,829 New York blacks served in regiments formed in other states. Three black regiments were raised in New York: the 20th, the 26th, and the 31st United States Colored Troops (USCT).[62] William C. Newark of Oneonta joined the 20th regiment of USCT, which was the first black regiment to be organized in New York State. While training at Rikers Island, Newark wrote a letter, dated January 29, 1864, that was published in the *Oneonta Herald*. Corporal Newark, who had himself doubted that colored men would make "good Solgers" was impressed with the progress made by the recruits. All was not well, however, as there had been a fight ("a mob fite") between the African American soldiers and a contingent of Irish troops.[63]

Congress authorized Lincoln to use black troops by passing the Militia Act of July 17, 1862. Initially, Lincoln had endorsed the acceptance of African Americans—whether free volunteer in the North, fugitive, or contraband in the South—as laborers and not soldiers. On August 6, he replied to an offer from Indiana to raise up two black regiments, "To arm the negroes would turn 50,000 bayonets from the loyal Border States against us that were for us."[64] But, after the implementation of the Emancipation Proclamation, efforts to recruit "as many persons of African descent" intensified.

In May of 1863, the War Department's General Order No. 143 centralized control of the USCT and made it possible for African American men to be mustered into the army directly. Many whites doubted that the "Negro" would fight, but African Americans were eager to prove their manhood. Frederick Douglass put it this way: "Once let the black man get upon his person the brass letters U.S., let him get an eagle on his button, and a musket on his shoulder and bullets in his pocket, and there is no power on earth which can deny that he has earned the right to citizenship in the United States."[65]

African American soldiers fought in 449 engagements during the Civil War. Of these, 39 were major battles. After Lincoln's endorsement of black troops, the *Buffalo Express* editorialized, "The state of New York could furnish 10,000 effective troops from the source, without much trouble or delay, and that would greatly relieve many Democrats who have trembled for months lest a draft might take them off."[66]

Massachusetts, not New York State, took the lead in raising "colored regiments." Douglass was one of a number of agents who were given the task of recruiting men for the Massachusetts 54th. Charles Remond Douglass and Lewis Henry Douglass were, according to their father, the first two recruits from the state of New York to help fill the quota of the 54th.[67] William Wells Brown, Henry Highland Garnet, Martin Delany, Charles Lenox Remond, and Jermain Wesley Loguen also joined in the effort to put a Yankee uniform on the black soldier and a pistol in his belt. But it was Douglass who was the most effective, recruiting more than one hundred men for the 54th. On March 6, 1863, he wrote to Gerrit Smith from Rochester: "I have visited Buffalo and obtained seven good men. I spoke here last night and got thirteen. I shall visit Auburn, Syracuse, Ithaca, Troy and Albany and other places in the state till I get one hundred men. Charley my youngest son was the first to put his name down as one of the company."[68]

Douglass spoke in Syracuse on March 11, 1863, from the pulpit of the A.M.E.Z. Church, with as much eloquence as he had ever mustered: "Who would be free themselves must strike the blow. I urge you to fly to arms and smite to death the power that would bury the government and your liberty in the same hopeless grave. This is your golden opportunity."[69] Ten men signed up that night.

Douglass returned on March 26th. Of that visit, the *Syracuse Journal* reported,

> The war meeting at Zion's Church last evening was largely attended. Frederick Douglass made an effective address and six recruits responded. There have been 23 colored recruits raised in this city and they will be sent forward next week. They have joined the colored regiment now being raised in Massachusetts, the 54th from that state. This regiment is to be organized the same as the others, except that the field and staff officers are to be whites.[70]

Douglass escorted the recruits to Boston and Camp Readville by way of Binghamton and New York City, where he also gathered up men willing to fight. Syracuse was not alone in sending recruits to Massachusetts. Five men from Chemung County walked from Elmira to Boston to join up with the 54th.[71]

The Massachusetts 54th mustered up on May 13, 1863. Alongside Douglass's sons were scores of men from North Star Country, most of them in their twenties. They had been farmers, barbers, waiters, cooks, seamen, hostlers, and common laborers. Now they were soldiers in an army of liberation but, contrary to Douglass's recruiting promise, they did not have benefits equal to those of white troops. Noncommissioned black soldiers received $7 a month instead of the $13 a month that their white counterparts were being paid by 1863. The black soldier's clothing allowance came in at $3, fifty cents less than that of white soldiers.

Colonel Robert Gould Shaw, a twenty-five-year-old from a Yankee abolitionist family, had to fight army bureaucrats to outfit his men with shoes and uniforms. More importantly, he had to fight for an opportunity to get onto the battlefield. Douglass was upset that African American soldiers were prohibited from rising to the rank of commissioned officer on the basis of merit but, as he told Gerrit Smith, wearing a United States uniform "was a very great advance."[72]

Shaw and his troops went South when summer came. On July 16, 1863, the troops found themselves on Morris Island, near Fort Wagner. The island was key to the Confederate defense of the Charleston, South Carolina, harbor. On the evening of July 18, Shaw's "smoked Yankees" spearheaded an attack on the well-defended fort with a charge up the open beach. Six hundred troops of the 54th rushed into history in one of the defining moments of the Civil War. With a small force of men, Shaw made it to the parapets before being cut down by a fuselage of Confederate shot and shells. Less than half of the original force survived the bloody attack.

Among the casualties: a twenty-nine-year-old black resident of Syracuse, named George Washington; a seaman who died on August 3, 1863, from the wounds he received on July 18; and twenty-one-year-old James P. Johnson of Oswego, formerly a barber, who was wounded at Fort Wagner and died of disease in Jacksonville, Florida, on April 4, 1864.[73] A dozen or so blacks from Syracuse's Eighth Ward were among the 20 killed, the 100 missing and presumed dead, and the 147 wounded.

The August 3, 1863, *Syracuse Journal* reported, "The 54th Massachusetts

Regiment, colored, which fought so bravely in the assault upon Fort Wagner, Morris Island, had 15 men in its ranks who enlisted from this city. Col. Shaw of Boston, commanding this regiment, was among the slain. To mark their despite for having to fight Negroes, the rebels buried the Col. in a pit with 20 of his men. Perhaps it will be all the same at the general resurrection."[74]

In his third and final autobiography, which was first published in 1881, Frederick Douglass contemplated the historic significance of the gallantry and courage of the men of the 54th.

> In that terrible battle, under the wing of night, more cavils in respect of the quality of Negro manhood were set at rest than could have been during a century of ordinary life and observation. After that assault we heard no more of sending Negroes to garrison forts and arsenals, to fight miasma, yellow-fever, and smallpox. Talk of his ability to meet the foe in the open field, and of his equal fitness with the white man to stop a bullet, then began to prevail.[75]

Douglass took special pride in the fact that his sons, Charles and Lewis, enlisted in the 54th.

Charles did not ship out of Boston Harbor with the 54th because of illness, but Lewis did. Along with his comrades, he marched down to Battery Wharf to the music of "John Brown's Body." On July 20, 1863, from the relative safety of Morris Island, Lewis wrote to his father and mother about the desperate charge on Fort Wagner two days earlier. "The splendid 54th is cut to pieces. . . . I had my sword sheath blown away while on the parapet of the Fort. The grape and canister, shell and minnies swept us down like chaff, still our men went on and on, and if we had been properly supported, we would have held the Fort, but the white troops could not be made to come up. The consequence was we had to fall back, dodging shells and other missiles."[76]

Sergeant Major Lewis Douglass informed his young wife, Amelia Loguen (daughter of Jermain Loguen), "A shell would explode and clear a space of twenty feet, our men would close up again, but it was no use we had to retreat, which was a very hazardous undertaking. How I got out of that fight alive I cannot tell, but I am here." "Should I fall in the next fight killed or wounded," Lewis avowed, "I hope to fall with my face to the foe." After listing some of the wounded and missing, Lewis closed, "My Dear girl I hope again to see you. I must bid you farewell should I be killed. Remem-

Lewis Henry Douglass (1840–1908). The eldest son of Frederick Douglass, Lewis Henry Douglass married Amelia Lougen, the daughter of Jermain and Caroline Loguen, in 1862. In March 1863 he enlisted in the Fifty-fourth Massachusetts Regiment and served at the noncommissioned rank of sergeant major. He survived the Union's ill-fated assault on Fort Wagner (July 18, 1863) but contracted typhoid fever and was discharged from active service in May 1864 because of ill health.
Courtesy of Moorland-Spingarn Research Center, Howard University, Washington, D.C.

ber if I die I die in a good cause. I wish we had a hundred thousand colored troops we would put an end to this war."[77]

Hermon Clarke and the 117th, or Fourth Oneida, arrived on Morris Island approximately two weeks after the first attack upon Fort Wagner. From the deck of the *S.S. Spaulding*, he heard the Union continuing its bombardment of the Confederate stronghold. On August 2, 1863, he wrote to his father, "Our men are shelling Wagner now. We shall see fighting now—we can't help it. I had hoped it never would be necessary for us to get in so tight a place as this, but it has come and we shall see what the 117th is made of."[78]

A week later, while encamped on Folly Island, Hermon wrote to his father of his first brush with death: "The bullets fell like rain some of the time. One of our men had his gunstock badly shivered by one." Of the black troops, Hermon reported, "There are three colored regiments on the Island, and they do good work. They fight well and do more fatigue duty than any white can. I am willing to let them fight and dig if they will; it saves so many white men." Concerning his fate and that of the 54th, Hermon ventured, "It may be with us as it was with the Colonel of the 54th Massachusetts. When his body was sent for the day after the battle they told them he was buried under two layers of his Negroes."[79]

African Americans had to fight to get into the military. Once in uniform they had to fight for equal treatment and equal pay. Congress finally increased the compensation for black privates to $13 per month, in June of 1864. Even then, some African American soldiers went without pay because of bureaucratic delays.

Thomas Sipple enlisted at Elmira in New York State. By late summer of 1864, he and the New York 20th Regiment were at Camp Parapet near New Orleans. After serving for seven months, Sipple and his black comrades had still not received any pay, not to mention compensation equal to white soldiers. In August 1864, he wrote to "My Dear and Worthy Friend MR. President," whom he described as "A friend to me and to all our Race." "I have a wife and 3 Children Neither one of them Able to thake Care of Themselfs and my wife is sick And she has sent to me for money And i have No way of getting Eney money to send to her Because i cant Get my Pay. And it gos very hard with me to think my family should be At home A suffering have money earnt and cant not get it."[80]

Sipple did not blame Lincoln for his troubles, but he did say, "I Don't Beleave the Government wants me eney how In fact i mean the New York 20th Regiment The Reasons why i say so is Because we are treated Like A Parcels of Rebs. . . . we came out to be true union soldiers the Grandsons of Mother Africa Never to Flinch from Duty." Sipple had escaped from Maryland in 1855. When the Union League Club "got up" the war effort, he had enlisted, "Promised All satisfaction Needful But it seem to Be A failure."[81] Attached to Sipple's letter, in different handwriting, was the following: "Mr President I Surtify that this I is jest what mr Rodgers sais and my other frend mr Sipele Nimrod Rowley Elmira Chemong CO.N.Y."[82]

Harriet Tubman served as spy, scout, and nurse during the Civil War. She also witnessed the memorable assault upon Fort Wagner and gave this poignant portrait: "And then we saw the lightning and that was the guns; and then we heard the rain falling, and that was the drops of blood falling and when we came to get in the crops it was dead men that we reaped."[83]

Tubman is said to have served Robert Gould Shaw his last breakfast before he led the 54th in the fatal charge upon the Confederate stronghold. Afterwards, she helped bind up the wounded. Tubman had been in the Sea Islands region since May of 1862, at the request of Governor John Andrew of Massachusetts. As Union forces moved in off the coast and took control of the plantations, Harriet worked among the contrabands (former slaves who were no longer under the "whip and the lash" but who were not technically free people). Like Sojourner Truth in the freedmen's camps of Washington, D.C., Harriet taught the ex-slaves practical skills such as homemaking and personal hygiene.

Charlotte Forten, daughter of a prominent Philadelphia black abolitionist family and a schoolteacher among the contrabands, visited Tubman in early 1863 and reported, "She is living in B[eaufort] now; keeping an eating house."[84] Harriet made gingerbread, pies, and root beer in the evenings as a way to support herself. Her hospital work exposed her to the virulent diseases that were prevalent in the swampy lowlands, and to smallpox. Her herbal remedy for dysentery was in great demand.

Harriet also provided valuable reconnaissance to Colonel James Montgomery of the black 2nd South Carolina Volunteers when that unit was engaged in guerrilla warfare. During the Combahee River expedition in June 1863, Harriet accompanied Montgomery and 150 black troops as they removed torpedoes, set fire to plantations, and carried away 756 slaves.[85] Later, Harriet reported to friends in Boston,

> In our late expedition up the Combahee river in coming on board the boat, I was carrying *two pigs* for a sick woman, who had a child to carry, and the order of "double quick" was given, and I started to run, stepped on my dress, it being rather long, and fell and tore it almost off, so that when I got on board the boat there was hardly anything left of it but shreds. I made up my mind then, I would never wear a long dress on another expedition of the kind, but would have a *bloomer* as soon as I could get it. So please make this known to the ladies, if you will, for I expect to have use for it very soon, probably before they can get it to me.[86]

Harriet had been away from Auburn for almost two years and was concerned about her parents, whom she described as old and feeble. Yet she felt she could not abandon her wartime labors. She served as matron and nurse at a hospital for contrabands and black soldiers in Beaufort, South Carolina, until 1864, when she went to another hospital at Fortress Monroe, Virginia.

When the war ended, Harriet returned to Auburn. In 1869, she married Nelson Davis, a young ex-soldier, who was reportedly afflicted with tuberculosis. Alice Brickler, a niece of Harriet Tubman, was interviewed in 1981. Then in her nineties, Brickler reminisced about hearing a Civil War veteran speak of his experiences. This was during a visit to the home for the elderly that Tubman had established on her property in Auburn. The veteran described the bloody attempt to capture Fort Wagner in vivid language—he may well have been a member of the Massachusetts 54th. When Tubman died in 1913, a picture of the attack upon Fort Wagner hung over her bed.[87]

Fort Wagner and the other Civil War battle sites were a long way from Upstate New York; present-day Woodlawn National Cemetery in Elmira is a vivid reminder of how close the Civil War came to North Star Country. Hundreds of Confederate soldiers are buried in this cemetery, soldiers whose bodies were not returned once the conflict ended and the Elmira prison camp closed.

The camp was established on July 6, 1864, at the site of barracks no. 3. The camp held thousands of prisoners who had been captured and sent north by Union forces. John Jones, who had been listed in Elmira's 1857 directory as a gardener, was the caretaker. When some of the 12,000 Con-

Elmira prison camp. The camp was originally a Union military depot and rendezvous station. It was established in May 1864 and occupied so-called Barracks 3 (a plot of about 30 acres running for 1,000 feet along W. Water St. from Hoffman and then extending south to River). It was enclosed by a twelve-foot plank fence and housed 11,916 prisoners, of whom 2,994 died; of that number, 2,973 were buried in the National Cemetery. From a postcard that shows prisoners in line for dinner. *Courtesy of the Chemung County Historical Society.*

federates who were brought to the Elmira prison died, Jones was asked to bury them in a field behind his farm, on what is now College Avenue. A monument which was erected in 1992 at the corner of Hoffman and West Water Streets in Elmira draws attention to the flagpole of the old Confederate prison.

Jones received $2.50 for each burial and interred nearly three thousand boys and men, with the help of twelve assistants. Jones recorded the name, rank, company and regiment, death date, and grave number on the lid of each coffin. He is said to have given all of the Confederate dead a respectful burial. Some of the Confederates still lie in the ground at Woodlawn today.

Jones himself died in 1900. In 1953, the city of Elmira honored him for his service as custodian of the prison cemetery and for his role as an agent of the Underground Railroad (credited with assisting nearly eight hundred on their flight northward) by naming a housing project after him.[88]

As in all wars when families are separated, Upstate New Yorkers attempted to lessen the distance between home front and battlefield so as to strengthen the bonds of intimacy. The Benjamin A. Fordyce family letters capture this well. When her physician father was at Camp Hubbard in Louisiana, Abbie Fordyce, who was almost ten, wrote of feeding the chickens, studying the physical geography of Asia, and going on a picnic with her friends. Abbie's little brother, George, was a constant pest. As she wrote, he often begged to be included in the letters meant for their father. Stella, who was two years older than Abbie, gave Dr. Fordyce a daughterly admonition, "Pa if you get to drinking with them Officers . . . I won't claim you as my Father when you come home."

Fordyce's wife wrote to him on August 30, 1863: "I went a blackberrying the other day and have made 12 pounds of jam do you think I could send you anything by Captain Corning write to him and see if he would take charge of a small box for you." By the following November, Fordyce was giving his wife, who had been left to manage the family farm and home, the following advice:

> About selling the cows, act your own judgment. The price offered is fair. If we sell the place we certainly do not want them. The fodder they would eat if sold in February or March would make the price good. I have got me a good warm overcoat and 2 pair of good drawers cotton flannel. I am glad to hear George is plump and healthy. I should very much like to see the little chub and hug and kiss him (some I guess). I need some good flannel shirts most of anything. Those I bought in Auburn have shrunk so that it is difficult to for me to wear them.

In December, Stella, without much attention to punctuation, wrote to her father:

> It snows quite hard now the snow is about three inches deep on the ground Grandpa and grandma and Elihu and Sally Slocum are going to quaker meeting ma wanted me to go but I had rather stay here and play chess with Abbie I can keep still just as well playing chess as I can in a quaker meeting house. The black horse is dead it had an awful sore leg and it rotted and they killed it Ma did not want me to write it grandma and grandpa and Uncle Giles would faint

if they knew it but I know that you would rather know it now than to have us keep it from you and tell you when you come home.

Stella closed her letter with "I will be in bed in less than 3 minutes" as if her father had just called "lights out!"[89]

Dr. Fordyce was still encamped in far off Louisiana and would not be home for Christmas. He had Christmas dinner with a Southern family, showing them pictures of his beloved daughters and writing to the girls afterwards to tell them that they had been much admired. As the new year approached and winter settled in on North Star Country, the Civil War surgeon implored his wife and children to "Remember the little fruit trees tread snow around them."[90]

Rural women like Mrs. Fordyce had to shoulder additional duties while their husbands were away. In some North Star Country communities, more than half of the adult men served in the Civil War, resulting in a chronic labor shortage and many a vacant chair around the family table.[91] Haying was an especially trying time for farm women, and the winters were long, cold, and lonesome.

In November 1862, Semira Merrill wrote to her husband, David, from their farm "in the woods" of Nanticoke (Broome County): "O dearest I hope you are not out to night on duty for it is A cold bad night here the ground is wight with snow today O how I wish you could be here by the fire with me to night than I could go to bed contented but now I cannot I keep thinking about how hard you have to fare and it makes me feel bad I cannot help it."[92]

Sickness and disease on the battlefield accounted for six out of ten deaths among Civil War soldiers. And the withering hand of illness and death did not spare loved ones at home. Semira informed her husband of the epidemic sweeping the Nanticoke Valley in the winter of 1862–63: "the dipthera rages real bad around here I have been so afraid our littel ones would get I dasent hardly lent them go out Enoch Spencer has tow little ones that is dead they are both to be berred tomorrow at one o'clock I should like to go if is was only well they died of dipthera and he has one more sick with it."[93] One can imagine David's anxiety upon reading this letter and understand his desire to return to his domestic circle as soon as possible.

Most soldiers who donned the Yankee blue went on active duty without hope of being reunited with their families until their periods of service were over. The fortunate ones came home on furlough, perhaps to serve as recruiting agents, but then went back to war. North Star Country had its deserters, slackers, and bounty hunters, but the majority of the men and boys soldiered because it was the necessary and honorable thing to do. Years later, they could look back, with pride, to the time that they took on the burdens of preserving the Union and ending slavery.

In 1931, the daughter of Owego resident Oscar Barton hosted a party for her father's 100th birthday. This descendent of free blacks from Rhode Island had been a drummer in Company B of the 26th New Colored Infantry. Although he had been a paralytic for thirty years, with no use of his arms and legs, Barton was still keen of mind and his eyesight undimmed.

Back in 1863, Oscar had been living south of Vestal. He, a half-brother, and five nephews all enlisted; he remained in service until the end of the war. Oscar's maternal grandfather, Thomas Reynolds, had soldiered in the Revolutionary War. Oscar had done so in the second American Revolution. This old veteran made his last public appearance in his drummer's dress when the Union fife and drum corps paraded by on July 4, 1892, during the dedication of the Soldiers' and Sailors' Civil War monument in Owego.[94]

Barton represents the thousands of North Star Country soldiers who fought without fanfare. Many of them came from homes where the word *abolitionist* was spoken with disdain, or with only lukewarm enthusiasm. Others belonged to households where "the plight of the slave" was a subject for earnest conversation at the dinner table; one such was Samuel Porter, the eighteen-year-old son of Rochester's activist Porter family, who joined Company F, 108th Regiment of New York State Volunteers, on August 9, 1862.[95] Whatever the background, if he was still alive when the guns silenced, the typical Civil War veteran returned home, picked up his life, and passed into history without much public notice.

Upstate New York is not, however, without its unique Civil War personalities. There was Doctor Mary Walker of Oswego, a graduate of Syracuse Medical College. She took on the cause of dress reform. In 1864, she appeared in her own form of uniform at the headquarters of the Army of the Cumberland in Chattanooga, Tennessee. A *Cincinnati Commercial* correspondent wrote that she was "dressed in gent's boots, pants, a ladies broadcloth cloak, and jaunty hat."[96] Walker's controversial outfit included a knee-length skirt and baggy trousers that were gathered at the ankle. This was known as the bloomer, after Amelia Jenks Bloomer. Walker was the first woman to receive the Congressional Medal of Honor, only to have it taken from her in 1917 when Congress upgraded the requirements and a review board found "nothing in the records to show the specific act or acts for which the decoration was originally awarded."[97] In 1977, at the request of Representative Les Aspin of Wisconsin, Congress placed Mary Walker's name back on the Medal of Honor list.

Historians still debate whether this dedicated supporter of women's rights was a good Samaritan or a charlatan. Walker was once imprisoned at Castle Thunder in Richmond on suspicion of being a spy but she was not officially recognized as a battlefield surgeon. After the Civil War, Walker toured England telling of her experiences, and then she joined a vaudeville company in the United States. She worked for a while at the Pension Bureau in Washington but was dismissed for failure to perform her duties as expected. Later she tried to set up an "Adam-less Eden," a retreat for women only, on her Oswego farm. Upon her death in 1919, at the age of eighty-six, Mary was buried in her black frock suit.[98]

North Star Country had its complement of less controversial Medal of Honor winners. For example, there was Henry A. Barnum of Onondaga County and the 12th New York regiment. A lawyer by trade, he fought at Malvern Hill, one of the Seven Days' Battles in 1862. He had a musket ball pass through his body, and a corpse which was mistaken for Barnum was buried on the battlefield, but he survived and was placed in Richmond's Libby Prison, which at one time held one thousand Union officers. After he was freed in a prisoner exchange, he went to New York City on a hospital ship and recovered sufficiently to lead the 149th New York Volunteers into the Battle of Gettysburg. Barnum was in Tennessee at the Battle of Lookout Mountain during which he suffered a second serious wound when a shot passed through his sword arm. His earlier wound had only partially healed, and a physician could pass an oakum rope entirely through Barnum's body. Nevertheless, this Medal of Honor winner went into the field again and was the first Union officer to enter Savannah with Sherman's Army.[99]

Myles Keogh was born of Roman Catholic parents in Carlow County, Ireland. Strange as it may seem, Civil War re-enactors recall this soldier-of-fortune during a Myles Keogh weekend each August in Auburn. A nine-foot-tall tombstone marks his grave in the same cemetery in which Harriet Tubman and William H. Seward are buried.

Keogh's connection to North Star Country came about in a curious way. After serving in the Papal Guard at the Vatican, Keogh persuaded Seward to help him get a commission in the Union Army. He fought at Second Bull Run, Antietam, Chancellorsville, and Gettysburg. In 1862, he befriended Captain Andrew J. Alexander of Auburn, who introduced him to Evelina Martin, daughter of the wealthy owners of the Willowbrook estate in the village. Evelina and Myles Keogh were married, but the adventuresome Keogh joined up with Custer's Seventh U.S. Cavalry. He was killed on June 25, 1876, at the Battle of Little Big Horn in Montana.[100]

Gerrit Smith was too old to take up a gun when the Civil War began, but this veteran peace advocate viewed the beginning of the conflict as inevitable and, ultimately, necessary. At a war meeting in Peterboro on April 27, 1861, he said, "The end of American slavery is at hand. That it is to end in blood does not surprise me. For fifteen years I have been constantly predicting that it would be. . . . *The first gun fired at Fort Sumter announced the fact that the last fugitive slave had been returned.*"[101]

Smith was active in the Loyal Leagues during the war, offered to contribute $3,000 to the fund that George L. Stearns was building to recruit black troops, and contributed $1,000 to the victims, black and white, of New York City's 1863 draft riots. Upon hearing of the Emancipation Proclamation, Smith expressed regret that it did not apply to the border states and was not effective immediately, but he was hopeful: "The President, who is both an able and an honest man, is doing his duty. He will do his whole duty."[102]

During the war years, the Sage of Peterboro continued to receive demands upon his purse. A certain Colonel S. T. Smith wrote and asked for $1,000 to raise a regiment of volunteers that would be known as the Smith legion—composed entirely of men bearing the name Smith. Gerrit dismissed this opportunity to bring honor and fame to Smiths everywhere by writing on the letter "A new Fancy."[103]

Women actively supported the war effort on the home front. They sewed bandages, packed thousands of pounds of preserves and other edibles for the soldiers, and sent many a petition heavenward for the safe return of the combatants. Some women were active in the various local and regional divisions of the USSC, and others took up the farm chores customarily done by men.

A few went off on wartime adventures of their own. Jane Higgins was the wife of Captain Benjamin L. Higgins, former chief of the Syracuse Fire Department. She accompanied her husband and the rifle company he recruited from among his fellow firemen. She went to camp with him, working as a nurse and cook. When Benjamin was wounded at Gettysburg, Jane built a large bed for him out of spare mattresses and sheets and nursed him back to health. Her nursing service has been memorialized on the monument to the 86th that stands on Sickles Avenue at the present-day Gettysburg National Military Park.[104]

By the beginning of 1865, North Star Country residents were weary of war and anxious to see the bloodshed end and to see slavery defeated. A string of Union victories gave them reason to hope, and they took note of Lincoln's plea for peace and moderation in his second inaugural address on March 4, 1865. The president urged all Americans to work together to bind up the nation's wounds, "with malice toward none; with charity for all."[105]

At that very moment, General Grant was laying siege to Richmond, capitol of the Confederacy. Upon hearing of the fall of Richmond, men, women, and children "all acting crazy as if they had not the remotest idea where they were or what they were doing" celebrated in Canandaigua. Caroline Richards tells us that villagers fired a cannon and guns, lit bonfires, and thronged the streets. Her grandmother elected not to light victory candles in the Richards home, preferring "to keep Saturday night and pity and pray for the poor suffering, wounded soldiers" whom she felt would be forgotten in the hoopla.[106]

One suspects that Caroline's grandmother set aside her reservations on April 10, 1865. On that morning, Caroline began her diary entry with a biblical reference, "Whether I am in the body, or out of the body, I know not, but one thing I know, Lee has surrendered! and all the people seem crazy in consequence. The bells are ringing, boys and girls, men and women are running through the streets wild with excitement; the flags are all flying, one from the top of our church, and such a 'hurrah boys' generally, I have never dreamed of." Caroline and family had been eating breakfast when, at around 7:00 o'clock, the village church bells began ringing. Raising a window to find out the cause, she caught the attention of a Captain Aldrich who came to the front door, where Caroline met him. "He almost shook my hand off and said, 'The war is over. We have Lee's surrender, with his own name signed.'"[107]

Frederick Douglass was in Boston when news came of the fall of Richmond. He joined in the celebration and spoke at Faneuil Hall, anticipating, as did others, that the end of the war was at hand. Douglass had been present when Lincoln was sworn in for a second term. He had clapped with "gladness and thanksgiving" when the president, standing there on the east portico of the Capitol, urged "let us strive to finish the work we are in, to bind up the nation's wounds, to care for him who shall have borne the battle, and for his widow and his orphans, to do all which may achieve and cherish a just and lasting peace among ourselves and with all nations." Douglass thought Lincoln's counsel contained "more vital substance" than anything he had "ever seen compressed in a space so narrow." Frederick was overjoyed, but as he looked about the crowd, he saw "expressions of widely different emotion" in the faces of others.[108]

Perhaps what Douglass saw was cousin to the spirit he had encountered earlier that inauguration day. While waiting for the ceremonies to begin, the veteran freedom fighter noticed Lincoln and Andrew Johnson conversing. Lincoln touched Johnson and then directed Johnson's attention toward Douglass.

> The first expression which came to his face, and which I think was the true index of his heart, was one of bitter contempt and aversion. Seeing that I observed him, he tried to assume a more friendly appearance, but it was too late; it is useless to close the door when all within has been seen. His first glance was the frown of the man; the second was the bland and sickly smile of the demagogue. I turned to Mrs. Dorsey [the wife of Thomas J. Dorsey] and said, 'Whatever Andrew Johnson may be, he certainly is no friend of our race.'[109]

Douglass also noted that, although it was early morning, Johnson was drunk.

When spring came that year, there was reason to hope that America's fratricidal war was almost over. In Johnson's face and demeanor Douglass saw an omen of what would follow if the cessation of hostilities was allowed to mark the end of the quest for black freedom and justice. This was a theme Douglass had emphasized in his remarks on the impending

Emancipation Proclamation. "Law and the sword can and will, in the end abolish slavery. But law and the sword cannot abolish the malignant slaveholding sentiment which has kept the slavery system in this country during two centuries."[110]

Even as Lee's army surrendered to Grant at Appomattox Court House on Palm Sunday, April 9, 1865, and the clouds of war began to dissipate, the crusade for freedom continued. The hour had come to ensure that the sacrifices that had been made on the battlefield and on the home front by North Star Country residents would count for something deeper than military conquest.

Epilogue
The Enduring Mission

The Civil War brought changes to North Star Country in ways that few who left their firesides for distant battlefields could have anticipated. There were economic benefits for the region. Rochester produced military boots and shoes. Elmira's textile factories turned out cloth for uniforms. Arms and ammunition came from the Remington plant in Ilion (Herkimer County). From 1861 to 1865, prices for farm products rose because of the need to feed marching armies and, although there was a want of labor in North Star Country, agricultural affairs prospered. Newly designed machines that could plant and harvest, mow and rake, were pressed into service. Curiously, bean production began to gain on wheat in Genesee country, even though it had lagged far behind as a staple crop in the previous two decades. Because Civil War troops developed a taste for the beans that were rationed to them, New York State became the nation's largest bean producer.[1]

This economic boom did not, however, become a lodestar for African Americans and, in many respects, the struggle for greater freedom and opportunity continued into the post–Civil War years. For some of the old abolitionists and their children, the call to follow the light of the North Star endured.

While some of the newly emancipated did migrate to North Star Country in the immediate post–Civil War period, there was no dramatic increase in the African American population. Farm land was already in the hands of whites, and little economic opportunity existed in central and western New York State towns and villages for blacks. Frederick Douglass urged the freedmen to remain in the South where they could, in the aggregate, exercise political influence and improve their lives by voting.[2]

A small number of ex-slaves found a niche in the existing social order. One was Jerry Freeman who was brought to Belfast in Allegany County by a returning Civil War officer named Burr. When it was suggested that Jerry, who didn't know his birth name, take the name Burr, he replied, "No, I'se now a free man and that's good enough for me."[3] Freeman became Belfast's town barber and wore a fireman's uniform with pride.

Because of Gerrit Smith's influence, Peterboro retained a number of black families long after the Civil War. Hanson Williams, a former slave and war veteran, worked on the Smith farm and was the foreman when the Holstein cattle owned by Gerrit Smith Miller were breaking records. In 1927, Jared Van Wagenen, Jr., visited the Peterboro estate and reported, "Today the servants and laborers—within the house and on the land outside are the descendants of slaves. Mr. Miller gave me the names of two colored families the members of which have served his people for four generations. Even today, the village has an unusual number of colored for a Northern community."[4]

Stories persist in the Mumford-Caledonia area south of Rochester about what has been called the Culpeper Connection. It is said that a Civil War captain named Frank Harmon had been stationed in the Culpeper, Virginia, area. When the war ended, Harmon encouraged newly emancipated blacks to migrate to central New York State where they worked on area farms. "Many Rochester area residents today," Eugene E. Du Bois wrote in 1994, "trace their family roots to these early settlers from Culpeper, VA."[5]

Although the ashes of war still smoldered, the phoenix of hope rose in the hearts of many who had advanced the freedom struggle as they watched the Thirteenth Amendment (outlawing slavery) make its way through Congress. President Abraham Lincoln called for a generous reconstruction in his final public address on April 11, 1865. Then, on April 14th, John Wilkes Booth shot Lincoln at Ford's Theater in Washington. A fellow conspirator stabbed Secretary of State William Henry Seward. Fortunately, Seward's wound was not fatal. Grief and anger now blanketed the nation, and the long-drawn-out funeral for Lincoln dramatized how deep a rift the Civil War had created. Only five days after Lee's surrender at Appomattox, the man who had led the country through its darkest hours had been cut down.

Anne Gertrude Sneller, who grew up in the rural community of Cicero (Onondaga County), was told by her mother how the news of Lincoln's death came. Grandfather ran toward the house early that April morning, tears streaming down his face. He was barely able to talk. "I came over to tell you. Lincoln—Lincoln is dead. He's been shot." Sneller's mother, who was then thirteen, and the others stared in disbelief. Grandfather voiced the fear, shared by others in the North, that, with Lincoln dead, the South would start up the war again. When Lincoln's funeral train reached Syracuse, Anne Sneller's grandfather and uncles were there to pay their respects. "It was thought proper by the family," the granddaughter wrote, "that all the menfolks should go out to meet the train, and no one thought of proposing that they should take with them the young sister who would have remembered it longest of all."[6]

Buffalo was one of eleven major urban centers chosen to conduct a funeral ceremony. But when Lincoln's funeral train reached Buffalo, the city's eighty thousand citizens were already exhausted from having conducted a mock funeral earlier. Now that the procession had a real coffin and body, Buffalo mourned again, using a hearse that was drawn by six white horses clothed in black. At St. James's Hall "the coffin was properly up-tilted and brilliantly lighted, and sweet voices sang, 'Rest, noble spirit, rest,' as one hundred thousand, until eight at night, moved decorously past."[7] The decorum and order with which the mourners conducted themselves contrasted sharply with the raw emotion of the first funeral. The mood of the crowd represented the grim reality of what was to come. The North might have won on the battlefield, but there was still much to be done on the home front.

In 1865, William Lloyd Garrison called for the dissolution of the AASS on the grounds that the work of the abolitionists had been finished with the coming of freedom.[8] Syracuse's Jermain Loguen believed that the silencing of the guns of war did not release the friends of liberty from their duty. As an escapee from the peculiar institution, and as someone who had refused to allow friends in Cortland to purchase his freedom from Manasseh Logue of Tennessee, Loguen fully understood that no piece of paper, not even the Thirteenth Amendment, could guarantee "manhood and personality." These were gifts from God. Humans had the responsibility of affirming everyone's self-worth.[9] Loguen defined the abolitionist mission as more than the destruction of slavery; it also entailed enabling the newly freed people to take their rightful place in a reconstructed South.

Once the Rebels laid down their arms, Loguen went to see for himself what could be done to help the freed people. He traveled to Tennessee in the summer of 1865 to find his family and to organize churches and schools among the ex-slaves. He spoke at a large 4th of July celebration in Nashville, and in Knoxville he organized a church that still bears his name.[10] Exhausted by nearly two months of incessant labor, Loguen returned to Salt City. On July 25, 1865, he reported in the *Weekly Anglo-African*, "It is almost impossible for a person to realize the changes brought about by this war without visiting the South. In place of slave-pens, you will see churches and schoolrooms filled with happy souls. In place of auctioneers there are missionaries who preach a full, free Gospel to the eager listening ones. They are anxious to learn to read and write, and the privilege to do so makes them appear happier than any other people in that part of the country." Loguen understood how precious and fragile freedom was and urged "every strong man and woman, preacher and teacher, who can leave for a time their Northern laboring fields, to go and spend all the time they can in the South."[11]

Edmonia Highgate was one of the many Upstate New Yorkers who responded to the appeal to aid those who had survived the House of Bondage. Born in Syracuse in 1844, she was the daughter of a barber and a member of Plymouth Congregational Church. She graduated from high school with honors, taught in Montrose, Pennsylvania, for a year, and then became principal of a black school in Binghamton. In January 1864, she wrote to the American Missionary Association (AMA), which had been founded in 1846 to oppose slavery, and asked to be placed in the South or Southwest: "I am about twenty years of age and strong and healthy. I know just what self-denial, self-discipline and domestic qualifications are needed for the work and modestly trust that with God's help I could labor advantageously in the field for my newly freed brethren.[12]

The AMA first appointed Highgate to Norfolk, Virginia, where she was deeply moved by the sufferings of the black men, women, and children who had waited so long for the chance to study geography and arithmetic. Emotionally exhausted from her labors, she returned to North Star Country in the summer of 1864. After recuperating, she traveled about the region seeking funds for her educational work. Loguen wrote to Gerrit Smith, asking him to help Highgate: "She has been a very worthy worker both North &

South among our Freed brethren. She enjoys the fullest confidence of this community and I must say she is much beloved by the freed men where she has been teaching in Norfolk and other places."[13] In October 1864, Highgate spoke about her work in front of the National Convention of Colored Men held in the Wesleyan Methodist Church in Syracuse. Such an opportunity was rarely given to women in the black conventions of the nineteenth century.[14]

Highgate returned to the South after a period of rest in Syracuse. In the spring of 1865, she worked briefly in Darlington, a rural town in Maryland. Her next assignment was Louisiana, where she served in New Orleans as the principal of Frederick Douglass School (housed in a former slave pen). White rioters attacked the Unionists in July 1866, forcing Highgate out of the city and into rural Lafayette Parish.[15] There she taught among the "French Creoles." Whites opposed her, threatened to burn her school and boarding place. She was shot at twice.

The next year, Highgate returned to New Orleans but resigned from teaching when the city's old rebel School Board proposed a segregated public school system. Determined that she would "rather starve than stoop once inch on that question," she moved to Enterprise, Mississippi, in 1868. In the fall of 1869, she returned to Upstate New York as a collection agent for the AMA. She raised funds to repair a church in Jackson, Mississippi, which was being used as a school. In February of 1870, she spoke before the Massachusetts Anti-Slavery Society, telling the abolitionists that their work was "not yet half done; and if it is not thoroughly done, it will have to be done over again."[16] Little else is known of this young woman's last years except that she was preparing to take a position at Tougaloo Normal School in Mississippi.

Edmonia wrote to Gerrit Smith on September 2, 1870, asking him to invite her sister, Carrie, to Peterboro. A teacher stationed in Jackson, Mississippi, Carrie had recently married A. T. Morgan, a white abolitionist and Mississippi state senator. Edmonia told Smith of how the couple had barely escaped being mobbed by whites on the night of their marriage. They were temporarily visiting Albany, New York, and were apprehensive about returning to Mississippi.[17]

Carrie and her husband had good reason to fear the worst, for their interracial marriage ran afoul of contemporary fears of amalgamation.

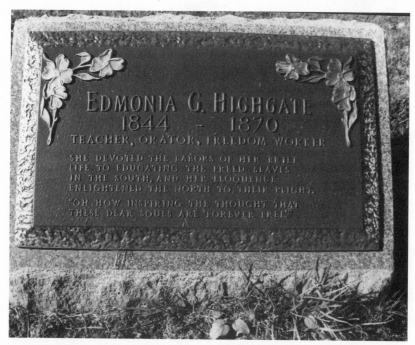

EDMONIA G. HIGHGATE
1844 - 1870
TEACHER, ORATOR, FREEDOM WORKER

SHE DEVOTED THE LABORS OF HER BRIEF
LIFE TO EDUCATING THE FREED SLAVES
IN THE SOUTH, AND HER ELOQUENCE
ENLIGHTENED THE NORTH TO THEIR PLIGHT.

"OH HOW INSPIRING THE THOUGHT THAT
THESE DEAR SOULS ARE 'FOREVER FREE'"

Edmonia Highgate's grave, Syracuse. After Highgate's burial site was rediscovered, the author participated in a memorial service that dedicated this marker (1988). At that time, a stone obelisk stood on the nearby grave of her brother Charles, but it is now missing. Jermain Loguen's grave is also located in Section 6 of Oakwood Cemetery, down the hill and to the west. *Photo by the author.*

Democratic apologists for slavery had coined the term *miscegenation* to stigmatize their Republican opponents and tried to use it against Lincoln in the election of 1864.[18]

Only the most progressive writers of the time dared to treat the theme of interracial love in fiction. Louisa May Alcott, the niece of the Reverend Samuel J. May, and a frequent visitor to Syracuse, did write about the theme in several stories that were published before her best-known novel, *Little Women*.[19]

On October 17, 1870, the *Syracuse Daily Courier* carried an item under the heading "Melancholy and Sudden Death."[20] Edmonia Highgate, age 26, had been found dead in Syracuse in the house of an abortionist. Her purse contained a ticket for a trunk of belongings which she had been forced to leave with a pawnbroker. Although the exact circumstances are unknown, she seems to have fallen in love with John Henry Vosburg, assistant editor of the *National Quarterly Review*, a learned quarterly that was published from 1860 to 1880. Vosburg's wife was in a mental institution and he, a poet in delicate health (a cripple, according to one source) with two children, was dependent upon his wife's family. These circumstances and public hostility toward their interracial romance proved too burdensome for Highgate. So her death was doubly tragic. A. T. Morgan wrote to Gerrit Smith to tell him that his sister-in-law had been preparing to return to the South and pick up her work again when he and Carrie last saw her. Yet, she had spoken to Carrie of "an overwhelming premonition that she should die soon."[21]

Edmonia is buried in Oakwood Cemetery, Syracuse, near the grave of her father and that of her brother Charles, who died April 2, 1865, of wounds received in a battle at Petersburg, Virginia.[22]

We remember Thomas James (1804–1891) as instrumental to organizing congregations for the A.M.E.Z. Church in North Star Country. He was also active in the South during and after the Civil War.[23] James left Rochester in 1862 as an agent of the AMA. He went to Kentucky, a difficult state to work in because blacks enjoyed only de facto freedom. Lincoln's Emancipation Proclamation permitted slave owners in the border states to maintain technical control over their "property." At Louisville, James came under the supervision of the federal government and worked among the homeless, mostly women and children, in a ten-acre camp on the edge of the city. He went to Louisville's five slave pens and, with the backing of General Burbage, brought out the inmates. James set up a Sunday school and a day school in the camp, and he held religious services. He rescued a girl named Laura from the cellar in which she had been shut up without food and drink. James tells us that he sent another girl, "rescued by me under somewhat similar circumstances," to Rochester to find a home with the family of a Colonel Klinck.

James remained at Louisville after the war to supervise a federal hospital, a dispensary, and a store. In 1878, he went to Ohio as a missionary preacher and, in 1880, he was posted to Kansas where he worked among the Exodusters under the auspices of the Topeka Relief Association. When he returned to Rochester, James sat down to sum up an eventful life. In 1886, he wrote,

Thomas James (1804–1891). An ex-slave himself, James helped found A.M.E.Z. churches in North Star Country and aided fellow freedom-seekers. After the Civil War, he worked among the newly liberated in Kentucky, and in 1886 he published an autobiography, "Life of Rev. Thomas James, By Himself." *Courtesy of the Rochester Public Library.*

You ask me what change for the better has taken place in the condition of the colored people of this locality in my day. I answer that the Anti-Slavery agitation developed an active and generous sympathy for the free colored man of the North, as well as for his brother in bondage. We felt the good effect of that sympathy and the aide and encouragement which accompanied it. But now, that the end of Anti-Slavery agitation has been fully accomplished, our white friends are inclined to leave us to our resources.[24]

The Highgate women and Thomas James were not the lone representatives of North Star County in the army of teachers and missionaries who worked among the freedmen. Nathan T. Condol of Geneva, son of a day laborer, taught in Mississippi's Black Belt from 1866 until 1878, when he died of yellow fever. Charles Douglass, son of Frederick Douglass, clerked in the War Department and taught among the freedmen for a year in Washington, D.C. At least one of the teachers from North Star Country stayed on in the South to participate in Reconstruction politics. Stephen A. Swails, a boatman from Elmira, and his wife, Sarah, worked among the freed people of South Carolina. Stephen was elected to the state legislature, and from 1872 to 1874 he was president pro tem of the state senate. He became a newspaper editor and served on the board of trustees of the University of South Carolina.[25]

Several score white men and women hailing from Upstate New York also went South under the auspices of the educational and missionary agencies. Among them was Sally Holley, daughter of Rochester's Myron Holley, who became a teacher at Lotsburgh, Virginia.[26] Some of Beriah Green's former students became officers in the freedmen's educational associations. John Alvord served as superintendent of Schools for Freedmen, Bureau of Refugees, Freedmen and Abandoned Lands; and George Whipple was secretary of the AMA. Both men belonged to the executive committee of the American Freedmen's Union Commission.[27] Homer's Erastus M. Cravath came from an abolitionist family with Underground Railroad connections in Cortland County. A graduate of Oberlin College, Erastus served a Congregational church in Ohio until resigning in 1863 to join the Union army. In 1865, he became field secretary of the AMA and was instrumental in founding what is now known as Fisk University in Nashville, Tennessee.[28]

Emily Howland (1827–1929) was born of a Quaker family living at Sherwood (Cayuga County). She dedicated her life to educating and assisting

the freed people. The Howland household embraced Garrisonian abolitionism and was a known station on the Underground Railroad. A temperance and women's rights advocate in her own right, Emily Howland taught
in the Miner School for Colored Girls in Washington, D.C., beginning in
1857. When the school's founder, Myrtilla Miner (a white woman originally
from Upstate New York), became ill, Howland replaced her. During the
Civil War, Howland worked as a teacher and a nurse in the contraband
camps surrounding the nation's capital. In 1866, Howland opened up a
school in Northumberland County, Virginia, on four hundred acres of land
that she had persuaded Slocum Howland, her father, to purchase. Howland
School was open to poor white and black children and financed by Emily's
father. Because of her father's ill health, Emily Howland was forced to
return to North Star County in 1870, but she continued to provide financial
support for the Howland School until 1921, when it became part of the Virginia public school system.[29]

Samuel J. May was especially active in the post–Civil War reconstruction
effort. A key figure in the Syracuse or Onondaga County freedmen's association, he corresponded with James Miller McKim regarding the placement
and support of young women who sought fulfillment of their own antislavery feelings in the crusade to educate blacks in the South. In 1866, May
wrote McKim about the needs of three teachers from the Syracuse area who
were stationed in Florida. The Syracuse Freedman's Relief Association was
prepared to pay half of the women's expenses, but they were in need of
additional support and better housing. May pleaded with McKim not to
remove Cornelia Smith from St. Augustine when her initial term expired,
saying of her, "She is a conscientious, sensible, diligent, enterprising, and
courageous woman. I consider her superior to any of the young ladies we
have sent from this part of the state."[30] About a year later, May wrote
McKim about Cloe Merrick, who was resigning her post because of her
impending marriage to Governor Reed of Florida. At the same time, May
instructed McKim to make sure that three boxes of schoolbooks that had
been collected in Syracuse be directed to teachers Thomas W. Cardozo at
Elizabeth City, North Carolina; Jennie Greene at Columbia, South Carolina; and Emma Norris (Merrick's successor) at New Bern, North Carolina.[31]

Sojourner Truth, who was illiterate, lacked the skills to teach reading and
writing, but she made an effort to move freed slaves away from dependence

on the federal government. While working for the National Freedmen's Relief Association in Washington, Truth received a request from Amy Post to send ex-slaves to Rochester and vicinity where they could be employed. The following advertisement appeared in local newspapers in March 1867:

> To the Public.—Sojourner Truth, the well known Mrs. Stowe's African Sybil, is now in Rochester, endeavoring to find employment for some of the Southern freed people, who are in Washington, several thousands of them supported by the Government and philanthropists, in idleness. They are willing and able to work, but there is none for them there.
>
> It is therefore proposed to establish a depot for some of them in Rochester, where the farmers and citizens can supply their great need of such help. They will be transported here without expense to the employer, but to pay expenses while in the city, fifty cents or a dollar may be required.
>
> We therefore solicit all who need help, and are willing to pay them such wages as they may earn, to immediately avail themselves of this opportunity, by writing Sojourner Truth, care of Isaac Post, Rochester; of what number and kind; whether men, women, or families, they desire.
>
> On or before the arrival of these people notice will be given in the city papers, that applicants may come and select for themselves.
>
> Sojourner Truth, who is the life and soul of this movement intends holding meetings in adjoining towns, in aid of this effort.[32]

Although prospective employers were numerous, they desired young women and men for domestic help and farm laborers. Children and the elderly were discouraged.[33]

Truth brought a small company of freed slaves to Rochester, but she found most occupants of the camps surrounding Washington unwilling to relocate to the wintry North. It did not help that Rochester's *Daily Union*, a Democratic paper, was warning whites that the ex-slaves Truth proposed to bring would take work from them. The newspaper also urged its readership to "look to your chicken-coops."[34] Mary H. Thomas, a Quaker woman from Union Springs, did not concern herself with the chickens when she wrote to Amy Post of the experience her family had with one of the freedmen:

> The man whom thou sent to us we liked very much. But as we were just papering, painting, and varnishing all through the house, we had no place to put him, and so we told him if he would go to the school, and work for his board a few days till we could make the arrangement, then he could come here and work for wages all the season.

But when we inquired for him we found he was gone back to Rochester without letting us now anything about it.

We are really disappointed for they tell us he worked very smart at the school and seems just such a one as we wanted. I hope as soon as his wife comes he will return here—we have a vacant house they can occupy—but unless she comes soon it may be rented to some one else.

I enclose a dollar as requested in Amy Post's letter if he did not remain here.[35]

The squalor in the freedmen's camps from which Truth tried to rescue ex-slaves was brought home to the RLASS in the vivid reports of Julia A. Wilbur, the society's agent. She described the lack of clothing and shelter among the freedmen at Alexandria, Virginia, and told of corruption in high places.[36]

The 1870s were the twilight years of the abolitionist generation that had led the freedom crusade in North Star Country. Nearly a half century had passed since Charles G. Finney set Upstate New York aflame with spiritual excitements. The veteran abolitionists of the Burned-over District had fought the good fight against the sin of slavery and its evil twin, racism, for almost four decades. Now the ranks of the old guard were thinning.

On the morning of May 4, 1874, Beriah Green walked from his house (called the Old Hive), located on Whitesboro's main street, to the Whitesboro Town Hall. While admonishing the Board of Excise to not grant any new liquor licenses, he fell backwards upon the floor and died almost instantly. He is buried in Grand View Cemetery, overlooking the Mohawk Flats upon which Oneida Institute once stood. On his gravestone is inscribed the text that Green used the day before he died when addressing a tiny congregation in his house: "He that doeth righteousness is righteous."[37] When news of Green's death reached John Greenleaf Whittier, the Quaker poet and veteran abolitionist penned a memorial to his fallen comrade. "I am pained to learn of the death of that noble man, Beriah Green. How thick the Cypress shadows fall, and how few are left of those whom I met at the anti-slavery convention in 1833."[38]

Gerrit Smith, ever his own man, continued to act his conscience after the Civil War, regardless of public opinion. In 1867 he, along with Cornelius Vanderbilt and Horace Greeley, signed the bail bond for Jefferson Davis, former president of the Confederacy. This brought a retort from the *Chica-*

go Tribune: "Gerrit Smith stands indebted to his sire for feeble intellect and large fortune."[39]

Smith spent the last years of his life trying, as always, to improve the world about him. He organized the Anti-Dramshop Party in New York State in 1869, though he voted for Grant and the Republicans in 1872. Smith continued to lead meetings at the Free Church in Peterboro until his health flagged. Ann Smith, Gerrit's wife, drifted into Spiritualism and talked with mediums, but he kept faith with rationalism.

On July 4, 1874, Smith went to Syracuse to advocate the peaceful acquisition of Cuba. One of those who heard Smith speak that day wrote that the old power was gone. "His glorious voice, which, earlier in life, rang out in eloquent denunciation of oppression and wrong, and which had great volume and power, besides being finely modulated and full of music, had now lost its best qualities, though it was still capable of being heard to quite a distance, even in the open air."[40] When Christmas came, the old reform warhorse went to New York City to visit his nephew and nieces. He became ill and lapsed into unconsciousness the day after his arrival. He died on December 27, 1874, at the age of 77.[41]

It was thirty degrees below zero when the night train carrying Smith's body reached Canastota on December 29th. His remains were taken by carriage to Peterboro and placed in the Smith mansion so that villagers could pay their respects. Thirty children, black and white, came from the orphan asylum that Smith had sponsored. They gathered 'round the coffin and sang one of his favorite hymns. The funeral services at the house and grave were simple and dignified, in keeping with the natural faith of a man who thought of the hereafter with confident hope. In 1852, when the Sage of Peterboro was at his prime, Frederick Douglass took pen in hand to write to Gerrit Smith. He thanked Smith for "notes and messages" sent during Douglass's recent illness and then added a note of commendation which confirms the abolitionist reputation of his friend and ally. "My heart leaped up, when I read your name among the counsel for the rescuers [of Jerry]. I assigned you a place in [the] trial which would send your name down in posterity beside that of Granville Sharpe. You were to be made (under God) the honored instrument of making the Soil of New York like that of England—too sacred to bear the footprints of a slave or a slave hunter."[42]

Still in his prime after the passage of the Thirteenth Amendment, Frederick Douglass was without a vocation. "The antislavery platform had performed its work, and my voice was no longer needed,"[43] he acknowledged. Douglass had a few thousand dollars saved from the publication of *My Bondage and My Freedom* in 1855, but it was not enough to retire with. So, he took up lecturing on ethnology to dispute the pseudo-scientific racial theories of the day. Something of the old agitator rose in him during the early years of Reconstruction, and he spoke out on questions of land and education for the freedmen. His suspicions regarding Andrew Johnson were borne out in the administration's policies, which were hostile to black civil rights. Douglass joined the Radical Republicans in advocating impeachment. In 1867, Douglass rejected President Johnson's offer to become head of the Freedmen's Bureau, judging it to be the political ploy that it was.[44]

Douglass, like Gerrit Smith, initially opposed the Fourteenth Amendment, passed in May 1866, because it did not include provisions for black suffrage. When the question of voting rights for black males first came before voters in the 1846 New York State referendum, most whites had opposed granting them access to the ballot box. The Civil War, emancipation, and the use of black troops, as historian Phyllis F. Field noted in her examination of the black suffrage struggle in New York State, changed minds and hearts. Most Republicans "were made to see that for the party of patriotism, union, and decency to triumph, changes would have to be made in the black man's status in America."[45]

In the national controversy over the Fifteenth Amendment, Frederick Douglass parted company with the white suffragists who feared that pressing for the black vote would divide their supporters. Though Douglass regretted his differences with the suffragists over tactics, he felt no shame in being, as he said, "denominated a woman's-rights man."[46] In reporting on the 1848 Seneca Falls convention for the *North Star,* Douglass had proclaimed, "We are free to say that in respect to political rights, we hold woman to be justly entitled to all we claim for man."[47] After the Fifteenth Amendment (giving voting rights to eligible black males) took effect in 1870, Douglass said, "I looked upon suffrage to the Negro as the only measure which could prevent him from being thrust back into slavery."[48]

Frederick Douglass's intimate ties to North Star Country came to an end on a late spring night in June of 1872. Douglass was in Washington, D.C., when he received a telegram that his South Avenue house on the hill (in Rochester) had burned. Attributed to an incendiary, the conflagration destroyed the only existing complete runs of the *North Star, Frederick Douglass's Paper*, and *Douglass's Monthly*.

Reflecting on the grievous loss of twelve volumes of his paper, Douglass wrote, "If I have at any time said or written that which is worth remembering or repeating, I must have said such things between the years 1848 and 1860, and my paper was a chronicle of most of what I said during that time."[49] A cow had died in the fire, but the family was safe. Once arrangements could be made, the Douglass family moved to Washington, D.C., where Frederick became president of the Freedman's Savings and Trust Company. Thus ended a quarter century in which the name of Frederick Douglass and North Star Country were synonymous.

Douglass died in Washington, D.C., on February 20, 1895, most likely of heart failure. His remains were brought to Rochester and placed in Mount Hope Cemetery. Today his grave is located not far from that of Amy Post,[50] the Upstate New Yorker who had been instrumental in encouraging "the Lion who wrote history," as Douglass has been called, to relocate to the Burned-over District nearly a half century earlier.[51] Elizabeth Cady Stanton summed up the freedom warrior's life as she recalled an abolitionist meeting many years earlier in Boston. Among all the speakers, Frederick Douglass "stood there like an African prince, majestic in his wrath."[52] Today a bronze statue of Douglass sits on the edge of Highland Park in Rochester. Set on a pedestal of westerly blue granite, the sculpture makes Douglass appear larger than life. This Frederick Douglass monument is known as the first public sculpture to be erected in the United States that honors an African American. It was designed by Sidney W. Edward and dedicated on June 9, 1899, by New York State Governor Theodore Roosevelt at its original location at Central Avenue and St. Paul Street. Susan B. Anthony complained about its orientation: "I wonder how the mistake was made of having it face the South. It ought not be so and I shall endeavor to have it changed. He always faced North; his paper was called *The North Star*, and I do not like to see him look to the South."[53] African American veterans of the Grand Army of the Republic held annual reunions at the foot of Douglass's monument for many years after the Civil War. In more recent times, concerns about the deterioration of the Central Avenue area and then the

Frederick Douglass's grave, Rochester. Visitors to historic Mt. Hope Cemetery can pay their respects to North Star Country's most eloquent voice for freedom in Section T of the cemetery. Myron Holly (1819–1841) and Susan B. Anthony (1820–1906) are also buried in Mt. Hope, as are the Posts and Porters (Rochester families who were active in the abolitionist cause). *Photo by the author.*

construction of Rochester's Inner Loop brought about the statue's removal to Highland Park, where it was rededicated in September 1941 and was turned to face North.[54]

Harriet Tubman outlived most of the freedom crusaders connected with Upstate New York. Her home remained in Auburn from 1857 until her death in 1913, though she was gone for three years during the Civil War when she worked as a cook and nurse among the contrabands. She returned to Auburn after the war and continued her labors on behalf of destitute children, the sick and the disabled, and women's rights. In response to the question "Do you really believe that women should vote?" Tubman said in 1911, "I have suffered enough to believe it."[55]

In 1890, after a long struggle to legitimize her claim, she began receiving a pension of $20 per month because her second husband, Nelson Davis, whom she married in 1869, had been a Union soldier.[56] The two biographies, *Scenes in the Life of Harriet Tubman* (1868) and *Harriet Tubman: The Moses of Her People* (1886), that were authored by Sarah Bradford helped to popularize Harriet as the Moses of her people, but brought neither fortune nor public acclaim in her declining years. Harriet Tubman died of pneumonia on March 10, 1913, in the fiftieth year since the Emancipation Proclamation. Moses was interred on a cold winter afternoon with military honors in Fort Hill Cemetery, Auburn.

When leading tired slaves out of bondage Harriet Tubman would tell them, "Children, if you are tired, keep going; if you are scared, keep going; if you are hungry, keep going; if you want to taste freedom, keep going." For nearly a century, Harriet had herself kept going—now she rests from her labors. Her last words before she died: "I Go to Prepare a Place for You."[57] Booker T. Washington was the featured speaker on June 12, 1914, when thousands of people, black and white, came to Auburn to honor the life and work of Harriet. A bronze tablet was unveiled by the Cayuga County Historical Society and placed at the entrance to the Cayuga County Court House. The inscription reads, in part, "Called the 'Moses of her people', she led over three hundred Negroes up from slavery to freedom, and rendered invaluable service as nurse and spy." Tubman herself is quoted: "On my underground railroad I nebber run my train off de track and I nebber los' a passenger."[58]

Jermain Loguen was elected to the office of bishop at the A.M.E.Z. General Conference in 1868, with responsibility for the Allegheny and Kentucky Conferences. Two years later, he assumed oversight of the Second District, a district which included his home Genesee Conference. In 1872, he was about to take up a new assignment to do mission work on the Pacific Coast when tuberculosis forced him to resign and seek a cure at the mineral springs in Saratoga Springs. It was there, on September 30, 1872, that Loguen died. Loguen's funeral was held in Syracuse's First Methodist Church on October 4, 1872, and he was buried in Oakwood Cemetery not far from the grave of Edmonia Highgate. In its obituary, the *Syracuse Jour-*

Frederick Douglass Memorial Monument, Rochester. The Frederick Douglass statue was dedicated in 1898 and was originally located at St. Paul Street and Central Avenue, near the New York Central Railroad Station. The statue is said to have been the first public monument in the United States to be dedicated to an African American. In 1941, the monument was relocated to Highland Park. *Photo by the author.*

nal noted that Loguen "enjoyed the respect of everybody in this community, and was welcome wherever his duty or social relations called him."[59] Loguen's own sentiment about the place where he had stood tall for freedom can be inferred from a letter he wrote. He was living in exile in Canada, following the Jerry Rescue, and he asked Governor Hunt for "the shield of protection in the free course of justice." "I have," Loguen declared, "resided long enough in her Britannic Majesty's dominions to have become a British subject; but having lived for many years in the State of New York, at Syracuse, as a minister of the Gospel and 'citizen of no mean city', I have never been able to produce any other certificate of freedom than the one which was indelibly written upon my constitutional nature, by the finger of the Almighty."[60]

William Henry Seward died in 1872 and is buried in the same cemetery, Auburn's Fort Hill, as Harriet Tubman.[61]

Samuel J. May died in 1871, two years after he summed up his involvement in the black freedom struggle with *Some Recollections of Our Antislavery Conflict.* In his recollections, May confessed that he had moved from Boston to Syracuse in 1845 because he feared that his ardor for the freedom cause might cool so far from the furnace of New England's brand of abolitionism. The Unitarian clergyman was pleased to find so many of his new neighbors and fellow citizens dedicated to immediatism, and he took special pleasure in his long association with Gerrit Smith, despite finding some of the Peterboro abolitionist's views "eccentric."[62]

May gave a detailed account of the Jerry Rescue of 1851 in his recollections, viewing it as the hallmark of North Star Country abolitionism. He was instrumental in organizing Syracuse's first Rescue of Jerry celebration in 1852. He had been personally drawn into the struggle when, but a year or two after moving to Syracuse, a freedom-seeker "accosted" him in the street, asking for help in getting his mother out of Virginia. May inquired how the man had found his way to Upstate New York and was told, "By the light of the north-star."[63]

In 1867, May preached a sermon in the Church of the Messiah, Syracuse, in which he recounted his forty-seven years in the ministry. At the age of seventy, he was contemplating the "termination of my temporal course."[64] May would live another four years, during which he continued to devote his energies to humanitarian causes. When May felt his work was done, he donated his extensive collection of antislavery pamphlets, books, and letters to Cornell University.[65]

William Lloyd Garrison ceased publication of the *Liberator* in 1865 and declared, "My vocation as an Abolitionist, thank God, is ended."[66] During the ensuing half decade, abolitionists debated whether or not their work was indeed done. The AASS did not dissolve until 1870. Then Wendell Phillips and the remaining "old abolitionists" followed Garrison's lead. The passage of the Fifteenth Amendment brought closure to a long and difficult struggle for the first-generation immediatists. They had endured many contentious debates among themselves over critical issues such as how to interpret the Constitution, the role of women in antislavery societies, and the need for the Liberty Party. But the coming of the Civil War brought most of the pioneering reformers back together in common cause.

Gerrit Smith, Frederick Douglass, Elizur Wright, Jr., William Goodell, and Theodore Dwight Weld, to name but a few, rejoined the AASS, and the rival AFASS quietly faded away. As historian Lawrence Friedman points out, the aging abolitionists "perceived themselves to be nearing the end." They were "drawing near the grave" and as one of them confessed, felt "'too worn and weary for active labor.'"[67] In 1874, veteran abolitionists, with the debates over the dissolution of the AASS behind them, gathered in Chicago for a three-day reunion convention. William Goodell was the only member of the Gerrit Smith circle from North Star Country to attend.[68] Frederick Douglass sent a letter of greeting, telling the gathering of the old guard that their work had been *the* great work of the century.[69]

Dead or in their declining years, the first generation abolitionists of North Star Country moved off center stage in the 1870s. Their exploits were remembered in stories about the Underground Railroad, but soldiers who fought in the Civil War were more apt to argue about old battles and recall what it felt like under the hot sun at Gettysburg than to tell of Gerrit Smith and Frederick Douglass.

North Star Country's special contributions to the struggle over slavery and freedom have been folded into the collective national memory of the Civil War. Mothers taught children the songs sung by their fathers in the Union armies, such as "We are coming, Father Abraham, A hundred thousand strong." Veterans brought back anthems representing the slave's rebellious spirit: "Oh, freedom! Freedom over me! And before I'd be a slave I'd be carried to my grave. And go home to my Master and be free."[70] Gertrude Sneller tells us that several soldiers returned with a black boy. He worked on a farm in the Cicero area and went to school with the other children. He sang beautifully and taught his schoolmates Southern war songs like "The Bonnie Blue Flag that Bears the Single Star."[71]

As a visit to most cemeteries in North Star Country will demonstrate, the graves of members of the Grand Army of the Republic are still marked. In helping to defeat the South, the G.A.R. veterans helped bring about the Second American Revolution. Whether they thought of themselves as abolitionists or not, they assumed honored places in North Star Country communities after the Civil War, and they dominated Republican politics for decades. They held annual campfires and observed Union Sunday. Gertrude Sneller gives us this picturesque account of the G.A.R. winter reunions she attended as a child growing up in northern Onondaga County:

> The veterans as hosts appeared in dark blue uniforms with the G.A.R. badge pinned to their coats, and their black slouch hats had a little laurel wreath in front made of real gold. Refreshments too were the same each year, supposedly what the soldiers had eaten. Very black coffee was served in tin cups such as the soldiers had used; baked beans and hardtack went with the coffee, and sometimes there was ham as a concession to nonmilitary appetites. The rest of the evening was spent in dancing the Lancers, Virginia Reel, Portland Fancy, a waltz or two, and square dances of intricate variety. The leader of the three-piece orchestra called off in the voice of a major general, and commanded the dancers to swing and circle and join hands.[72]

Speakers told of how it felt to have "fit" and bled for the Union, and local talent, including the children, were pressed into service to recite patriotic poetry. On a spring Sunday in May, the G.A.R. members gathered with their families for a union church service. Sneller recalls, "Methodists, Presbyterians, and Universalists forgot their three-sided distrust of one another's doctrines and remembered that they had a common country even if there was no likelihood that they would occupy a common heaven."[73]

The death of so many abolitionist stalwarts by the time of America's centennial in 1876, the removal of Frederick Douglass to Washington, and the return of the Union veterans to their homes and farms brought the end of an era in the history of North Star Country which is deserving of perpetual care. Charles G. Finney, whose revivals sparked a host of reform endeavors in the region, died in 1875, having lived out his last years quietly in Oberlin, Ohio. Theodore Dwight Weld once said of Finney in a letter to Lewis Tappan, "I know Finney is not a perfect man, . . . but yet take him for all in all, when shall we look upon his like again?"[74] The same can be said of the host of abolitionists, black and white, who took Finney's evangelical legacy and directed it toward emancipating the slaves and securing their rights. Though some were perfectionists, ever watchful for the cardinal sin of self-pride, none of them were perfect. Nevertheless, they deserve our best efforts to be the caring stewards of the bright shining star that inspired them.

Appendix

Notes

Bibliography

Index

Appendix

African Americans in New York State, 1790–1870

County	1790 Slave	1790 Free	1800 Slave	1800 Free	1810 Slave	1810 Free	1820 Slave	1820 Free	1830[1] Free	1840[2] Free	1850 Free	1860 Free	1870 Free
Albany[3]	3,924	170	1,808	353	772	866	413	858	1,593	1,314	1,194	938	1,095
Allegany	—[4]	—	—	—	21	0	17	12	79	142	128	264	349
Broome	—	—	—	—	23	30	25	63	96	223	431	464	481
Cataraugus	—	—	—	—	—	—	2	4	21	38	102	151	164
Cayuga	—	—	53	19	75	86	48	191	369	435	543	451	657
Chautauqua	—	—	—	—	—	—	3	10	100	124	140	205	195
Chemung	—	—	—	—	—	—	—	—	—	113	286	572	793
Chenango	—	—	16	40	13	76	7	189	266	273	264	263	302
Clinton	17	16	59[5]	62[6]	29	32	2	96	82	86	112	128	128
Columbia	1,623	55	1,501	490	879	850	761	1,053	1,582	1,556	1,312	1,380	1,312
Cortland	—	—	—	—	0	2	3	48	38	46	42	16	58
Delaware	—	—	16	30	55	77	56	82	203	190	201	186	232
Dutchess	1,856	440	1,609	931	1,262	1,124	772	1,685	2,486	2,270	1,970	2,051	2,113
Erie	—	—	—	—	—	—	—	—	243	608	825	878	858
Essex	—	—	—[5]	—[5]	0	3	3	28	60	78	50	123	80
Franklin	—	—	—	—	3	0	0	0	24	3	62	19	27
Fulton	—	—	—	—	—	—	—	—	—	114	102	185	221
Genesee	—	—	—	—	11	14	35	82	92	115	77	84	153
Greene	—	—	548	69	367	371	134	637	994	893	895	819	629
Hamilton	—	—	—	—	—	—	1	1	1	3	2	3	1
Herkimer	—	—	61	8	64	77	72	188	352	287	203	251	226
Jefferson	—	—	—	—	0	40	5	135	139	141	191	209	236
Kings	1,432	46	1,479	332	1,118	735	879	882	2,007	2,843	4,065	4,999	5,653
Lewis	—	—	—	—	4	25	0	43	83	53	42	39	54
Livingston	—	—	—	—	—	—	—	—	134	140	209	184	215
Madison	—	—	—	—	35	177	10	182	227	223	298	300	313
Monroe	—	—	—	—	—	—	—	—	465	655	699	567	605
Montgomery	588	41	466	8	712	365	349	571	685	588	474	357	351
New York	2,369	1,101	2,876	3,506	1,686	8,137	518	10,368	13,959	16,358	13,815	12,574	13,072
Niagara	—	—	—	—	8	31	15	67	102	241	317	517	448
Oneida	—	—	50	73	81	130	9	368	453	644	672	638	590
Onondaga	—	—	11	18	50	114	59	195	492	477	613	555	707

(table continues)

County	1790 Slave	1790 Free	1800 Slave	1800 Free	1810 Slave	1810 Free	1820 Slave	1820 Free	1830[1] Free	1840[2] Free	1850 Free	1860 Free	1870 Free
Ontario	11	6	57	109	212	299	0	727	455	664	610	639	539
Orange	966	201	1145	534	966	927	1,125	969	2,223	2,292	2,464	2,112	2,524
Orleans	—	—	—	—	—	—	—	—	27	69	108	131	172
Oswego	—	—	—	—	—	—	0	32	144	215	215	335	306
Otsego	—	—	48	44	74	133	16	235	264	222	175	207	229
Putnam	—	—	—	—	—	—	49	166	160	167	138	183	120
Queens	2,309	808	1,540	1,431	809	2,354	559	2,648	3,108	3,509	3,451	3,387	3,791
Rensselaer	—	—	898	113	750	362	433	632	1,036	1,190	1,019	1,058	783
Richmond	759	127	675	83	437	274	532	78	552	483	590	659	787
Rockland	—	—	551	68	316	292	124	412	451	432	596	549	728
Saratoga	—	—	358	73	107	565	123	504	592	649	618	691	683
Schenectady	—	—	—	—	318	188	102	454	304	410	388	241	168
Schoharie	—	—	354	11	316	235	302	264	567	493	478	484	426
Schuyler	—	—	—	—	—	—	—	—	—	—	—	100	186
Seneca	—	—	—	—	101	44	84	180	177	199	181	213	239
Steuben	—	—	22	0	87	29	46	130	208	288	371	475	383
St. Lawrence	—	—	—	—	5	17	8	14	60	35	39	59	72
Suffolk	1,098	1,126	886	1,016	413	1,373	323	1,166	2,013	2,177	2,117	1,798	1,806
Sullivan	—	—	—	—	43	11	69	33	119	80	100	94	99
Tioga	—	—	17	32	61	39	104	32	163	162	197	248	359
Tompkins	—	—	—	—	—	—	6	66	234	253	325	297	401
Ulster	2,906	157	2,257	336	1,437	1,066	1,523	597	1,770	1,804	1,585	1,609	1,433
Warren	—	—	—	—	—	—	7	10	22	32	46	58	54
Washington	47	3	280	119	315	2,815	150	254	385	272	350	259	379
Wayne	—	—	—	—	—	—	—	—	188	222	268	270	344
Westchester	1,419	358	1,260	482	982	948	205	1,638	2,115	2,300	2,075	2,270	2,513
Wyoming	—	—	—	—	—	—	—	—	—	—	64	52	82
Yates	—	—	—	—	—	—	—	—	106	134	165	157	166
STATE TOTAL	21,324	4,682	20,903	10,374	15,017	25,333	10,088	29,279	44,870	50,027	49,069	49,005	52,081

1. The 1830 census reported 75 slaves (Albany, 2; Chenango, 3; Montgomery, 26; New York, 17; Oneida, 15; Putnam, 4; and Washington, 8). Slaves could be brought into New York State by their owners until 1841.

2. The 1840 census reported 4 slaves (Kings, 3, and Putnam, 1).

3. The twenty-eight italicized counties are not included in North Star Country as defined, approximately, by the boundaries of the Burned-over District.

4. The dash (—) indicates a county that was not yet organized as of the decennial census.

5. Known as Clinton/Essex County in 1800.

Adapted from the tables titled "Free Colored" and "Slave" in the Ninth Census, Vol. I, of *The Statistics of the Population of the United States for 1870* (Washington, D.C.: Government Printing Office, 1872), pp. 51–52.

Notes

Introduction

1. *North Star,* Jan. 7, 1848. Pennington, like Douglass, was a refugee from slavery as it existed along Maryland's Eastern Shore. In 1848, Pennington was pastor of Talcott Street Congregational Church in Hartford, Connecticut. His *Textbook of the Origin and History of the Colored People* (1841) is thought to be the earliest African American history.

2. William S. McFeely, *Frederick Douglass* (New York: Norton, 1991), 148.

3. William Lloyd Garrison to the *Liberator,* May 14, 1847, "No Union with Slave-holders, 1841–1849," in vol. 3 of Garrison, *The Letters of William Lloyd Garrison,* ed. Walter M. Merrill (Cambridge Mass.: Harvard Univ. Press, 1973), 477–80.

4. *North Star,* Dec. 3, 1847. In 1851, Douglass replaced the title of *North Star* with *Frederick Douglass' Paper,* which lasted until 1860. *Douglass' Monthly,* also published in Rochester, appeared before January 1859 as a supplement to *Frederick Douglass' Paper* and continued until 1863.

5. Quotation cited in McFeely, *Frederick Douglass,* 149.

6. Whitney R. Cross, *The Burned-over District: The Social and Intellectual History of Enthusiastic Religion in Western New York, 1800–1850* (Ithaca: Cornell Univ. Press, 1950). Judith Wellman discusses the reverberations of Cross's classic study on subsequent scholarship in "Crossing Over Cross: Whitney Cross's Burned-over District as Social History," *Reviews in American History* 17 (Mar. 1989): 159–74.

7. Ralph V. Harlow, *Gerrit Smith: Philanthropist and Reformer* (1939; reprint, New York: Russell & Russell, 1972). This most recent attempt at a full-scale biography of Smith was published in 1940, at a time when the reputation of the abolitionists as overly self-righteous and quarrelsome was at its height.

8. *North Star,* Dec. 8, 1848.

9. W. E. B. DuBois, *The Souls of Black Folk* (1903; reprint, New York: Fawcett Publications, 1961), 158–59. For information about Alexander Crummell, see Wilson Jeremiah Moses, *Alexander Crummell: A Study of Civilization and Discontent* (New York: Oxford Univ. Press, 1989).

10. Milton C. Sernett, *Abolition's Axe: Beriah Green, Oneida Institute, and the Black Freedom Struggle* (Syracuse: Syracuse Univ. Press, 1986).

11. Samuel R. Ward, Cortlandville, Feb. 1849, *North Star,* Feb. 9, 1849.

12. Elizabeth Smith, cited in Helene C. Phelan, *And Why Not Every Man?: An Account of Slavery, the Underground Railroad, and the Road to Freedom in New York's Southern Tier* (Interlacken, N.Y.: Heart of the Lakes Publishing, 1987), 177.

13. T. S. Eliot, *Little Gidding,* pt. 5, in "Four Quartets," in *The Complete Poems and Plays: 1909–1950* (New York: Harcourt-Brace-Jovanovich, 1953), 119.

1. Slavery and the Burned-over District

1. Austin Steward, *Twenty-Two Years a Slave, and Forty Years a Freeman* (1857; reprint, New York: Negro Univ. Press, 1968), 107.

2. "Bath: Its Slave Population in Olden Time," *Bath Plaindealer,* Jan. 24, 1885. For more information about Captain Helm, see *Bath Plaindealer,* Feb. 7 and 14, 1885; Steward, *Twenty-Two Years a Slave,* 62.

3. Silas Bowker visited the Onondaga Salines in 1774 and reported, "the manufacture of salt was wholly in the hands of two Negro men, deserters from their master in Esopus, who used brass kettles for this purpose and whose only customers were the neighboring Indians." The salt springs on the bank of Onondaga Lake soon attracted white squatters to the lands of the Iroquois Confederacy, and some settlers brought their slaves with them. Isaac Wales, the "property" of John Fleming, came in 1810. He learned to read and write, worked on the construction of the Erie Canal, and purchased his own freedom. He eventually obtained a lot and a house in Syracuse and advertised his services as a chimney sweep. Timothy C. Cheney, *Reminiscences of Syracuse* (Syracuse: Onondaga Historical Association, 1914), 136.

4. Thomas J. Davis, "New York's Long Black Line: A Note on the Growing Slave Population, 1626–1790," *Afro-Americans in New York Life and History* 2 (Jan. 1978): 41–59. See also David Kobrin, *The Black Minority in Early New York* (Albany, N.Y.: Office of State History, 1971).

5. A. J. William-Myers, "The African Presence in the Mid-Hudson Valley Before 1800: A Preliminary Historiographical Sketch," *Afro-Americans in New York Life and History* 8 (Jan. 1984): 31–39. See also Ralph Watkins, "A Survey of the African American Presence in the History of the Downstate New York Area," *Afro-Americans in New York Life and History* 15 (Jan. 1991): 53–55.

6. Carleton Mabee with Susan Mabee Newhouse, *Sojourner Truth: Slave, Prophet, Legend* (New York: New York Univ. Press, 1993), 5. See also Nell Irvin Painter, *Sojourner Truth: A Life, A Symbol* (New York: W. W. Norton & Company, 1997), Chapter 2.

7. Edgar J. McManus, *A History of Negro Slavery in New York* (Syracuse: Syracuse Univ. Press, 1966), 12–13.

8. In 1712, twenty-four slaves recently brought from Africa armed themselves, set fire to a building on the northern outskirts of Manhattan, and then took refuge in the woods. Twenty-one of the alleged conspirators were tried, convicted, and put to death in the medieval manner: burned alive, racked and broken on the wheel, and gibbeted. McManus, *Negro Slavery in New York,* 122–26. The panic of 1741 began after the burglary of a white tobacconist. It was fueled by rumors that slaves were plotting to burn New York City and massacre whites. Fourteen slaves were burned at the stake, eighteen were hanged, and seventy-two alleged conspirators were banished from the province. McManus, *Negro Slavery in New York,* 126–39; Daniel Horsmanden, *The New York Conspiracy* (Boston: Beacon Press, 1971); and Kobrin, *Black Minority,* 26–29.

9. Kobrin, *Black Minority,* 10.

10. On the work of the New York Manumission Society, as well as other early efforts to ameliorate slavery, see McManus, *Negro Slavery in New York,* chapters 8 and 9.

11. McManus, *Negro Slavery in New York,* 149–50, 174.

12. See E. Anne Schaetzke, "Slavery in the Genesee Country (also known as Ontario County) 1789 to 1827," *Afro-Americans in New York Life and History* 22 (Jan. 1998): 7–40.

13. The 1820 census was the first to list blacks who were held as slaves by name. In previous counts, African American slaves were enumerated as belonging to the households of whites. See the decennial totals in the Appendix to this book. All subsequent references to state and county census data draw upon this chart. I have calculated totals for the counties that will comprise the Burned-over District by the 1820s. For the names of free blacks, see Alice Eichholz and James M. Rose, *Free Black Heads of Households in the New York State Federal Census, 1790–1830* (Detroit: Gale Research Company, 1981).

14. The law retroactively provided uncompensated emancipation for approximately 10,000 individuals held as slaves. A few slaves do appear in the census materials after 1827 because nonresidents were still allowed to bring slaves into the state; an 1841 statute outlawed this practice. On the legislative history, see Carl Nordstrom, "The New York Slave Code," *Afro-Americans in New York Life and History* 4 (Jan. 1980): 7–25; Edgar J. McManus, "Antislavery Legislation in New York," *Journal of Negro History* 46 (Oct. 1961): 207–15; and Arthur Zilversmit, *The First Emancipation: The Abolition of Slavery in the North* (Chicago: Univ. of Chicago Press, 1967), 213.

15. Steward, *Twenty-Two Years a Slave,* 113.

16. Colonel Nathaniel Rochester, a reformed slaveholder from Maryland, brought a small number of African Americans to New York State. They were freed in Dansville and came to Rochester in 1818, nearly concurrent with Steward's arrival. Thus began Rochester's free black population.

17. Peter Wheeler, *Chains and Freedom; or, The Life and Adventures of Peter Wheeler, a Colored Man Yet Living, a Slave in Chains, a Sailor on the Deep, and a Sinner at the Cross* (New York: E.S. Arnold and Co., 1839).

18. In Sydney H. Gallwey, *Peter Webb: Slave-Freeman-Citizen of Tompkins County, New York* (Ithaca: DeWitt Historical Society, 1960), 3. See also Tendai Muntunhu, "Peter Webb of Tompkins County, Central New York," *Negro History Bulletin* 45 (Jan.-Feb.-Mar. 1982): 48–49.

19. Federal Writers' Project, Works Progress Administration, State of New York, *Rochester and Monroe County* (Rochester: Scrantom's, 1937), 289. Most African Americans who were held as slaves prior to statewide emancipation in 1827 do not enter the historical record except in census materials. A few left testimonials of another sort. Rsearchers for the American Guide Series of the Federal Writers' Project of the Works Progress Administration scoured Monroe County in the 1930s. They came across evidence of the presence of African American slaves which was more than a century old. The town of Perinton, southeast of Rochester, was still orchard country. The Ellsworth farm, south of Fairport at the crossing of Turk Hill and Ayrault Roads, then had the distinction of ancient apple trees that had been planted by slaves around 1810. Surrounded by an equally ancient stone wall, which is said to have been erected by African Americans held as slaves, the orchard reportedly also served as a slave cemetery.

20. Robin Winks, *Blacks in Canada* (New Haven, Conn.: Yale Univ. Press, 1971), chapter 4. The Imperial Act of 1793 was a gradual emancipation statute. It stipulated that slaves' children born after July 9, 1793, would be free at age twenty-five, and that children born of these children were automatically free. It also prohibited the import of slaves into Upper Canada.

21. The free black population in New York State in 1820 totaled 29,279.

22. Thomas James, *Wonderful Eventful Life of Rev. Thomas James. By Himself* (3rd ed.;

Rochester, N.Y.: Post-Express Printing Company, 1887). Republished as "The Autobiography of Rev. Thomas James," *Rochester History* 37 (Oct. 1975): 21–32.

23. Steward, *Twenty-Two Years a Slave*, 114. On early schools, including Sunday schools for blacks, see Carleton Mabee, *Black Education in New York State: From Colonial to Modern Times* (Syracuse: Syracuse Univ. Press, 1979), chapters 1–3.

24. James, "Autobiography," 5.

25. Thomas J. Davis, "Three Dark Centuries Around Albany: A Survey of Black Life in New York's Capital City Area Before World War I," *Afro-Americans in New York Life and History* 7 (Jan. 1983): 10–11. Also, McManus, *Negro Slavery in New York*, 187–88.

26. Nathaniel Paul, "An Address, Delivered on the Celebration of the Abolition of Slavery, in the State of New York, July 5, 1827," in *Afro-American Religious History: A Documentary Witness*, ed. Milton C. Sernett (Durham, N.C.: Duke Univ. Press, 1985), 181, 185, 187.

27. *Ithaca Chronicle*, July 11, 1827, as quoted by Field Horne, "Ithaca's Black Community," in *A Heritage Uncovered: The Black Experience in Upstate New York, 1800–1925*, ed. Cara Sutherland (Elmira, N.Y.: Chemung County Historical Society, 1988), 19.

28. Steward, *Twenty-Two Years a Slave*, 163.

29. James W. Darlington, "Peopling the Post-revolutionary New York Frontier," *New York History* 74 (Oct. 1993): 341–81.

30. The section from Rochester to Albany was open by 1823. By the late 1830s, 500,000 barrels of wheat traveled along the canal.

31. Ronald E. Shaw, *Erie Water West: A History of the Erie Canal, 1792–1854* (Lexington: Univ. of Kentucky Press, 1966), chapter 12. See also Carol Sheriff, *The Artificial River: The Erie Canal and the Paradox of Progress, 1817–1862* (New York: Hill & Wang, 1996), chapter 1.

32. The classic formulation of the Yankee-Yorker typology was done by Dixon Ryan Fox, *Yankees and Yorkers* (New York: New York Univ. Press, 1940). See also David Maldwyn Ellis, "The Yankee Invasion of New York, 1783–1860," *New York History* 32 (Jan. 1951): 3–17.

33. Donald W. Meinig, "New York and Its Neighbors: Some Problems of Regional Interpretation," in *New Opportunities in a New Nation: The Development of New York After the Revolution*, ed. Manfred Jones and Robert V. Wells (Schenectady, N.Y.: Union College Press, 1982), 84.

34. For more on the commercial development of the "teeming west," see Shaw, *Erie Water West*, chapter 14; Sheriff, *Artificial River*, chapter 5.

35. Mary P. Ryan, *Cradle of the Middle Class: The Family in Oneida County, New York, 1790–1865* (New York: Cambridge Univ. Press, 1981). For more on women's reform activities in Rochester, see Nancy A. Hewitt, *Women's Activism and Social Change: Rochester, New York, 1822–1872* (Ithaca: Cornell Univ. Press, 1984).

36. Paul E. Johnson, *A Shopkeeper's Millennium: Society and Revivals in Rochester, New York 1815–1837* (New York: Hill and Wang, 1978), 138. Also, James I. McElroy, "Social Control and Romantic Reform in Antebellum America: The Case of Rochester, New York," *New York History* 58 (Jan. 1977): 17–46.

37. William C. Cochran, *Charles G. Finney: Memorial Address* (Philadelphia: Lippincott, 1908), 13.

38. Keith J. Hardman, *Charles Grandison Finney, 1792–1875: Revivalist and Reformer* (Syracuse: Syracuse Univ. Press, 1987), 41–43; Charles G. Finney, *The Memoirs of Charles G. Finney: The Complete Restored Text*, (1875), ed. Garth M. Rosell and Richard A. G. Dupuis (Grand Rapids, Mich.: Zondervan, 1989).

39. Cited in Hardman, *Finney*, 55.

40. Cochran, *Finney*, 16.

41. Cited in Hardman, *Finney*, 47–48.

42. Michael Barkun, *Crucible of the Millennium: The Burned-Over District of New York in the 1840s* (Syracuse: Syracuse Univ. Press, 1986), 24.

43. Howard Alexander Morrison, "The Finney Takeover of the Second Great Awakening During the Oneida Revivals of 1825–1827," *New York History* 59 (Jan. 1978): 27–53. See also David K. McMillan, "To Witness We Are Living: A Study of Charles Finney and the Revival of Religion in and about Utica, New York, During the Winter and Spring of 1826" (B.D. thesis, Union Theological Seminary, 1961); Tyler O. Hendricks, "Charles Finney and the Utica Revival of 1826: The Social Effect of a New Religious Paradigm" (Ph.D. diss., Vanderbilt Univ., 1983).

44. Although he was renowned for his physical stamina, not even Finney could manage such a "protracted meeting" alone. A reserve force of eight or nine ministers and evangelists assisted him. McElroy, "Social Control and Romantic Reform," 25.

45. John L. Hammond, *The Politics of Benevolence: Revival Religion and American Voting Behavior* (Norwood, N.J.: Ablex, 1979), 48–49.

46. Whitney R. Cross, *The Burned-over District: The Social and Intellectual History of Enthusiastic Religion in Western New York, 1800–1850* (Ithaca: Cornell Univ. Press, 1950), 155.

47. Henry Brewster Stanton, *Random Recollections* (Johnstown, N.Y.: Blunck and Leaning, 1885), 43.

48. Elizabeth Cady Stanton, *Eighty Years and More: Reminiscences, 1815–1897* (1898; reprint, New York: Schocken Books, 1971), 422–43.

49. General histories of this remarkable flowering of religious and reform energy include Timothy L. Smith, *Revivalism and Social Reform in Mid-Nineteenth-Century America* (1957; reprint, New York: Harper & Row, 1965); William G. McLoughlin, *Modern Revivalism: Charles Grandison Finney to Billy Graham* (New York: Ronald, 1959); and Bernard A. Weisberger, *They Gathered at the River: The Story of the Great Revivalists and their Impact upon Religion in America* (Boston: Little, Brown, 1958).

50. This was especially the case in rural areas and villages where revivalism was intense. See the detailed study of Cortland County by Curtis D. Johnson, *Islands of Holiness: Rural Religion in Upstate New York, 1790–1860* (Ithaca: Cornell Univ. Press, 1989).

51. Cross, *Burned-over District*, 158.

52. Cross, *Burned-over District*, 4. The Whitney R. Cross Papers (Collection #1678, Rare and Manuscript Collections, Kroch Library, Cornell Univ., Ithaca, New York) contain a sketch map that Cross labeled "A Tentative Location of the Burnt District." It is conveniently reproduced in James D. Folts, "The Fanatic and the Prophetess: Religious Perfectionism in Western New York, 1835–1839," *New York History* 72 (Oct. 1991): 359.

53. Mapping North Star Country is an imprecise science. Although I have chosen a region comprised of thirty-two counties as they are demarcated on today's New York

State map, abolitionist zeal was not evenly distributed across these counties. Antiabolitionist sentiment could be found within many of the same towns and villages where the friends of the slave planted their abolitionist standard.

54. Randolph A. Roth, *The Democratic Dilemma: Religion, Reform, and the Social Order in the Connecticut Valley of Vermont, 1791–1850* (New York: Cambridge Univ. Press, 1987). Linda K. Pritchard compares Upstate New York with the upper Ohio River Valley region in "The Burned-Over District Reconsidered: A Portent of Evolving Religious Pluralism in the United States," *Social Science History* 8 (Summer 1984): 243–65.

55. Judith Wellman, "Crossing Over Cross: Whitney Cross's Burned-over District as Social History," *Reviews in American History* 17 (1989): 159.

56. Richard H. Shryock, "Sylvester Graham and the Popular Health Movement, 1830–1870," *Mississippi Valley Historical Review* 18 (Sept. 1931): 172–83.

57. On Noyes, see Robert D. Thomas, *The Man Who Would Be Perfect: John Humphrey Noyes and the Utopian Impulse* (Philadelphia: Univ. of Pennsylvania Press, 1977).

58. Charles G. Finney, *Lectures on Revivals of Religion*, ed. William G. McLoughlin (Cambridge: Harvard Univ. Press, 1960), 403–4.

59. Alexander Campbell's observation, cited in Gordon S. Wood, "Evangelical America and Early Mormonism," *New York History* 61 (Oct. 1980): 380. Alexander Campbell, like Smith, sought a way out of the confusing snarl of religious claims in the aftermath of the Second Great Awakening. Campbell, again like Smith, ironically ended up founding a new religious group that became just another, albeit homegrown, denomination: the Disciples of Christ. For more on Mormonism's Upstate New York origins, see Cross, *Burned-over District*, chapter 8; Leonard J. Arrington, "Mormonism: From Its New York Beginnings," *New York History* 61 (Oct. 1980): 387–410; and Marvin S. Hill, "The Rise of Mormonism in the Burned-over District: Another View," *New York History* 61 (Oct. 1980): 411–30.

60. Miller gave the date as "about 1843" for many years, but when 1843 passed, he endorsed a recalculation based on the Jewish calendar and set the end of the world for October 22, 1844. Millerism and the millenarian impulse is the focus of Barkun, *Crucible of the Millennium*, and David L. Rowe, *Thunder and Trumpets: Millerites and Dissenting Religion in Upstate New York, 1800–1850* (AAR Studies in Religion, no. 38. Decatur, Ga.: Scholars Press, 1985). Whitney Cross reminds us that expectations of an early advent of Christ's Second Coming (the Day of Judgment) began outside the Burned-over District in northeastern New York, Vermont, and western Massachusetts. Though Adventism was an import, Cross felt that Millerites in the Burned-over District eventually "may nearly have equaled New England." Cross, *Burned-over District*, 288.

61. Cited in Hardman, *Finney*, 273–74.

62. James David Essig, "The Lord's Free Man: Charles G. Finney and His Abolitionism," *Civil War History* 24 (Mar. 1978): 25–45; Hardman, *Finney*, 275 ff. In his *Lectures to Professing Christians*, published in 1837, Finney said, "It can be demonstrated absolutely, that slavery is unlawful, and ought to be repented of, and given up, like any other sin." As to those who continued to hold slaves while doubting slavery's lawfulness, Finney said, "they are condemned before God, and we may be sure their sin will find them out, and God will let them know how He regards it." What of those who doubted the lawfulness of holding slaves and of emancipating them? Here Finney applied the moral reasoning

of Jonathan Edwards. They must seek the truth and meanwhile educate their slaves in order to "put them in a state where they can be set at liberty." Finney, *Lectures on Professing Christians* (London: Milner and Company, 1837), 36–37.

63. Cited in Robert V. Remini, *Andrew Jackson and the Course of American Freedom*, vol. 2: 1822–1832 (New York: Harper & Row, 1981), 235.

64. *David Walker's Appeal in Four Articles; Together with a Preamble to the Coloured Citizens of the World, But in Particular, and Very Expressly to Those of the United States of America*, ed. Charles M. Wiltse (New York: Hill & Wang, 1965), Article III. See also Donald M. Jacobs, "David Walker and William Lloyd Garrison: Racial Cooperation and the Shaping of Boston Abolition," in *Courage and Conscience: Black & White Abolitionists in Boston*, ed. Donald M. Jacobs (Bloomington: Indiana Univ. Press, 1993), 1–20.

65. Henry Highland Garnet, "A Brief Sketch of the Life and Character of David Walker," in *Walker's Appeal in Four Articles* with *An Address to the Slaves of the United States of America* (1848; reprint, New York: Arno Press, 1969), 8.

66. David B. Davis, *The Problem of Slavery in the Age of Revolution, 1770–1823* (Ithaca: Cornell Univ. Press, 1975). On the ACS, see Philip J. Staudenraus, *The African Colonization Movement: 1861–1865* (New York: Columbia Univ. Press, 1961).

67. *Liberator*, Aug. 17, 1833. On immediatism as a surrogate religion, see Anne C. Loveland, "Evangelicalism and 'Immediate Emancipation' in American Thought," *Journal of Southern History* 32 (May 1966): 172–88.

2. The Awakening

1. Lundy met Garrison in 1828 while Lundy was lecturing against slavery in New England. Lundy later convinced Garrison to come to Baltimore. For Garrison's attack on Todd, see *The Genius of Universal Emancipation*, Nov. 13, 1829; Garrison to Todd, May 13, 1830, in Garrison, *The Letters of William Lloyd Garrison*, ed. Walter M. Merrill (Cambridge, Mass: Harvard Univ. Press, 1971), 1:94. Garrison's Latin, loosely translated, reads, "He who profits from crime, himself does injury."

2. Cited in Henry Mayer, *All on Fire: William Lloyd Garrison and the Abolition of Slavery* (New York: St. Martin's Press, 1998), 94.

3. *Liberator*, Jan. 1, 1831. The paper was co-published with Isaac Knapp until dissolution of the partnership in December 1835. Garrison continued as editor and Knapp became sole publisher.

4. Part 2 of Garrison's *Thoughts on African Colonization* (Boston: Garrison and Knapp, 1832) gathers statements from African American individuals and organizations who were opposed to colonization. *Thoughts* sold 2,750 copies during the first nine months of publication. On black support for the *Liberator*, see Garrison to Simeon S. Jocelyn, May 30, 1831, in Garrison, *Letters* 1: 119; Philip J. Staudenraus, *The African Colonization Movement, 1816–1865* (New York: Columbia Univ. Press, 1961).

5. Garrison to Henry E. Benson, July 30, 1831, in Garrison, *Letters* 1: 124.

6. Robert H. Abzug, "The Influence of Garrisonian Abolitionists' Fears of Slave Violence on the Antislavery Argument, 1829–1840," *Journal of Negro History* 55 (Jan. 1970): 15–28. On Nat Turner's insurrection, see Stephen B. Oates's fine narrative history, *The Fires of Jubilee: Nat Turner's Fierce Rebellion* (New York: Harper & Row, 1975). See also Henry Irving Tragle, *The Southampton Slave Revolt of 1831: A Compilation of Source Material* (Amherst: Univ. of Massachusetts Press, 1971).

7. John Demos, "The Antislavery Movement and the Problem of Violent 'Means,'" *New England Quarterly* 36 (Dec. 1964): 503. See also Carleton Mabee, *Black Freedom: The Nonviolent Abolitionists from 1830 through the Civil War* (London: Macmillan, 1970).

8. Henry Mayer's outstanding biography of Garrison, *All on Fire*, which was published in 1998, discusses these themes at length in the context of Garrison's personal experiences. A more theoretical examination of the Garrison philosophy and a classic in its own right is Aileen Kraditor's *Means and Ends in American Abolitionism: Garrison and His Critics on Strategy and Tactics, 1834–1850* (New York: Vintage Books, 1970).

9. James L. McElroy, "Social Control and Romantic Reform in Antebellum America: The Case of Rochester, New York," *New York History* 58 (Jan. 1977): 31.

10. See Donald M. Scott, "Abolition as a Sacred Vocation," in *Anti-Slavery Reconsidered: New Perspectives on the Abolitionists*, ed. Lewis Perry and Michael Fellman (Baton Rouge, La.: Louisiana State Univ. Press, 1979), 51–74. On the family backgrounds and upbringing of these youthful reformers, see James Brewer Stewart, *Holy Warriors: The Abolitionists and American Slavery* (New York: Hill & Wang, 1976), 37–41.

11. Robert H. Abzug, *Passionate Liberator: Theodore Dwight Weld and the Dilemma of Reform* (New York: Oxford Univ. Press, 1980), 47–51.

12. George Gale, *Autobiography (to 1834) of George Washington Gale (1789–1861)* (New York: n.p., 1964), 276–90. This printed version is derived from an original manuscript transcribed by Gale's daughter, Margaret Gale Hitchcock. It stops in mid-sentence as Gale is describing how the Oneida Institute campus appeared in 1834. On Gale's educational and theological views, see Wallace G. Lamb, "George Washington Gale: Theologian and Educator" (Ph.D. diss., Syracuse Univ., 1949).

13. Paul Goodman, "The Manual Labor Movement and the Origins of Abolitionism," *Journal of the Early Republic* 13 (fall 1993): 355–88.

14. Gale, *Autobiography*, 305. Gale left Whitesboro in 1835 and went to Illinois where he helped to found a colony, later named Galesburg, and a school, known today as Knox College. See Hermann R. Muelder, *Fighters for Freedom: The History of Anti-Slavery Activities of Men and Women Associated with Knox College* (New York: Columbia Univ. Press, 1959).

15. For a fuller account of the founding and transformation of Oneida Institute as well as Beriah Green's work as educator, reformer, and abolitionist, see Milton C. Sernett, *Abolition's Axe: Beriah Green, Oneida Institute, and the Black Freedom Struggle* (Syracuse: Syracuse Univ. Press, 1986).

16. Beriah Green to the Reverend Simeon S. Jocelyn, New Haven, Conn., Nov. 5, 1832, *Abolitionist* 1 (Feb. 1833): 29.

17. Beriah Green, *Four Sermons, Preached in the Chapel of the Western Reserve College, On Lord's Days, November 18th and 25th, and December 2nd and 9th, 1832* (Cleveland: The Office of the Herald, 1833), 45. For information on the early history of Western Reserve College, see Carroll Cutler, *A History of Western Reserve College, 1826–1876* (Cleveland: Crocker Publishing House, 1876).

18. *Liberator*, Nov. 30, 1833.

19. Green to "Brother Cummings," Apr. 12, 1833, *Liberator*, Aug. 17, 1833.

20. Green to Elizur Wright, Jr., Apr. 22, May 3, 1833, Hudson, Ohio, Elizur Wright Jr. Papers, Library of Congress.

21. On the struggle at Lane and the role of Weld and the students from Oneida Institute, see Abzug, *Passionate Liberator*, chapters 5 and 6; Lawrence T. Lesick, *The Lane*

Rebels: Evangelicalism and Antislavery in Antebellum America (Metuchen, N.J.: Scarecrow, 1980).

22. Oberlin College's founding is discussed by Robert S. Fletcher, *A History of Oberlin College from Its Foundation Through the Civil War*, vol. 1 (Oberlin, Ohio: Oberlin College, 1943). Were there space enough to sketch out the connections, we could show that Oneida Institute contributed to the establishment of a number of other schools (in addition to Oberlin and Knox Colleges) which had the reputation of being progressive on the question of antislavery. Several of the founders of Berea College in Berea, Kentucky, had ties to Oneida Institute; the Reverand John Frost of Whitesboro's Presbyterian Church who, as a trustee supported Green's presidency of Oneida Institute, joined the faculty of Berea College. Grinnell College, in Grinnell, Iowa, is named after Josiah B. Grinnell, a prominent Iowa state senator and antislavery activist. Grinnell belonged to one of the last Oneida Institute classes prior to the school's closing in 1845.

23. "V. R. V." to William Goodell, Nov. 1833, *Emancipator*, Dec. 21, 1833.

24. *Circular of the Executive Committee of the Whitestown and Oneida Institute Societies* (1833), May Anti-Slavery Collection, Rare and Manuscript Collections, Kroch Library, Cornell Univ., Ithaca, N.Y.

25. Alice Henderson, "The History of the New York State Anti-Slavery Society" (Ph.D. diss., Univ. of Michigan, 1963), 389–406. The absence of abolition societies in a cluster of downstate counties (Albany, Columbia, Kings, New York, Putnam, Queens, Rensselaer, Rockland, Sullivan, and Ulster) underscores the significance of the link between the cultural and social patterns of the Burned-over District and antislavery activism.

26. Cited in Stewart, *Holy Warriors*, 43.

27. Abzug, *Passionate Liberator*, 4–5.

28. Abzug, *Passionate Liberator*, 87; Sernett, *Abolition's Axe*, 21.

29. Henderson, "New York State Anti-Slavery Society," 30; Christopher Densmore, "The Dilemma of Quaker Anti-Slavery: The Case of Farmington Quarterly Meeting, 1836–1860," *Quaker History* 82 (fall 1993): 80–91.

30. Gerald Sorin, *The New York Abolitionists: A Case Study of Political Radicalism* (Westport, Conn.: Greenwood, 1971), 79.

31. John G. Whittier, "The Anti-slavery Convention of 1833" (1874), in *The Writings of John Greenleaf Whittier in Seven Volumes*, vol. 7 (Riverside edition; Boston: Houghton, Mifflin and Company, 1889), 174–75.

32. Phillip Green Wright and Elizabeth Q. Wright, *Elizur Wright, The Father of Life Insurance* (Chicago: Univ. of Chicago Press, 1937), 31. Samuel J. May, one of those present at the 1833 meeting, recalled that this was the first time in his life that he had heard the voice of a woman in a public deliberative assembly. Until Mott was invited to come forward by Green, the women who were present had modestly seated themselves in the rear of the hall. See May's speech in *Proceedings of the American Anti-Slavery Society, at its Second Decade, Held in the City of Philadelphia, Dec. 3rd, 4th, and 5th, 1853* (New York: American Anti-Slavery Society, 1854), 9.

33. May's speech, *American Anti-Slavery Society Proceedings*, 27.

34. Cited in Whittier, "The Anti-Slavery Convention of 1833," 186.

35. Charles Denison to Garrison, Jan. 14, 1834, William Lloyd Garrison Papers, Boston Public Library.

36. From a broadside *Declaration of the Anti-Slavery Convention Assembled in Philadelphia*, Dec. 3, 1833, illus. R[euben] S. Gilbert (Philadelphia: Merrihew and Gunn, 1833). Rare Books and Special Collections Division, Library of Congress.

37. John Montieth, attached to letter written by Timothy D. Weld to James Birney, Oct. 30, 1835, *Letters of James Gillespie Birney, 1831–1857*, vol. 1, ed. Dwight L. Dumond (New York: Appleton-Century Co., 1938): 254–55.

38. Stewart, *Holy Warriors*, 43.

39. *Colored American,* Aug. 25, 1838; John R. McKivigan and Jason H. Silverman, "Monarchial Liberty and Republican Slavery: West Indies Emancipation Celebrations in Upstate New York and Canada West," *Afro-Americans in New York Life and History* 10 (Jan. 1986): 7–18.

40. On the transatlantic connection, see Betty Fladeland, *Men & Brothers: Anglo-American Antislavery Cooperation* (Urbana: Univ. of Illinois Press, 1972) and R. J. M. Blackett, *Building an Anti-Slavery Wall: Black Americans in the Atlantic Abolitionist Movement 1830–1860* (Baton Rouge, La.: Louisiana State Univ. Press, 1983).

41. Sernett, *Abolition's Axe*, 40; John L. Myers, "The Beginning of Anti-Slavery Agencies in New York, 1833–1836," *New York History* 43 (Apr. 1962): 155.

42. Anthony J. Barker, *Captain Charles Stuart: Anglo-American Abolitionist* (Baton Rouge, La.: Louisiana State Univ. Press, 1986), 88. Stuart was a licensed Presbyterian minister and member of the Oneida Presbytery.

43. Stuart was sometimes confused with another Englishman, George Thompson. Thompson signed on as an agent for the AASS and arrived in America in the summer of 1834. He began lecturing in New York City but then moved up the Hudson River Valley and into the Albany-Troy-Schenectady area, where he often spoke along with Amos Phelps at antislavery rallies. Subjected to continual harassment and, at times threatened with bodily harm, Thompson was forced to return to England in December 1835.

44. Cited in Barker, *Captain Charles Stuart*, 119. For more on Stuart, see Myers, "Beginning of Anti-Slavery Agencies," 156–58.

45. Myers, "Beginning of Anti-Slavery Agencies," 158–61.

46. Rochester had a black women's antislavery society as early as March 1834. See the *Liberator,* Mar. 8, 1834. White women in Rochester set up an auxiliary to the AASS in 1835. There were male antislavery societies in Rochester (1833) and Monroe County (1834). See Nancy Hewitt, "The Social Origins of Women's Antislavery Politics in Western New York," in Alan M. Kraut, ed. *Crusaders and Compromisers: Essays on the Relationship of the Antislavery Struggle to the Antebellum Party System* (Westport, Conn.: Greenwood, 1983), 206, 208.

47. Myers, "Beginning of Anti-Slavery Agencies," 161–65.

48. For additional details on the organization of antislavery societies in the Burned-over District, see John Lytle Myers, "The Agency System of the Anti-Slavery Movement, 1832–1837, and Its Antecedents in Other Benevolent and Reform Societies" (Ph.D. diss., Univ. of Michigan, 1961).

49. Myers, "Beginning of Anti-Slavery Agencies," 169.

50. Theodore Weld to the Reverend Ray Potter, June 11, 1836, *Letters of Theodore Dwight Weld, Angelina Grimké Weld and Sarah Grimké, 1822–1844,* ed. Gilbert H. Barnes and Dwight L. Drummond (New York: Appleton-Century, 1934), 1: 309–10. Weld's difficulties are reported in the *Friend of Man,* June 23, 1836 and July 14, 1836.

51. Weld to the Reverend Ray Potter, Troy, June 11, 1836, *Letters of Theodore Dwight Weld*, 1: 309–10; Abzug, *Passionate Liberator*, 147–49.

52. Luke 10:1 (King James Version).

53. Myers, "Beginning of Anti-Slavery Agencies," 173–76. Weld met Angelina Grimké at the agents' convention in December. During his stay in New York he escorted her to various antislavery meetings. Angelina and her older sister, Sarah, were the daughters of a Charleston, South Carolina, slaveholder. Converted to Quakerism and abolitionism, the Misses Grimké challenged the male abolitionists to consider taking up the issue of the rights of women. Theodore and Angelina married in May of 1838. In March of 1840, they bought a house and a fifty-acre farm near Belleville, New Jersey, on the Passaic River. They established the Weld Institute where they taught children of prominent abolitionists such as Gerrit Smith, James G. Birney, and Henry B. Stanton. Abzug, *Passionate Reformer*, chapters 10 and 12.

54. On their labors and those of others in Upstate New York, see John L. Myers, "The Major Effort of National Anti-Slavery Agents in New York State, 1836–1837," *New York History* 46 (Apr. 1965): 162–86. Stuart's description of Weld is cited by Gilbert H. Barnes, *Anti-Slavery Impulse, 1830–1844* (1933; reprint, Gloucester, Mass.: Peter Smith, 1973), 105.

55. Gerald Sorin, *The New York Abolitionists: A Case Study of Political Radicalism* (Westport, Conn.: Greenwood, 1971), 63–67.

56. Phelps to Smith, Oct. 2, 1835, cited in Barker, *Captain Charles Stuart*, 115.

57. *Emancipator*, Jan. 27, 1835.

58. Myers, "Beginning of Anti-Slavery Agencies," 150.

59. Esther C. Loucks, "The Anti-Slavery Movement in Syracuse from 1839–1851" (M.A. thesis, Syracuse Univ., 1934), 6.

60. Phelps to Mrs. Phelps, Aug. 11, 22, 1835, cited in Barker, *Captain Charles Stuart*, 114.

61. Lewis Perry, *Radical Abolitionism: Anarchy and the Government of God in Antislavery Thought* (Ithaca: Cornell Univ. Press, 1973), xi.

62. Smith possessed considerable wealth and enough land to be embarrassed by it. His father, Peter Smith, had been a partner of John Jacob Astor in the fur trade and land speculation that took place after the War for Independence. Gerrit took over the administration of his father's business empire in 1819. Seven years later, he underwent a religious conversion and thereafter saw himself as a steward of the Lord with the responsibility to do good works with his wealth. Gerrit Smith contributed tens of thousands of dollars to public causes ranging from temperance reform to women's rights. He also gave generous amounts to churches, schools, and private individuals during his lifetime. The Garrisonians, Beriah Green in particular, argued that anyone who gave rhetorical support, time, or money to the ACS was an unwitting ally of the enemies of freedom (*North Star*, July 7, 1848). (Banks was a West Indian who operated a clothing shop and tailoring business in Detroit.)

63. Gerrit Smith to Leonard Bacon, Mar. 31, 1834, Gerrit Smith Papers, Syracuse Univ.

64. Smith, *Journal*, July 12, 1834, quoted by Octavius Brooks Frothingham, *Gerrit Smith: A Biography* (1878; reprint, New York: Negro Univ. Press, 1969), 163–64.

65. Wright to Amos G. Phelps, Oct. 27, 1834, Elizur Wright, Jr., Papers, Library of Congress.

66. Garrison to Smith, Feb. 7, 1835, in Garrison, *Letters* 1: 445.

67. Garrison to Smith, Jan. 31, 1835, in Garrison, *Letters* 1: 438–39. The "Gerrit Smith

vs. Gerrit Smith" columns begin with Garrison to Smith, Feb. 7, 1835, in Garrison, *Letters* 1: 448–53. They continue in Garrison to Smith, Feb. 28, 1835, in Garrison, *Letters* 1: 456. In the final and fourth letter of the series, Garrison reiterated the doctrine of immediate emancipation of which Smith approved and challenged him to find support for it in any of the publications of the ACS. Garrison to Smith, Mar. 7, 1835, in Garrison, *Letters* 1: 457–63.

68. In addition to wanting Smith to rid himself of ties to the colonization scheme, Green had another motive for trying to enlist Smith in the immediatist campaign. Shortly after becoming president of Oneida Institute, Green wrote to Smith and requested that the Peterboro philanthropist aid in the financial support of his "poor boys' school." Smith attracted Green's interest because he too had shown concern for the education of "colored youth." As early as 1827, Smith floated a proposal for a school in Peterboro which would prepare American blacks to go to Africa as missionaries under the auspices of the ACS. He seems to have abandoned the plan until 1834. Then he announced the opening of a manual labor "high school." Smith wrote Leonard Bacon, a colonizationist leader, "I hope my first class, limited to 15, will have members who will go to Africa with a sound education of head and heart" (Gerrit Smith to Bacon, Mar. 31, 1834, Gerrit Smith Papers, Syracuse Univ.). (For a description of the Peterboro Manual Labor School, see *African Repository* 10 [Dec. 1834]: 312–13.) A handful of students actually came. Housed in a small frame structure, the Peterboro Manual Labor School had but one instructor, Colquhoun Grant, brother of one of Green's faculty. Supported only by Smith's benevolence, the school closed in early 1835. Green gave a sigh of relief. He had written Smith a year earlier, "For one I am from principal opposed to the cord of caste wherever it may appear. Away with caste! It has strangled its thousands. . . . Till we have white and black together in our schools, the cord of caste will remain" (Beriah Green to Gerrit Smith, Mar. 25, 1824, Gerrit Smith Papers, Syracuse Univ.). Years later when Smith went to Michigan to visit his brother-in-law, James G. Birney, the Kentucky slaveholder who converted to abolitionism and stood as the Liberty Party presidential candidate of 1840, the Peterboro philanthropist discovered two of the former students of his "colored school" living in Detroit. Concerning Robert Banks and George R. Symes, Smith wrote to Frederick Douglass: "They are very worthy men." (Smith, *Journal*, July 12, 1834, quoted by Frothingham, *Gerrit Smith*, 163–64. For more on an endorsement of the Peterboro Manual Labor School by the ACS, see *African Repository* 10 (Dec. 1834), 312–13.

69. Mary S. Bull, "Gerrit Smith," *Good Company* 6 (Nov. 1880), 241.

70. John R. McKivigan and Madeleine L. McKivigan, "'He Stands Like Jupiter': The Autobiography of Gerrit Smith," *New York History* 65 (Apr. 1984), 199.

71. Ibid.

3. Into the Storm

1. Quoted by Howard Alexander Morrison, "Gentlemen of Proper Understanding: A Closer Look at Utica's Anti-Abolitionist Mob," *New York History* 62 (Jan. 1981): 61.

2. *Proceedings of the New York Anti-Slavery Convention, Held at Utica, October 21, and New York Anti-Slavery Society, Held at Peterboro, October 22, 1835* (Utica: Standard & Democrat Office, 1835), 8.

3. In addition to Morrison, "Gentlemen of Proper Understanding," see Lorman Rat-

ner, *Powder Keg: Northern Opposition to the Antislavery Movement, 1831–1840* (New York: Basic Books, 1968) and Leonard Richards, *"Gentlemen of Property and Standing": Anti-Abolition Mobs in Jacksonian America* (New York: Oxford Univ. Press, 1970).

4. Cited in Morrison, "Gentlemen of Proper Understanding," 61.

5. The structure merited a place on the national and state registers in 1994.

6. "Speech of Mr. Gerrit Smith," *Proceedings of the New York Anti-Slavery Convention*, 21.

7. Smith, *Journal*, Oct. 25, 1835, quoted in Octavius Brooks Frothingham, *Gerrit Smith: A Biography* (1878; reprint, New York: Negro Univ. Press, 1969), 66.

8. Smith to Cox, Nov. 12, 1835, *Emancipator*, Nov. 1835. The *Liberator* (Feb. 6, 1836) pointed out that Smith sent a check for $3,000 to cover pledges previously made to the ACS while simultaneously breaking with the organization. In a brief autobiography that was most likely written during the summer or fall of 1856 when Smith was the presidential candidate of the radical American Abolition Society, Peterboro's prince of good causes claimed that his conversion to immediatism was simultaneous with his religious conversion in 1826. As we have seen, Smith did not make a decisive break from the ACS until after the Utica riot of 1835.

9. Beriah Green to Gerrit Smith, Aug. 19, 1835, Gerrit Smith Papers, Syracuse Univ.

10. Garrison to George W. Benson, Oct. 26, 1835, in Garrison, *Letters* 1: 477–80.

11. Garrison to George W. Benson, Nov. 27, 1835, in Garrison *Letters* 1: 561.

12. *Proceedings of the New York Anti-Slavery Convention*, 39.

13. Alice Henderson, "The History of the New York State Anti-Slavery Society" (unpublished Ph.D. diss., Univ. of Michigan, 1963), 65–68.

14. *Friend of Man*, Nov. 1, 1837.

15. *Friend of Man*, July 11, 1838.

16. George W. Clark, *The Liberty Minstrel* (New York City, 1844), as quoted in Amy Hanmer-Croughton, "Anti-Slavery Days in Rochester," *Rochester Historical Society Publications* 14 (1936): 120.

17. Shirley Cox Husted, "'Black & White together!': Paths Towards Freedom on the Underground Railroad," in *Sweet Gift of Freedom: A Civil War Anthology*, ed. Shirley Cox Husted (Rochester: County of Monroe, 1986), 14. See also *American Antislavery Songs: A Collection and Analysis*, ed. Vicki L. Eaklors (Westport, Conn.: Greenwood, 1988).

18. Samuel Ringgold Ward, *Autobiography of a Fugitive Negro* (1855; reprint, New York: Arno Press, 1968), 54–56.

19. Beriah Green, *Sermons and Other Discourses with Brief Biographical Hints* (New York: S. W. Green, 1860). S. W. Green was Samuel W. Green, Beriah's son.

20. *Ohio Reporter*, Sept. 16, 1859. Lucy N. Colman, *Reminiscences* (Buffalo: H. L. Green, Publisher, 1891).

21. Colman, *Reminiscences*, 50.

22. On one occasion, Gerrit Smith was lecturing in Cooperstown, home of one of America's best-known authors, James Fenimore Cooper. Smith, an aristocrat by monetary standards, was pleased to see that many of the "leading gentlemen of the village" had come to hear him. He felt that their presence lent an aura of "dignity and respectability" to the meeting, even though four or five of the men opposed him. Cooper spoke for four or five hours against Smith's abolitionist ideas, but the Peterboro reformer came away impressed with the "kindness, delicacy, and refinement" with

which his opponents had treated him. Smith to William Goodell, Apr. 5, 1838, in *Friend of Man*, Apr. 11, 1838.

23. *Emancipator*, May 19, 1836.

24. *New York Tribune*, Dec. 3, 1863.

25. Skaneateles *Columbian*, Aug. 18, 1839; Reverend W[illiam] M. Beauchamp, *Notes of Other Days in Skaneateles* (Syracuse: Dehler Press, 1915).

26. Cited in Henderson, "New York State Anti-Slavery Society," 55.

27. Luther Lee, *Autobiography of the Rev. Luther Lee, D.D.* (1882; reprint, New York: Garland, 1984), 170–74.

28. For general accounts of women abolitionists, see Julie Roy Jeffrey, *The Great Silent Army of Abolitionism: Ordinary Women in the Antislavery Movement* (Chapel Hill: Univ. of North Carolina Press, 1998); Alma Lutz, *Crusade for Freedom: Women of the Antislavery Movement* (Boston: Beacon Press, 1968); and Shirley J. Yee, *Black Women Abolitionists: A Study in Activism, 1828–1860* (Knoxville: Univ. of Tennessee Press, 1992.)

29. Nancy A. Hewitt, "On Their Own Terms: A Historiographical Essay," in Jean Fagan Yellin and John C. Van Horne, eds., *The Abolitionist Sisterhood: Women's Political Culture in Antebellum America* (Ithaca: Cornell Univ. Press, 1994), 26–27. See also Nancy A. Hewitt, "The Social Origins of Women's Anti-slavery Politics in Western New York," in *Crusaders and Compromisers: Essays on the Relationship of the Antislavery Struggle to the Antebellum Party System*, ed. Alan M. Kraut (Westport, Conn.: Greenwood, 1983), 205–33.

30. From a notice for an antislavery fair to be held in Rochester, Dec. 17 and 18, 1847; *North Star*, Dec. 3, 1847.

31. Cited from Hewitt, "On Their Own Terms," 224. Records of the Rochester Ladies' Anti-Slavery Society can be found at the William L. Clements Library, Univ. of Michigan, Ann Arbor, Mich.

32. *North Star*, Dec. 29, 1848.

33. Cited in Wilbur H. Siebert, *The Underground Railroad from Slavery to Freedom* (1898; reprint, New York: Russell & Russell, 1967), 77.

34. On the debate over suffrage and women's property rights, see Judith Wellman, "Women's Rights, Republicanism, and Revolutionary Rhetoric in Antebellum New York State," *New York History* 69 (Oct. 1988): 353–84.

35. Deborah Bingham Van Broekhoven, "'Let Your Names Be Enrolled': Method and Ideology in Women's Antislavery Petitioning," in Yellin and Van Horne, eds., *The Abolitionist Sisterhood*, 179–99.

36. Benjamin Quarles, *Black Abolitionists* (New York: Oxford Univ. Press, 1969), 177–78.

37. Michael D. Pierson, "'Guard the Foundation Well': Antebellum New York Democrats and the Defense of Patriarchy," *Gender & History* 7 (Apr. 1995): 25–40.

38. *Impartial Citizen*, Sept. 5, 1849.

39. Ward, *Autobiography of a Fugitive Negro*, 42–43.

40. Austin Steward, *Twenty-Two Years a Slave, and Forty Years a Freeman* (1856; reprint, New York: Negro Univ. Press, 1968), 107.

41. Quarles, *Black Abolitionists*, 98.

42. Little is known of Dawkins, but James Duffin, the son of John and Susannah Duffin, came to Geneva from Canada as early as 1829. Susannah may have been a fugi-

tive from Maryland. James attended the African American Sunday school operated by Geneva's First Presbyterian Church and was an agent for the *Colored American*. Duffin was active in the black convention, temperance, and suffrage movements. He supported the Liberty Party and helped Gerrit Smith identify worthy recipients for the land that Smith gave away to African Americans in the late 1840s. Duffin was given lots of land in Hamilton County, but he remained in Geneva where he operated a barber shop. James and his wife named their son, born in March 1847, Gerrit Smith Duffin.

43. *Colored American*, Oct. 14, 1837.

44. Communication, dated Feb. 17, 1836, in *Colored American*, Mar. 4, 1837.

45. *Freedom's Journal*, Feb. 15, 1828.

46. Cited in William S. McFeeley, *Frederick Douglass* (New York: W. W. Norton & Company, 1991), 160.

47. The objector was Horatio G. Warner, a prominent Rochester attorney with strong antiblack and proslavery sympathies. He built a castellated house, still known as "Warner Castle," on Mt. Hope Avenue. After the Civil War, Warner bought a home in Georgia and died there. Amy Hanmer-Croughton, "Anti-Slavery Days in Rochester," 130.

48. *North Star*, Aug. 17, 1849.

49. Douglass hated discrimination so strongly that he held all race-specific institutions, black or white, to a higher standard. In his crusade to abolish the separate and unequal system in Rochester, Douglass was aided by Samuel D. Porter. Hanmer-Croughton, "Anti-Slavery Days in Rochester," 130.

50. Carleton Mabee, *Black Education in New York State: From Colonial to Modern Times* (Syracuse: Syracuse Univ. Press, 1979).

51. Vincent W. Howell, *History of the St. James A.M.E. Zion Church, Ithaca, N.Y.* (Ithaca: n.p., 1986).

52. Milton C. Sernett, "On Freedom's Threshold: The African American Presence in Central New York, 1760–1940," *Afro-Americans in New York Life and History* 19 (Jan. 1995): 49–50; Monroe Fordham, "Origins of the Michigan Street Baptist Church, Buffalo, New York," *Afro-Americans in New York Life and History* 21 (Jan. 1997): 7–18.

53. For Garnet's essay, "Self-help. The Wants of Western New York," see *North Star*, Jan. 19, 1849.

54. Letter to the editor, signed "G. G. R.," *New York Tribune*, Aug. 1, 1848.

55. Kenneth R. Short, "New York Central College: A Baptist Experiment in Integrated Higher Education, 1848–61," *Foundations* 3 (July 1962): 250–56.

56. Catherine M. Hanchett, "'What Sort of People & Families . . .' : The Edmondson Sisters," *Afro-Americans in New York Life and History* 6 (July 1982): 21–37. See also Thomas Fleming, "The Flight of the Pearl," *American Legacy* 6 (summer 2000): 65–72.

57. Lewis was of both African American and Native American (Chippewa) ancestry. Questions still persist as to the place and date of her birth. Ohio and New York (the Albany or Greenbush area) are likely possibilities, and the years 1843 or 1845 appear in some sources. Lewis went from New York Central College to Oberlin Institute in Ohio and then to a notable career in sculpture that took her to Europe. Lynda Roscoe Hartigan, *Sharing Traditions: Five Black Artists in Nineteenth-Century America* (Washington, D.C.: Smithsonian Institution Press, 1985), 85–98.

58. Reason was hired in September 1849 at the age of 31 and taught at New York Central College for three years. Born in New York City, of Haitian immigrants, Reason

(1818–1893) left the McGrawville institution to direct the Institute for Colored Youth in Philadelphia. He began a long career as a teacher in New York City's black public schools in 1855. Reason was active in the New York Association for the Political Elevation and Improvement of People of Color.

59. William G. Allen to Henry Bibb, Aug. 4, 1851, *Voice of the Fugitive*, Aug. 27, 1851.

60. William G. Allen, *The American Prejudice Against Color. An Authentic Narrative, Showing how Easily the Nation Got into an Uproar. By W. G. Allen, a Refugee from American Despotism* (London: W. and F. G. Cash, 1853), 13–14; William G. Allen, *A Short Personal Narrative* (London: R. Chapman, 1860); R. J. M. Blackett, "William G. Allen: The Forgotten Professor," *Civil War History* 26 (Mar. 1980): 38–52; Milton C. Sernett, *Abolition's Axe*, 59–61.

61. The land upon which students had done manual labor was sold off. In 1868 the Union School District took over the remaining property. In 1896 the college's old main building was damaged by a fire and dismantled. All that remained was the college cupola which could be seen on a local farmer's barn a century later. Wright, *Cornell's Three Precursors: vol. 1, New York Central College*, 104.

62. Alexander Crummell, "Eulogium on Henry Highland Garnet, D.D.," 1882, in *Africa and America: Addresses and Discourses* (Springfield, Mass.: Wiley and Co., 1891), 281. Crummell graduated from Oneida Institute in 1838, became an Episcopalian priest and earned a B.A. from Queen's College, Cambridge, England, in 1853.

63. Crummell, "Henry Highland Garnet," 283.

64. Quoted by Crummell, "Henry Highland Garnet," 287.

65. Henry Bibb letter, Jan. 29, 1849, *North Star*, Feb. 16, 1849. Bibb estimated that Geneva, like Syracuse, had an African American population of about 200.

66. Jane H. Pease and William H. Pease, *Bound with Them in Chains: A Biographical History of the Antislavery Movement* (Westport, Conn.: Greenwood, 1972), 167. Clara Merritt DeBoer, *Be Jubilant My Feet: African American Abolitionists in the American Missionary Association, 1839–1861* (New York: Garland, 1994), 210–16.

67. Pease and Pease, *Bound with Them in Chains*, 170.

68. Cited from "Atrocious Outrage on Henry H. Garnet," *North Star*, July 7, 1848.

69. Reprinted from the *New York Tribune*, in the *North Star*, July 7, 1848.

70. Garrison to Mrs. Hannah Fifield, Nov. 21, 1837, in vol. 2 of Garrison, *Letters*, 328. Fifield was corresponding secretary of the Female Emancipation Society of Weymouth, Mass.

71. Beriah Green, *The Martyr: A Discourse on Commemoration of the Martyrdom of the Rev. Elijah P. Lovejoy, Delivered in Broadway Tabernacle, New York, and in the Bleecker Street Church, Utica* (New York: American Anti-Slavery Society, 1838), 15–16.

72. *Sixth Annual Report of the Executive Committee of the American Anti-Slavery Society* (New York: American Anti-Slavery Society, 1839), 20.

73. Stewart believed that duties on the export of manufactured goods protected Northern business. The cotton growers of the South, dependent on the same manufactured products, advocated low tariffs. Stewart also believed in the necessity of a national banking system, federal financing of internal improvements (roads, canals, and railroads), and a public education system.

74. *Friend of Man*, Oct. 2, 1839.

75. Gerrit Smith to Lewis Tappan, Mar. 14, 1840, Gerrit Smith Papers, Syracuse Univ.

76. Beriah Green to Gerrit Smith, June 9, 1840, Gerrit Smith Papers, Syracuse Univ.

77. From the *Liberty Press*, as cited in Gregory P. Lampe, *Frederick Douglass: Freedom's Voice, 1818–1845* (East Lansing, Mich.: Michigan State Univ. Press, 1998), 175.

78. Frederick Douglass, *Life and Times of Frederick Douglass* (1892; rev. ed., New York: Collier Books, 1962), 227.

79. Douglass, *Life and Times*, 227.

80. Douglass, *Life and Times*, 228.

4. Trouble in God's House

1. The Wesleyan Methodist Society of Syracuse building became the First Gospel Church of Syracuse in 1965. In the 1980s, the structure went up for sale, then stood vacant for a number of years. More recently it housed a restaurant. Douglas V. Armstrong and Lou Ann Wurst, "'Faces' of the Past: Archaeology of an Underground Railroad Site in Syracuse, New York," *Syracuse Univ. Archaeological Report* 10 (Jan. 1998), 81 pp. This is a detailed and judicious examination of the sculpted faces in their historical and archaeological contexts. Preservationists removed the faces in February 1999 with the intent of putting them on permanent display at the Onondaga Historical Association museum in Syracuse. "Church Carvings are Preserved," *History Highlights* 12 (summer 1999): 1.

2. Cited from Edwin Scott Gaustad, *Historical Atlas of Religion in America* (rev. ed., New York: Harper & Row, 1976), 42.

3. Donald G. Mathews, "The Second Great Awakening as an Organizing Process, 1780–1830: An Hypothesis," *American Quarterly* 21 (spring 1969): 23–43; C. C. Goen, *Broken Churches, Broken Nation: Denominational Schisms and the Coming of the Civil War* (Macon, Ga.: Mercer Univ. Press, 1985), 57.

4. There were 1,231 Methodist, 781 Baptist, and 671 Presbyterian churches in New York State in 1850. Methodists led in the nation as a whole, followed by Baptists, Presbyterians, and Congregationalists. Richard Swainson Fisher, *A New and Complete Statistical Gazetteer of the United States of America Founded and Compiled from Official Federal and State Returns and the Seventh National Census* (New York: J. H. Cotton, 1858).

5. On Scott's abolitionist work, see Lucius C. Matlack, *The Life of Rev. Orange Scott: In Two Parts* (1848; reprint, Freeport, N.Y.: Books for Libraries Press, 1971) and Donald G. Mathews, "Orange Scott: The Methodist Evangelist as Revolutionary," in *The Antislavery Vanguard: New Essays on the Abolitionists*, ed. Martin Duberman (Princeton: Princeton Univ. Press, 1965), 71–101.

6. Cited in Mathews, "Orange Scott," 86.

7. On the relationship between Lee's abolitionism and evangelical revivalism, see William C. Kostlevy, "Luther Lee and Methodist Abolitionism," *Methodist History* 20 (1982): 90–103.

8. Cited in Luther Lee, *Autobiography of the Rev. Luther Lee, D.D.* (1882; reprint, New York: Garland, 1984), 103. So seriously did Lee take his charge to unmask the doctrinal errors of the Universalists that he wrote a three-hundred-page attack on those who held the notion that all would be saved. Luther Lee, *UNIVERSALISM EXAMINED AND REFUTED and the doctrine of the endless punishment of such as do not comply with the conditions* (Watertown, N.Y.: By the Author, 1836).

9. Lee, *Autobiography*, 134. For an extended treatment of Lee's battles with fellow

Methodists, see Paul Leslie Kaufman, "'Logical' Luther Lee and the Methodist War against Slavery" (Ph.D. diss., Kent State Univ., 1994).

10. The name Wesleyan derived from the English religious dissenters, John and Charles Wesley, who founded the Methodist movement a half century earlier. Lee, *Autobiography*, 141.

11. Lee, *Autobiography*, 154–55.

12. Lee, *Autobiography*, 164.

13. Lee, *Autobiography*, 189.

14. Lee, *Autobiography*, 252.

15. *North Star*, Jan. 14, 1848.

16. The two-story addition on the east side of the church and the brick tower over the western entrance were constructed in 1858. A spire was added to the tower in 1878. In 1855, after three years in Syracuse, Lee took charge of the Wesleyan Church at Fulton. In 1856, he moved to Michigan to become professor of theology at Leoni College. The fledgling Wesleyan school was unable to pay Lee a regular salary, so he resigned and took a pastorate at Felecity (Clermont County), Ohio. While stationed there, Middlebury College, Vermont, awarded him the title of Doctor of Divinity. In 1859, Lee moved to Chagrin Falls, Ohio, where he served a combined congregation of Wesleyan Methodists and Congregationalists. In 1860, he relocated his family back to Syracuse and took up the work of a traveling missionary for the Wesleyans, with a "light charge" in his old stomping ground at Sprague's Corners, on the line between Jefferson and St. Lawrence Counties. Lee was now sixty years old and anxious to be out of the eye of the storm. In 1864, he took up a theological professorship in Adrian College, Adrian, Michigan.

17. Frederick Douglass gave this sardonic account of the sectional split in Methodism while he was lecturing in England in 1846:

> A slaveholding bishop, Bishop Andrew of South Carolina, married a slaveholding wife and became the possessor of fifteen slaves. At this time the Methodist Church in the North was of the opinion that bishops should not hold slaves. They remonstrated with the Conference to induce Bishop Andrew to emancipate his slaves. The Conference did it in this way. A resolution was brought in, when the Bishop was present, to the following effect: "Whereas Bishop Andrew has connected himself with slavery, and has thereby become guilty, or has done a great wrong," but "has thereby injured his itinerancy as a bishop, we therefore resolve that Bishop Andrew be, and he hereby is,"—what?— "requested to suspend his labors as a bishop until he can get rid of"—what?—slavery?—"his impediment." (Laughter.) This was the name given to slavery. One might have inferred from the preamble that it was to get rid of his wife. (Laughter and loud cheers.)

From *Report of a Public Meeting Held at Finsbury Chapel, Moorfields, to receive Frederick Douglass, An American Slave on Friday, May 22, 1846* (London, 1846), 16, as cited in Benjamin Quarles, "Abolition's Different Drummer: Frederick Douglass," in *The Antislavery Vanguard*, ed. Duberman, 129.

18. Cited in Mathews, "Orange Scott," 98.

19. Shortly after Finney became a professor of theology at Oberlin, he wrote Theodore D. Weld, "Now if abolition can be made an append[a]ge of a general revival of religion all is well. I fear no other form of carrying this question will save our country or the liberty or soul of the slave. One most alarming fact is that the absorbing abolitionism has drunk up the spirit of some of the most efficient moral men and is fast doing so [to] the rest, and many of our abolition brethren seem satisfied with nothing less. This I have

been trying to resi[s]t from the beginning as I have all along foreseen that should that take place, the church and the world, ecclesiastical and state leaders, will become embroiled in one common infernal squabble that will roll a wave of blood over the land." Finney to Weld, July 21, 1836, in vol. 2 of *Letters of Theodore Dwight Weld, Angelina Grimké Weld, and Sarah Grimké,* ed. Gilbert Barnes and Dwight L. Dumond (New York: Appleton-Century, 1934), 319.

20. P. H. Fowler, *Historical Sketch of Presbyterianism Within the Bounds of the Synod of Central New York* (Utica: Cross and Childs, 1877), 154.

21. Minutes, June 26, 1834, *Oneida Presbytery Records,* vol. 6, 1833–1838, Presbyterian Historical Society, Philadelphia.

22. *Records of the Session of the Presbyterian Church, Whitesboro, New York,* vol. 3, Dec. 11, 1835.

23. David L. Ogden, *Review of a Pamphlet Entitled "Reply of the Congregational Church in Whitesboro to a Question of the Oneida Presbytery"* (Utica: R. Northway, 1839), 7.

24. Ibid., 8.

25. [Beriah Green], *Reply of the Congregational Church in Whitesboro, to a Question of the Oneida Presbytery* (Whitesboro, N.Y.: Press of the Oneida Institute, 1839), 5–6.

26. Ogden, *Review of a Pamphlet,* 9–10.

27. Beriah Green, *Things for Northern Men to Do: A Discourse Delivered Lord's Day Evening, July 17, 1836, in the Presbyterian Church* (Whitesboro, N.Y.: Published by Request, 1836), 22.

28. Beriah Green to Gerrit Smith, Aug. 2, 1857, Gerrit Smith Papers, Syracuse Univ.

29. David L. Ogden, *Thoughts on Men and Things,* Clements Library, Univ. of Michigan, Ann Arbor, entries for August 2 and 3, 1837. Of these journals, written while Ogden was a minister in Whitesboro, 1837–1843, three manuscripts survive. Volumes two and three cover the Whitesboro years.

30. *New York Observer,* Sept. 30, 1837. West's letter is reprinted in *Friend of Man,* Nov. 15, 1837.

31. Presbyterian Church *Session Minutes,* Nov. 15, 1837.

32. Green to Smith, Jan. 6, 1838, Simon Gratz Collection, Pennsylvania Historical Collection, Philadelphia.

33. Beriah Green to Gerrit Smith, Mar. 19, 1839, Gerrit Smith Papers, Syracuse Univ.

34. James Logan McElroy, "Social Reform in the Burned-over District: Rochester, N.Y., as a Test Case, 1830–1854" (Ph.D. diss., S.U.N.Y. Binghamton, 1974), 155.

35. Ogden, *Thoughts on Men and Things,* Aug. 8, 1837.

36. Smith wrote to Green on April 4, 1842, "Green Smith was born ½ past 2 P.M. this day. Who is Green Smith?, you will ask. He is my only son, named after my beloved brother Beriah Green." (Gerrit Smith to Beriah Green, Apr. 4, 1842, Letter Copybook, Gerrit Smith Papers, Syracuse Univ.) Beriah's namesake is sometimes referred to as Greene Smith, as on his grave marker in the Peterboro cemetery, but Smith clearly meant for his son to honor his abolitionist colleague and friend. To the embarrassment of his father, and the disappointment of his namesake, Greene Smith was an indifferent student. Smith sent his son to the Weld Institute run by Theodore Dwight Weld, his wife Angelina, and her sister Sarah, with the hope that he would develop character. Young Greene came home pretending to be a spiritualist medium. Shortly before the Civil War,

Smith was forced to call his son back to Peterboro from Cambridge, Massachusetts, where Greene was preparing for college, because of reports of "bad conduct" associated with liquor and tobacco. In later life, Greene Smith became a respected amateur ornithologist. Portions of Greene's ornithology collection are still intact and can be seen at the historical society in Peterboro.

37. Printed copy of Smith's address to the Christian Union Convention, Syracuse, Aug. 21, 1838, Gerrit Smith Papers, Syracuse Univ.

38. Ralph Volney Harlow, *Gerrit Smith: Philanthropist and Reformer* (1939; reprint, New York: Russell & Russell, 1972), 199.

39. Gerrit Smith to William Goodell, Jan. 22, 1842, Letter Copybook, Gerrit Smith Papers, Syracuse Univ.

40. Silas E. Persons, *Historical Sketch of the Religious Denominations of Madison County* (Cazenovia, N.Y.: Madison County Historical Society, 1908), 14–15.

41. Gerrit Smith to Rand, Sept. 8, 9, 1847, Letter Copybook, Gerrit Smith Papers, Syracuse Univ.; Harlow, *Gerrit Smith*, 207–14.

42. Ironically, Smith adopted the seventh day or Saturday as the "true" Sabbath in November 1849, and he observed it religiously for the remaining twenty-five years of his life. Harlow, *Gerrit Smith*, 214.

43. The Reverend Michael Strieby served Plymouth until 1864 when he became corresponding secretary of the American Missionary Association. Formed in 1846, the nonsectarian AMA brought Christian abolitionists into a missionary fellowship which, after the Civil War, worked directly among the newly freed slaves. Strieby also helped found schools such as Fisk University in Nashville, Tennessee, and Hampton Institute in Hampton, Virginia. Upon his death in 1899, Oberlin College trustees memorialized Strieby as follows: "He was often at the front immediately after the war encouraging despondent teachers, gathering about him a great mass of negroes just freed from bondage, seeking to inspire them with purposes of self-control and self-direction. And to him it was given to see the full and complete victory of the principles for which he suffered in early manhood and to whose realization he struggled with tireless energy in midlife." Cited from George Bain, "Congregationalists formed association for abolition; local pastors played roles," Syracuse *Herald-American*, Feb. 8, 1998, D6. On Plymouth Congregational Church, see Evamaria Hardin, *Syracuse Landmarks* (Syracuse: Onondaga Historical Association/Syracuse Univ. Press, 1993), 121, 136–38.

44. On Luther Myrick's career, see Whitney R. Cross, *The Burned-over District: The Social and Intellectual History of Enthusiastic Religion in Western New York, 1800–1850* (Ithaca: Cornell Univ. Press, 1950), 191–93, 279. Cross uses Myrick to exemplify the progression from revivalism to perfectionism, then to antislavery agitation, and finally to the radical position that all comeouters belonged to the one sinless church.

45. Daniel C. Knowlton, "The Founding and Evolution of a Nineteenth Century Community Church, 1798–1959," typescript in author's possession, 134–35.

46. David McMillan, "James Richards and Auburn Theological Seminary," unpublished research paper, Cleveland, July 1983, 165, in author's possession. John Quincy Adams, *A History of Auburn Theological Seminary, 1818–1918* (Auburn, N.Y.: Auburn Seminary Press, 1918).

47. *Friend of Man*, June 22, 1841.

48. As reported by John Frost in the *Friend of Man*, Aug. 31, 1841. Emphasis in original.

49. "Auburn Convention," by John Frost, *Friend of Man*, Sept. 14, 1831. A furious exchange of letters ensued, pitting supporters of Richards against his critics. John Frost, though a confirmed abolitionist, thought Richards had been unfairly treated and pointed out that by the high standard applied to him, both Gerrit Smith and James Birney would be guilty. See Frost's essay, "Case of Dr. Richards," *Friend of Man*, Oct. 5, 1841.

50. Ward, *Autobiography of a Fugitive Negro*, 69. Ward had made reference to James Gillespie Birney's *The American Churches: The Bulwarks of American Slavery* (1842) and the antislavery sentiment of Albert Barnes, author of *The Church and Slavery* (1857) and *An Inquiry into the Scriptural Views of Slavery* (1846).

51. On antislavery Baptists, see Douglas M. Strong, *Perfectionist Politics: Abolitionism and the Religious Tensions of American Democracy* (Syracuse: Syracuse Univ. Press, 1999), 105–13.

52. Goen, *Broken Churches, Broken Nation*, 90–98.

53. Howard D. Williams, *A History of Colgate University, 1819–1969* (New York: Van Nostrand Reinhold Company, 1969), 68–70.

54. Quoted in Cross, *Burned-over District*, 224.

55. Isaac K. Brownson, "Diary," Aug. 4 and 7, 1838, Colgate University Archives, Hamilton; Williams, *History of Colgate University*, 68–69.

56. Cited in Nellie K. Edmonston, "Anti-Slavery Activist in Hamilton," in *Roots of our Past: The First 100 Years of the Village of Hamilton,* a supplement created by *The Chenango Valley News*, Mar. 3, 1995, 9; Williams, *History of Colgate University*, 136–37.

57. "Circular and Appeal in Behalf of Clinton Seminary," *Liberty Press*, Jan. 31, 1843; Stewart report, *Liberty Press*, Jan. 3, 1843.

58. *Liberty Press*, Oct. 26, 1844.

59. *Fiftieth Anniversary of Whitestown Seminary, June 20, 1878* (Utica: Ellis H. Roberts & Co., 1878).

60. Kenneth R. Short, "New York Central College: A Baptist Experiment in Integrated Higher Education, 1848–61," *Foundations* 5 (July 1962): 250–56.

61. Strong, *Perfectionist Politics*, Appendix A.

62. M. Leon Perkal, "William Goodell: Radical Abolitionist," *Centerpoint* 2 (spring 1977): 17–25. Goodell moved from the free church movement into Liberty Party politics and was the author of two influential abolitionist works: *Slavery and Anti-Slavery: A History of the Great Struggle in Both Hemispheres: With a View of the Slavery Question in the United States* (New York: William Goodell, 1855) and *American Slave Code in Theory and Practice* (New York: American and Foreign Anti-Slavery Society, 1853).

63. On the Wesleyan Methodists, see Lucius Matlack, *The History of American Slavery and Methodism, From 1780 to 1849: And History of the Wesleyan Methodist Connection of America; in Two Parts, With an Appendix* (New York: Lucius C. Matlack, 1849) and Chris Padgett, "Hearing the Antislavery Rank-and-File: The Wesleyan Methodists Schism of 1843," *Journal of the Early Republic* 12 (spring 1992): 63–84. On the Franckean Lutherans, see Milton C. Sernett, "Lutheran Abolitionism in New York State: A Problem in Historical Explication," *Essays and Reports, Lutheran Historical Conference, 1982* 10 (1984), 16–37, and Paul Kuenning, *The Rise and Fall of American Lutheran Pietism* (Macon, Ga.: Mercer Univ. Press, 1988).

64. John R. McKivigan, "The Antislavery 'Comeouter' Sects: A Neglected Dimension of the Abolitionist Movement," *Civil War History* 26 (1980): 143. See also John R. Mc-Kivigan, "Vote As You Pray and Pray As You Vote: Church-Oriented Abolitionism and

Antislavery Politics," in *Crusaders and Compromisers: Essays on the Relationship of the Antislavery Struggle to the Antebellum Party System,* ed. Alan M. Kraut (Westport, Conn.: Greenwood, 1983), 179–203.

65. Ronald G. Walters, *The Antislavery Appeal: American Abolitionism after 1830* (Baltimore: Johns Hopkins Univ. Press, 1978), chapter 3.

66. Whitney R. Cross, *The Social and Intellectual History of Enthusiastic Religion in Western New York, 1800–1850* (Ithaca: Cornell Univ. Press, 1950), 333.

67. Cross, *Burned-over District,* 335.

68. James Brewer Stewart, *Holy Warriors: The Abolitionists and American Slavery* (rev. ed., New York: Hill & Wang, 1996), 91.

69. According to one report, Noyes's paper, the *Perfectionist,* spread "like lightening" among the students at Oneida Institute. See *Religious Experience of John Humphrey Noyes,* ed. George Wallingford Noyes (New York: The Macmillan Company, 1923), 188. On Green's low opinion of the perfectionists, see Elizur Wright, Jr., to Green, Oct. 17, 1837, Elizur Wright, Jr., Papers, Library of Congress; and Green to Amos Phelps, Mar. 29, 1838, Phelps Papers, Boston Public Library.

70. Quoted in J. H. Noyes, *History of American Socialisms* (1870; reprint, New York: Dover Publications, 1966), 167.

71. Quoted in Noyes, *American Socialisms,* 177.

72. *The Communist,* Sept. 18, 1845, as quoted in Noyes, *American Socialisms,* 170–71. John L. Thomas discusses Collins with reference to other utopian groups in antebellum America in "Antislavery and Utopia," in *The Antislavery Vanguard,* ed. Duberman, Chapter 11. For a detailed report on conditions in the Skaneateles community as of August 1845, see the letter by the British utopian John Finch, reprinted in H. Roger Grant, ed., "The Skaneateles Community: A New York Utopia," *Niagara Frontier* 22 (autumn 1975), 68. When Finch visited the colony in 1845, it consisted of 11 adult male members, 8 female adults, and 7 children. All lived on fruit, vegetables, and milk.

73. Samuel J. May, Jr., to Richard D. Webb, July 12, 1864, May Papers, Boston Public Library, quoted in Louis Filler, *The Crusade Against Slavery: Friends, Foes, and Reforms 1820–1860* (Algonac, Mich.: Reference Publications, 1986), 141, n. 6.

74. Lewis Perry, *Radical Abolitionism: Anarchy and the Government of God in Antislavery Thought* (Ithaca: Cornell Univ. Press, 1973), 95.

75. Green's speech in *First Annual Report of the American Anti-Slavery Society* (New York: Dorr & Butterfield, 1834), 13.

76. Garnet's speech in *Seventh Anniversary of the American Anti-Slavery Society* (New York: American Anti-Slavery Society, 1840), 5.

77. Mary Mathews to Charles G. Finney, June 22, 1836, Finney Papers, as cited in McElroy, "Social Reform," 155.

78. Weld to Tappan, Feb. 22, 1836, in vol. 1 of *Letters of Theodore Dwight Weld, Angelina Grimké Weld, and Sarah Grimké, 1822–1844,* ed. Gilbert Barnes and Dwight L. Dumond (New York: Appleton-Century, 1934), 265.

79. Samuel J. May, *Some Recollections of Our AntiSlavery Conflict* (Boston: Fields, Osgood & Co., 1869), 332.

80. For a more detailed discussion of this important demurral to the notion that Finney's theology and radical utopianism were linked, see Leonard J. Sweet, "The View of Man Inherent in New Measures Revivalism," *Church History* 45 (June 1976): 206–21.

5. Bible Politics

1. Cited in John Niven, *The Coming of the Civil War 1837–1861* (Arlington Heights, Ill.: Harlan Davidson, 1990), 18–19. On Van Buren's political views, see Donald B. Cole, *Martin Van Buren and the American Political System* (Princeton: Princeton Univ. Press, 1959), and Robert V. Remini, *Martin Van Buren and the Making of the Democratic Party* (New York: Columbia Univ. Press, 1959).

2. Used as early as 1834 by Henry Clay of Kentucky to describe an anti-Democratic coalition of anti-Masons, National Republicans, and states' rights Democrats, the Whig Party included northeastern industrialists and merchants, western businessmen, supporters of internal improvements, and Southern planters who believed in Clay's American System of protective tariffs, federally sponsored roads and railways, and a national bank. The Whigs, who had borrowed the name Whig from opponents to royal prerogatives in Great Britain, fell apart on the rising tide of sectionalism by 1854. Most Northern Whigs joined the new Republican Party in the 1856 presidential election. The standard source is Michael F. Holt, *The Rise and Fall of the Whig Party: Jacksonian Politics and the Onset of the Civil War* (New York: Oxford Univ. Press, 1999).

3. Lawrence J. Friedman, *Gregarious Saints: Self and Community in American Abolitionism, 1830–1870* (New York: Cambridge Univ. Press, 1982), 115.

4. Lewis Perry, *Radical Abolitionism: Anarchy and the Government of God in Antislavery Thought* (Ithaca: Cornell Univ. Press, 1973).

5. *Liberator,* Nov. 6, 1836.

6. Wright to Beriah Green, Oct. 17, 1837, cited in Richard H. Sewell, *Ballots for Freedom: Antislavery Politics in the United States 1837–1860* (New York: Oxford Univ. Press, 1976), 28.

7. Beriah Green to Gerrit Smith, Oct. 19, 1838, Gerrit Smith Papers, Syracuse Univ.

8. *Friend of Man,* Oct. 17, 1838.

9. Beriah Green to Gerrit Smith, Nov. 29, 1838, Gerrit Smith Papers, Syracuse Univ.

10. *Friend of Man,* Feb. 12, 1840; Sewell, *Ballots for Freedom,* 44–45. Smith was not, however, a newcomer to politics. He was a nominee on the anti-Masonic state ticket in 1827 and attended a Whig State Convention in 1834.

11. Sewell, *Ballots for Freedom,* 49–50. A biography of Stewart has yet to be written, but see Luther R. Marsh, *Writings and Speeches of Alvan Stewart on Slavery* (New York: A. B. Burdick, 1860).

12. Stewart to E. W. Clarke, Sept. 14, 1839, cited in Gerald Sorin, *The New York Abolitionists* (Westport, Conn.: Greenwood, 1971), 50.

13. Stewart to wife, May 7, 1838, cited in Sorin, *New York Abolitionists,* 51.

14. Clay's speech was given on Feb. 7, 1839, as cited in Sewell, *Ballots for Freedom,* 48.

15. Stewart to Myron to Edwin W. Clarke, Sept. 14, 1839, cited in Sewell, *Ballots for Freedom,* 51.

16. [Elizur Wright, Jr.], *Myron Holley; and What He Did for Liberty and True Religion* (Boston: Elizur Wright, 1882), 243.

17. "Speech of Myron Holley at Perry, July 4, 1839," *Friend of Man,* Aug. 14, 1839. Holley died in 1841, only a year after the formation of the Liberty Party, the purest expression of the Bible politics he advocated. Abolitionists in North Star Country sought to erect a monument honoring him in Rochester's Mt. Hope Cemetery. James C. Jackson, Corresponding Secretary of the New York State Anti-Slavery Society, wrote that the

monument was to "pay respect to the man who by common consent, has awarded to him the Honor of having organized and brought into shape the Liberty Party of the United States." *Albany Patriot,* Apr. 10, 1844. Gerrit Smith wrote the inscription: "The Liberty Party of the United States of America have erected this monument to the memory of Myron Holley, the friend of the slave and the most effective, as well as one of the very earliest, of the founders of the party." Cited in Amy Hanmer-Croughton, "Anti-Slavery Days in Rochester," *Rochester Historical Society Publications* 14 (1936): 124.

18. Cited in James B. Stewart, "The Aims and Impact of Garrisonian Abolitionism, 1840–1860," *Civil War History* 15 (Sept. 1969): 198.

19. Henry Mayer, *All on Fire: William Lloyd Garrison and the Abolition of Slavery* (New York: St. Martin's Press, 1998), 214.

20. Beriah Green to Gerrit Smith, Aug. 28, 1837, Gerrit Smith Papers, Syracuse Univ.

21. Sorin, *New York Abolitionists,* 47–52.

22. Cited in William Birney, *James G. Birney and His Times* (New York: D. Appleton & Co., 1890), 12.

23. Birney to Ralph R. Gurley, July 12, 1832, in *Letters of James Gillespie Birney, 1831–1857,* ed. Dwight L. Dumond (1938; reprint, Gloucester, Mass.: Peter Smith, 1966), 1:12.

24. Theodore D. Weld to Birney, May 28, 1834, in *Letters of Birney,* 1:113.

25. Birney to Lewis Tappan, Mar. 19, 1835, in *Letters of Birney,* 1:186. Birney began writing to Smith in 1834, urging the Madison County philanthropist to rid himself of ties to the ACS. Weld, who had moved on to Oberlin, wrote Birney on February 16, 1835, "I am glad to hear that you and Gerrit Smith are corresponding, hold on to him by all means. If we gain *him,* it will be an *immense accession to our cause,* and he will be more influenced by you than by all others." Theodore D. Weld to Birney, Feb. 16, 1835, in *Letters of Birney,* 1:182.

26. Matilda was being returned as a fugitive.

27. Birney to Lewis Tappan, July 5, 1837, in *Letters of Birney,* 1:392.

28. Henry B. Stanton to Birney, Aug. 7, 1837, in *Letters of Birney,* 1:411.

29. Birney to Myron Holley, Joshua H. Darling, and Josiah Andrews, Dec. 17, 1839, in *Letters of Birney,* 1:514–16.

30. Francis J. LeMoyne to Birney, in *Letters of Birney* 1:514.

31. Smith to Joshua Leavitt, Dec. 24, 1839, in *Emancipator,* Jan. 9, 1840.

32. *Liberator,* Mar. 27, 1840.

33. On the founding of the Liberty Party, see Richard Sewell's excellent study, *Ballots for Freedom,* chapter 3.

34. Cited in *Letters of Birney,* 1:550, n. 2.

35. Smith to William Goodell, Feb. 8, 1840, in *Friend of Man,* Feb. 19, 1840.

36. Beriah Green to Gerrit Smith, Mar. 26, 1840, Gerrit Smith Papers, Syracuse Univ.

37. Cited in Mayer, *All on Fire,* 280.

38. For a detailed interpretation of the schism which argues that the Garrisonians did not take over the AASS at the annual meeting in May 1840 "but resisted an atempt either to oust them or dissolve the organization," see Mayer, *All on Fire,* 278–83.

39. Hiram H. Kellogg to Birney, May 5, 1840, in *Letters of Birney,* 1:560–61. The Sabbath issue was an important one to many abolitionists, especially those who came out of a revivalist background. They had honed their organizational skills in the movement to

purge Sunday of various secular activity, including government distribution of the mail.

40. Douglas M. Strong, "Partners in Political Abolitionism: The Liberty Party and the Wesleyan Methodist Connection," *Methodist History* 23 (Jan. 1985): 99–100. For a detailed analysis of the correlation between abolitionism and comeouter churches in Upstate New York, which was typified in support for the Liberty Party, see Douglas M. Strong, *Perfectionist Politics: Abolitionism and the Religious Tensions of American Democracy* (Syracuse: Syracuse Univ. Press, 1999), especially Appendix A.

41. Garrison angered the clerical abolitionists further, in 1848, when he became involved in the anti-Sabbatarian movement, because he felt that the compulsory restriction of nonreligious activities on Sunday was spiritual tyranny. Mayer, *All on Fire,* 376–77.

42. *Friend of Man,* Extra, July 23, 1840.

43. See Richard Carwardine, "Evangelicals, Whigs and The Election of William Henry Harrison," *Journal of American Studies* 17 (Apr. 1983): 47–75.

44. James L. Sundquist, *Dynamics of the Party System: Alignment and Realignment of Political Parties in the United States* (Washington, D.C.: The Brookings Institution, 1973), 45.

45. Beriah Green to Gerrit Smith, June 11, 1842, Gerrit Smith Papers, Syracuse Univ.

46. Smith to President of National Liberty Convention, Aug. 10, 1843, quoted in the *Albany Weekly Patriot,* Sept. 12, 1843.

47. Green tried to convince Birney to send his six sons to Oneida Institute, and he complained in particular that Joshua Leavitt, editor of the *Emancipator,* and John Rankin, a New York City merchant associated with the Tappans in the antislavery and the free church movements, had not done so. He also thought it strange that Arthur Tappan should have a daughter living in Utica but that she had no connection with local abolitionists. Beriah Green to Birney, Feb. 27, 1840, in *Letters of Birney,* 1:534–35; Beriah Green to Birney, Mar. 10, 1840, in *Letters of Birney,* 1:538–39.

48. *Emancipator,* May 15, 1840.

49. Benjamin Quarles, *Black Abolitionists* (New York: Oxford Univ. Press, 1969), 183–85.

50. National conventions began in 1830 and were held annually through 1835, generally in Philadelphia. After 1835, they were held intermittently until 1865. See Howard H. Bell, ed., *Minutes of the Proceedings of the National Negro Conventions, 1830–1865* (New York: Arno Press, 1969). New York blacks held a state convention from 1836 to 1850. For the minutes, see Philip S. Foner and George E. Walker, eds. *Proceedings of the Black State Conventions, 1840–1865, Volume I: New York, Pennsylvania, Indiana, Michigan, Ohio* (Philadelphia: Temple Univ. Press, 1979), 2–101.

51. H. H. Garnet to Mrs. Maria W. Chapman, Nov. 11, 1843, cited in Carter G. Woodson, *Mind of the Negro as Reflected in Letters Written During the Crisis, 1800–1860* (Washington, D.C.: Associated Publishers, 1920), 194.

52. Garnet's speech is most readily available in its entirety as document 60 in vol. 3 of *The Black Abolitionist Papers,* ed. Peter Ripley (Chapel Hill, N.C.: Univ. of North Carolina Press, 1991), 403–13.

53. Minutes of the *National Convention of Colored Citizens* (Buffalo: New York, 1843). William S. McFeely, *Frederick Douglass* (New York: W. W. Norton, 1991), 106.

54. Beriah Green, *Sketch of the Life and Writings of James Gillespie Birney* (Utica: Jack-

son and Chaplin, 1844), 117–18. Green had made reference to the year 1839 when Birney, after his father's death, voluntarily emancipated the slaves—adults and children—that he had inherited. Birney describes them by name in an "inclosure" attached to a letter to Lewis Tappan, Sept. 12, 1839, in *Letters of Birney*, 1:498–501.

55. Frederick Merk, *Slavery and the Annexation of Texas* (New York: Alfred A. Knopf, 1972).

56. Samuel J. May, *A Brief Account of His Ministry: Given in a Discourse, Preached to the Church of the Messiah, in Syracuse, N.Y., Sept. 15th, 1867* (Syracuse: Masters & Lee, 1867), 38.

57. Green to Gerrit Smith, Esq., and Smith to President Green, letters in *Albany Patriot*, Feb. 19, 1845.

58. Douglass was addressing the fourteenth anniversary meeting of the AASS held at Broadway Tabernacle. Douglass, "The Triumphs and Challenges of the Abolitionist Crusade: An Address Delivered in New York, New York, on 9 May 1848," in John W. Blassingame, ed. *The Frederick Douglass Papers* (New Haven: Yale Univ. Press, 1982), 2:126.

59. Douglass, "Abolitionists and Third Parties: An Address Delivered in Boston, Massachusetts on January 26, 1842," in Blassingame, ed., *Douglass Papers*, 1:15. Douglass was referring to opposition generated in Upstate New York toward the AASS after the split of 1840.

60. Douglass, "American Slavery, American Religion, and the Free Church of Scotland: An Address Delivered in London, England on 22 May 1846," in Blassingame, ed., *Douglass Papers* 1:286.

61. Douglass, "American Slavery, American Religion," 1:290–91.

62. *Liberator*, Apr. 17, Apr. 24, May 1, 1846.

63. Mayer, *All on Fire*, 444–45.

64. William Goodell, *Views of American Constitutional Law in Its Bearing upon American Slavery* (Utica: Jackson and Chaplin, 1844), 11.

65. Intricacies of the development of antislavery constitutionalism can be followed in William M. Wiecek, *The Sources of Antislavery Constitutionalism in America, 1760–1848* (Ithaca: Cornell Univ. Press, 1977).

66. "Is the Constitution Pro-Slavery? A Debate between Frederick Douglass, Charles C. Burleigh, Gerrit Smith, Parker Pillsbury, Samuel Ringgold Ward, and Stephen S. Foster in Syracuse, New York, on 17 January 1850," in Blassingame, ed., *Douglass Papers*, 2:229.

67. Douglass, "What to the Slave is the Fourth of July?: An Address Delivered in Rochester, New York, On 5 July 1852," in Blassingame, ed., *Douglass Papers*, 2:385. It originally appeared as Frederick Douglass, *Oration, Delivered in Corinthian Hall, Rochester . . . July 5th, 1852* (Rochester: Lee, Mann & Co., 1852).

68. Beriah Green to Gerrit Smith, Sept. 15, 1846, Gerrit Smith Papers, Syracuse Univ.

69. Beriah Green to Birney, Sept. 23, 1846, in *Letters of Birney*, 2:1027.

70. Birney to John V. Smith, Apr. 20, 1846, in *Letters of Birney*, 2:1011.

71. During the political battles of the late 1830s, a faction of radical Democrats that was known as *Loco Focos* in New York State, broke with their conservative counterparts and with the Whigs by supporting the Independent Treasury Act, which called for federal depositories. The Loco Focos allied themselves with the radical Barnburner Democrats in the 1840s.

72. Alan M. Kraut and Phyllis F. Field, "Politics versus Principles: The Partisan Response to 'Bible Politics' in New York State," *Civil War History* 25 (June 1979): 116.

73. Wesley Bailey to Gerrit Smith, June 5, 1847, Gerrit Smith Papers, Syracuse Univ.

74. Richard H. Sewell, *John P. Hale and the Politics of Abolition* (Cambridge: Harvard Univ. Press, 1965).

75. Democrats in New York State were split into two groups. The radicals, called Barnburners, supported the Wilmot Proviso. Their leader was Martin Van Buren. The conservative Democrats, called Hunkers because of their alleged hankering or hungering after patronage, sided with the Polk administration and opposed the Wilmot Proviso, thereby helping to block it and to boost the tenet of popular sovereignty over that of Free Soil. The Barnburners, who were so named because their uncompromising politics, reminded critics of the Dutch farmer who torched his barn to rid it of rats, joined progressive Whigs and the ex-Liberty Party voters to support Martin Van Buren, the Free Soil candidate in the 1848 presidential campaign. Sundquist, *Dynamics of the Party System*, 50–51; Mark L. Berger, *The Revolution in the New York Party Systems, 1840–1860* (Port Washington, N.Y.: Kennikat Press, 1973), 140.

76. Sewell, *Ballots for Freedom*, 156.

77. Leavitt to John. P. Hale, Aug. 22, 1848, John P. Hale Papers, New Hampshire Historical Society, Concord, N.H.. Cited in Sewell, *Ballots for Freedom*, 158.

78. Sernett, *Abolition's Axe*, 120–26. Green became enamored with the antidemocratic writings of Thomas Carlyle, the Scottish essayist and moralist who touted the virtues of the "great man" theory of history.

79. *North Star*, Aug. 25, 1848.

80. Mayer, *All on Fire*, 384.

81. Eric Foner, "Racial Attitudes of New York Free Soilers," *New York History* 46 (Oct. 1965): 311–29.

82. *North Star*, Sept. 1, 1848.

83. Sewell, *Ballots for Freedom*, 161.

84. *North Star*, Mar. 25, 1849.

85. John M. Taylor, *William Henry Seward: Lincoln's Right Hand* (New York: Harper Collins, 1991).

86. Cited in Sewell, *Ballots for Freedom*, 233.

87. Mayer, *All on Fire*, 407.

88. Douglass, "Do not Send Back the Fugitive: An Address Delivered in Boston, Massachusetts, on 14 October 1850," in Blassingame, ed., *Douglass Papers*, 2:246.

89. Frederick Douglass, *Life and Times of Frederick Douglass, Written by Himself* (1892; reprint, London: Collier-Macmillan Ltd., 1962), 280.

90. Douglass, "Slavery and the Slave Power: An Address Delivered in Rochester, New York, on 1 December 1850," in Blassingame, ed., *Douglass Papers*, 2:259.

6. The Turbulent 1850s

1. Cited in Hugh C. Humphreys, "'Agitate! Agitate! Agitate!': The Great Fugitive Slave Law Convention and Its Rare Daguerreotype," *Madison County Heritage*, 19 (1994): 9. Approved by President Millard Filmore on September 18, 1850, the Fugitive Slave Law was more accurately termed "An Act Respecting Fugitives from Justice, and Persons Escaping from the Service of Their Masters."

2. Ibid., 10.

3. Humphreys, "Great Fugitive Slave Convention," 43. Gerrit Smith was the treasurer of the Chaplin fund and gave over $12,000 to meet Chaplin's bail. Chaplin's abolitionist friends expected him to return to Washington for his trial in the District, and to conduct a lecture tour to reimburse his supporters. Chaplin failed to do either and, in the words of historian Ralph V. Harlow, "gave himself up to a long continued misconduct with a lady of questionable means." Ralph V. Harlow, *Gerrit Smith, Philanthropist and Reformer* (1939; reprint, New York: Russell & Russell, 1972), 293. This is a puzzling comment. Humphreys says that Chaplin married Theodosia Gilbert at Glen Haven in 1851. She died in childbirth in 1855.

4. Mary and Emily attempted to escape on the night of April 15, 1848, when seventy-seven slaves from Washington City, Georgetown, and Alexandria, Virginia, sailed down the Potomac aboard the *Pearl*, a schooner headed for Philadelphia. Lawmen gave chase and caught the Pearl, which was becalmed and no match for the pursuing steamboat. The girls were put up for sale in the slave pens of Alexandria for the sum of $2,250. William Chaplin purchased their freedom with funds raised by the Reverend Henry Ward Beecher and his congregation in New York City. Humphreys, "Great Fugitive Slave Convention," 17–18. See also Catherine M. Hanchett, "What Sort of People & Families . . . : The Edmondson Sisters," *Afro-Americans in New York Life and History* 6 (July 1982): 21–37.

5. Cited in Humphreys, "Great Fugitive Slave Convention," 23.

6. The location is at 9 Sullivan Street, currently the site of the Cherry Valley Apartments.

7. For a detailed decoding of the daguerreotype and for a discussion of the Cazenovia meeting, see Humphreys, "Great Fugitive Slave Convention," especially 32–33.

8. *North Star*, Sept. 5, 1850, cited in Humphreys, "Great Fugitive Slave Convention," 31.

9. Newspaper citations from Humphreys, "Great Fugitive Slave Convention," 31–35.

10. W. H. Burleigh to Gerrit Smith, Oct. 17, 1850, Gerrit Smith Papers, Syracuse Univ. Library.

11. Jermain W. Loguen, *The Rev. J. W. Loguen, As a Slave and As a Freeman* (1859; reprint, New York: Negro Univ. Press, 1968), 394–95.

12. Loguen, *The Rev. J. W. Loguen*, 391, 393–94.

13. Milton C. Sernett, "'A Citizen of No Mean City': Jermain W. Loguen and the Antislavery Reputation of Syracuse," *Syracuse Univ. Library Associates Courier* 22 (fall 1987), 33–55; Loguen, *The Rev. J. W. Loguen*, 394.

14. Daniel Webster, *The Writing and Speeches of Daniel Webster* (Boston: Little, Brown, 1903), 13:420; Robert F. Dalzell, Jr., *Daniel Webster and the Trial of American Nationalism, 1843–1852* (Boston: Houghton-Mifflin, 1973).

15. May, *Some Recollections*, 374.

16. Lucy Watson was sixteen at the time of the rescue. Her statement, first published in 1894, is contained in Earl E. Sperry, *The Jerry Rescue* (Syracuse: Onondaga Historical Association, 1924), 42. Sperry's account made use of contemporary newspapers and included testimonies from eyewitnesses and informants who had Jerry Rescue stories passed on to them. My reconstruction of the events of October 1, 1851, is compiled from the Loguen, May, and Ward autobiographies. They sometimes vary on details, as does

the press of the day. Useful secondary sources, in addition to the Sperry volume, are W. Freeman Galpin, "The Jerry Rescue," *New York History* 26 (Jan. 1945): 19–34 and Jayme Sokolow, "The Jerry McHenry Rescue and the Growth of Northern Anti-Slavery Sentiment during the 1850s," *Journal of American Studies* 16 (Dec. 1982): 427–45. Constance Robertson wrote a fascinating book-length fictional account of the Jerry Rescue using many primary sources. See her *Fire Bell in the Night* (New York: Henry Holt and Company, 1944).

17. May, *Some Recollections,* 375. William Henry of North Carolina claimed ownership of Jerry's mother and may possibly have been his father. Sometime after 1818 the Henry family and slaves moved to Missouri and settled near Hannibal in Marion County. In 1843, Jerry escaped, with the intention of finding refuge in Canada, but during the winter of 1849–1850 he apparently made his way to Syracuse because of its reputation for racial tolerance and economic opportunity. In 1845, William Henry sold Jerry (*in absentia*) to a Mr. Miller. Henry then died four days later. His widow married John McReynolds, to whom Miller resold Jerry on July 8, 1851, at a time when Jerry was already in Syracuse. Somehow McReynolds found out that Jerry was living in Upstate New York and authorized James Lear to bring him back to Missouri. Lear arrived in mid-September, but Commissioner Joseph F. Sabine demanded proof of McReynolds's claim to ownership. Sheriff Samuel Smith of Marion County, Missouri, showed up at midnight on September 30 with the required deed of sale and other papers.

18. Ward, *Autobiography of a Fugitive Negro,* 117–28.

19. Cited from Loguen, *The Rev. J. W. Loguen,* 409.

20. May, *Some Recollections,* 377; Donald Yacovone, *Samuel Joseph May and the Dilemmas of the Liberal Persuasion, 1791–1871* (Philadelphia: Temple Univ. Press, 1991), 145.

21. Loguen, *The Rev. J. W. Lougen,* 402.

22. The Syracuse *Daily Standard,* a Whig paper, claimed that the crowd numbered ten thousand, but this figure may be more a reflection of the paper's pro-rescue sympathies than accurate reporting. See the issues of Oct. 4 and 5, 1851.

23. Cited from Watson's statement in Sperry, *Jerry Rescue,* 42–43.

24. Cited from the statement of Ella B. Moffett, published in the *Syracuse Herald,* and included in Sperry, *Jerry Rescue,* 44.

25. The Orson Ames Greek Revival woodframe home is located at 58 West Main Street.

26. John Jackson Clarke, "Memories of the Anti-Slavery Movement and the 'Underground Railway,'" typescript, Dec. 29, 1931, Oswego County Historical Society, Oswego, New York, 3. Clarke has this additional reference (2–3) to Jerry.

> The news of his flight was telegraphed to all points and officers and Southern agents were watching all avenues of escape to Canada. He arrived at the farm on a dark night in custody of a trusty servant in uncle's employ and remained hidden for four days, awaiting a favorable chance to pass him on. On the fourth day father found a vessel tied up on the west side near where the enormous lumber yards used to be, that was to sail that night, and made arrangements with the captain to carry him across.

On Jackson's recollections, see Melanie K. Jackson, "Oswego-area man's memoir tells of Underground Railroad," Madison Accent section to the Syracuse *Herald-Journal,* Mar., 5, 1997.

27. Elizabeth Simpson, *Mexico, Mother of Towns* (Buffalo, N.Y.: J. W. Clement Co., 1949), 353. It is not clear where Simpson got her information regarding Jerry's place of burial and date of death. Efforts to locate the grave have been unsuccessful. It is possible that Jerry was placed in an unmarked grave.

28. Sokolow, "Jerry McHenry Rescue," 429.

29. Sokolow, "Jerry McHenry Rescue," 440–41, 444–45. For a diligent attempt to sort out the conflicting evidence regarding the number of rescuers and their ethnic and social class identities, see Carol M. Hunter, *To Set the Captives Free: Reverend Jermain Wesley Loguen and the Struggle for Freedom in Central New York, 1835–1872* (New York: Garland Publishing, 1993), 129–33. Hunter counts forty-two white participants, fourteen of whom were indicted, and twelve African Americans, all of whom were indicted.

30. Samuel Joseph May, *Speech of the Rev. Samuel J. May, to the Convention of Citizens of Onondaga County* (Syracuse: Agan & Summers, Printers, 1851), 2.

31. Attorney General John J. Crittenden to United States Attorney James R. Lawrence, Oct. 6, 1851, quoted in the Syracuse *Daily Standard,* Nov. 3, 1851.

32. Sperry, *Jerry Rescue,* 27–28. Sperry reports that Ira H. Cobb, Moses Summers, W. S. Salmon, James Davis, Stephen Porter, Harrison Allen, William Thompson and Prince Jackson were indicted at Auburn. Allen, Thompson, and Jackson were African Americans. Indicted at Buffalo were William L. Crandall, L. H. Salisbury, J. B. Brigham, Montgomery Merrit, and Enoch Reed, an African American.

33. Samuel J. May to William Lloyd Garrison, Nov. 23, 1851, in W. P. and F. Garrison, *William Lloyd Garrison 1805–1879: The Story of His Life Told by His Children,* 4 vols. (New York: Century Company, 1889), 3: 336.

34. Hunter, *To Set the Captives Free,* 135–38.

35. "Every person who shall, without the authority of law, forcibly remove, or attempt to remove from this State any fugitive from service or labor, or any person who is claimed as such a fugitive, shall forfeit the sum of five hundred dollars to the party aggrieved, and shall be deemed guilty of the crime of kidnaping, and, upon conviction of such offence, shall be punished by imprisonment in the State Prison for a period not exceeding ten years." —New York State Personal Liberty Law of 1840. See Thomas D. Morris, *Free Men All: The Personal Liberty Laws of the North, 1780–1861* (Baltimore: The Johns Hopkins Univ. Press, 1974).

36. "Abstract of Gerrit Smith's Argument," in *Trial of Henry W. Allen, U.S. Deputy Marshal, for Kidnaping, with Arguments of Counsel & Charge of Justice Marvin, on the Constitutionality of the Fugitive Slave Law, in the Supreme Court of New York* (Syracuse: Power Press of the Daily Journal Office, 1852), 9–10.

37. Lucy Stone was a women's rights activist and antislavery lecturer who was active in the American Woman Suffrage Association and American Equal Rights Association after the Civil War. Lucretia Mott was a Quaker reformer who helped found the Philadelphia Female Anti-Slavery Society and the Anti-Slavery Convention of American Women.

38. Cited in Yacovone, *Samuel Joseph May,* 151.

39. Samuel J. May, *A Brief Account of His Ministry: Given in a Discourse Preached to the Church of the Messiah, in Syracuse, N.Y., September 15th, 1867* (Syracuse: Masters & Lee, 1867), 40. This is how May, an avowed disciple of nonresistance, rationalized his participation in the forcible rescue of Jerry: "I declared that I had no confidence in the

use of deadly weapons, that I would not carry even my cane to the rescue of one, who should be seized under the Law. I would *hold* a man who was attempting to execute it, if I could, overpower him if I had strength so to do: but not intentionally harm a hair of his head." May, *Brief Account of his Ministry*, 51.

40. Jermain Wesley Loguen to Washington Hunt, Dec. 2, 1851, C. Peter Ripley, ed., *The Black Abolitionist Papers* (Chapel Hill, N.C.: Univ. of North Carolina Press, 1986), 2:195.

41. Quoted from a letter written by Loguen to Rev. Joseph Johnson, representative of the American Missionary Association and one of Jerry's rescuers by Hunter, *To Set the Captives Free*, 136.

42. Loguen, *The Rev. J. W. Loguen*, 365. The Loguen narrative continues: "We called this female companion 'another white lady,' because nothing in her complexion, dress, or deportment, and nothing in the treatment of her that was publicly seen, designated her as one of the abject race."

43. Elizabeth Cady Stanton, *Eighty Years and More*, 62–63.

44. Elizabeth Cady Stanton, *Eighty Years and More*, 63.

45. The Harriet Powell circular, a copy of which is in the Onondaga Historical Association archives, Syracuse, is reproduced in Barbara S. Davis, *A History of the Black Community of Syracuse* (Syracuse: n.p., 1980) 6; and in Sperry, *Jerry Rescue*, 60–61.

46. Elizabeth Cady Stanton, *Eighty Years and More*, 63.

47. Cited in Elizabeth Cady Stanton, *Eighty Years and More*, 64. Many years later, Elizabeth Smith Miller, daughter of the celebrated abolitionist, revealed that Harriet, whom she referred to as the "White Slave," had been taken by Federal Dana (Smith's clerk) from her father's house directly to Cape Vincent. From there Dana wrote, "I saw her pass the ferry this morning into Canada." Letter from Miller to Siebert, September 21, 1896, cited in Wilbur H. Siebert, *The Underground Railroad from Slavery to Freedom* (1898; reprint, New York: Russell & Russell, 1967), 12.

48. Douglass, *Life and Times*, 281.

49. Ibid., 282; Jonathan Katz, *Resistance at Christiana: The Fugitive Slave Rebellion, Christiana, Pennsylvania, September 11, 1851, A Documentary Account* (New York: Crowell, 1974).

50. "The Trial of Van Tuyl—His Conviction and Sentence," *Gazette* (Geneva), Apr. 22, 1859. Obituary cited in Kathryn Grover, *Make a Way Somehow: African-American Life in a Northern Community, 1790–1965* (Syracuse: Syracuse Univ. Press, 1995), 36.

51. *The Voice of the Fugitive*, Nov. 5, 1851; Fred Landon, "The Negro Migration to Canada after the Passing of the Fugitive Slave Act," *Journal of Negro History* 5 (Jan. 1920): 22–36.

52. Douglass, *Life and Times*, 279.

53. Shirley Cox Husted, "'Black & White Together!': Paths Towards Freedom on the Underground Railroad," in *Sweet Gift of Freedom*, ed. Shirley Cox Husted (Rochester: County of Monroe, 1986), 5; Eugene E. Du Bois, *The City of Frederick Douglass: Rochester's African-American People and Places* (Rochester: The Landmark Society of Western New York, 1994), 12.

54. Earl Smith, "Document: William Cooper Nell on the Fugitive Slave Act of 1850," *Journal of Negro History* 66 (spring 1981): 38.

55. *Frederick Douglass' Paper*, Aug. 20, 1852. In 1854, Douglass again indicated how far he had come from the nonresistance doctrine taught by William Lloyd Garrison: "*A*

good revolver, a steady hand, and a determination to shoot down any man attempting to kidnap. Let every colored man make up his mind to this, and live by it, and if needs be, die by it. This will put an end to kidnaping and to slaveholding, too. We blush to our very soul when we are told that a negro is so mean and cowardly that he prefers to live under the slave driver's whip—to the loss of life for liberty. Oh! that we had a little more of the manly indifference to death, which characterized the Heroes of the American Revolution." *Frederick Douglass' Paper*, June 9, 1854.

56. *Liberator*, Apr. 5, 1850.

57. Josiah Henson was born in 1789 in Charles County, Maryland, and escaped to Upper Canada in 1830. Of the claim that he was the model for Mrs. Stowe's Uncle Tom, the editors of the Canadian volume of *The Black Abolitionist Papers* have this to say: "Today Henson is remembered less for his antislavery activity and his work at Dawn than for the myth that he was the model for Uncle Tom in Harriet Beecher Stowe's *Uncle Tom's Cabin*. Despite early hesitation by Henson and Stowe to acknowledge his identification with Uncle Tom, that identification became generally accepted in the public mind. It enlarged Henson's reputation and made him one of the best known Canadian black leaders. It also enhanced Canada's image as a prejudice-free haven for blacks. Henson made a final trip to England in 1876 and was received by Queen Victoria and large crowds wishing to hear 'Uncle Tom' speak." C. Peter Ripley, ed., *Canada, 1830–1865*, vol. 2 of *The Black Abolitionist Papers* (Chapel Hill, N.C.: Univ. of North Carolina Press, 1986), 107. Henson's own story is told in Josiah Henson, *The Life of Josiah Henson, Formerly A Slave, Now an Inhabitant of Canada, as Narrated by Himself* (Boston: Arthur D. Phelps, 1849). It was republished in 1965 by Uncle Tom's Cabin Museum, Dresden, Ontario, Canada. On the impact of Mrs. Stowe's novel, see Moira Davison Reynolds, *Uncle Tom's Cabin and Mid-Nineteenth Century United States: Pen and Conscience* (Jefferson, N.C.: McFarland & Co., 1985).

58. Cited in William S. McFeely, *Frederick Douglass* (New York: W. W. Norton & Company, 1991), 166.

59. Douglass, *Life and Times*, 282–91. African American leaders voiced support for a black industrial college at both a national convention (held in Rochester in 1853) and a state convention (held in Syracuse in 1854). The initiative was opposed by those who felt a separate institution would increase prejudice and by those who believed there was sufficient room for black students in the existing white schools and colleges. The initiative died when it was voted down at the national black convention in 1855. Douglass's support for the proposed "industrial college," given his opposition to separate institutions in general, may be explained by his hope that it would be located in Rochester. Carleton Mabee, *Black Education in New York State* (Syracuse: Syracuse Univ. Press, 1979), 163–65.

60. Sarah Bradford, *Scenes in the Life of Harriet Tubman* (Auburn, N.Y.: W. J. Moses, 1869), 22.

61. *Frederick Douglass' Paper* said nothing of Delany's *Condition, Elevation, Emigration and Destiny of the Colored People of the United States* (1852), much to Delany's displeasure. Douglass kept to his antiemigrationist position even during the darkest years of the 1850s when black nationalism crested in the wake of the Fugitive Slave Bill.

62. Leon Litwack, *North of Slavery* (Chicago: Univ. of Chicago Press, 1961), 273.

63. *Frederick Douglass' Paper*, Sept. 1, 1854.

64. David W. Blight, *Frederick Douglass' Civil War: Keeping Faith in Jubilee* (Baton Rouge. La.: Louisiana State Univ. Press, 1989), 49.

65. D. Reid Ross, "Kansas Minutemen: Missouri's Saviors," *America's Civil War* 7 (Nov. 1994): 42–48.

66. B. R. Wood to Gerrit Smith, Nov. 5, 1852, as cited in Harlow, *Gerrit Smith*, 315.

67. *Liberator*, Nov. 12, 1852.

68. Cited in Harlow, *Gerrit Smith*, 332.

69. Octavius Brooks Frothingham, *Gerrit Smith: A Biography* (1878; reprint New York: Negro Univ. Press, 1969), 213.

70. *Radical Abolitionist* 1 (Aug. 1855): 7.

71. Leon M. Perkal, "American Abolition Society: A Viable Alternative to the Republican Party?" *Journal of Negro History* 65 (1980): 57–71.

72. Garrison to Samuel J. May, Mar. 21, 1856, in *The Letters of William Lloyd Garrison*, ed. Louis Ruchames (Cambridge, Mass.: Harvard Univ. Press, 1971), 4: 391.

73. In the 1860 presidential campaign, the minuscule Radical Abolitionist party was merely a goad to keep the Republicans true to their antislavery rhetoric. Frederick Douglass announced that he intended to vote for Gerrit Smith, again the presidential candidate of the Radical Abolitionists, but privately he hoped for Lincoln's victory.

74. Robert T. Oliver, "William H. Seward on the 'Irrepressible Conflict,' October 25, 1858," in *Antislavery and Disunion, 1858–1861*, ed. J. Jeffery Auer (New York: Harper & Row, 1963), 31–50.

75. Glyndon G. Van Deusen, *William Henry Seward* (New York: Oxford Univ. Press, 1967), 123. Seward relied on content not technique to make his case. Of his speaking abilities, Van Deusen says, "Seward was not, in the popular sense, a great orator. He had no well-calculated gestures, his voice was husky, and he often gave the impression of communing with himself rather than addressing an audience." Van Deusen, *William Henry Seward*, 122.

76. William E. Gienapp, *The Origins of the Republican Party, 1852–1856* (New York: Oxford Univ. Press, 1987).

77. Henry Schramm, *Central New York: A Pictorial History* (Norfolk, Va.: The Donning Company, 1987), 37.

78. For an argument that New York State's "vortex of politicking" actually retarded the growth of antislavery Republicanism, see Robert J. Rayback, "New York State in the Civil War," *New York History* 59 (Jan. 1961): 56–70. See also Hendrick Booraem, *The Formation of the Republican Party in New York: Politics and Conscience in the Antebellum North* (New York: New York Univ. Press, 1983) and Mark L. Berger, *The Revolution in the New York Party Systems* (Port Washington, N.Y.: National Univ. Publications, 1973).

79. Cited in Aida DiPace Donald, "The Decline of Whiggery and the Formation of the Republican Party in Rochester: 1848–1856," *Rochester History* 20 (July 1858): 13.

80. Cited in Berger, *New York Party Systems*, 136.

81. Berger, *New York Party Systems*, 135; Dale Baum and Dale T. Knobel, "Anatomy of a Realignment: New York Presidential Politics, 1848–1860," *New York History* 65 (Jan. 1984): 61–81.

82. Ralph Harlow, *Gerrit Smith: Philanthropist and Reformer* (1939; reprint, New York: Russell & Russell, 1972), 381.

83. Cited in Berger, *New York Party Systems*, 136.

84. Cited in Sernett, *Abolition's Axe*, 139.

85. Cited from Paul Finkelman, ed., *Dred Scott v. Sanford: A Brief History with Documents* (Boston: Bedford Books, 1997), 174. The Frederick Douglass Monument in Rochester's Highland Park displays an extract from his speech on the Dred Scott Decision: "I know of no soil better adapted to the growth of reform than American soil. I know of no country where the conditions for effecting great changes in the settled order of things, for the development of right ideas of liberty and humanity are more favorable than here in these United States."

86. Landon, "Negro Migration to Canada," 22–25.

87. Samuel Ringgold Ward to Henry Bibb, Oct. 16, 1851, *Voice of the Fugitive*, Nov. 5, 1851, as reprinted in *Black Abolitionist Papers*, ed. C. Peter Ripley (Chapel Hill, N.C.: Univ. of North Carolina Press, 1986), 2:177.

88. Ibid., 177.

89. "Report by Samuel Ringgold Ward," Mar. 24, 1853, *Black Abolitionist Papers*, 2: 257. This appeared originally in the *Provincial Freeman* (Windsor, Canada West), Mar. 24, 1853. On Hiram Wilson, see William H. Pease and Jane H. Pease, *Bound with Them in Chains: A Biographical History of the Antislavery Movement* (Westport, Conn., Greenwood Press, 1972), 115–39.

90. Samuel Ringgold Ward to Henry Bibb, Nov. 6, 1851, *Voice of the Fugitive*, as republished in *Black Abolitionist Papers*, 2:182.

91. Samuel Ringgold Ward, "Founding the *Provincial Freeman*," editorial in *Black Abolitionist Papers*, 2:265.

92. Ward, *Autobiography*. Shortly after the publication of his narrative, Ward went to Jamaica where he ministered to a small congregation and settled on a modest lot given him while in England. He died about 1866. His last years were rumored to have been preoccupied with attempts to fend off the grip of alcoholism and poverty. See also Ronald K. Burke, *Samuel Ringgold Ward: Christian Abolitionist* (New York: Garland, 1995).

93. William Wells Brown, *The Narrative of William W. Brown, a Fugitive Slave. And a Lecture Delivered before the Female Anti-Slavery Society of Salem* (1847; reprint, Reading, Mass.: Addison-Wesley Pub., 1969); William Wells Brown, *Clotel, or, The President's Daughter: A Narrative of Slave Life in the United States,* with introduction by William Edward Farrison (New York: Carol Publishing Group, 1989).

94. This is in reference to George Higgins, a white Kentuckian whom Brown claimed was the half-brother of his first master. William Edward Farrison, *William Wells Brown, Author and Reformer* (Chicago: Univ. of Chicago Press, 1969), 5.

95. William Wells Brown, "The Colored People of Canada," as reprinted in *Black Abolitionist Papers*, 2: 465–66. This first appeared as a series of articles for *Pine and Palm* (Boston, Mass.), the journal of James Redpath's Haytian Emigration Bureau. I am citing the section on St. Catharines.

7. Moses and Her People

1. Runaways were told to "follow the drinkin' gourd" in reference to the constellation of stars known as the Big Dipper. They could find the North Star or Polaris (pole star) by drawing an imaginary line through the two outer stars in the bowl of the Big Dipper.

Polaris is the first bright star that the line comes to over the bowl, at a distance of about three times the distance between the two "pointer" stars. The North Star is less than one degree from the celestial pole and so effectively marks the north pole star. The point on the horizon directly below it is thus true north of the observer. No doubt on many nights the meteorological conditions in Upstate New York were such that Polaris was difficult to locate precisely. When this happened, fugitives looked to the "the drinkin' gourd."

2. Helpful contemporary studies of the Underground Railroad include Charles L. Blockson, "Escape from Slavery: The Underground Railroad," *National Geographic* (July 1984): 3–39; Charles L. Blockson, *The Underground Railroad* (New York: Berkley Books, 1989); and Larry Gara, *The Liberty Line: The Legend of the Underground Railroad* (Lexington: Univ. of Kentucky Press, 1961). The National Park Service has published a handbook on the Underground Railroad with excellent essays, photographs, and illustrations, available from its Division of Publications: *Underground Railroad* (Washington, D.C.: National Park Service, 1998). *North Star to Freedom: The Story of the Underground Railroad,* by the Canadian author Gena K. Gorrell (New York: Delacorte Press, 1997), is attractively written and illustrated for general readers. On Quaker involvement, see Larry Gara, "Friends and the Underground Railroad," *Quaker History* 51 (Spring 1962): 3–19.

3. On the difficulties of assessing the size of the fugitive slave exodus, see Robin W. Winks, *The Blacks in Canada: A History* (New Haven: Yale Univ. Press, 1971), 233–40. Winks points out that estimates of the black population in Canada often did not distinguish between "fugitive slaves" and "free blacks." After carefully sorting out conflicting claims, Winks says that "by 1860 the black population of Canada West alone may have reached forty thousand, three-quarters of whom had been or were fugitive slaves or their children, and therefore beneficiaries of the Underground Railroad" (page 240). See also Michael Wayne, "The Black Population of Canada West on the Eve of the American Civil War: A Reassessment Based on the Manuscript Census of 1861," *Social History* 28 (Nov. 1995): 465–81.

4. *North Star,* Apr. 14, 1848.

5. *Weekly Anglo-African,* Nov. 24, 1860, cited in Blockson, *Underground Railroad,* 226.

6. In 1848, Hiram Wilson wrote an article for the *Liberator,* reprinted in Douglass's *North Star,* describing conditions in Canada West: "The colored population of Canada has been variously estimated at from fifteen to twenty-five thousand. As the laws here know no man by the color of his skin, there has never been a distinct census taken of them. I think the number would fall a little short of 20,000; some have emigrated to the West Indies, and many returned to the Northern States, where they are comparatively safe, though not constitutionally so. As an asylum for the fugitive slave, Canada West is a desirable country, much more so than is generally supposed. The climate is mild and salubrious, the soil is unusually fertile and productive, and bountifully rewards the hand of industry." *North Star,* Apr. 14, 1848. Wilson mentioned several Americans who were assisting the fugitives. Among them was Mrs. Loranna Parker of Oneida County who was in charge of the juvenile school at Dawn in western Ontario.

7. Carlton Rice to William H. Siebert, Sept. 2, 1896, in W. H. Siebert Collection, New York Underground Railroad Materials, Columbus, Ohio: Ohio Historical Society, 1999. The New York State component of Siebert's extensive collection of primary and secondary sources is now available on three microfilm reels. Some of the items date from as late

as the 1930s, long after the publication of Siebert's classic study, and demonstrate his lifelong interest in obtaining as complete a picture as possible of how the Underground Railroad worked.

8. The National Park Service has produced several excellent guides to studying the Underground Railroad, the first of which is its report to Congress. See National Park Service, *Underground Railroad Special Resource Study*, U.S. Department of the Interior, National Park Service, Denver Service Center, Sept., 1995; National Park Service, *Underground Railroad Resources in the United States Theme Study*, National Historic Landmarks Survey (Washington, D.C.: U.S. Department of the Interior, 1998); National Register of Historic Places, National Park Service, *Exploring a Common Past: Researching and Interpreting the Underground Railroad* (Washington, D.C.: U.S. Government Printing Office, 1998).

9. In addition to the submission of a study report conducted by the Schomburg Center for Research in Black Culture of The New York Public Library to the New York State Department of Education, a New York State Freedom Trail Commission was formed for the purpose of coordinating activities related to a proposed marked New York State Freedom Trail in the areas of tourism, education, research and preservation, and development. See *New York State Freedom Trail Program Study: Commission Report* (New York: Schomburg Center for Research in Black Culture, 1999). For a summary of the report, see the New York State Freedom Trail internet site (http://www.nysfreedom.nysed.gov).

10. See Carol Kammen's essay "The UGRR and Local History" in the special issue, "Slavery and Resistance," of *CRM* 21 (1998): 11–13, published by the National Park Service, U.S. Department of the Interior. I quote from p. 11.

11. Arch Merrill, Upstate New York's widely published folklorist and storyteller with a journalist's eye for facts, devoted his twenty-first book to the network of "stations" known as the Underground Railroad. "A complete, documented history of the Underground's operations in Central-Western New York," Merrill wrote in the early 1960s, "is impossible to write. . . . Any researcher runs against a wall of secrecy and silence." Arch Merrill, *The Underground, Freedom's Road, and Other Upstate Tales* (New York: American Book-Stratford, 1963), 1. In addition to Merrill's collection of Underground Railroad stories, readers interested in details (always subject to additional review) about stations and operators in Upstate New York can consult Helen C. Phelan, *And Why Not Every Man?: An Account of Slavery, the Underground Railroad, and the Road to Freedom in New York's Southern Tier* (Almond, N.Y.: n.p., 1987) and *Underground Railroad Tales with Routes Through the Finger Lakes Region* (Rochester, N.Y.: Friends of the Finger Lakes Publishing, 1997) by Emerson Klees, with illustrations by Dru Wheelin. Klees responds to the verification question by categorizing houses in three groups: those with New York State historical markers, those authenticated by historical organizations, and those identified in written reference material.

12. Examples of other sites with New York State historical markers are the Edwards House, Fruit Valley (Oswego), the Hanford House, Etna, the Pliny Sexton house, Palmyra, the Salisbury-Pratt House, Little York, and the Warrant Homestead, Brighton. See Klees, *Underground Railroad Tales*, 112.

13. Diane M. Ames, "The Underground Railroad" (Cortland County), May 1994, unpublished manuscript in author's possession.

14. The marker reads, "Here Stood a Station of Underground R.R. in Which Catherine Harris Did Heroic Service for Fugitive Slaves." Harris, a domestic worker, also pioneered in establishing the first black church in Jamestown. Phelan, *And Why Not Every Man?* 91–92.

15. Melane Hirsch, "Along the Underground Railroad," *Post-Standard, North Neighbors* (Syracuse), Feb. 4, 1988, 3, 5.

16. David Kobrin, *The Black Minority in Early New York* (Albany, N.Y.: Office of State History, 1971), 34–35.

17. Austin Steward, *Twenty-Two Years a Slave, and Forty Years a Freeman* (1857; reprint, New York: Negro Univ. Press, 1968), 139–40.

18. Steward, *Twenty-Two Years a Slave,* 140–44.

19. Charles L. Blockson, *The Underground Railroad in Pennsylvania* (Jacksonville, N. C.: Flame International, 1981). See especially chapters 7–9 on Pennsylvania's northern counties. Maps of suspected Underground Railroad routes in North Star Country can be found in Phelan, *And Why Not Every Man?* and in Klees, *Underground Railroad Tales.*

20. Sernett, *Abolition's Axe,* 62.

21. Phelan, *And Why Not Every Man?* 141–42; Tendai Mutunhu, "John W. Jones: Underground Railroad Station-Master," *Negro History Bulletin* 41 (1978): 814–18; Abner C. Wright, "Underground Railroad Activities in Elmira," *The Chemung County Historical Journal* 14 (Sept. 1968): 1755–58.

22. John Jones to William Still, June 6, 1860, in William Still, *The Underground Rail Road* (1872; reprint, Chicago: Johnson Publishing Company, Inc., 1970), 554.

23. J. W. Loguen, Oct. 5, 1856, in Still, *Underground Railroad,* 153. Loguen added this interesting information about Underground Railroad activities in North Star Country: "Miss F. E. Watkins left our house [in Syracuse] yesterday for Ithaca, and other places in that part of the State. Frederick Douglass, Wm. J. Watkins and others were with us last week; Gerritt [sic] Smith with others. Miss Watkins is doing great good in our part of the State. We think much indeed of her. She is such a good and glorious speaker, that we are all charmed by her. We have had thirty-one fugitives in the last twenty-seven days; but you, no doubt, have had many more than that. I hope the good Lord may bless you and spare you long to do good to the hunted and outraged among our brethren" (153–54). William J. Watkins was a black abolitionist who moved to Rochester from Toronto in 1853 and became associate editor of *Frederick Douglass' Paper.* A free black active in antislavery politics in Baltimore before settling in Toronto in 1852 and opening a grocery, he assisted Douglass with the care of fugitives who arrived in Rochester.

24. Letter, Warren G. Olin, Tioga County Historian, to Milton Sernett, July 12, 1988, in author's possession. See also Thomas Townsend and Jack Shay, "When They Spirited the Runaway Slaves into Broome and Tioga," *Sunday Press* (Binghamton), Nov. 20, 1977; and Eric Anderson, "Owego Houses Have Railroad Homes," *Press & Sun-Bulletin* (Binghamton), Jan. 3, 1988.

25. Klees, *Tales of the Underground Railroad,* 127–28.

26. Muriel G. Kappeler, "Tier Had Underground During Abolition Era," *Sunday Press* (Binghamton), July 26, 1953; "Mecklenburg House has Aura of History," *Journal of the Schuyler County Historical Society* 5 (Apr. 1969): 27–28.

27. Cited in Phelan, *And Why Not Every Man?* 127.

28. Vincent V. Harlow, *History of St. James A.M.E. Zion Church* (Ithaca: A.M.E. Zion Church, 1986); Tendai Mutunhu, "Tompkins County: An Underground Railroad Transit in Central New York," *Afro-Americans in New York Life and History* 3 (July 1979): 21. See also Sidney Gallwey, *Underground Railroad in Tompkins County* (Ithaca: DeWitt Historical Society of Tompkins County, 1963).

29. Samuel R. Ward, *Autobiography of a Fugitive Negro: His Anti-Slavery Labours in the United States, Canada, and England* (1855; reprint, New York: Arno Press, 1968); Ronald K. Burke, "The Antislavery Activities of Samuel Ringgold Ward in New York State," *Afro-Americans in New York Life and History* 2 (Jan. 1978): 17–28; Ronald K. Burke, *Samuel Ringgold Ward: Christian Abolitionist* (New York: Garland Publishing, 1995).

30. *Friend of Man*, July 2, 1839; Gerald Sorin, *The New York Abolitionists: A Case Study of Political Radicalism* (Westport, Conn.: Greenwood, 1971), 34.

31. Gerrit Smith to S. Worthington, Esq., Aug. 25, 1841, Gerrit Smith Papers, Syracuse Univ.

32. Gerrit Smith and Ann C. Smith to Samuel and Harriet Russell, Oct. 1, 1841, Gerrit Smith Letter copy book, 1827 and 1843, vol. 1, Gerrit Smith Papers, Syracuse Univ.

33. Gerrit Smith to James C. Fuller, Nov. 12, 1841, Gerrit Smith Papers, Syracuse Univ.

34. Raymond P. Ernenwein, *The Borough of Peter* (Sherburne, N. Y.: Heritage Press, 1970), 29; Donna Burdick, "Malvina Russell and Her Family," *Snippets* 2 (1995): 7. Malvina Russell died on April 16, 1925, at the age of eighty-five. Her funeral was held in the parlor of the Smith-Miller mansion, and the mourners sang her favorite hymns, "Nearer My God to Thee" and "Shall We Meet Beyond the River."

35. Cited in Ralph V. Harlow, *Gerrit Smith: Philanthropist and Reformer* (1939; reprint, New York: Russell & Russell, 1972), 43.

36. As demonstrated in the case of the Russells, Smith was prepared to put his personal reputation and his purse on the line to secure the freedom of as many slaves as possible. But he also worked in company with other abolitionists to spirit away fugitives. He and Lewis Tappan aided Dr. Alexander Milton Ross, a Canadian abolitionist, who went to New Orleans on a mission to help escapees. "Whenever a slave succeeded in making his or her escape," Ross testified, "I was to send them the information, and they in turn notified our friends north of the Ohio river to be on the lookout for 'packages of hardware' (men) or 'dry-goods' (females), and these Ohio friends concealed the fugitives for a time, if necessary, until they could be safely sent to Canada. . . ." Cited from Blockson, *Underground Railroad*, 32–33.

37. Birdseye to Smith, Jan. 25, 1841, Gerrit Smith Papers, Syracuse Univ.

38. Ward to Smith, Apr. 18, 1842, Gerrit Smith Papers, Syracuse Univ.

39. Mason to Smith, June 21, 1842, Gerrit Smith Papers, Syracuse Univ.

40. Mason to Smith, Mar. 15, 1843, Gerrit Smith Papers, Syracuse Univ.

41. Ambush to Smith, June 30, 1843, Gerrit Smith Papers, Syracuse Univ.

42. Walton to Smith, May 1844, Gerrit Smith Papers, Syracuse Univ.

43. Edwards to Smith, Apr. 22, 1852, Gerrit Smith Papers, Syracuse Univ.

44. Edwards to Gerrit Smith, Mar. 19, 1860, Gerrit Smith Papers, Syracuse Univ.

45. Judith Wellman, "'Bound by Duty': Abolitionists in Mexico, New York, 1830–1842," *Journal of the Oswego County Historical Society* (1973): 1–30; Frieda Schuelke,

"Activities of the Underground Railroad in Oswego County," *Fourth Publication of the Oswego Historical Society* (1940), 1–14; Charles M. Synder, "The Anti-slavery Movement in the Oswego Area," *Eighteenth Publication of the Oswego County Historical Society* (1973): 1–30.

46. On Grant and other African American escapees who settled in Upstate New York, see Judith Wellman, "This Side of the Border: Fugitives from Slavery in Three Central New York Communities," *New York History* 79 (Oct. 1998): 359–92.

47. Klees, *Underground Railroad Tales,* 140–41.

48. Eber M. Pettit, *Sketches in the History of the Underground Railroad* (Fredonia, N. Y.: W. McKinstry & Son, 1879, republished with introduction and notes by Paul Leone, Westfield, N.Y.: Chautauqua Region Press, 1999), 105.

49. "Rev. J. W. Loguen's Letter," *Frederick Douglass' Paper,* June 8, 1855. Abner Bates was a tanner, store owner, and member of the abolitionist First Congregational Church, founded in 1838 as a comeouter congregation from Syracuse's First Presbyterian Church. He also belonged to the Vigilance Committee of thirteen set up to oppose the Fugitive Slave Law.

50. May, *Some Recollections.* On May's extensive reform career, see Jane H. Pease and William H. Pease, "The Gentle Humanitarian: Samuel Joseph May," in *Bound with Them in Chains* (Westport, Conn.: Greenwood, 1972), chapter 12, and Donald Yacovone, *Samuel Joseph May and the Dilemmas of the Liberal Persuasion, 1797–1871* (Philadelphia: Temple Univ. Press, 1991).

51. *Syracuse Standard,* June 22, 1857.

52. Benjamin Quarles, *The Black Abolitionists* (New York: Oxford Univ. Press, 1969), 157, 159.

53. From the *Syracuse Standard,* Sept. 28, 1857.

54. *Douglass' Monthly,* May 1859. There is an undated note in the Rochester Ladies' Anti-Slavery Society papers regarding the link between Syracuse and Rochester. William Oliver writes to Maria Porter from "Fred'k Douglass' Office" one Thursday morning, "Will you please attend to this man—a fugitive from Maryland. He came here this morning, directed here by Mr. J W Loguen of Syracuse. Both Mr. Douglass and Watkins are absent from the city." Rochester Ladies' Anti-Slavery Society Records, William L. Clements Library, Univ. of Michigan.

55. Cited in the *Post Standard* (Syracuse), Nov. 28, 1857.

56. Mansfield to Still, Dec. 15, 1856, in Still, *Underground Railroad,* 540.

57. Loguen's autobiography, probably ghost-written by the Syracuse white abolitionist John Thomas, appeared in 1859. Proceeds went to offset the cost of running the Syracuse station. See Loguen, *The Rev. J. W. Loguen.* For more on Loguen's activities in Syracuse, see Sernett, "A Citizen of No Mean City," 33–55. Loguen's biographer is Carol M. Hunter, *To Set the Captives Free: Reverend Jermain Wesley Loguen and the Struggle for Freedom in Central New York 1835–1872* (New York: Garland Publishing, 1993).

58. For a list of "Underground Railroad Stops Documented by Eye Witnesses" in Monroe County, see Shirley Cox Husted, "'Black & White Together!': Paths Towards Freedom on the Underground Railroad," in *Sweet Gift of Freedom: A Civil War Anthology,* 18.

59. Siebert, *Underground Railroad,* 414–15.

60. William S. McFeely, *Frederick Douglass* (New York: W. W. Norton, 1991), p. 146.

61. McFeely, *Frederick Douglass,* 172.

62. Douglass, *Life and Times,* 266–67.

63. Douglass to Siebert, Mar. 27, 1893, letter in Siebert Collection, New York State Underground Railroad materials.

64. Cited in Merrill, *The Underground Freedom's Road,* 50; Husted, "Black & White Together," 6.

65. Amy Post, "The Underground Railroad at Rochester," undated typescript in Siebert Collection, New York State Underground Railroad Materials, 2–3.

66. Douglass, *Life and Times,* 266–67.

67. In 1860 Anne Douglass, Frederick Douglass's ten-year old daughter, died. Samuel Porter had Anne buried in the Porter family plot in Mt. Hope Cemetery because her parents had no lot of their own.

68. William Bloss kept a tavern at Brighton along the Erie Canal until his conversion to temperance. He lived from 1830 to 1860 in a brick house on East Avenue. The Bloss residence (moved to 636 Broadway in 1880) is described in as "one of the few authenticated local stations of the Underground Railroad now in existence." See Amy Hanmer-Croughton, "Anti-Slavery Days in Rochester," *Rochester Historical Society Publication Fund Series* 14 (1936): 120, 133. Hanmer-Croughton quotes Joseph B. Bloss's recollections from a paper, "The Underground Railroad," Bloss read in 1921 before the William Clough Bloss Club.

69. The farm of Asa Anthony on Rochester's outskirts is mentioned in Douglass's memoirs as a station. Douglass reported that a fugitive from Maryland was working on the Anthony farm when word came that his master had filed papers with a United States commissioner charged with enforcing the Fugitive Slave Law of 1850. Warned in advance, the young man was "on the free waves of Lake Ontario, bound to Canada" before the papers could be served. See Douglass, *Life and Times,* 267. Asa Anthony was Susan B. Anthony's uncle. Arch Merrill concluded that there is no evidence that the famous woman's rights crusader participated directly in the Underground Railroad, however Shirley Husted says that the home of Lucy and Daniel Anthony (Susan B. Anthony's parents) on Brooks Avenue (formerly Rapids Street) was a "station" on the Underground Railroad. For more information on Underground Railroad stations in Rochester and immediate vicinity, see Arch Merrill, *The Underground Freedom's Road,* Chapter 9, and Husted's essay, "Black & White Together!" 1–24.

70. McFeely, *Frederick Douglass,* 172.

71. Douglass, *Life and Times,* 329–30.

72. Quarles, *Black Abolitionists,* 149.

73. Cited in Pettit, *Sketches in the History of the Underground Railroad,* ix.

74. Pettit, *Sketches in the History of the Underground Railroad,* 53.

75. Ibid., 54.

76. "The Underground Railroad: Celebrate the Niagara Frontier role in a dramatic American story," *Buffalo News,* Jan. 19, 1998.

77. William Wells Brown, *The Narrative of William W. Brown, A Fugitive Slave, Written by Himself* (1847; reprint, Reading, Mass.: Addison-Wesley Publishing Co., 1969), 107–8.

78. Mike Vogel, "Michigan Street Baptist: Historic Church to be Preserved," *Buffalo News*, July 14, 1996, B1, B8. Monroe Fordham, "Origins of the Michigan Street Baptist Church, Buffalo, New York," *Afro-Americans in New York Life and History* 21 (Jan. 1997): 7–18. Jack Edwards, "Freedom and the Lakes," *Great Lakes Cruiser* 3 (Sept. 1996), 38–43.

79. Of his emotions upon reaching Canada on October 28, 1830, Henson said, "My first impulse was to throw myself on the ground, and giving way to the riotous exultation of my feelings, to execute sundry antics which excited the astonishment of those who were looking on. A gentleman of the neighborhood, Colonel Warren, who happened to be present, thought I was in a fit, and as he inquired what was the matter with the poor fellow, I jumped up and told him I was free. 'O,' said he, with a hearty laugh, 'is that it? I never knew freedom make a man roll in the sand before.'" Josiah Henson, *The Life of Josiah Henson, Formerly a Slave, Now an Inhabitant of Canada, As Narrated by Himself* (Boston: Arthur D. Phelps, 1849), 54–55. Henson lived for a while in the "Little Africa" community at Fort Erie. See Owen A. Thomas, *Niagara's Freedom Trail: A Guide to African-Canadian History on the Niagara Peninsula* (Thorold, Ontario: Niagara Economic and Tourism Corporation, 1996), 10.

80. Buffalo *Commercial Advertiser*, Oct. 1, 1847; Buffalo *Daily Courier*, Oct. 1, 1847.

81. Cited in Siebert, *Underground Railroad*, 80.

82. For details on Tubman's early years, I am following an article written by Frederick B. Sanborn in 1863 and published in the *Boston Commonwealth*. He also sent a letter to Bradford as she was preparing her account of Tubman's life and was seeking verification of what Tubman had told her. Sanborn was a well-known Massachusetts abolitionist who met Harriet on several of the trips she made to New England. On one occasion, Sanborn hosted her in his home in Concord and introduced her to other area abolitionists. Sanborn's letter is in Sara Bradford, *Harriet Tubman: The Moses of Her People* (2nd ed, 1886; reprint, Secaucus, N.J.: The Citadel Press, 1961), 106–19. See also Earl Conrad, *Harriet Tubman* (Washington, D.C.: Associated Publishers, 1943), Chapter 2, especially pp. 30–31.

83. Bradford, *Harriet Tubman*, 1886, 27–28.

84. Cited in Still, *Underground Railroad*, 305. On Garrett, see James A. McGowan, *Station Master on the Underground Railroad: The Life and Letters of Thomas Garrett* (Moylan, Pa.: The Whimsie Press, 1977).

85. Still, *Underground Railroad*, 306.

86. Conrad, *Harriet Tubman*, 59–61; Elizabeth Cady Stanton, *Eighty Years and More*, 51.

87. Cited in Bradford, *Harriet Tubman*, 39.

88. W. E. Abbott to Maria G. Porter, Nov. 29, 1856, Rochester Ladies' Anti-Slavery Society Records, William L. Clements Library, Univ. of Michigan, Ann Arbor.

89. Tubman may also have crossed over on the suspension bridge constructed in 1851 between Lewiston, New York, and Queenston, Ontario. On early bridges across the Niagara River, see "Niagara River," *Niagara Frontier* 27 (1980): 17–19.

90. Bradford, *Harriet Tubman*, 48–51. While Tubman lived in St. Catharines she attended Salem Chapel (now at 92 Geneva St.), a congregation of the British Methodist Episcopal denomination, the Canadian equivalent of the African Methodist Episcopal denomination in the U.S. St. Catharines also is the site of the burial place of Anthony

Burns, whose arrest under the Fugitive Slave Act in Boston in 1854 caused immense consternation in abolitionist ranks.

91. The house at 33 South Street, Auburn, was built in 1816–1817 in the federal style and is registered as a National Historic Landmark. It has thirty rooms. Upon Seward's death in 1872, the house became the property of his son, William H. Seward, a brigadier general in the Civil War.

92. Glydon G. Van Deusen, *William Henry Seward* (New York: Oxford Univ. Press, 1967). Paul Finkelman, "The Protection of Black Rights in Seward's New York," *Civil War History* 34 (Sept. 1988), 211–34.

93. Bradford, *Harriet Tubman,* 119–28. Scott Christianson, "The Battle for Charles Nalle," *American Legacy* 2 (Winter 1997), 31–35.

94. Sarah Bradford's *Scenes in the Life of Harriet Tubman* was published privately in 1869. A revised and enlarged edition with the title *Harriet Tubman: The Moses of Her People* was privately printed by Bradford in 1886 (Reprint, Secaucus, N.J.: The Citadel Press, 1961). Bradford's work served as an important resource for subsequent attempts to tell Tubman's story, though Earl Conrad did extensive research of his own. See Earl Conrad, *Harriet Tubman* (Washington, D.C.: Associated Publishers, 1943). The Bradford-Conrad material is the primary source for more recent biographies: Dorothy Sterling, *Freedom Train: The Story of Harriet Tubman* (Garden City, N.Y.: Doubleday and Co., 1954), and Ann Petry, *Harriet Tubman: Conductor on the Underground Railroad* (New York: Thomas Y. Crowell Co., 1955). For an insightful analysis of the shaping of Tubman's oral testimony by Bradford, see Jean M. Humez, "In Search of Harriet Tubman's Spiritual Autobiography," in *This Far by Faith: Readings in African-American Women's Religious Biography,* ed. Judith Weisenfeld and Richard Newman (New York: Routledge, 1996), 239–61.

95. In 1873 Tubman acquired the property where her parents first settled on South Street in the Town of Fleming, perhaps by paying off a second mortgage from Frederick W. and Anna Seward, the son and daughter-in-law of William H. Seward. There was a wood frame house on this 6.253 acre parcel until about 1875. The presently existing red brick house (at 208 South St.) where Harriet and her second husband, Nelson Davis, lived until his death in 1888, was built sometime after 1875. In June 1896, Tubman bid $1,250 at auction for an additional twenty-five acres adjoining the brick residence and located on either side of the Auburn-Fleming line. After Harriet's death, the brick house and smaller parcel fell into private hands. The second or 25.508-acre parcel contained one brick structure, which Harriet christened "John Brown Hall," two frame cottages, and two barns. In 1903, ten years prior to her death, Tubman deeded the second parcel to the African Methodist Episcopal Zion Church. The white-frame house visitors are shown today as the Harriet Tubman Home was formally opened on June 22, 1908, to shelter the aged and the poor. Questions remain regarding its date of construction and relationship to the two frame cottages noted above. Harriet moved into it when she could no longer care for herself. The house was vacant from 1928 and restored and rededicated in 1953 by the A.M.E.Z. denomination. The brick building known as John Brown Hall was damaged in a fire in 1949 and subsequently demolished. The Department of Anthropology of Syracuse University set up an archeological field site to explore the ruins of John Brown Hall in October 1998 and during the summer of 1999.

The red brick house (at 208 South St.) was purchased in 1990 from the Norris estate and added to the Harriet Tubman second or twenty-five-acre parcel to comprise today's historic site. See "Harriet Tubman Home and Christening of John Brown Hall," *Auburn Daily Advertiser,* June 20, 1903, 8; "Dedication of Harriet Tubman Home," *Auburn Daily Advertiser,* June 24, 1908, 5; "Tubman Home Open," *Auburn Citizen,* June 24, 1908, 7; Charley Hannagan, "House linked to Tubman offered for sale," Syracuse *Herald-American,* Feb. 25, 1990, C1, C6; Monroe Fordham, "The Harriet Tubman Home and Museum, Auburn, New York," *Afro-Americans in New York Life and History* 1 (Jan. 1977): 105–11; Judy Holmes, "Students unearth the past at Auburn's Tubman Home," *Syracuse Record,* July 26, 1999, Supplement, A1, A4–A5.

96. Douglass to Harriet Tubman, Aug. 29, 1868. The entire letter is reprinted in the Appendix to Bradford's *Harriet Tubman,* 1886 edition, 134–35.

97. On dating the brick structure known as John Brown Hall, see Bonnie Crarey Ryan and Douglas V. Armstrong, *Archeology of John Brown Hall at the Harriet Tubman Home: Site Report,* Syracuse Univ. Archeology Research Report, vol. 13 (Syracuse, N.Y.: Syracuse Univ. Anthropology Department, 2000).

98. "Harriet Tubman Home and Christening of John Brown Hall," *Auburn Daily Advertiser,* June 20, 1903, 8. See also Molly Fennell Manchenton, "Tubman's Home for Aged aided Poor," Syracuse *Herald-Journal,* Feb. 1, 1999, B1.

8. John Brown's Body

1. Mary Brown's heart bore a triple burden. During the raid upon the Federal armory at Harpers Ferry, two of her sons, Owen and Watson, had been killed. Their remains, buried in a mass unmarked grave after the ill-fated assault, were not disinterred and brought to North Elba until 1899.

2. Franklin Benjamin Sanborn, ed., *The Life and Letters of John Brown, Liberator of Kansas, and Martyr of Virginia* (3rd edition; Concord, Mass.: F. B. Sanborn, 1910), 623.

3. Thomas Wentworth Higginson, the New England abolitionist who commanded the all-black Massachusetts 54th during the Civil War, came to North Elba to be with Mary once her husband was captured. He gives this description of the site as it looked in 1859: "The Notch seems beyond the world, North Elba and its half-dozen houses are beyond the Notch, and there is a wilder little mountain road which rises beyond North Elba. But the house we seek is not even on that road, but behind it and beyond it; you ride a mile or two, then take down a pair of bars; beyond the bars faith takes you across a half-cleared field, through the most difficult of wood-paths, and after half a mile of forest you come out upon a clearing. There is a little frame house, unpainted, set in a girdle of black stumps, and with all heaven about it for a wider girdle; on a high hillside, forests on north and west, —the glorious line of the Adirondacks on the east, and on the south one slender road leading off to Westport, a road so straight that you could sight a United States marshal for five miles." Quoted in James Redpath, *Public Life of Captain John Brown* (Boston: Thayer and Eldrige, 1860), 61. New York State has owned the property since 1895. Today it is maintained and staffed by the New York State Department of Parks, Recreation and Historic Preservation. The Brown cabin has been restored to how it might have looked about 1859. Some of the original furnishings remain. A small barn is also on the property. The large boulder at the grave site was placed there about 1900,

and the statue of Brown and a young African American boy was erected by the now defunct John Brown Memorial Association.

4. See Wendell Phillips, *Speeches, Lectures, and Letters* (Boston: Lee and Shepard, 1894), 290.

5. Robert Gordon, "A Mournful Trip," *Adirondack Life* 15 (Jan.–Feb. 1984): 16–18; 29–32. Oswald Garrison Villard, *John Brown, 1800–1859: A Biography Fifty Years After* (Boston: Houghton Mifflin Company, 1911), 561–62. John Anthony Scott and Robert Alan Scott, *John Brown of Harper's Ferry* (New York: Facts on File, 1988), 160–61. For an especially poetic account of the funeral, using eye-witness accounts by reporters from the *New York Herald* and the *New York Tribune,* see Chapter 17, "Body in Transit," by Truman Nelson, *The Old Man: John Brown at Harper's Ferry* (New York: Holt, Rinehart and Winston, 1973), 281–304. According to Christopher Densmore, former archivist at the State Univ. of New York at Buffalo, "Blow Ye Trumpet Blow" written by Charles Wesley and sung to the tune of "Lenox" stems from the Sacred Harp tradition.

6. Sanborn, ed., *Life and Letters of John Brown,* 111–12. Scott and Scott, John Brown, 74.

7. Lyman Epps also sang "Blow Ye The Trumpets Blow" in 1896 during the ceremony marking the transfer of the John Brown homestead to New York State. Connecticut-born, Epps was a professional Adirondacks guide who helped establish the Lake Placid Public Library and the local Baptist church. He died in 1897. His son, also named Lyman, was interviewed in 1936 at the age of 83 and recalled singing "Blow Ye The Trumpets Blow" at the funeral. See Amy Godine, "Home Truth: The Saga of African-Americans in the Adirondack Park," *Adirondack Life* 25 (Jan./Feb. 1994): 50; Alfred W. Santway, *A Brief Sketch of John Brown, The Martyr—Emancipator* (Watertown, N.Y.: n.p., 1936).

8. Quotations from Brown's letters as cited in Richard O. Boyer, *The Legend of John Brown: A Biography and a History* (New York: Alfred A. Knopf, 1973), 393.

9. James H. Henderson to H. H. Garnet, Jan. 29, 1849, *North Star,* Feb. 16, 1849.

10. From Sanborn, ed., *Life and Letters of John Brown,* 97.

11. *North Star,* Apr. 21, 1848.

12. Zita Dyson, "Gerrit Smith's Efforts in Behalf of the Negroes in New York," *Journal of Negro History* 3 (Oct. 1918): 354–59. In 1849 Smith devised another plan to give farms to a thousand white males and $50 in money to white women who avoided intoxicating liquors and were landless. See Charles A. Hammond, *Gerrit Smith: The Story of a Noble Life* (Geneva, N.Y.: W. F. Humphrey, 1908), 40.

13. Emma Corinne Brown, "The Lore of the Negro in Central New York State" (Ph.D. dissertation, Cornell Univ., 1943), 148–49.

14. Printed Circular, cited in Ralph V. Harlow, *Gerrit Smith: Philanthropist and Reformer* (1939; reprint, New York: Russell & Russell, 1972), 245.

15. Austin Steward, *Twenty-Two Years a Slave, and Forty Years a Freeman* (1857; reprint, New York: Negro Universities Press, 1968), 167.

16. *North Star,* Dec. 22, 1848.

17. *North Star,* Mar. 2, 1849.

18. Bibb letter, *North Star,* Feb. 16, 1849.

19. *North Star,* Mar. 16, 1849.

20. Smith letter, Dec. 8, 1847 in *North Star,* Jan. 7, 1848.

21. *North Star,* Feb. 18, 1848.

22. Gerrit Smith to Ray, Nov. 16, 1848, Gerrit Smith Papers, Syracuse Univ.

23. *North Star,* Mar. 24, 1848.

24. A. C. Van Epps to Gerrit Smith, Oct. 24, 1851, Gerrit Smith Papers, Syracuse Univ.

25. Quoted in Villard, *John Brown,* 74.

26. Quoted in Sanborn, ed., *Life and Letters of John Brown,* 99.

27. Letter to wife, Nov. 18, 1850, from Sanborn, ed., *Life and Letters of John Brown,* 106–7.

28. Quoted in Villard, *John Brown,* 75.

29. Sanborn, ed., *Life and Letters of John Brown,* 111–12. Scott and Scott, *John Brown,* 74.

30. Harlow, *Gerrit Smith,* 339–41.

31. Douglass, *Life and Times,* 303.

32. Cited from Amy Hammer-Croughton, "Anti-Slavery Days in Rochester," *Rochester Historical Society Publications* 14 (1936): 141.

33. Doy was taken from a Kansas jail to St. Joseph, Missouri, where abolitionists rescued him. He brought back his rifle (one of "Beecher's Bibles") and the hunting knife he carried (known as "John Brown's Peacemaker") and exhibited them in the office of the *Rochester Telegraph.* See Shirley Cox Husted, "In the Eagle's Claw . . . The Irrepressible Conflict," in *Sweet Gift of Freedom: A Civil War Anthology,* ed. Shirley Cox Husted, (Rochester: County of Monroe, 1986), 27–29.

34. The two best studies of this group are Jeffery Rossbach, *Ambivalent Conspirators: John Brown, The Secret Six, and a Theory of Slave Violence* (Philadelphia: Univ. of Pennsylvania Press, 1982), and Otto Scott, *The Secret Six: John Brown and the Abolition Movement* (New York: Times Books, 1979).

35. Smith to Sanborn, Jan. 22, 1859, in Sanborn, ed., *Life and Letters of John Brown,* 482.

36. Douglass, *Life and Times,* 271.

37. Douglass, *Life and Times,* 272–73.

38. Douglass, *Life and Times,* 316.

39. Ibid.

40. Villard, *John Brown,* 55.

41. Quoted in Smith to Hyatt, July 25, 1857, Kansas State Historical Society, as cited in Harlow, *Gerrit Smith,* 394.

42. Brown to Higginson, Feb. 12, 1858, Boston Public Library, as cited in Harlow, *Gerrit Smith,* 396.

43. Sanborn, ed., *Life and Letters of John Brown,* 439. Rossbach, *Ambivalent Conspirators,* 141–43.

44. Cited in Harlow, *Gerrit Smith,* 397.

45. Smith to Giddings, Mar. 25, 1858, as cited in Harlow, *Gerrit Smith,* 399.

46. Smith to Sanborn, July 26, 1858, in Sanborn, ed., *Life and Letters of John Brown,* 466.

47. Cited from a letter Brown wrote April 8, 1858 to his son, in Sanborn, ed., *Life and Letters of John Brown,* 452.

48. Loguen to Brown, May 6, 1858, Kansas State Historical Society, reprinted in *Blacks on John Brown,* ed. Benjamin Quarles (Urbana: Univ. of Illinois Press, 1972), 6.

49. Quarles, *Allies for Freedom*, 49.

50. Green, who was almost captured on his way to Brown's Maryland hideout, is described as bold and impetuous, "the Zouave" of John Brown's band. See Husted, "In the Eagle's Claw," 29.

51. Morton to Sanborn, Apr. 13, 1858, printed in Sanborn, ed., *Life and Letters of John Brown*, 1: 161–62.

52. Cited in Villard, *John Brown*, 340.

53. Cited in Douglass, *Life and Times*, 320.

54. Douglass, *Life and Times*, 320.

55. Loguen, *The Rev. J. W. Loguen*, 451.

56. Earl Conrad, *Harriet Tubman* (New York: Associated Publishers, 1943), 126.

57. Cited in Sanborn, ed., *Life and Letters of John Brown*, 620.

58. Douglass, *Life and Times*, 307.

59. William S. McFeely, *Frederick Douglass* (New York: W. W. Norton & Company, 1991), 199. The mark of the chisel with which the desk drawer was opened remained for many years as evidence of Douglass's involvement with John Brown.

60. Reprinted in Quarles, ed., *Blacks on John Brown*, 7–10. See also, Douglass, *Life and Times*, 312.

61. Husted, "In the Eagle's Claw," 33. Ruth Rosenberg-Naparsteck, "A Growing Agitation: Rochester Before, During, and After The Civil War," *Rochester History* 46 (Jan. and Apr., 1984): 11. On the reputation of John Brown among African Americans, see Quarles, ed., *Blacks on John Brown*.

62. An ex-soldier of fortune from Great Britain, Forbes served as Brown's military aid during the Kansas conflict. He proved to be a traitor by revealing Brown's plans to some members of Congress.

63. Octavius Brooks Frothingham, *Gerrit Smith: A Biography* (1878; reprint, New York: Negro Universities Press, 1969), 243.

64. Cited from Harlow, *Gerrit Smith*, 408.

65. *New York Herald*, Nov. 2, 1859.

66. Frothingham, *Gerrit Smith*, 244.

67. George Thomas, Esq., of Utica visited Smith in June 1859 and later published his recollections of the house and grounds to which John Brown and so many other North Star Country advocates of black freedom were welcomed: "On my arrival at Peterboro I first saw Mr. Smith at his office—a plain and substantial full sized edifice for the purpose situated a few rods from his dwelling. Very soon he showed me the way to his stately mansion, and seated me in his library room, where Mrs. Smith was engaged in drawing. This is a very large room entered (from) the large hall and fronts Main Street—had an extensive library, but he remarked that he had found time to read but a few of the volumes it contained. He passed me around through the mansion containing many large and smaller rooms, some 12 ft. high in the lower story—all in good order and richly but plainly furnished. The wide piazza on the southerly side of the house was converted into a large conservatory with a glass front and filled with choice flowers in great variety and heated in winter from a furnace in the basement of the mansion. After such examination Mr. Smith remarked that his father had built the mansion when he was a child and before settlements even made near it to any extent—said he had

improved and added somewhat to it and *feelingly* remarked that he venerated it with the poplars that surrounded it as the work of his *father.* We were now called to dinner and when seated around the table Mr. Smith with much *unction* invoked God's blessing upon the poor slave and the dinner was served. After dinner he conducted me over the grounds attached to his mansion consisting of 25 A of land through which was flowing a never failing stream of water of sufficient size to operate a mill just below the premises. A strong stone wall above high water mark extending along the sides of the stream protected the banks from the action of the water the summit of the banks being some 15 ft. above the walls. The ground was graded forming an even gradual slope to the height of the walls. On the one side of the stream was a beautiful green lawn. On the other side were five terraces some fifteen to 20 rods in length rising each about 3 ft. above the other to the summit. These terraces were planted with grapevines of several varieties all in a flourishing condition. At the end of the terraces was a large greenhouse or grapery made of glass at a cost of $4000 in which the most choice foreign grapes were produced. Some ten rods in the rear of the mansion is a beautiful summer house, near which is a fine artificial fountain of living water. The whole grounds were in a state of high cultivation, abounding in fruit and ornamental trees and flowers, producing abundance of vegetables in great variety, melons, etc. The grounds were carefully laid out, with neat gravel walks passing in different directions with a design for convenience and ornament and they exhibited good taste." From *Personal Recollections of Gerrit Smith* by George Thomas, Esq., Utica, Jan. 5, 1875. Onondaga County Public Library, Syracuse.

68. "Interview of John Brown with His Wife," Gerrit Smith Papers, Syracuse Univ.

69. Cited from his suit against the *Chicago Tribune,* in Gerrit Smith Papers, Syracuse Univ.

70. For the "Manifesto" including Douglass's letter, see Frothingham, *Gerrit Smith,* 253–59.

71. Harlow, *Gerrit Smith,* 421–22. The *National Intelligencer* carried this item on November 24, 1859, dated from Utica on November 11: "The Hon. Gerrit Smith, ex-Member of Congress, has been confined in the Lunatic Asylum here since Monday last. . . . It was only by stratagem that his friends succeeded in getting him here. He has been, ever since the arrest of Brown . . . , haunted with the idea that he was culpably responsible for all the lives that have and will be sacrificed; and so much have this reflection and the fear of being called on to answer at the bar of justice preyed upon him, that his mind, never exempt from a tendency to be unhinged, gave way. . . . For some days . . . he manifested a most nervous anxiety to anticipate the requisition which he expected would be made upon him, and to proceed to Virginia and surrender himself. . . . When it was resolved to place him under restraint, this anxiety of his was taken advantage of. His friends pretended to chime in with his notion, and when he set out for Utica he was under the impression he was on his way to Richmond or Charlestown." Cited from Edward Stone, ed., *Incident At Harper's Ferry* (Englewood Cliffs, N. J.: Prentice-Hall, Inc., 1956), 102.

72. John R. McKivigan and Madeleine Leveille, "The 'Black Dream' of Gerrit Smith, New York Abolitionist," *Syracuse Univ. Library Associates Courier* 20 (Fall 1985): 76. For the view that Gerrit Smith was a "criminal accomplice" of John Brown, see Ralph Volney

Harlow, "Gerrit Smith and the John Brown Raid," *American Historical Review* 38 (Oct. 1932): 32–60.

73. Cited in Frothingham, *Gerrit Smith*, 247.

74. May, *Some Recollections*, 387.

75. Cited in W. Freeman Galpin, *Central New York: An Inland Empire* (New York: Lewis Historical Publishing Company, 1941), 2: 193.

76. *New York Times*, Dec. 1, 1859.

77. Galpin, *Central New York*, 2: 194.

78. Cited from Hanmer-Croughton, "Anti-Slavery Days in Rochester," 147.

79. The American poet Stephen Vincent Benét has given us a powerful book-length poem inspired by the life and death of John Brown. In Benét's rendition, when Brown was awaiting the judgment of men at Charles Town he jotted down the essentials to be inscribed on the family monument at North Elba. "Oliver Brown born 1839 was killed at Harpers Ferry, Va. Nov. 17th, 1859. Watson Brown born 1835 was wounded at Harpers Ferry Nov. 17th and died Nov. 19th 1859. (My Wife can) supply blank dates to above. John Brown born May 9th 1800 was executed at Charleston Va. December 2nd 1859." The tombstone of which the poem speaks was brought to North Elba from Canton, Connecticut, by John Brown in April 1858. It was the old grave marker of his grandfather, Captain John Brown the Revolutionary soldier. The name of Frederick Brown, the son who lost his life in the Kansas prelude to the Civil War, preceded those of father and brothers on the old marker. Stephen Vincent Benét, *John Brown's Body* (New York: Rinehart & Company, Inc., 1941), 57. See also Villard, *John Brown*, 553.

80. Douglass, *Life and Times*, 275.

81. Garrison explained his position, one seemingly at odds with his longstanding nonresistance principles, by declaring that once a contest between the oppressed and the oppressor actually begins, he must side with the oppressed. Portions of his speech, given at Tremont Temple in Boston, can be found in Wendell Phillips Garrison and Francis Jackson Garrison, *William Lloyd Garrison, 1805–1879: The Story of His Life told by His Children* (1885; reprint, New York: Negro Universities Press, 1969), 3: 491.

82. Green to Phillips, Dec. 29, 1859, Phillips Papers, Houghton Library, Harvard Univ.

83. This letter is also in Frothingham, *Gerrit Smith*, 240–41.

84. *New York Times*, Oct. 20, 1859.

85. Speech delivered on November 1, 1859 in Henry Ward Beecher's Church of the Pilgrims, Brooklyn, New York, in *Wendell Phillips on Civil Rights and Freedom*, Louis Filler, ed., (New York: Hill & Wang, 1965), 96. This speech was published in the *New York Times*, Nov. 2, 1859.

86. *New York Herald*, Oct. 20, 1859.

87. From the *Washington Constitution*, as reprinted in *New York Times*, Oct. 21, 1859.

88. *New York Times*, Oct. 24, 1859.

89. Douglass, *Life and Times*, 306.

9. Battlefields and Home Fronts

1. Caroline Cowles Richards, *Village Life in America 1852–1872*, intro. by Margaret E. Sangster (Williamstown, Mass.: Corner House Publishers, 1972), 130–31.

2. Henry Conklin, *Through "Poverty's Vale": A Hardscrabble Boyhood in Upstate New York, 1832–1862,* intro. by Wendell Tripp (Syracuse: Syracuse Univ. Press, 1974), 212.

3. The Mohawk Rangers went to Albany where the unit joined with the Seven Oswego Companies to become the 81st Regiment of Infantry. Conklin served in Company C, was wounded in the Battle of Seven Pines during the Peninsular Campaign of 1862, and spent ten weeks in a hospital at Annapolis, Maryland. Barely able to walk, he was discharged in December and returned to Upstate New York. Conklin moved his family to Attica, New York, and later to Indiana, but he eventually settled on acreage in the Town of Wilmurt in Herkimer County. On the 81st, which was the first regiment of infantry to enter the Confederate capitol of Richmond and had the task of releasing Union prisoners confined in Castle Thunder and Libby Prison, see Charles McCool Synder, *Oswego County, New York in the Civil War* (Oswego, N.Y.: Yearbook of the Oswego County Historical Society and the Oswego County Civil War Centennial Committee, 1962), chapter 4.

4. David Golightly Harris, *Piedmont Farmer: The Journals of David Golightly Harris, 1855–1870,* edited with intro. by Philip N. Racine (Knoxville: Univ. of Tennessee Press, 1990), 190.

5. Quoted from Geoffrey C. Ward, *The Civil War: An Illustrated History* (New York: Alfred A. Knopf, 1990), 55.

6. Ibid., 238.

7. Cited in Ralph K. Andrist, ed., *The American Heritage History of the Making of the Nation* (American Heritage Publishing Co., Inc.), 380.

8. Blassingame, ed. *Douglass Papers,* 3:437, 445.

9. Smith, diary May 18, 1861, quoted in Ralph V. Harlow, *Gerrit Smith: Philanthropist and Reformer* (1939; reprint, New York: Russell & Russell, 1969), 429.

10. *Liberator,* Apr. 19, 1860.

11. Cited in Milton C. Sernett, *Abolition's Axe: Beriah Green, Oneida Institute, and the Black Freedom Struggle* (Syracuse: Syracuse Univ. Press, 1986), 144.

12. Henry Hall, *The Story of Auburn* (Auburn, N.Y.: Dennis Bro's & Co., 1869), 397.

13. This editorial by Ira Brown of the Republican *Times* of Oswego is typical of the patriotic calls which filled the North Star Country press after the firing on Fort Sumter: "Grim visaged war is upon us. Our dispatches today disclose the fact that the rebel authorities have assumed the responsibility of opening a causeless, senseless warfare upon the government of the United States. The days of bullying are passed. The slaveholders who for the past 10 years have kept this otherwise peaceful country in a constant uproar, have at last proceeded to the dire extremity of war. . . . Men of the North! Are you ready to accept the issue? The noble government of your fathers is assailed with armed force. Will you in this hour forget whose sons you are, whose inheritance you possess? . . . . The die is cast. Let party differences be thrown to the winds. Perish dissension when our country is in peril! All together let us stand ready to accept the consequences and do our duty like men in whose minds yet linger the recollection of Bunker Hill, Yorktown and Saratoga. To arms! Down with the rebel flag—up with the good old banner which our fathers have carried in triumph on the road to glory!" Cited in Snyder, *Oswego County,* 7.

14. Newton Martin Curtis, *From Bull Run to Chancellorsville: The Story of the Six-teenth New York Infantry together with Personal Reminiscences* (New York: G. P. Putnam's Sons, 1906), vi.

15. Gerrit Smith to George C. Becksmith, Secretary of the American Peace Society, May 18, 1861, cited in Harlow, *Gerrit Smith*, 429.

16. Cited from editorial "Sudden Revolution in Northern Sentiment," *Douglass' Monthly,* May 1861.

17. Syracuse *Standard,* Nov. 14, 1861; republished in Blassingame, ed. *Douglass Papers* 1:xliii.

18. May, *Some Recollections,* 389–95. W. Freeman Galpin, *Central New York: An Inland Empire* (New York: Lewis Historical Publishing Company, Inc., 1941), 194–96. Evamaria Hardin, *Syracuse Landmarks: An AIA Guide to Downtown and Historic Neighborhoods* (Syracuse: Onondaga Historical Association/Syracuse Univ. Press, 1993), 141.

19. James Sullivan, ed., *History of New York State, 1523–1927* (New York: Lewis Histor-ical Publishing Company, Inc., 1927), 3: 1149, 1155. [William G. Tyrell], *The Civil War and the Community* (Albany: The State Education Department, The Univ. of the State of New York, 1961), 7. William A. Price, *The Civil War Handbook* (Arlington, Va.: Litho-graph Co., 1961), 11.

20. Sullivan, *History of New York State,* III: 1177. James A. Frost, "The Home Front in New York during the Civil War," *New York History* 59 (July 1961): 273.

21. Cited in Helen C. Phelan, *And Why Not Every Man?: An Account of Slavery, the Underground Railroad, and the Road to Freedom in New York's Southern Tier* (Interlaken, N.Y.: Heart of the Lakes Publishing, 1987), 198.

22. Cited in J. N. Larned, *A History of Buffalo* (New York: The Progress of the Empire State Company, 1911), 1: 67.

23. Cited in Phelan, *And Why Not Every Man?,* 199.

24. C. Dale Marshall, "The 50th New York Engineers were invaluable bridge builders during the various campaigns against Lee," *America's Civil War* 8 (Nov. 1995): 10–18.

25. Letter reproduced in David K. Parsons, *Bugles Echo Across the Valley: Oswego County, New York and the Civil War,* ed. Marie K. Parsons (Sandy Creek, N. Y.: Write to Print, 1994), 16.

26. Ibid.

27. Price, *Civil War Handbook,* 11.

28. Parsons, *Bugles Echo Across the Valley,* 31.

29. Ibid., 52.

30. Ibid., 23.

31. Ibid., 31.

32. J. A. Mowris, *A History of the One Hundred and Seventeenth Regiment N.Y. Volun-teers, (Fourth Oneida), from the Date of Its Organization, August 1862, Till That of Its Muster Out, June 1865* (Hartford, Conn.: Case, Lockwood and Company, 1866), 23.

33. Harry F. Jackson and Thomas F. O'Donnell, *Back Home in Oneida: Hermon Clarke and His Letters* (Syracuse: Syracuse Univ. Press, 1965), 41–42.

34. Ibid., 46–47.

35. Ibid., 66.

36. Ibid., 113–14.

37. Ibid., 116.

38. The orphanage's 233 children escaped, thanks to an evacuation plan prepared in advance and protection given them by New York City firemen who were themselves Irish. For details on the riots see James McCague, "Long Hot Summer: 1863," *Mankind* 1 (Aug. 1968): 11–17, 47–49; and Joseph P. Fried, "Story of the New York Draft Riots," *Civil War Times Illustrated* 4 (Aug. 1965): 4–10, 28–31.

39. Lydia P. Hect, ed., *Echoes from the Letters of a Civil War Surgeon* (n.p.: Bayou Publishing, 1996), 42.

40. Douglass, *Life and Times,* 354–56.

41. Cited from Kathleen Cochrane Kean, "George Tipping, The Corcoran Irish Legion, and the Civil War," *Niagara Frontier* 24 (Autumn 1977): 63.

42. Cited in David Herbert Donald, *Lincoln* (New York: Simon & Schuster, 1995), 368.

43. For a discussion of events leading to Lincoln's decision, see Stephen B. Oates, "The Slaves Freed," *American Heritage* 32 (Dec. 1980): 74–83. On the debate about Lincoln's motives, see Caesar A. Roy, "Was Lincoln the Great Emancipator?" *Civil War Times Illustrated* 33 (May/June 1994): 46–49.

44. *Douglass' Monthly,* Jan. 1863.

45. Douglass, *Life and Times,* 352–53.

46. Douglass, *Life and Times,* 351–52.

47. William S. McFeely, *Frederick Douglass* (New York: W. W. Norton, 1991), 217.

48. Herb S. Crumb and Katherine Dhalle, eds., *No Middle Ground: Thomas Ward Osborn's Letters from the Field (1862–1864)* (Hamilton, N.Y.: Edmonston Publishing, Inc., 1993), p. 105. Osborne commanded Battery D of the First New York Light Artillery Regiment, made up of Upstate New York Country "boys." In 1863 he was made chief of artillery in the Federal Army of the Tennessee.

49. Crumb and Dhalle, eds., *No Middle Ground,* 99.

50. Richards, *Village Life in America,* 150.

51. Richards, *Village Life in America,* 151.

52. Richards, *Village Life in America,* 151–55.

53. Richards, *Village Life in America,* 155.

54. On the USSC, see William Quentin Maxwell, *Lincoln's Fifth Wheel: The Political History of the United States Sanitary Commission* (New York: Longmans, Green and Co., 1956).

55. Jim Reilly, "Flags kept in courthouse are little-known historical gems," *Syracuse Herald Journal,* Feb. 2, 1996, B2; John Doherty, "Historic Flag at End of Its Rope," *Herald American* (Syracuse), June 14, 1998, B2. The monument to the 149th of New York is located at Gettysburg on North Slocum avenue. Kathleen R. George, *The Location of the Monuments, Markers, and Tablets on the Battlefield of Gettysburg* (Gettysburg, Pa.: Gettysburg National Military Park, 1982), 11.

56. Katherine Wilcox Thompson, "A Gentlemen's War!: Civil War Days Remembered," in *Sweet Gift of Freedom,* ed. Shirley Cox Husted (Rochester: County of Monroe, 1986), 42–43. Blake McKelvey, *Rochester: A Brief History* (New York: The Edwin Mellen Press, 1984), 31–32.

57. Carol M. Hunter, *To Set the Captives Free: Reverend Jermain Wesley Loguen and the Struggle for Freedom in Central New York 1835–1872* (New York: Garland Publishing, Inc., 1993), 225.

58. *Syracuse Journal,* Apr. 23, 1861.

59. *Syracuse Courier,* May 7, 1861.

60. On the Massachusetts 54th, see Peter Burchard, *One Gallant Rush: Robert Gould Shaw and his Brave Black Regiment* (New York: St. Martin's Press, 1965), and Clinton Cox, *Undying Glory: The Story of the Massachusetts 54th Regiment* (New York: Scholastic Inc., 1991). Useful histories of the black presence on the battlefield include, Dudley Taylor Cornish, *The Sable Arm: Black Troops in the Union Army, 1861–1865* (Lawrence: Univ. Press of Kansas, 1987), and James M. McPherson, *Marching Toward Freedom: The Negro in the Civil War, 1861–1865* (New York: Random House, 1967). On the historical validity of the movie about the Massachusetts 54th see James M. McPherson, "The 'Glory' Story," *The New Republic* 202 (Jan. 8 & 15, 1990): 22–23, 26–27.

61. Douglass, "Men of Color to Arms," Mar. 2, 1863, included in Douglas, *Life and Times,* 339–41.

62. The New York black regiments had 574 war-induced casualties. Frederick Phister, *New York in the War of the Rebellion: 1861–1865* (Albany, N.Y.: J. B. Lyon, 1912), 22, 62, 91, 283, 305, 307. Geoffrey C. Ward with Ric Burns and Ken Burns, *The Civil War: An Illustrated History* (New York: Alfred A. Knopf, 1990), xix. Harry Bradshaw Matthews, *Honoring New York's Forgotten Soldiers: African Americans of the Civil War* (Oneonta, N.Y.: Hartwick College, 1998), 2.

63. The letter is reproduced in Matthews, *Honoring New York's Forgotten Soldiers,* p. 4.

64. Cited in Jack Fincher, "The hard fight was getting into the fight at all." *Smithsonian* 20 (Oct. 1990): 49.

65. Douglass, "Address for the Promotion of Colored Enlistments," speech in Philadelphia, July 6, 1863, in: *The Life and Writings of Frederick Douglass,* ed. Philip S. Foner (New York: International Publishers, 1950), 3: 344–45.

66. As reprinted in Rochester's *Union and Advertiser,* Feb. 9, 1863, and cited by Ruth Rosenberg-Naparsteck, "A Growing Agitation: Rochester Before, During, and After The Civil War," *Rochester History* 46 (Jan. and Apr. 1984), 29–30.

67. Douglass, *Life and Times,* 342.

68. Frederick Douglass to Gerrit Smith, Mar. 6, 1863, Gerrit Smith Papers, Syracuse Univ.

69. Douglass, as cited in John Doherty, "Syracuse blacks fought to enlist in Union Army," *Herald-Journal* (Syracuse), Feb. 15, 1996, 1. This was language reminiscent of Douglass's famous essay "Men of Color, To Arms," which appeared first in the *North Star,* Mar. 2, 1863, and can be found in Douglass, *Life and Times,* 339–41.

70. *Syracuse Journal,* Mar. 27, 1863.

71. Ellen McTiernan, "Our Melting Pot: Eight 'Minorities'," in *Chemung County 1890–1975* (Elmira, N.Y.: Chemung County Historical Society, Inc., 1976), 519.

72. Frederick Douglass to Gerrit Smith, Mar. 6, 1863, Gerrit Smith Papers, Syracuse Univ.

73. Luis F. Emilio, *History of the Fifty-fourth Regiment of Massachusetts Volunteer Infantry, 1863–1865* (1894; reprint, New York: Johnson Reprint Corp., 1968), 348.

74. *Syracuse Journal,* Aug. 3, 1863.

75. Douglass, *Life and Times,* 342.

76. Lewis Douglass to "My Dear Father and Mother," July 20th, 1863, in *Douglass'*

Monthly, Aug. 1863, reprinted in *The Black Abolitionist Papers,* ed. C. Peter Ripley (Chapel Hill: Univ. of North Carolina Press, 1992), 5: 241.

77. Lewis H. Douglass to Amelia Loguen, July 20, 1863. The full letter can be found in *The Mind of the Negro as Reflected in Letters Written During the Crisis, 1800–1860,* ed. Carter G. Woodson (Washington, D.C.: Associated Publishers, 1926), 544. See also James M. McPherson, *The Negro's Civil War: How American Negroes Felt and Acted during the War for the Union* (New York: Random House, 1965), 190. Lewis served as the original Recruiting Sergeant Major.

78. Jackson and O'Donnell, *Back Home in Oneida,* 96–97.

79. Ibid., 99–100.

80. Thomas Sipple letter, [Aug.] 1864, in *Free at Last: A Documentary History of Slavery, Freedom, and the Civil War,* ed. Ira Berlin, Barbara J. Fields, Steven F. Miller, Joseph P. Reidy, and Leslie S. Rowland (New York: The New Press, 1992), pp. 475–76. George Rodgers and Samuel Sampson also signed the letter.

81. Ibid., 476.

82. Ibid., 477. Black troops encountered widespread discrimination and poor treatment. In the case of the 89th U. S. Colored Infantry, mustered into service on October 8, 1863, conditions were so bad under the command of General Nathaniel Banks that the unit's white officers, including John B. Weber of Buffalo, resigned in protest in June 1864. J. N. Larned, *A History of Buffalo* (New York: The Progress of the Empire State Company, 1911), 1: 78.

83. Quoted in Phelan, *And Why Not Every Man?* 202.

84. Charlotte Forten, *The Journal of Charlotte Forten,* ed. Ray Allen Billington (New York: Collier Books, 1961), 180. On the Port Royal "experiment" see, Willie Lee Rose, *Rehearsal for Reconstruction* (New York: Vintage Books, 1967).

85. Earl Conrad, *Harriet Tubman* (Washington, D.C.: Associated Publishers, 1943), 169–71. Sara Bradford, *Harriet Tubman: The Moses of Her People* (2nd ed., 1886, reprint, Secaucus, N. J.: The Citadel Press, 1961), 138, 140.

86. Harriet Tubman to "Boston Friends," June 30, 1863, appearing in *Commonwealth* (Boston, Mass.), July 17, 1863, republished in Ripley, ed., *Black Abolitionist Papers,* 5: 220.

87. Tom Boudreau, "Education into a Painful Past," unpublished manuscript, Syracuse Univ., Dec. 12, 1981, in author's possession. See also Benjamin Quarles, "Harriet Tubman's Unlikely Leadership," in *Black Leaders of the Nineteenth Century,* ed. Leon Litwack and August Meier (Urbana: Univ. of Illinois Press, 1988), 43–57.

88. Thomas E. Byrne, "Elmira's Black History," *Chemung Historical Journal* 14 (Sept. 1968): 1747–49. Abner C. Wright, "Underground Railroad Activities in Elmira," *Chemung Historical Journal* 14 (Sept. 1968): 1755–58. Carol Kammen, "Gateway to Freedom: A Black History Trail," *Heritage* 9 (Summer 1993): 17–18.

89. Citations from Hect, ed., *Letters of a Civil War Surgeon,* 55–56, 63, 110, and 113–14.

90. Hect, ed., *Letters of a Civil War Surgeon,* 125.

91. For more on the impact of the Civil War on Union volunteers away from home and their families, see Reid Mitchell, *The Vacant Chair: The Northern Soldier Leaves Home* (New York: Oxford Univ. Press, 1993).

92. Cited in Nancy Grey Osterud, "Rural Women during the Civil War: New York's Nanticoke Valley, 1861–65," *New York History* 62 (Oct. 1990): 360.

93. Ibid., 363, n. 3.

94. *Owego Gazette,* Nov. 3, 1931; Laurence Leamer, "Blacks in Vestal," 1984, 5, typescript by Vestal town historian, in author's possession.

95. Samuel was wounded four times during the Civil War—at Antietam, Gettysburg, Bristoe Station, and at the Battle of the Wilderness. His letters from the battlefield to the home front are in the Porter Family Papers, Rare Book and Manuscripts Division, Rodent Library, Univ. of Rochester, Rochester.

96. Quoted from Albert Castel, "Mary Walker: Samaritan or Charlatan?," *Civil War Times Illustrated* 33 (May/June 1994): 42.

97. Quoted in Castel, "Mary Walker," 64.

98. Charles McCool Snyder, *Dr. Mary Walker: The Little Lady in Pants* (New York: Vantage Press, 1962), 151.

99. Sullivan, *History of New York State,* 3: 1181–82.

100. John S. Manion, "Myles Keogh Had Close Auburn Connections," in *200 Years of History, 1793–1993* (Auburn, N.Y.: Auburn Bicentennial Committee, 1992), 59, 61.

101. Cited in Octavius Brooks Frothingham, *Gerrit Smith: A Biography* (1878; reprint, New York: Negro Universities Press, 1969), 270.

102. Cited in Harlow, *Gerrit Smith,* 436.

103. Harlow, *Gerrit Smith,* 430.

104. Henry W. Schramm, *Central New York: A Pictorial History* (Norfolk, Va.: The Donning Company, 1987), 39.

105. Cited from Donald, *Lincoln,* 567.

106. Richards, *Village Life,* 178–79.

107. Ibid., 180.

108. Douglass, *Life and Times,* 364.

109. Douglass, *Life and Times,* 364.

110. *Douglass' Monthly,* Jan. 1863.

Epilogue

1. Daniel Fink, *Barns of the Genesee Country, 1790–1915: Including an Account of Settlement and Changes in Agricultural Practices* (Geneseo, N.Y.: James Brunner, 1988), 246; Ulysses Prentiss Hedrick, *A History of Agriculture in the State of New York* (Albany, N.Y.: New York State Agricultural Society, 1933), 215; *Country Gentleman* 22 (Sept. 10, 1863): 169.

2. William S. McFeely, *Frederick Douglass* (New York: W. W. Norton, 1991), 299–300.

3. Cited in Helene C. Phelan, *And Why Not Every Man?: An Account of Slavery, the Underground Railroad, and the Road to Freedom in New York State's Southern Tier* (Interlaken, N.Y.: Heart of the Lakes Publishing, 1987), 208.

4. Jared Van Wagenen, Jr., "The Story of Gerrit Smith: Reflections from a Visit to a Home where History was Made," *American Agriculturalist,* Dec. 3, 1927.

5. Eugene E. Du Bois, *The City of Frederick Douglass: Rochester's African-American People and Places* (Rochester: The Landmark Society of Western New York, 1994), 43.

6. Anne Gertrude Sneller, *A Vanished World* (Syracuse: Syracuse Univ. Press, 1964), 27–29. Lincoln's funeral procession back to Illinois took fourteen days and traveled 1,662 miles. The train bearing the President's coffin came up from New York City to Albany

where a somber parade took place on April 26, 1865. It then crossed the Empire State to Buffalo, slowing down or halting in towns and villages along the way so that their residents could honor the fallen president.

7. Cited from Dorothy Meserve Kunhardt and Philip B. Kunhardt, Jr., *Twenty Days: A Narrative in Text and Pictures of Abraham Lincoln and the Twenty Days and Nights that Followed-The Nation in Mourning, the Long Trip Home to Springfield* (New York: Harper & Row, 1965), 219.

8. Gerrit Smith, Beriah Green, and Frederick Douglass, among others, challenged Garrison's call to disband and gave their support to Wendell Phillips, who assumed leadership of the AASS and edited the *Standard* after the *Liberator* ceased and Garrison withdrew. See Lawrence J. Friedman, *Gregarious Saints: Self and Community in American Abolitionism 1830–1870* (Cambridge, Mass.: Cambridge Univ. Press, 1982), 264–68.

9. Loguen, *The Rev. J. W. Loguen* 303; Carol M. Hunter, *"To Set the Captives Free": Reverend Jermain Wesley Loguen and the Struggle for Freedom in Central New York 1835–1872* (New York: Garland Publishing, 1993), 209–10.

10. Ibid., 227. Logan Temple in Knoxville uses a modernized spelling.

11. Loguen to "Mr. Editor," July 25, 1865, in *The Black Abolitionist Papers*, ed. C. Peter Ripley (Chapel Hill: Univ. of North Carolina Press, 1992), 5: 354–55.

12. Edmonia Highgate to George Whipple, Jan. 18, 1864, in Dorothy Sterling *We Are Your Sisters: Black Women in the Nineteenth Century*, ed. Dorothy Sterling (New York: W. W. Norton, 1984), 294–95.

13. Jermain Loguen to Gerrit Smith, Apr. 27, 1865, Gerrit Smith Papers, Syracuse Univ.

14. *Proceedings of the National Convention of Colored Men Held in the City of Syracuse, N. Y., October 4, 5, 6, and 7, 1864* (Boston: J. S. Rock and George L. Ruffin, 1864).

15. Joe M. Richardson, *Christian Reconstruction: The American Missionary Association and Southern Blacks, 1861–1890* (Athens: Univ. of Georgia Press, 1986), 196–97. On the beginnings of educational efforts for blacks in New Orleans, see Patricia Brady, "Trials and Tribulations: American Missionary Association Teachers and Black Educators in Occupied New Orleans, 1863–1864," *Louisiana History* 31 (Winter 1990): 5–20.

16. Cited in Sterling, ed., *We Are Your Sisters*, 301.

17. Edmonia Highgate to Gerrit Smith, Sept. 2, 1870, Gerrit Smith Papers, Syracuse Univ. Edmonia included a clipping from the *Syracuse Journal* which described Carrie as a quadroon, "finely educated" and "remarkably beautiful."

18. Sidney Kaplan, "The Miscegenation Issue in the Election of 1864," *Journal of Negro History* 31 (July 1949): 274–343.

19. See the collection of Alcott's abolitionist interracial romances edited by Sarah Elbert, *Louisa May Alcott on Race, Sex, and Slavery* (Boston: Northeastern Univ. Press, 1997).

20. The notice reads in part: "Last Friday morning Undertakers Ryan were notified that a woman died suddenly at the house of a woman named Mrs. Paine, residing at No. 67 Taylor street. They immediately proceeded to the place designated and removed the body to their rooms, and notified the Coroner, who held a post-mortem examination Saturday which showed that the woman was *enceinte* and died from the effects of treatment for abortion. The body of the unfortunate victim who thus lost her life while endeavoring to hide her shame, was identified as that of Miss Edmonia Highgate, a

mulatto, aged about thirty, and a school teacher by profession. She was seen in the city a week ago last Saturday so that the story about her arriving from Binghamton last Tuesday is untrue. She was dressed in a brown suit, with a black silk overskirt. She also wore a gray balmoral skirt with a plaid border. She had with her a satchel, filled with underclothing. In the satchel were found her wallet, containing something over $5 in money and a pawn ticket issued by Lewis Taylor of this city, on the 19th of October, she having pawned her trunk and contents for $16.55. . . . Miss Highgate was well-known in this city, as she was born and educated here, and at one time taught school in the Eighth Ward. She then moved to Binghamton, and from there went to the South, where she was engaged for a long time teaching the impoverished sons and daughters of her own race. We are informed that her last occupation was that of a book agent. But she has now fallen a victim to her own shame and guilt, and is a sad warning to others to beware how they trifle with their lives, as God often visits the death penalty upon those who would act contrary to both the laws of nature and to nature's God. We hope that the guilty miscreant who administered the antidote that caused the death of the unfortunate woman will be discovered and get what he justly merits." Syracuse *Daily Courier,* Oct. 17, 1870.

21. A. T. Morgan to Gerrit Smith, Oct. 21, 1870, Gerrit Smith Papers, Syracuse Univ.

22. Ronald E. Butchart, "'We Best Can Instruct Our Own People': New York African Americans in the Freedmen's Schools, 1861–1875," *Afro-Americans in New York Life and History* 12 (Jan. 1988): 30, 35; [Gary Paul Weinstein], "Edmonia Highgate of Syracuse, New York (1844–1870): Teacher, Orator, Crusader, Freedom Worker," pamphlet of The Edmonia Highgate Memorial Fund (in author's possession). I participated in a dedicatory ceremony in 1988 at the unveiling of a headstone and dedication plaque at Edmonia's grave. The plaque contains a line from one of Edmonia's letters reporting on her work: "Oh how inspiring the thought that these dear souls are 'Forever Free.'"

23. Born a slave at Canajoharie, Montgomery County, James was once exchanged for a yoke of steers. He escaped to Canada and afterwards found work in the warehouse of the Hudson and Erie Line in Rochester. He built a small church and taught in a Sunday school for black children, though as a slave he "knew nothing of letters or religion." He was ordained by Bishop Christopher Rush of the Zion connection in 1833. "I had been called Tom as a Slave, and they called me Jim at the warehouse," he wrote in an autobiographical sketch in 1886. "I put both together when I reached manhood, and was ordained as Rev. Thomas James." [Thomas James], "The Autobiography of Rev. Thomas James," *Rochester History* 37 (Oct. 1975): 5.

24. Ibid., 29.

25. Butchart, "We Best Can Instruct Our Own People," 34–35, 38. See also Robert C. Morris, *Reading, 'Riting, and Reconstruction: The Education of Freedmen in the South, 1861–1870* (Chicago: Univ. of Chicago Press, 1981).

26. Amy Hanmer-Croughton, "Anti-Slavery Days in Rochester," *Rochester Historical Society Publications* 14 (1936): 124.

27. Henry Lee Swint, *The Northern Teacher in the South, 1862–1870* (New York: Octagon Books, 1967), 143 and 169.

28. Joe M. Richardson, *A History of Fisk University* (University: Univ. of Alabama Press, 1980).

29. Judith Colucci Breault, *The World of Emily Howland: Odyssey of a Humanitarian*

(Millbrae, Calif.: Less femmes Publishers, 1976). For letters written to Howland by students enrolled in the School for Colored Girls, see Sterling, ed., *We Are Your Sisters,* 191–213, 286–94, and 380–81. Sidney Ann Taliaferro, one of Howland's African American protégées who later attended Howard Univ., spent several winters living with the Howland family in Sherwood. See Mildred D. Myers, *Miss Emily* (Charlotte Harbor, Fl.: Tabby House, 1998), a biographical novel based on Howland's diaries and letters.

30. Samuel J. May to J. M. McKim, July 26, 1866, Samuel J. May Anti-Slavery Collection, Kroch Library, Cornell Univ. The other two women were Eliza J. Smith and Fannie J. Botts. May to McKim, July 9, 1866, May Anti-Slavery Collection, Cornell.

31. May to McKim, July 20, 1867, May Anti-Slavery Collection, Cornell.

32. Rochester *Daily Democrat,* Mar. 13, 14, 1867; *Rochester Evening* Express, Mar. 13, 14, 1867, cited from Carleton Mabee, "Sojourner Truth Fights Dependence on Government: Moves Free Slaves Off Welfare in Washington to Jobs in Upstate New York," *Afro-Americans in New York Life and History* 14 (Jan. 1990): 12.

33. The Freed Slaves section of the Isaac and Amy Post Papers at the University of Rochester contains letters written by North Star families in 1867 asking Sojourner Truth for help in obtaining former slaves to work on the farms and in the homes of Upstate New York. Post (Isaac and Amy) Papers, Rare Books and Manuscripts Division, Rodent Library, Univ. of Rochester.

34. *Rochester Daily Union and Advertiser,* Mar. 14, 16, 1867, quoted in Mabee, "Sojourner Truth Fights Dependence," 14.

35. Cited in Mabee, "Sojourner Truth Fights Dependence," 16. For more on Truth's effort to place refugees in Rochester and elsewhere in the North, see Nell Irvin Painter, *Sojourner Truth: A Life, A Symbol* (New York: W. W. Norton, 1996), chapter 22.

36. Wilbur's letters are in the Rochester Ladies' Anti-Slavery Society Records, William L. Clements Library, Univ. of Michigan, Ann Arbor. There are also letters from Daniel Breed pertaining to the Rochester School for Freedmen in Washington, D.C., which the Society sponsored.

37. Milton C. Sernett, *Abolition's Axe: Beriah Green, Oneida Institute, and the Black Freedom Struggle* (Syracuse: Syracuse Univ. Press, 1986), 146.

38. Cited in "Beriah Green," undated clipping from the Utica press, probably February 1904.

39. Quoted from Ralph V. Harlow, *Gerrit Smith: Philanthropist and Reformer* (1939; reprint, New York: Russell & Russell, 1969), 450. The insult of "feeble intellect" alludes to the history of mental instability within the Smith family line. Gerrit's father and brother are said to have exhibited the trait.

40. Charles A. Hammond, *Gerrit Smith: The Story of a Noble Life* (Geneva, N.Y.: W. F. Humphrey, 1908), 97.

41. On the evening before he breathed his last, Gerrit Smith dictated four letters. Octavius Brooks Frothingham, entrusted by the family to write the life story of one of North Star Country's brightest luminaries, tells us: "The first was to his old housekeeper at Peterboro, charging her not to neglect his poor in the village, to see that the children of the orphan asylum had their holiday supplies, and that papers were sent to the free reading room which he maintained; the other three were kindly answers to applications for charity." Octavius Brooks Frothingham, *Gerrit Smith: A Biography* (1878; reprint, New York: Negro Universities Press, 1969), 354.

42. Frederick Douglass to Gerrit Smith, Feb. 5, 1852, Gerrit Smith Papers, Syracuse Univ.

43. Douglass, *Life and Times*, 373.

44. David W. Blight, *Frederick Douglass' Civil War: Keeping Faith in Jubilee* (Baton Rouge: Louisiana State Univ. Press, 1989), chapter 9.

45. Phyllis F. Field, *The Politics of Race in New York: The Struggle for Black Suffrage in the Civil War Era* (Ithaca: Cornell Univ. Press, 1982), 222.

46. Douglass, *Life and Times*, 472.

47. *North Star*, July 28, 1848.

48. Douglass, *Life and Times*, 396.

49. Douglass, *Life and Times*, 265.

50. Isaac Post died in 1872, the year Frederick Douglass left Rochester. Amy Post lived until 1889. The indomitable Posts had been faithful advocates of abolitionism since coming to Rochester from Long Island in 1836. Their home on Sophia Street was a busy station on the Underground Railroad. Amy attended the woman's rights convention in 1848 at Seneca Falls. She was active in the American Equal Rights Association and in the temperance movement. Both she and Isaac embraced spiritualism and were members of the original group of five people who met at the house of the Fox sisters to investigate the "Rochester Rappings."

51. Laurel Gabel, "Mount Hope Cemetery: A 196-Acre Classroom," *Epitaph: The Friends of Mount Hope Cemetery* 16 (Summer 1996): 4–6.

52. Quoted in McFeely, *Frederick Douglass*, 383; Frederick S. Voss, *Majestic in his Wrath: A Pictorial Life of Frederick Douglass* (Washington, D.C.: Smithsonian Institution, 1995).

53. Cited from Eugene E. Du Bois, *The City of Frederick Douglass: Rochester's African-American People and Places* (Rochester, N.Y.: The Landmark Society of Western New York, 1994), 32.

54. The Douglass monument was spared the fate of the old Douglass house at 297 Alexander Street when Rochester's new highway system necessitated the leveling of the site. The location of Douglass's second home, the one which burned in 1872, is now a parking lot belonging to the James P.B. Duffy School at 999 South Avenue. Today, pilgrims from near and far must pay their respects to Rochester's most famous freedom fighter by visiting the Douglass monument in Highland Park and his grave in nearby Mt. Hope Cemetery. As late as the 1940s when Rochester celebrated "Douglass Day," two of the old warrior's granddaughters came as special guests. See "Douglass Day to be Marked," *Rochester Democrat and Citizen*, July 4, 1943. See also "Negroes Honor Douglass in Church Rites, Cemetery," *Rochester Democrat and Citizen*, June 9, 1939; J. W. Thomas, *An Authentic History of the Douglass Monument* (Rochester: Herald Press, 1903). Douglass's son Charles served as the model for the sculpture.

55. Earl Conrad, *Harriet Tubman* (Washington, D.C.: Associated Publishers, 1943), 217.

56. Harriet's first husband, John Tubman, whom she married in 1844, had refused to leave the South. He was killed in Maryland in 1867. Neither the Tubman or the Davis marriages resulted in children.

57. *Auburn Citizen*, Mar. 11, 1913.

58. William Donald Mitchell, "Describes Tablet to be Unveiled in Memory of Harriet Tubman," Auburn *Advertiser-Journal,* May 25, 1914, 5; "Memorial to Harriet Tubman to be Unveiled; Booker T. Washington to Deliver Address," Auburn *Advertiser-Journal,* June 12, 1914, 5.

59. *Syracuse Journal,* Oct. 1 & 4, 1872; Hunter, *To Set the Captives Free,* 227–28.

60. Loguen to Washington Hunt, Dec. 2, 1851, *Liberator,* May 14, 1852, as cited in Sernett, "A Citizen of No Mean City," 45. Loguen is buried in Lot No. 55, Section 6 of Oakwood Cemetery, Syracuse. His wife Caroline died of consumption August 17, 1867, and is also buried in Oakwood.

61. Sixteen rooms of the Seward House at 33 South Street in Auburn are open to the public. A registered national historic landmark, it is furnished much as it was when Seward was active in public affairs. The Seward Memorial Statute, dedicated in 1888, stands outside. It bears the inscription from Seward's speech in the Senate, March 11, 1850, in the debate over the Fugitive Slave Law: "The Constitution regulates our stewardship; the Constitution devotes the domain to union, to justice, to welfare and to liberty. But there is a higher law than the Constitution, which regulates our authority over the domain, and devotes it to the same noble purposes." Quoted from a pamphlet entitled *The Seward House* (Auburn, N.Y.: The Foundation Historical Association, 1990), 28. William H. Seward II, a brigadier general in the Civil War, head of the Auburn banking firm of William H. Seward & Co., lived in the house after his father's death in 1872. The house was left as a memorial to his grandfather by William H. Seward III, its last occupant, in 1951.

62. May, *Some Recollections,* 323–29.

63. Ibid., 279. May attempted to help Sanford and sent money to John Needles of Baltimore who engaged a fellow Quaker in Virginia to make an offer for Aunt Bess or Old Bess, as Sanford's mother was called. But her owner spurned the money, which was more than the market-value of the elderly woman.

64. Samuel J. May, *A Brief Account of his Ministry: Given in a Discourse, Preached to the Church of the Messiah, Syracuse, N.Y., September 15th, 1867* (Syracuse, N.Y.: Masters & Lee, 1867), 3.

65. The May collection is in the Division of Rare and Manuscript Collections, Kroch Library, Cornell Univ., Ithaca.

66. Cited in Friedman, *Gregarious Saints,* 265.

67. Ibid., 257, 276.

68. William Goodell (1792–1878) is buried in Berea, Kentucky. That his final resting place should be so far from the region where he had been active as an abolitionist editor and pastor (without ordination) of a comeouter church is suggestive of the radiating reform influence of North Star Country. Goodell's legacy was that of theorist and writer. His *American Slave Code in Theory and Practice Slavery* (1853) and *Anti-Slavery: A History of the Great Struggle in Both Hemispheres* (1855) are valuable resources for the contemporary scholar (William Goodell, *American Slave Code in Theory and Practice* [New York: American Foreign Anti-Slavery Society, 1853], and William Goodell, *Slavery and Anti-Slavery: A History of the Great Struggle in Both Hemispheres: With a View of the Slavery Question in the United States* [New York: William Goodell, 1855].) Goodell's anti-slavery interpretation of the American Constitution, an argument most abolitionists

dismissed in 1844 when his pamphlet *Views of the American Constitutional Law in its Bearing upon American Slavery* appeared, enjoyed substantial support when Lincoln and the Republican Party had to counter secessionist states' rights arguments. Goodell's biographer claims that this native Upstate New Yorker "was the first abolitionist who called on the government to turn the war and its aftermath into a 'Second American Revolution' to achieve complete economic and political equality" (M. Leon Perkal, "William Goodell: Radical Abolitionist," *Centerpoint* 2 [1977]: 17). Goodell pressed the federal government to grant the freed people economic assistance and legal protection. Disillusioned with the progress made towards black equality, Goodell deserted the Republicans and endorsed Gen. John C. Frémont in his battle with President Lincoln regarding the status of slaves fighting for the Confederacy in Missouri.

69. Ibid., 278.

70. Sneller, *A Vanished World*, 32–33.

71. Ibid., 34.

72. Ibid., 35.

73. Ibid., 37.

74. Weld to Lewis Tappan, Apr. 5, 1836, in *Letters of Theodore Dwight Weld, Angelina Grimké Weld, and Sarah Grimké, 1822–1844*, ed. Gilbert Barnes and Dwight L. Dumond, ed. (New York: Appleton-Century, 1934), 1:288–89.

Bibliography

Newspapers and manuscript collections have been noted in chapter endnotes.

Selected Published Primary Sources

Barnes, Gilbert, and Dwight L. Dumond, eds. *Letters of Theodore Dwight Weld, Angelina Grimké Weld, and Sarah Grimké, 1822–1844.* 2 vols. New York: Appleton-Century, 1934.

Blassingame, John, ed. *Frederick Douglass Papers.* 3 vols. New Haven: Yale Univ. Press, 1985.

Brown, William Wells. *The Rising Son, or the Antecedents and Advancement of the Colored Race.* Boston: A. G. Brown, 1874.

Calloway-Thomas, Carolyn. "William G. Allen: On 'Orators and Oratory.'" *Journal of Black Studies* 18 (Mar. 1988): 313–336.

Colman, Lucy. *Reminiscences.* Buffalo: H. L. Green, 1891.

Crumb, Herb S., and Katherine Dhalle, eds. *No Middle Ground: Thomas Ward Osborn's Letters from the Field (1862–1864).* Hamilton, N.Y.: Edmonston Publishing, Inc., 1993.

Douglass, Frederick. *The Frederick Douglass Papers.* 3 vols. Edited by John W. Blassingame. New Haven and London: Yale Univ. Press, 1985.

———. *Life and Times of Frederick Douglass Written by Himself.* 1892. Reprint, London: Collier-Macmillan Ltd., 1962.

———. *The Life and Writings of Frederick Douglass.* Edited by Philip S. Foner. New York: International Publishers, 1950.

———. *My Bondage and My Freedom.* New York and Auburn: Miller, Orton & Mulligan, 1855.

———. *Narrative of the Life of Frederick Douglass, An American Slave, Written by Himself.* Edited by David W. Blight. Boston and New York: Bedford Books of St. Martin's Press, 1993.

Drew, Benjamin. *A North Side View of Slavery or the Narratives of Fugitive Slaves in Canada with an Account of the History and Condition of the Colored Population of Upper Canada.* 1856. Reprint, New York: Negro Univ. Press, 1968.

DuBois, Ellen Carol, ed. *The Elizabeth Cady Stanton–Susan B. Anthony Reader: Correspondence, Writings, Speeches.* Boston: Northeastern Univ. Press, 1992.

Dumond, Dwight L., ed. *Letters of James Gillespie Birney, 1831–1857.* 2 vols. New York: Appleton-Century, 1938.

Finney, Charles G. *The Memoirs of Charles G. Finney: The Complete Restored Text.* 1875. Edited by Garth M. Rosell and Richard A. G. Dupuis. Grand Rapids, Mich.: Zondervan, 1989.

Foner, Philip S., and George E. Walker, eds. *Proceedings of the Black State Conventions, 1840–1865.* Vol. 1, *New York, Pennsylvania, Indiana, Michigan, Ohio.* Philadelphia: Temple Univ. Press, 1979.

Garrison, William Lloyd. *The Letters of William Lloyd Garrison.* 6 vols. Edited by Walter M. Merrill and Louis Ruchames. Cambridge, Mass.: Harvard Univ. Press, 1971–1981.

Goodell, William. *Slavery and Anti-slavery: A History of the Great Struggle in Both Hemispheres, with a View of the Slavery Question in the United States.* 1852. Reprint, New York: Negro Univ. Press, 1968.

Green, Beriah. *The Miscellaneous Writings of Beriah Green.* Whitesboro, N.Y.: Oneida Institute, 1841.

———. *Sermons and Other Discourses with Brief Biographical Hints.* New York: S. W. Green, 1860.

Grinnell, Josiah Bushnell. *Men and Events of Forty Years.* Boston: D. Lothrop Company, 1891.

Hect, Lydia, ed. *Echoes from the Letters of a Civil War Surgeon.* N.p.: Bayou Publishing, 1996.

Jackson, Harry F., and Thomas F. O'Donnell. *Back Home in Oneida: Hermon Clarke and His Letters.* Syracuse: Syracuse Univ. Press, 1965.

James, Thomas. *Wonderful Eventful Life of Rev. Thomas James, By Himself.* 3rd ed. Rochester N.Y.: Post-Express Printing Co., 1887 (pamphlet). Reprinted in *Rochester History* 37 (Oct. 1975): 21–32.

Lee, Luther. *Autobiography of the Rev. Luther Lee.* New York: Phillips and Hunt, 1882. Reprint, New York: Garland, 1984.

Loguen, Jermain W. *The Rev. J. W. Loguen, As a Slave and As a Freeman.* Syracuse: Truair & Co., 1859. Reprint, New York: Negro Univ. Press, 1968.

Matlock, Lucius. *Slavery and Methodism from 1780–1849 and History of the Wesleyan Methodist Connection of America.* New York: Spruce Street Pub., 1849.

May, Samuel J. *The Fugitive Slave Law and Its Victims.* New York: American Antislavery Society, 1856.

———. *Some Recollections of Our Anti-Slavery Conflict.* Boston: Fields, Osgood, and Co., 1869.

McKivigan, John R., and Madeleine L. McKivigan. "'He Stands Like Jupiter': The Autobiography of Gerrit Smith." *New York History* 65 (Apr. 1984): 189–200.

Paul, Nathaniel. *An Address, Delivered on the Celebration of the Abolition of Slavery, in the State of New York, July 5, 1827.* Albany, N.Y.: John B. Van Steenbergh, 1827.

Pettit, Eber M. *Sketches in the History of the Underground Railroad Comprising Many Thrilling Incidents of the Escape of Fugitives from Slavery and the Perils of Those who Aided Them.* 1879. Reprinted, with an introduction and notes by Paul Leone, Westfield, N.Y.: Chautauqua Region Press, 1999.

Richards, Caroline Cowles. *Village Life in America, 1852–1872.* 1908. Reprint, Williamstown, Mass.: Corner House Publishers, 1972.

Ripley, C. Peter, ed. *The Black Abolitionist Papers.* 5 vols. Chapel Hill, N.C.: Univ. of North Carolina Press, 1985–1992.

Sanborn, Franklin B., ed. *The Life and Letters of John Brown, Liberator of Kansas, and Martyr of Virginia.* 3rd ed. Concord, Mass.: F. B. Sanborn, 1910.

Smith, Earl. "Document: William Cooper Nell on the Fugitive Slave Act of 1850." *Journal of Negro History* 66 (spring 1981): 37–40.

Sneller, Anne Gertrude. *A Vanished World.* Syracuse: Syracuse Univ. Press, 1964.

Stanton, Elizabeth Cady. *Eighty Years and More (1815–1897); Reminiscences.* 1898. Reprint, with an introduction by Gail Parker, New York: Schocken Books, 1971.

Stanton, Henry. *Random Recollections.* New York: Harper and Bros., 1887.

Sterling, Dorothy, ed. *Speak out in Thunder Tones: Letters and Other Writings by Black Northerners, 1787–1865.* New York: De Capo Press, 1998.

———, ed. *We Are Your Sisters: Black Women in the Nineteenth Century.* New York: W.W. Norton, 1984.

Steward, Austin. *Twenty-Two Years a Slave, and Forty Years a Freeman.* 1857. Reprint, New York: Negro Univ. Press, 1968.

Stewart, Alvan. *Writings and Speeches of Alvan Stewart on Slavery.* New York: A.B. Burdick, 1860.

Still, William. *The Underground Rail Road.* 1872. Reprint, Chicago: Johnson Publishing Company, 1970.

Ward, Samuel Ringgold. *Autobiography of a Fugitive Negro: His Anti-Slavery Labours in the United States, Canada, and England.* 1855. Reprint, New York: Arno Press, 1968.

Articles & Essays

Armstrong, Douglas V., and Louann Wurst. "Faces of the Past: Archaeology of an Underground Railroad Site in Syracuse, New York." *Syracuse University Archaeological Research Center Report* 10 (Jan. 1998): 81 pp.

Bailey, William S. "Underground Railroad in Southern Chautauqua County." *New York History* 33 (Jan. 1935): 53–63.

Banner, Lois W. "Religion and Reform in the Early Republic: The Role of Youth." *American Quarterly* 23 (Dec. 1971): 677–95.

Barber, Charles W. "Elmira As Civil War Depot and Prison Camp." *The Chemung Historical Journal* 6 (Sep. 1960): 753–59.

Baum, Dale, and Dale T. Knobel. "Anatomy of a Realignment: New York Presidential Politics, 1848–1860." *New York History* 65 (Jan. 1984): 61–81.

Bell, Howard H. "National Negro Conventions of the Middle 1840's: Moral Suasion vs. Political Action." *Journal of Negro History* 42 (1957): 247–60.

Bilotta, James D. "A Quantitative Approach to Buffalo's Black Population of 1860." *Afro-Americans in New York Life and History* 12 (July 1988): 19–34.

Blackett, R. J. M. "William G. Allen: The Forgotten Professor." *Civil War History* 26 (Mar. 1980): 38–52.

Blockson, Charles L. "The Underground Railroad." *National Geographic* 166 (July 1984): 3–39.

Brady, Patricia. "Trials and Tribulations: American Missionary Association Teachers and Black Educators in Occupied New Orleans, 1863–1864." *Louisiana History* 31 (winter 1990): 5–20.

Burke, Ronald K. "The Antislavery Activities of Samuel Ringgold Ward in New York State." *Afro-Americans in New York Life and History* 2 (Jan. 1978): 17–28.

Butchart, Ronald. "'We Best Can Instruct Our Own People': New York African Americans in the Freedmen's Schools, 1861–1875." *Afro-Americans in New York Life and History* 12 (Jan. 1988): 27–49.

Byrne, Thomas E. "Elmira's Civil War Prison Camp: 1864–65." *The Chemung Historical Journal* 10 (Sep. 1964): 1298–1300.

Castle, Musette S. "A Survey of the History of African Americans in Rochester, New York; 1800–1860." *Afro-Americans in New York Life and History* 13 (July 1989): 7–32.

Darlington, James W. "Peopling the Post-Revolutionary New York Frontier." *New York History* 74 (Oct. 1993): 341–81.

Davis, David Brion. "The Emergence of Immediatism in British and American Antislavery Thought." *The Mississippi Valley Historical Review* 49 (Sept. 1962): 209–30.

Davis, Thomas J. "New York's Long Black Line: A Note on the Growing Slave Population, 1626–1790." *Afro-Americans in New York Life and History* 2 (Jan. 1978): 41–59.

———. "Three Dark Centuries Around Albany: A Survey of Black Life in New York's Capital City Area Before World War I." *Afro-Americans in New York Life and History* 7 (Jan. 1983): 7–60.

Densmore, Christopher. "The Dilemma of Quaker Anti-Slavery: The Case of the Farmington Quarterly Meeting, 1836–1860." *Quaker History* 82 (Fall 1993): 80–91.

Dyson, Zita. "Gerrit Smith's Effort in Behalf of the Negroes in New York." *Journal of Negro History* 3 (Oct. 1918): 354–59.

Ellis, David Maldwyn. "Conflicts Among Calvinists: Oneida Revivalists in the 1820s." *New York History* 71 (Jan. 1990): 25–44.

———. "Whitestown: From Yankee Outpost to Cradle of Reform." *New York History* 65 (Jan. 1984): 32–59.

———. "The Yankee Invasion of New York, 1783–1860." *New York History* 32 (Jan. 1951): 3–17.

Essig, James David. "The Lord's Free Man: Charles G. Finney and His Abolitionism." *Civil War History* 24 (Mar. 1978): 25–45.

Farley, Ena L. "Afro-American Presence in the History of Western New York." *Afro-Americans in New York Life and History* 14 (Jan. 1990): 27–89.

———. "The Denial of Black Equality Under the States Rights Dictum: New York, 1865 to 1873." *Afro-Americans in New York Life and History* 1 (Jan. 1977): 9–23.

Farrison, William Edward. "William Wells Brown in Buffalo." *Journal of Negro History* 60 (Oct. 1954): 299–314.

Finkelman, Paul. "The Protection of Black Rights in Seward's New York." *Civil War History* 34 (Sept. 1988): 211–34.

Fischer, Donald M. "The Civil War Draft in Rochester." *Rochester History* 53 (1991): 3–30.

Folts, James D. "The Fanatic and the Prophetess: Religious Perfectionism in Western New York, 1835–1839." *New York History* 72 (Oct. 1991): 357–87.

Foner, Eric. "Racial Attitudes of the New York Free Soilers." *New York History* 46 (Oct. 1965): 311–29.

Fordham, Monroe. "The Harriet Tubman Home and Museum, Auburn, New York." *Afro-Americans in New York Life and History* 1 (Jan. 1977): 105–11.

———. "Origins of the Michigan Street Baptist Church, Buffalo, New York." *Afro-Americans in New York Life and History* 21 (Jan. 1997): 7–18.

Formisano, Ronald P., and Kathleen Smith Kutolowski. "Antimasonry and Masonry: The Genesis of Protest, 1826–1827." *American Quarterly* 29 (summer 1977): 139–65.

Fraser, James W. "Abolitionism, Activism, and New Models for Ministry." *American Presbyterians* 66 (1988): 89–103.

Friedman, Lawrence J. "The Gerrit Smith Circle: Abolitionism in the Burned-over District." *Civil War History* 26 (Mar. 1980): 18–38.

Frost, James A. "The Home Front in New York During the Civil War." *New York History,* 59 (July 1961): 273–97.

Galpin, W. Freeman. "The Jerry Rescue." *New York History* 26 (Jan. 1945): 19–34.

———. "Samuel Joseph May, God's Chore Boy." *New York History* 21 (Apr. 1940): 139–50.

Gara, Larry. "Friends and the Underground Railroad." *Quaker History* 51 (spring 1962): 3–19.

Gee, Clarence S. "The Stone on John Brown's Grave." *New York History* 59 (Apr. 1961): 157–68.

George, Carol V. R. "Widening the Circle: The Black Church and the Abolitionist Crusade, 1830–1860." In *AntiSlavery Reconsidered: New Perspectives on the Abolitionists,* edited by Lewis Perry and Michael Fellman, 75–95. Baton Rouge, La.: Louisiana State Univ. Press, 1979.

Godine, Amy. "Home Truth: The Saga of African-Americans in the Adirondack Park." *Adirondack Life* 25 (Jan./Feb. 1994): 47–53, 63.

Goodheart, Lawrence B. "'The Chronicles of Kidnapping in New York': Resistance to the Fugitive Slave Law, 1834–35." *Afro-Americans in New York Life and History* 8 (Jan. 1984): 7–15.

Goodman, Paul. "The Manual Labor Movement and the Origins of Abolitionism." *Journal of the Early Republic* 13 (fall 1993): 355–88.

Gordon, Robert. "A Mournful Trip." *Adirondack Life* (Jan./Feb. 1984): 16–18, 29–32.

Grant, H. Roger, ed. "The Skaneateles Community: A New York Utopia." *Niagara Frontier* 22 (autumn 1975): 68–72.

Hammond, John L. "Revival Religion and Antislavery Politics." *American Sociological Review* 39 (Apr. 1974): 175–86.

Hanchett, Catherine M. "Agitators for Black Equality and Emancipation: Cortland Country, 1837–1855." In *From Many Roots: Immigrant and Ethnic Groups in the History of Cortland County,* edited by Louis Varnaria, 87–99. Cortland, N.Y.: Cortland County Historical Society, 1986.

———. "'What Sort of People & Families . . .': The Edmondson Sisters." *Afro-Americans in New York Life and History* 6 (July 1982): 21–37.

Hanmer-Croughton, Amy. "Anti-slavery Days in Rochester." *Rochester Historical Society Publications* 14 (1936): 113–55.

Harlow, Ralph V. "Gerrit Smith and the Free Church Movement." *New York History* 18 (July 1937): 269–87.

———. "Gerrit Smith and the John Brown Raid." *American Historical Review* 38 (Oct. 1932): 32–60.

Hill, Marvin S. "The Rise of Mormonism in the Burned-over District: Another View." *New York History* 61 (Oct. 1980): 411–30.

Hirsch, Leo H., Jr. "The Negro and New York, 1783 to 1865." *Journal of Negro History* 16 (Oct. 1931): 383–473.

Hoefer, Jean M. "They Called Her 'Moses.'" *Civil War Times Illustrated* 26 (1988): 36–41.

Huch, Ronald K. "Patriotism Versus Philanthropy: A Letter From Gerrit Smith to Frederick Douglass." *New York History* 49 (July 1968): 327–35.

Humez, Jean M. "In Search of Harriet Tubman's Spiritual Autobiography." In *Thus Far by Faith: Readings in African-American Women's Religious Biography,* edited by Judith

Weisenfeld and Richard Newman, 239–61. New York: Routledge, 1996.

Humphreys, Hugh C. "'Agitate! Agitate! Agitate!': The Great Fugitive Slave Law Convention and Its Rare Daguereotype." *Madison County Heritage* 19 (1994): 3–64.

Hunter, Carol M. "'The Rev. Jermain Loguen: A Narrative of Real Life.'" *Afro-Americans in New York Life and History* 13 (July 1989): 33–46.

Johnson, James E. "Charles G. Finney and a Theology of Revivalism." *Church History* 38 (Sept. 1969): 338–58.

Kammen, Carol. "The UGRR and Local History." *CRM* 21 (1998): 11–13.

Kean, Kathleen Cochrane. "George Tipping, The Corcoran Irish Legion, and the Civil War." *Niagara Frontier* 24 (autumn 1977): 53–65.

Kostlevy, William C. "Luther Lee and Methodist Abolitionism." *Methodist History* 20 (1982): 90–103.

Kraut, Alan M. "The Forgotten Reformers: A Profile of Third Party Abolitionists in Ante-Bellum New York." In *Anti-Slavery Reconsidered: New Perspectives on the Abolitionists*, edited by Lewis Perry and Michael Fellman, 119–45. Baton Rouge, La.: Louisiana State Univ. Press, 1979.

———, and Phyllis F. Field. "Politics Versus Principles: The Partisan Response to 'Bible Politics' in New York State." *Civil War History* 25 (June 1979): 101–18.

Kuenning, Paul P. "New York Lutheran Abolitionists: Seeking a Solution to a Historical Enigma." *Church History* 58 (Mar. 1989): 52–65.

Landon, Fred. "The Negro Migration to Canada after the Passing of the Fugitive Slave Act." *Journal of Negro History* 5 (Jan. 1920): 22–36.

Larson, C. Kay. "Bonnie Yank and Ginny Reb." *Minerva: Quarterly Report on Women and the Military* 8 (1990): 33–48.

Levine, Robert S. "Uncle Tom's Cabin in Frederick Douglass' Paper: An Analysis of Reception." *American Literature* 64 (Mar. 1992): 71–93.

Loveland, Anne C. "Evangelicalism and 'Immediate Emancipation' in American Antislavery Thought." *Journal of Southern History* 32 (May 1966): 172–88.

Mabee, Carleton. "A List of the First Black Schools in Each Place in New York State, from Colonial Times to 1945." *Afro-Americans in New York Life and History* 2 (July 1978): 9–14.

———. "Sojourner Truth Fights Dependence on Government: Moves Freed Slaves Off Welfare in Washington to Jobs in Upstate New York." *Afro-Americans in New York Life and History* 14 (Jan. 1990): 7–25.

———. "Toussaint College: A Proposed Black College for New York State in the 1870s." *Afro-Americans in New York Life and History* 1 (Jan. 1977): 25–35.

Maynard, Douglas H. "The World's Anti-Slavery Convention of 1840." *The Mississippi Valley Historical Review* 47 (Dec. 1960): 452–71.

McBride, David. "Fourteenth Amendment Idealism: The New York State Civil Rights Law, 1873–1918." *New York History* 71 (Apr. 1990): 207–33.

McElroy, James I. "Social Control and Romantic Reform in Antebellum America: The Case of Rochester, New York." *New York History* 58 (Jan. 1977): 17–46.

McKivigan, John R. "The Antislavery 'Comeouter' Sects: A Neglected Dimension of the Abolitionist Movement." *Civil War History* 26 (1980): 142–60.

———, and Jason H. Silverman. "Monarchial Liberty and Republican Slavery: West

Indies Emancipation Celebrations in Upstate New York and Canada West." *Afro-Americans in New York Life and History* 10 (Jan. 1986): 7–18.

———, and Madeline Leveille McKivigan. "The 'Black Dream' of Gerrit Smith, New York Abolitionist." *Syracuse University Library Associates Courier* 20 (fall 1985): 51–76.

McManus, Edgar J. "Antislavery Legislation in New York." *Journal of Negro History* 46 (Oct. 1961): 207–15.

Morrison, Howard Alexander. "The Finney Takeover of the Second Great Awakening During the Oneida Revivals of 1825–1827." *New York History* 59 (Jan. 1978): 27–53.

———. "Gentlemen of Proper Understanding: A Closer Look at Utica's Anti-Abolitionist Mob." *New York History* 62 (Jan. 1981): 61–81.

Mutunhu, Tendai. "John W. Jones: Underground Railroad Station-Master." *Negro History Bulletin* 41 (March-April 1978): 814–18.

———. "Peter Webb of Tompkins County, Central New York." *Negro History Bulletin* 45 (January-March 1982): 48–49.

———. "Tompkins County: An Underground Railroad Transit in Central New York." *Afro-Americans in New York Life and History* 3 (July 1979): 15–33.

Myers, John L. "The Beginning of Anti-Slavery Agencies in New York, 1833–1836." *New York History* 43 (Apr. 1962): 149–81.

———. "The Major Effort of National Anti-Slavery Agents in New York State, 1836–1837." *New York History* 46 (Apr. 1965): 162–86.

———. "Organization of 'The Seventy': To Arouse the North Against Slavery." *Mid-America* 48 (1966): 29–46.

Nizalowski, Edward. "The Forgotten Burial Ground." *Afro-Americans in New York Life and History* 9 (Jan. 1985): 19–25.

Nogee, Joseph. "The Prigg Case and Fugitive Slavery, 1842–1850." *Journal of Negro History* 29 (July 1954): 185–205.

Nordstrom, Carl. "The New York Slave Code." *Afro-Americans in New York Life and History* 4 (Jan. 1980): 7–25.

Oliver, Robert T. "William H. Seward on the 'Irrepressible Conflict,' October 25, 1858." In *Antislavery and Disunion, 1858–1861,* edited by J. Jeffery Auer, 31–50. New York: Harper & Row, 1963.

Osterud, Nancy Grey. "Rural Women during the Civil War: New York's Nanticoke Valley, 1861–1865." *New York History* 62 (Oct. 1990): 357–85.

Padgett, Chris. "Hearing the Antislavery Rank-and-File: The Wesleyan Methodists Schism of 1843." *Journal of the Early Republic* 12 (spring 1992): 63–84.

Pearson, Ralph L. "A Quantitative Approach to Buffalo's Black Population of 1860." *Afro-Americans in New York Life and History* 12 (July 1988): 19–34.

Pease, Jane H., and William H. Pease. "The Gentle Humanitarian: Samuel Joseph May." In *Bound with Them in Chains.* Westport, Conn.: Greenwood Press, 1972.

Perkal, M. Leon. "American Abolition Society: A Viable Alternative to the Republican Party?" *Journal of Negro History* 65 (Fall 1980): 57–71.

———. "William Goodell: Radical Abolitionist." *Centerpoint* 2 (spring 1977): 17–25.

Phillips, Betty S. "Upstate and Downstate in New York." *Names* 31 (1983): 41–50.

Prichard, Linda K. "The Burned-Over District Reconsidered: A Portent of Evolving Religious Pluralism in the United States." *Social Science History* 8 (summer 1984): 243–65.

Priebe, Paula J. "Central and Western New York and the Fugitive Slave Law of 1850." *Afro-Americans in New York Life and History* 16 (Jan. 1992): 19–29.

Purvis, Thomas L. "The National Origins of New Yorkers in 1790." *New York History* 67 (Apr. 1986): 133–53.

Quarles, Benjamin. "Letters from Negro Leaders to Gerrit Smith." *Journal of Negro History* 27 (Oct. 1942): 432–53.

Rayback, Robert J. "New York State in the Civil War." *New York History* 59 (Jan. 1961): 56–70.

Reed, Harry A. "The Slave As Abolitionist: Henry Highland Garnet's Addresss to the Slaves of the United States of America." *Centennial Review* 20 (1976): 385–94.

Riforgiato, Leonard R. "Bishop Timon, Buffalo, and the Civil War." *Catholic Historical Review* 73 (Jan. 1987): 62–80.

Roach, George W. "The Presidential Campaign of 1844 in New York State." *New York History* 19 (Apr. 1938): 153–72.

Rosenberg-Naparsteck, Ruth. "A Growing Agitation: Rochester Before, During, and After the Civil War." *Rochester History* 46 (Jan. and Apr. 1984): 3–39.

Rowe, David L. "A New Perspective on the Burned-over District: The Millerites in Upstate New York." *Church History* 47 (Dec. 1978): 408–20.

Ruchkin, Judith Polgar. "The Abolition of 'Colored Schools' in Rochester, New York: 1832–1856." *New York History* 51 (Apr. 1970): 377–93.

Sanborn, Franklin Benjamin. "Gerrit Smith and John Brown." *The Critic* 47 (Oct. 1905): 349–56.

Schaetzke, E. Anne. "Slavery in the Genesee Country (also known as Ontario County) 1789 to 1827." *Afro-Americans in New York Life and History* 22 (Jan. 1998): 7–40.

Scharer, Laura Lynee. "African-Americans in Jefferson County, New York, 1810–1910." *Afro-Americans in New York Life and History* 19 (Jan. 1995): 7–16.

Schmitt, Victoria Sandwick. "Goin' North." *Rochester History* 54 (winter 1992): 3–31.

Schuelke, Frieda. "Activities of the Underground Railroad in Oswego County." *Fourth Publication of the Oswego Historical Society* (1940): 1–14.

Scott, Donald M. "Abolition as a Sacred Vocation." In *Antislavery Reconsidered: New Perspectives on the Abolitionists,* edited by Lewis Perry and Michael Fellman, 51–74. Baton Rouge, La.: Louisiana State Univ. Press, 1979.

Scruggs, Otey. "The Meaning of Harriet Tubman." In *Remember the Ladies: New Perspectives on Women in American History—Essays in Honor of Nelson Manfred Blake,* edited by Carol V. R. George, 110–21. Syracuse: Syracuse Univ. Press, 1975.

Seraile, William. "The Struggle to Raise Black Regiments in New York State, 1861–1864." *New York Historical Quarterly* (July 1974): 215–33.

Sernett, Milton C. "'A Citizen of No Mean City': Jermain W. Loguen and the Antislavery Reputation of Syracuse." *Syracuse University Library Associates Courier* 22 (fall 1987): 33–55.

———. "Common Cause: The Antislavery Alliances of Gerrit Smith and Beriah Green." *Syracuse University Library Associates Courier* 21 (fall 1986): 55–76.

———. "First Honor: Oneida Institute's Role in the Fight Against American Racism and Slavery." *New York History* 66 (Apr. 1985): 197–209.

———. "Lutheran Abolitionism in New York State: A Problem in Historical Explication." *Essays and Reports, Lutheran Historical Conference, 1982,* 10 (1984): 16–37.

———. "On Freedom's Threshold: The African American Presence in Central New York, 1760–1940." *Afro-Americans in New York Life and History* 19 (Jan. 1995): 43–91.

Sevitsh, Benjamin. "The Well-Planned Riot of Oct. 21, 1835: Utica's Answer to Abolitionism." *New York History* 50 (July 1969): 251–63.

Short, Kenneth R. "New York Central College: A Baptist Experiment in Integrated Higher Education, 1848–1861." *Foundations* 5 (July 1962): 250–56.

Silverman, Jason H. "Monarchial Liberty and Republican Slavery: West Indies Emancipation Celebrations in Upstate New York and Canada West." *Afro-Americans in New York Life and History* 10 (Jan. 1986): 7–18.

Simpson, Elizabeth. "Two Famous Abolitionists of Oswego County." *Fourth Publication of the Oswego Historical Society* (1940): 81–91.

Smith, Robert P. "William Cooper Nell: Crusading Black Abolitionist." *Journal of Negro History* 55 (July 1970): 185–99.

Snyder, Charles M. "The Antislavery Movement in the Oswego Area." *Eighteenth Publication of the Oswego County Historical Society* (1955): 2–12.

———. "Oswego County's Response to the Civil War." *New York History* 59 (Jan. 1961): 71–92.

Sokolow, Jayme. "The Jerry Mchenry Rescue and the Growth of Northern Anti-Slavery Sentiment During the 1850s." *Journal of American Studies* 16 (Dec. 1982): 427–45.

Stanke, Michael J. "New York Black Abolitionist Bibliography." *Afro-Americans in New York Life and History* 3 (Jan. 1979): 45–50.

Stewart, James B. "The Aims and Impact of Garrisonian Abolitionism, 1840–1860." *Civil War History* 15 (Sept. 1969): 197–209.

———. "Peaceful Hopes and Violent Experiences: The Evolution of Reforming and Radical Abolitionism, 1831–1857." *Civil War History* 17 (Dec. 1971): 293–309.

Strong, Douglas M. "Partners in Political Abolitionism: The Liberty Party and the Wesleyan Methodist Connection." *Methodist History* 23 (Jan. 1985): 99–115.

Sweet, Leonard I. "The View of Man Inherent in New Measures Revivalism." *Church History* 45 (June 1976): 206–21.

Tanner, Edwin Platt. "Gerrit Smith, An Interpretation." *New York Historical Society Quarterly* 5 (Jan. 1924): 21–39.

Thompson, Priscilla. "Harriet Tubman, Thomas Garrett, and the Underground Railroad." *Delaware History* 22 (spring-summer 1986): 1–21.

Watkins, Ralph. "A Survey of African American Presence in the History of Downstate New York Area." *Afro-Americans in New York Life and History* 15 (Jan. 1991): 53–79.

Wayne, Michael. "The Black Population of Canada West on the Eve of the American Civil War: A Reassessment Based on the Manuscript Census of 1861." *Historic sociale/Social History* 28 (Nov. 1995): 465–81.

Wellman, Judith. "'Bound By Duty': Abolitionists in Mexico, New York, 1830–1842." *Journal of the Oswego County Historical Society* (1973): 1–30.

———. "Crossing Over Cross: Whitney Cross's Burned-over District As Social History." *Reviews in American History* 17 (Mar. 1989): 159–74.

———. "This Side of the Border: Fugitives from Slavery in Three Central New York Communities." *New York History* 79 (Oct. 1998): 359–92.

———. "Women and Radical Reform in Antebellum Upstate New York: A Profile of

Grassroots Female Abolitionists." In *Clio Was a Woman: Studies in the History of American Women*, edited by Mabel E. Durtrich and Virginia C. Purdy, 112–27. Washington, D.C.: Howard Univ. Press, 1980.

———."Women's Rights, Republicanism, and Revolutionary Rhetoric in Antebellum New York State." *New York History* 69 (July 1988): 353–83.

Wesley, Charles. "The Negroes of New York in the Emancipation Movement." *Journal of Negro History* 24 (Jan. 1969): 65–103.

Williams-Myers, A. J. "The African Presence in the Mid-Hudson Valley Before 1800: A Preliminary Historiographical Sketch." *Afro-Americans in New York Life and History* 8 (Jan. 1984): 31–39.

Wright, Abner C. "Underground Railroad Activities in Elmira." *Chemung County Historical Journal* 14 (Sept. 1968): 1755–58.

Books

Abzug, Robert H. *Passionate Liberator: Theodore Dwight Weld and the Dilemma of Reform.* New York: Oxford Univ. Press, 1980.

Altschuler, Glenn C., and Jan M. Saltzgaber. *Revivalism, Social Conscience and Community in the Burned-over District: The Trial of Rhoda Bement.* Ithaca: Cornell Univ. Press, 1983.

Barker, Anthony J. *Captain Charles Stuart: Anglo-American Abolitionist.* Baton Rouge, La.: Louisiana State Univ. Press, 1986.

Barkun, Michael. *Crucible of the Millennium: The Burned-Over District of New York in the 1840s.* Syracuse: Syracuse Univ. Press, 1986.

Barnes, Gilbert H. *The Antislavery Impulse 1830–1844.* 1933. Reprint, Gloucester, Mass.: Peter Smith, 1973.

Berger, Mark L. *The Revolution in the New York Party Systems, 1840–1860.* Port Washington, N.Y.: Kennikat Press, 1973.

Blackett, R. J. M. *Building an Anti-Slavery Wall: Black Americans in the Atlantic Abolitionist Movement, 1830–1860.* Baton Rouge, La.,: Louisiana State Univ. Press, 1983.

Blight, David W. *Frederick Douglass' Civil War: Keeping Faith in Jubilee.* Baton Rouge, La.,: Louisiana State Univ. Press, 1989.

Blockson, Charles L. *Hippocrene Guide to the Underground Railroad.* New York: Hippocrene Books, 1994.

———. *The Underground Railroad.* New York: Prentice Hall, 1987.

Blue, Frederick J. *The Free Soilers: Third Party Politics, 1848–54.* Urbana, Ill.,: Univ. of Illinois Press, 1973.

Booraem, Hendrik. *The Formation of the Republican Party in New York: Politics and Consciences in the Antebellum North.* New York: New York Univ. Press, 1983.

Boyer, Richard O. *The Legend of John Brown: A Biography and a History.* New York: Alfred Knopf, 1973.

Bradford, Sara. *Harriet Tubman: The Moses of Her People.* 2d ed. 1886. Reprint, Secaucus, N.J.: The Citadel Press, 1961.

———. *Scenes in the Life of Harriet Tubman.* Auburn, N.Y.: W. J. Moses, 1869.

Bramble, Linda. *Black Fugitive Slaves in Early Canada.* St. Catharines, Ont.: Vanwell, 1988.

Breault, Judith. *The World of Emily Howland: Odyssey of a Humanitarian.* Milbrae, Calif.: Les Femmes Publishers, 1976.

Burchard, Peter. *One Gallant Rush: Robert Gould Shaw and his Brave Black Regiment.* New York: St. Martin's Press, 1965.

Burke, Ronald K. *Samuel Ringgold Ward: Christian Abolitionist.* New York: Garland Publishing, 1995.

Campbell, Stanley. *The Slave Catchers: Enforcement of the Fugitive Slave Law.* New York: W.W. Norton, 1972.

Coles, Howard W. *The Cradle of Freedom: A History of the Negro in Rochester, Western New York and Canada.* Rochester: Oxford Press, 1941.

Conrad, Earl. *Harriet Tubman.* Washington, D.C.: Associated Publishers, 1943.

———. *Mr. Seward for the Defense.* New York: Rinehart, 1956.

Cross, Whitney R. *The Burned-over District: The Social and Intellectual History of Enthusiastic Religion in Western New York, 1800–1850.* Ithaca: Cornell Univ. Press, 1950.

Davis, Barbara S. *A History of the Black Community of Syracuse.* Syracuse: N.p., 1980.

DeBoer, Clara Merritt. *Be Jubilant My Feet: African American Abolitionists in the American Missionary Association, 1839–1861.* New York: Garland Publishing, 1994.

———. *His Truth is Marching On: African Americans Who Taught the Freedmen for the American Missionary Association, 1861–1877.* New York: Garland Publishing, 1995.

Diedrich, Maria. *Love Across Color Lines: Ottilie Assing and Frederick Douglass.* New York: Hill and Wang, 1999.

Dillon, Merton L. *The Abolitionists: The Growth of a Dissenting Minority.* DeKalb, Ill.: Northern Illinois Univ. Press, 1974.

Donovan, Herbert D. A. *The Barnburners: A Study of the Internal Movements in the Political History of New York State and of the Resulting Changes in Political Affiliation 1830–1852.* Philadelphia: Porcupine Press, 1974.

Douglas, Marilyn. *New York State Census Records, 1790–1925.* Albany, N.Y.: State Education Department, 1981.

DuBois, Eugene E. *The City of Frederick Douglass: Rochester's African-American People and Places.* Rochester: The Landmark Society of Western New York, 1994.

DuBois, W. E. Burghardt. *John Brown.* 1909. Reprint, New York: International Publishers, 1972.

Dumond, Dwight L. *Antislavery: The Crusade for Freedom in America.* Ann Arbor, Mich.: Univ. of Michigan Press, 1961.

Eaklors, Vicki L., ed. *American Antislavery Songs: A Collection and Analysis.* Westport, Conn.: Greenwood, 1988.

Eichholz, Alice. *Free Black Heads of Household in the New York State Federal Census, 1790–1830.* Detroit, Mich.: Gale Research Co., 1981.

Emilio, Luis F. *History of the Fifty-Fourth Regiment of Massachusetts Volunteer Infantry, 1863–1865.* 1894. Reprint, New York: Johnson Reprint Corp., 1968.

Ernenwein, Raymond P. *The Borough of Peter.* Sherburne, N.Y.: Heritage Place, 1970.

Farley, Ena L. *The Underside of Reconstruction New York: The Struggle Over the Issue of Black Equality.* New York: Garland Press, 1995.

Farrison, William Edward. *William Wells Brown, Author and Reformer.* Chicago: Univ. of Chicago Press, 1969.

Field, Phyllis F. *The Politics of Race in New York: The Struggle for Black Suffrage in the Civil War Era.* Ithaca: Cornell Univ. Press, 1982.

Filler, Louis. *The Crusade Against Slavery: Friends, Foes, and Reforms 1820–1860.* Algonac, Mich.: Reference Publications, Inc., 1986.

Fladeland, Betty. *James Gillespie Birney: From Slaveholder to Abolitionist.* Ithaca: Cornell Univ. Press, 1955.

———. *Men & Brothers: Anglo-American Antislavery Cooperation.* Urbana, Ill.: Univ. of Illinois Press, 1972.

Foner, Philip. *Frederick Douglass on Women's Rights.* Westport, Conn.: Greenwood, 1976.

Fordham, Monroe, ed. *The African American Presence in New York State History: Four Regional Surveys.* Albany: The New York African American Institute, 1989.

Fowler, P. H. *Historical Sketch of Presbyterianism Within the Bounds of the Synod of Western New York.* Utica, N.Y.: Cross and Childs, 1877.

Fox, Dixon Ryan. *Yankees and Yorkers.* New York: New York Univ. Press, 1940.

Friedman, Lawrence J. *Gregarious Saints: Self and Community in American Abolitionism, 1830–1870.* New York: Cambridge Univ. Press, 1982.

Frothingham, Octavius Brooks. *Gerrit Smith: A Biography.* 1878. Reprint, New York: Negro Univ. Press, 1969.

Gallwey, Sydney H. *Early Slaves and Freeman of Tompkins County.* Ithaca: N.p., 1962.

———. *Peter Webb: Slave-Freeman-Citizen of Tompkins County, New York.* Ithaca: DeWitt Historical Society of Tompkins County, 1960.

———. *Underground Railroad in Tompkins County.* Ithaca: Dewitt Historical Society of Tompkins County, 1963.

Gara, Larry. *The Liberty Line: The Legend of the Underground Railroad.* Lexington, Ky.: Univ. of Kentucky Press, 1961.

Gerber, David A. *The Making of an American Pluralism: Buffalo, New York, 1825–1860.* Urbana, Ill.: Univ. of Illinois Press, 1989.

Goen, C. C. *Broken Churches, Broken Nation: Denominational Schism and the Coming of the Civil War.* Macon, Ga.: Mercer Univ. Press, 1985.

Griffith, Elisabeth. *In Her Own Right, the Life of Elizabeth Cady Stanton.* New York: Oxford Univ. Press, 1984.

Grover, Kathryn. *Make a Way Somehow: African-American Life in a Northern Community, 1790–1965.* Syracuse: Syracuse Univ. Press, 1994.

Hammond, Charles A. *Gerrit Smith: The Story of a Noble Life.* Geneva, N.Y.: Press of W. F. Humphrey, 1908.

Hammond, John L. *The Politics of Benevolence: Revival Religion and American Voting Behavior.* Norwood, N.J.: Ablex, 1979.

Hardman, Keith J. *Charles Grandison Finney, 1792–1875: Revivalist and Reformer.* Syracuse: Syracuse Univ. Press, 1987.

Harlow, Ralph V. *Gerrit Smith: Philanthropist and Reformer.* 1939. Reprint, New York: Russell & Russell, 1972.

Harlow, Vincent V. *History of St. James A.M.E. Zion Church.* Ithaca: St. James A.M.E. Zion Church, 1986.

Hewitt, Nancy A. *Women's Activism and Social Change: Rochester, New York, 1822–1872.* Ithaca: Cornell Univ. Press, 1984.

Higgins, Ruth L. *Expansion in New York with Especial Reference to the Eighteenth Century.* Columbus, Ohio: Ohio State Univ., 1931.

Hill, Daniel G. *The Freedom Seekers: Blacks in Early Canada.* Agincourt, Ont.: Book Society of Canada, 1981.

Holzer, Harold, ed. *The Union Preserved: A Guide to the Civil War Records of the New York State Archives.* New York: Fordham Univ. Press and the New York State Archives Partnership Trust, 1999.

Horton, James Oliver, and Lois E. Horton. *In Hope of Liberty: Culture, Community and Protest Among Northern Free Blacks, 1700–1860.* New York: Oxford Univ. Press, 1997.

Huggins, Nathan Irvin. *Slave and Citizen: The Life of Frederick Douglass.* Boston: Little, Brown, 1980.

Humphreyville, Frances T. *Harriet Tubman: Flame of Freedom.* Boston: Houghton Mifflin Co., 1967.

Hunter, Carol M. *To Set the Captives Free: Reverend Jermain Wesley Loguen and the Struggle for Freedom in Central New York 1835–1872.* New York: Garland Publishing, 1993.

Husted, Shirley Cox, ed. *Sweet Gift of Freedom: A Civil War Anthology.* Rochester: County of Monroe, 1986.

Jeffrey, Julie Roy. *The Great Silent Army of Abolitionism: Ordinary Women in the Antislavery Movement.* Chapel Hill, N.C.: Univ. of North Carolina Press, 1998.

Johnson, Curtis D. *Islands of Holiness: Rural Religion in Upstate New York, 1790–1860.* Ithaca: Cornell Univ. Press, 1989.

Johnson, Paul E. *A Shopkeeper's Millennium: Society and Revivals in Rochester, New York 1815–1837.* New York: Hill and Wang, 1978.

Jonas, Manfred, and Robert V. Wells, eds. *New Opportunities in a New Nation: The Development of New York After the Revolution.* Schenectady, N.Y.: Union College Press, 1982.

Kammen, Carol. *The Peopling of Tompkins County: A Social History.* Interlaken, N.Y.: Heart of the Lakes Publishing, 1985.

Kobrin, David. *The Black Minority in Early New York.* Albany: Office of State History, 1971.

Kraditor, Aileen S. *Means and Ends in American Abolitionism: Garrison and His Critics on Strategy and Tactics, 1834–1850.* New York: Vintage Books, 1970.

Kraut, Alan M., ed. *Crusaders and Compromisers: Essays on the Relationship of the Antislavery Struggle to the Antebellum Party System.* Westport, Conn.: Greenwood, 1983.

Klees, Emerson. *People of the Finger Lakes Region.* Rochester: Friends of the Finger Lakes Publishing, 1995.

———. *Underground Railroad Tales with Routes Through the Finger Lakes Region.* Rochester: Friends of the Finger Lakes Publishing, 1997.

Krutz, David P. *Distant Drums: Herkimer County in the War of the Rebellion.* Utica, N.Y.: North Country Books, 1997.

Kuenning, Paul P. *The Rise and Fall of American Lutheran Pietism: The Rejection of an Activist Heritage.* Macon, Ga.: Mercer Univ. Press, 1988.

Lesick, Lawrence T. *The Lane Rebels: Evangelicalism and Antislavery in Antebellum America.* Metuchen, N.J.: Scarecrow, 1980.

Litwack, Leon F. *North of Slavery: The Negro in the Free States, 1790–1860.* Chicago: Univ. of Chicago Press, 1961.

Lutz, Alma. *Crusade for Freedom: Women of the Antislavery Movement.* Boston: Beacon Press, 1968.

Mabee, Carleton. *Black Education in New York State: From Colonial to Modern Times.* Syracuse: Syracuse Univ. Press, 1979.

———. *Black Freedom: The Nonviolent Abolitionists from 1830 through the Civil War.* London: Macmillan, 1970.

Mabee, Carleton, with Susan Mabee Newhouse. *Sojourner Truth: Slave, Prophet, Legend.* New York: New York Univ. Press, 1993.

Magdol, Edward. *The Antislavery Rank and File: A Social Profile of the Abolitionists' Constituency.* New York: Greenwood, 1986.

Marsden, George M. *The Evangelical Mind and the New School Presbyterian Experience.* New Haven: Yale Univ. Press, 1970.

Martin, Waldo E., Jr. *The Mind of Frederick Douglass.* Chapel Hill, N.C.: Univ. of North Carolina Press, 1984.

Matthews, Harry Bradshaw. *Honoring New York's Forgotten Soldiers: African Americans of the Civil War, with Research Examples A–Z, a Case Study in Historiographic Genealogy.* Oneonta, N.Y.: Hartwick College, 1998.

Mayer, Henry. *All on Fire: William Lloyd Garrison and the Abolition of Slavery.* New York: St. Martin's Press, 1998.

McFeely, William S. *Frederick Douglass.* New York: W. W. Norton & Company, 1991.

McKay, Ernest A. *The Civil War and New York City.* Syracuse: Syracuse Univ. Press, 1990.

McKivigan, John R. *The War Against Proslavery Religion, Abolition and the Northern Churches, 1830–1865.* Ithaca: Cornell Univ. Press, 1984.

McManus, Edgar J. *Black Bondage in the North.* Syracuse: Syracuse Univ. Press, 1973.

———. *A History of Negro Slavery in New York.* Syracuse: Syracuse Univ. Press, 1966.

Merrill, Arch. *The Underground Freedom's Road and Other Upstate Tales.* New York: American Book-Stratford Press, 1963.

Merrill, Walter M. *Against Wind and Tide: A Biography of William Lloyd Garrison.* Cambridge: Harvard Univ. Press, 1963.

Mitchell, Reid. *The Vacant Chair: The Northern Soldier Leaves Home.* New York: Oxford Univ. Press, 1993.

Moravek, John R. *The Developer's Frontier: The Making of the Western New York Landscape.* New Haven: Yale Univ. Press, 1988.

Morris, Thomas D. *Free Men All: The Personal Liberty Laws of the North, 1780–1861.* Baltimore: The Johns Hopkins Univ. Press, 1974.

Moses, Wilson Jeremiah. *Alexander Crummell: A Study of Civilization and Discontent.* New York: Oxford Univ. Press, 1989.

Nichols, Robert Hastings. *Presbyterianism in New York State: A History of the Synod and Its Predecessors.* Edited by James Hastings Nichols. Philadelphia: Westminster Press, 1963.

Oates, Stephen. *To Purge This Land in Blood: A Biography of John Brown.* New York: Harper and Row, 1970.

Ofari, Earl. *"Let Your Motto Be Resistance": The Life and Thought of Henry Highland Garnet.* Boston: Beacon Press, 1972.

Ottley, Roi, and William J. Weatherby, eds. *The Negro in New York; An Informal Social History.* Dobbs Ferry, N.Y.: Oceana Publications, 1967.

Painter, Nell Irvin. *Sojourner Truth: A Life, A Symbol.* New York: W.W. Norton & Company, 1997.

Parsons, David K. *Bugles Echo Across the Valley: Oswego County, New York and the Civil War.* Edited by Marie K. Parsons. Sandy Creek, N.Y.: Write to Print, 1994.

Pease, Jane H., and William H. Pease. *Bound with Them in Chains: A Biographical History of the Antislavery Movement.* Westport, Conn.: Greenwood, 1972.

———. *They Who Would Be Free: Blacks' Search for Freedom, 1830–1861.* New York: Atheneum, 1974.

Phelan, Helene C. *And Why Not Every Man?: An Account of Slavery, the Underground Railroad, and the Road to Freedom in New York State's Southern Tier.* Interlaken, N.Y.: Heart of the Lakes Publishing, 1987.

Phister, Frederick. *New York in the War of the Rebellion: 1861–1865.* Albany, N.Y.: J. B. Lyon, 1912.

Quarles, Benjamin. *Allies for Freedom: Blacks and John Brown.* New York: Oxford Univ. Press, 1984.

———. *Black Abolitionists.* New York: Oxford Univ. Press, 1969.

———, ed. *Blacks on John Brown.* Urbana, Ill.: Univ. of Illinois Press, 1972.

Ratner, Lorman. *Powder Keg: Northern Opposition to the Antislavery Movement, 1831–1840.* New York: Basic Books, 1968.

Richards, Leonard L. *"Gentlemen of Property and Standing": Anti-Abolition Mobs in Jacksonian America.* New York: Oxford Univ. Press, 1970.

Ripley, C. Peter, ed. *Witness for Freedom: African American Voices on Race, Slavery, and Emancipation.* Chapel Hill, N.C.: Univ. of North Carolina Press, 1993.

Robertson, Constance. *Fire Bell in the Night.* New York: Henry Holt and Company, 1944.

Rohman, D. Gordon. *Here's Whitesboro.* New York: Stratford House, 1949.

Rossbach, Jeffery. *Ambivalent Conspirators: John Brown, the Secret Six, and a Theory of Slave Violence.* Philadelphia: Univ. of Pennsylvania Press, 1982.

Rowe, David L. *Thunder and Trumpets: Millerites and Dissenting Religion in Upstate New York, 1800–1850.* AAR Studies in Religion, no. 38. Decatur, Ga.: Scholars Press, 1985.

Ryan, Mary P. *Cradle of the Middle Class: The Family in Oneida County, New York, 1790–1865.* New York: Cambridge Univ. Press, 1981.

Schor, Joel. *Henry Highland Garnet: A Voice of Black Radicalism in the Nineteenth Century.* Westport, Conn.: Greenwood, 1977.

Scott, John Anthony, and Robert Alan Scott. *John Brown of Harper's Ferry.* New York: Facts on File, 1993.

Scott, Otto J. *The Secret Six: John Brown and the Abolition Movement.* New York: Times Books, 1979.

Sernett, Milton C. *Abolition's Axe: Beriah Green, Oneida Institute, and the Black Freedom Struggle.* Syracuse: Syracuse Univ. Press, 1986.

Sewell, Richard H. *Ballots for Freedom: Antislavery Politics in the United States, 1837–1860.* New York: Oxford Univ. Press, 1976.

Shaw, Ronald E. *Erie Water West: A History of the Erie Canal, 1792–1854.* Lexington, Ky.: Univ. of Kentucky Press, 1966.

Sheriff, Carol. *The Artificial River: The Erie Canal and the Paradox of Progress, 1817–1862.* New York: Hill & Wang, 1996.

Siebert, Wilbur H. *The Underground Railroad from Slavery to Freedom.* 1898. Reprint, New York: Russell & Russell, 1967.

Silverman, Jason H. *Unwelcome Guests: Canada West's Response to American Fugitive Slaves, 1800–1865.* Port Washington, N.Y.: Associated Faculty Press, 1985.

Simpson, Elizabeth M. *Mexico, Mother of Towns.* Buffalo: J.W. Clement Company, 1949.

Smith, Theodore Clarke. *The Liberty and Free Soil Parties in the Northeast.* New York: Longmans, Green, 1897.

Smith, Timothy L. *Revivalism and Social Reform: American Protestantism on the Eve of the Civil War.* 1957. Reprint, New York: Harper & Row, 1965.

Snyder, Charles McCool. *Dr. Mary Walker: The Little Lady in Pants.* New York: Vantage Press, 1962.

———. *Oswego County, New York, in the Civil War.* Oswego, N.Y.: Yearbook of the Oswego County Historical Society and the Oswego County Civil War Centennial Committee, 1962.

Sorin, Gerald. *The New York Abolitionists: A Case Study of Political Radicalism.* Westport, Conn.: Greenwood, 1971.

Sperry, Earl E. *The Jerry Rescue.* Syracuse: Onondaga Historical Association, 1924.

Staudenraus, Philip J. *The African Colonization Movement, 1816–1865.* New York: Columbia Univ. Press, 1961.

Sterling, Dorothy. *Freedom Train: The Story of Harriet Tubman.* Garden City, N.Y.: Doubleday and Co., 1954.

Stewart, James B. *Holy Warriors: The Abolitionists and American Slavery.* Rev. ed., New York: Hill and Wang, 1996.

Strong, Douglas M. *Perfectionist Politics: Abolitionism and the Religious Tensions of American Democracy.* Syracuse: Syracuse Univ. Press, 1999.

Sutherland, Cara, ed. *A Heritage Uncovered: The Black Experience in Upstate New York, 1800–1925.* Elmira, N.Y.: Chemung County Historical Society, 1988.

Sweet, Leonard I. *Black Images of America, 1784–1870.* New York: W.W. Norton & Company, Inc., 1976.

Taylor, John M. *William Henry Seward: Lincoln's Right Hand.* New York: Harper Collins, 1991.

Thomas, Benjamin P. *Theodore Weld: Crusader for Freedom.* New Brunswick, N.J.: Rutgers Univ. Press, 1950.

Thomas, Owen A. *Niagara's Freedom Trail: A Guide to African-Canadian History on the Niagara Peninsula.* Thorold, Ontario: Niagara Economic and Tourism Corporation, 1996.

Thomas, Robert D. *The Man Who Would Be Perfect: John Humphrey Noyes and the Utopian Impulse.* Philadelphia: Univ. of Pennsylvania Press, 1977.

Thompson, John L. *The Liberator: William Lloyd Garrison.* Boston: Little, Brown, 1963.

Thompson, John W. *An Authentic History of the Douglass Monument.* Rochester: Rochester Herald Press, 1903.

Van Deusen, Glydon G. *William Henry Seward.* New York: Oxford Univ. Press, 1967.

Vanderhof, E. W. *Historical Sketches of Western New York.* 1907. Reprint, New York: AMS, 1972.

Villard, Oswald Garrison. *John Brown, 1800–1859: A Biography Fifty Years After.* Boston: Houghton Mifflin Co., 1911.

Walters, Ronald G. *The Antislavery Appeal: American Abolitionism after 1830.* Baltimore: The Johns Hopkins Press, 1978.

Wiecek, William M. *The Sources of Antislavery Constitutionalism in America, 1760–1848.* Ithaca: Cornell Univ. Press, 1977.

Winks, Robin W. *The Blacks in Canada: A History.* New Haven, Conn.: Yale Univ. Press, 1971.

Wright, Albert Hazen. *Cornell's Three Precursors: I. New York Central College.* Ithaca: New York State College of Agriculture, Cornell Univ., 1960.

Wyatt-Brown, Bertram. *Lewis Tappan and the Evangelical War Against Slavery.* New York: Atheneum, 1971.

Wyckoff, William. *The Developer's Frontier: The Making of the Western New York Landscape.* New Haven: Yale Univ. Press, 1988.

Yacovone, Donald. *Samuel Joseph May and the Dilemmas of the Liberal Persuasion, 1791–1871.* Philadelphia: Temple Univ. Press, 1991.

Yee, Shirley J. *Black Women Abolitionists: A Study in Activism, 1828–1860.* Knoxville, Tenn.: Univ. of Tennessee Press, 1992.

Yellin, Jean Fagan, and John C. Van Horne, eds. *The Abolitionist Sisterhood: Women's Political Culture in Antebellum America.* Ithaca: Cornell Univ. Press. 1994.

Zilversmit, Arthur. *The First Emancipation: The Abolition of Slavery in the North.* Chicago: Univ. of Chicago Press, 1967.

Dissertations and Theses

Baglier, Janet Dorothy. "The Niagara Frontier: Society and Economy in Western New York and Upper Canada." Ph.D. diss., State Univ. of Buffalo, 1993.

Bilotla, James D. "The Sectional Controversy in Western New York, 1840–1860." M.A. thesis, Buffalo State College, 1972.

Dorn, Adelaide Elizabeth. "A History of the Anti-Slavery Movement in Rochester and Vicinity." M.A. thesis, Univ. of Buffalo, 1932.

Ellis, Walter J. "Editorial Attitudes of the Onondaga Standard on Slavery from 1829–1848." M.A. thesis, Syracuse Univ., 1942.

Ellithorpe, Susan J. "Early Development of the Anti-Slavery Crusade with Special Reference to New York." M.A. thesis, Syracuse Univ., 1934.

Graf, Hildegarde Francis. "Abolition and Antislavery in Buffalo and Erie County." M.A. thesis, Univ. of Buffalo, 1939.

Henderson, Alice. "The History of the New York State Anti-Slavery Society." Ph.D. diss., Univ. of Michigan, 1963.

Hendricks, John R. "History of the Liberty Party in New York State, 1838–1848." Ph.D. diss., Fordham Univ., 1958.

Hendricks, Tyler Owen. "Charles Finney and the Utica Revival of 1826: The Social Effect of a New Religious Paradigm." Ph.D. diss., Vanderbilt Univ., 1983.

Hixson, Charles Robert III. "Antimasonry in Western New York: A Social and Political Analysis." Ph.D. diss., Univ. of California, 1983.

Johnson, James E. "The Life of Charles Grandison Finney." Ph.D. diss., Syracuse Univ., 1959.

Kaufman, Paul Leslie. "'Logical' Luther Lee and the Methodist War against Slavery." Ph.D. diss., Kent State Univ., 1994.

Lamb, Wallace G. "George Washington Gale: Theologian and Educator." Ph.D. diss., Syracuse Univ., 1949.

Loucks, Esther C. "The Anti-Slavery Movement in Syracuse from 1839–1851." M.A. thesis, Syracuse Univ., 1934.

McElroy, James. "Social Reform in the Burned-over District: Rochester, New York, as a Test Case, 1830–1854." Ph.D. diss., State Univ. of New York at Binghamton, 1974.

Myers, John Lytle. "The Agency System of the Anti-Slavery Movement, 1832–1837, and Its Antecedents in Other Benevolent and Reform Societies." Ph.D. diss., Univ. of Michigan, 1961.

Pease, Jane H. "William Henry Seward and Slavery, 1801–1861." M.A. thesis, Univ. of Rochester, 1957.

Perkal, M. Leon. "William Goodell: A Life of Reform." Ph.D. diss., City Univ. of New York, 1972.

Pritchard, Linda K. "Religious Change in a Developing Region: The Social Contexts of Evangelicalism in Western New York and the Upper Ohio Valley During the Mid-Nineteenth Century." Ph.D. diss., Univ. of Pittsburgh, 1980.

Rice, Arthur Harry. "Henry B. Stanton as a Political Abolitionist." Ph.D. diss., Columbia Univ., 1968.

Wellman, Judith. "The Burned-over District Revisited: Benevolent Reform and Abolitionism in Mexico, Paris, and Ithaca, New York, 1825–1842." Ph.D. diss., Univ. of Virginia, 1974.

Index

Italic page numbers denote illustrations.

North Star Country: Upstate New York and the Crusade for African American Freedom was composed in 10.5/14 Minion by Kachergis Book Design; printed by sheet-fed offset on 60-pound Writers Offset and Smyth-sewn and bound over binder boards in Arrestox B-grade cloth, and notch-bound with paper covers printed in 3 colors by Thomson-Shore of Dexter, Michigan; designed by Kachergis Book Design of Pittsboro, North Carolina; published by Syracuse University Press, Syracuse, New York 13244-5160.

6498